ICE, STEEL AND FIRE

BRITISH EXPLORERS IN PEACE AND WAR
1921-45

Linda Parker

Helion & Company Ltd

Helion & Company Limited
26 Willow Road
Solihull
West Midlands
B91 1UE
England
Tel. 0121 705 3393
Fax 0121 711 4075
Email: info@helion.co.uk
Website: www.helion.co.uk

Published by Helion & Company 2013

Designed and typeset by Farr out Publications, Wokingham, Berkshire
Cover designed by Euan Carter, Leicester (www.euancarter.com)
Printed by Gutenberg Press Limited, Tarxien, Malta

ISBN 978-1-908916-49-5

British Library Cataloguing-in-Publication Data.
A catalogue record for this book is available from the British Library.

For details of other military history titles published by Helion & Company Limited contact the above address, or visit our website: http://www.helion.co.uk.

We always welcome receiving book proposals from prospective authors.

Contents

List of Illustrations

List of Maps

Abbreviations

ALC	Assault Landing Craft
ASDIC	Sonar, orig. from Anti-Submarine Detection Investigation Committee
AU	Assault Unit
BK	Balli Kombetar (Albanian National Front)
BARRE	British Arctic Air Route Expedition
BEM	British Empire Medal
BGLE	British Graham Land Expedition
BNLO	British Naval Liaison Officer
DD	Duplex Drive
DSC	Distinguished Service Cross
DSM	Distinguished Service Medal
DSO	Distinguished Service Order
ISSU	Inter-Service Signals Unit
LCI	Landing Craft, Infantry
LCR	Landing Craft, Rubber
LDV	Local Defence Volunteers
LNC	Levizja Nacional Clirimtare (Albanian National Liberation Movement)
LST	Landing Ship, Tank
MAS	*Motorscafi Antisommergibili*
MBE	Member of the British Empire
MC	Military Cross
MGB	Motor Gun Boat
MI (R)	Military Intelligence (Research)
ML	Motor Launch
MTB	Motor Torpedo Boat
OBE	Order of the British Empire
OR	Other Rank(s)
OSS	Office of Strategic Services
PT	Patrol Boat
RAF	Royal Air Force
RE	Royal Engineers
RN	Royal Navy
RNR	Royal Naval Reserve
RNVR	Royal Naval Volunteer Reserve
SHAEF	Supreme Headquarters Allied Expeditionary Force
SIS	Secret Intelligence Service
SOE	Special Operations Executive
STS	Special Training School

Acknowledgements

I would like to acknowledge the invaluable help and support given to me by the families of some of the men who are the subject of this book.

Mrs Julia Korner willingly gave me access to, and permission to quote from, the private papers and photographs of her father, Andrew Croft, and provided a warm welcome to her house in order to study them.

The images of Freddie Spencer Chapman have been included with the permission of the Spencer Chapman Family and, where noted, the images in the chapter on Peter Fleming have been used with the permission of the Peter Fleming Estate. Permission to quote from Peter Fleming's books has also kindly been given by the Peter Fleming Estate.

Lt General Jonathon Riley was very helpful in pointing my research on his cousin Quintin Riley in the right direction and allowing me to quote from his book *Pole to Pole* and Quintin Riley's papers.

The Reverend Canon Lisle Ryder kindly provided access to, and permission to quote from, his father, R.E.D. Ryder's, diaries and documents and photographs. The families have also been assiduous in reading drafts and making suggestions.

I would like to thank the staff of Imperial War Museum for their assistance on several visits and similarly the staff of the Liddell Hart Centre for Military Archives at King's College, London, the Scott Polar Research Institute at Cambridge and the Pitt Rivers Museum, Oxford.

Mrs Anne Stevens has been a patient and efficient proofreader. Duncan Rogers from Helion and Company has been, as usual, a tower of strength in the ups and downs of production, from the original idea to publication. My husband Nigel has provided the loyal support and assistance without which the writing of *Ice Steel and Fire* would not have been possible

Introduction

The generation born in the first decades of the twentieth century, which was reaching maturity in the inter-war years, grew up surrounded with tales of heroism and sacrifice in the Great War. Fathers and uncles had died and men returning from the war had their stories to tell. This generation was to reach its prime in time to fight against Hitler's Germany.

In addition to being imbued with stirring ideas of heroism and wartime action, these men would have also been aware of the exciting and courageous stories of polar exploration. The 'heroic' age of polar adventure had produced such personalities and role models as Scott, Shackleton and Amundsen. Scott's journey, in particular had entered into the popular consciousness as a sacrifice worthy of comparison with those made in the Great War, which started only just over a year after news of his death reached Britain. Polar and cultural historian Stephanie Barczewski explains in her book on Scott and Shackleton, *Arctic Destinies*, how the death of Scott resonated in a wartime society which was attempting to come to terms with death on a large scale. She contends that Scott's death was seen "as an exemplar of heroic sacrifice, a concept that had profound implications as people grappled with the human consequences of war."[1] Andrew Croft, whose story is told in Chapter Four, wrote in 1939 that the tragedy of Scott "stirred the public imagination more than any other single event of its kind."[2]

Notwithstanding the example set by the 'heroic' age explorers, the next generation of polar travellers of the 1920s and 1930s were to develop a very different style of expedition. The concept of heroic, sacrificial exploration, heavily financed and manned, led by autocratic leaders gave way to leaner, scantily financed expeditions led by university men in a spirit of adventure, scientific discovery and exploration. The journeys of Vilhjalmur Stefansson between 1913-1917 had shown that it was possible to regard the Arctic as an hospitable place, rather than an implacable foe, and that it was possible to live off the land, adopting Eskimo methods of survival. In the economic climate of the inter-war years, expeditions had much less money to spend, and were therefore slimmed down and functional in all respects. They were run on much more democratic lines by men who placed much emphasis of a cooperative effort without an autocratic leader. The benchmark of such expeditions was set by George Binney during his Spitsbergen expeditions 1921-24. He commented in the foreword to his book describing the expeditions, *With Seaplane and Sledge and in the Arctic*, on his aims: "my interests have centred around expedition-craft, in building them on sound lines and on developing new methods and safeguards of exploration."[3] He wanted to "foster the old spirit" but he hoped the book would point "beyond the old methods of Arctic exploration". His expeditions have been called "a school for explorers".[4] Binney's efficient and successful expeditions to Spitsbergen in which no catastrophes or heroics were

---

1   S. Barczewski, *Antarctic Destinies: Scott, Shackleton and the Changing Face of Heroism* (London, 2007), p.116.
2   A. Croft, *Polar Exploration* (London, 1939), p.186.
3   G. Binney, *With Seaplane and Sledge in the Arctic* (London, 1925), p.23.
4   W.J. Solas in the preface to *With Seaplane and Sledge in the Arctic* (London, 1925).

emphasised set the tone for the expeditions of the inter-war years. Alexander Glen, when planning the first of his expeditions to Spitsbergen in 1933, emphasised the importance of facilitating the work of the scientists in safety: "risk ... must be fully allowed for, if only to ensure that time ... is not wasted. In short, the element of luck must be eliminated."[5]

Perhaps the epitome of this new school of polar explorers was Gino Watkins who, although he died in 1932, exercised an enormous influence on his contemporaries who were to employ and adapt his leadership methods and philosophy in exploration and warfare. Augustine Courtauld, writing after Watkins's death, said, "Gino would say that, on a well run expedition there should be no adventures and if there were he would not speak of them."[6] The emphasis was on cooperation and resourcefulness, with every member of the expedition expected to take some responsibility for leadership. Several times he delegated responsibility for decisions, however important, to the man on the spot, on the grounds that they were in a better position to make the decision. An example of this was the delegating of responsibility to Freddie Spencer Chapman to decide who should be left at the ice cap station on Greenland in the winter of 1930-1931. This ability to take the lead and make tough decisions independently was one which would serve him and Quintin Riley well when serving in Special Forces during the war.

An interesting feature of the Binney and Watkins expeditions was their determination to make use of the latest technology or theory, from the use of radio to the experimenting with small aircraft to improve the success of the expedition. Binney pioneered the use of aircraft in exploration and Watkins used his aircraft to enhance his meteorological survey, which was to prove important in the development of transatlantic flight. Both explorers experimented with the practical use of radio communication in arctic conditions, adding thereby to the development of efficient equipment and methods of use.

The motivation of the explorers and expedition leaders in the inter-war years was varied and individualistic, including a range of personal, political and strategic factors. Peter Fleming's adventures in Brazil were very much in the 'heroic' mould, his journey to find out what happened to Colonel Fawcett being reminiscent of the searches for Sir John Franklin in the 19th century. His objective in all his journeys was to provide interesting information and scoops for *The Times* newspaper, and providing good material for his travel books. However, his travels in China and the Far East, especially his journey from China to India through Tartary, shed light on inaccessible areas where the complicated political situation remained obscure as no one had managed to go there. The situation in Sinkiang, for example, was one which the British Government was anxious to understand. Fleming rightly considered this journey 'political exploration' as well as geographical exploration.

The voyage 'the wrong way' around the world, from Hong Kong to Britain of Martyn Sherwood and R. E. D Ryder in the *Tai mo Shan* is creditable as an example of young naval officers attempting an unusual feat in a spirit of adventure. The question of whether they were spying on the Japanese security arrangements and navy, particularly around the Kurile Islands, is one that is still causing controversy, but from the accounts of Ryder, it is clear that, even if no espionage took place, the possibility was planned for and equipment from the British Government provided.

The expeditions to Spitsbergen led by Alexander 'Sandy' Glen in 1933 and 1935-1936 with Andrew Croft second-in-command, followed on from Binney's visits in the early

5   A. Glen, *Young Men of the Arctic* (London, 1934), p.21.
6   Augustine Courtauld in the introduction to *Watkins's Last Expedition* (London, 1934), p.14.

1920s. On Glen's second expedition, the first overwintering in Spitsbergen took place, with the object of expanding knowledge of Arctic survival techniques and enabling a consistent monitoring of climatic and ice conditions. Both these features of the expedition were to be valuable to operations in the Arctic and on Spitsbergen during the war and in the routing of the Atlantic convoys. The research into the ionosphere, the layer of the earth's atmosphere that is responsible for the long distance propagation of wireless waves, was to prove helpful in the development of radar. Glen was not fully aware of the security aspects of the equipment being tested, as he received a telling off from the Admiralty on his return for having proudly shown a visiting Norwegian hunting ship, with two German guests on board, around the meteorological equipment. The knowledge that Glen gained of Barentsberg and Ice Fjord on his first expedition was to become crucial in the Allied operations Gauntlet, Fritham and Gearbox on Spitsbergen during the war.

The British Graham Land expedition, in which Quintin Riley and R.E.D. Ryder took part, was more in the mould of 'heroic' polar exploration as the expedition was away three years and fulfilled its aim of finding and mapping new sea and land areas. It was under-financed, which had implications in the quality of the expedition ship *Penola*, causing many problems for its captain, Ryder. The expedition proved beyond doubt that that Graham Land is a peninsula, not an archipelago, and discovered the George VI Sound. The use of an aeroplane greatly enhanced the planning of the route and communications and broke new ground in the use of aircraft in Antarctic exploration, which as to be put to good use by the Falklands Islands Dependencies Survey in Operation Tabarin, which was a small British expedition in 1943 to establish permanently occupied bases in the Antarctic. It is possible that the expedition was suggested to its leader, John Rymill, as the presence of a long term British expedition in the area would strengthen Britain's claim to what was, and still is, a disputed area of the South Atlantic and Antarctica.

In the inter-war period British mountaineers were also to be among those who developed skills which would be used by the special services during the war. H. W. 'Bill' Tilman was among the most famous of the pre war generation of climbers, having been the first to scale Nanda Devi and had been also the leader of the 1938 Everest expedition. At the age of 45 he was parachuted as part of SOE missions, firstly into Albania and then Italy and consolidated his reputation for rugged tenacity. Spencer Chapman, after his arctic experiences, made the first ascent of Mount Chomolhari, in the Himalayas.

The main characters of these inter-war expeditions went on to fight in the Second World War in a variety of theatres, and they all used their experiences and skills gained in this time to good effect in their wartime careers. Interestingly and perhaps inevitably these main figures, who know each other from exploration circles before the war, ended up serving together at various points, and some had remarkably similar career paths during the conflict. The 'Phoney War' saw the formation of the 5th Battalion Scots Guards, a specialist battalion which was to be made ready to send to Norway in response to the threat posed by the Russian attack on Finland. This battalion was to be trained quickly in Arctic warfare, and Quintin Riley, Martin Lindsay, J.M. Scott and Freddie Spencer Chapman found themselves posted to Chamonix to implement this training. In the event the unit was stood down on the capitulation of the Finnish army.

The Allied invasion of Norway saw Peter Fleming, Lindsay, Croft and Riley engaged in action at Namsos and Narvik. Sherwood was involved in the evacuation of Namsos in his ship, HMT *Cape Passaro*. At the threat of German invasion, Fleming and Croft became involved in the organisation of the auxiliary or 'left behind' units who were trained to harass the enemy from hidden positions behind the lines if Kent or Essex were invaded.

Some of the main protagonists of this book were, almost inevitably in view of their skills and courage, involved in the formation of commando units formed on Churchill's orders to harass the coasts of occupied Europe. Croft, Riley, Spencer Chapman and Courtauld were involved in the training of commandos in arctic skills and also in small boat handling, essential for raiding parties. Ryder famously won the Victoria Cross for his leadership of the raid on St Nazaire. Croft was to use his boat handling skills as part of Operation Balaclava, dropping agents into enemy occupied territory. He was then parachuted into the south of France to help the *Maquis* behind enemy lines. Riley became the leader of 30 Commando, following the frontline troops into Sicily on raids to 'snatch' enemy intelligence. Lancelot Fleming spent the war on battleships as a naval chaplain. Spencer Chapman survived three and a half years behind Japanese lines in the Malayan jungle harassing the Japanese forces and training guerrilla fighters. Martin Lindsay saw the long march of the allies across Europe after D-Day. Peter Fleming, after his experiences in Norway, was engaged in the defence and evacuation of Greece before spending the rest of the war in Intelligence deception in South East Asia.

The story of these inter war explorers in the Second World war is illuminating as they covered between them most theatres of war. When their pre-war record is examined it is not too much to suppose that their physical bravery and psychological endurance was born of their experiences in ice, mountain, ocean and jungle in times of peace.

1

George Binney

'A School for Explorers' 1921–24

George Binney's expeditions to Spitsbergen in 1921, 1923 and 1924 have been described as opening a new era in arctic and antarctic exploration. J. Gordon Hayes, in his overview of arctic exploration, wrote of the Oxford expeditions to Spitsbergen as "important, not only on account of their results, but also because, with the contemporary Cambridge ventures, they inaugurated a new school of British explorers."[1] The expeditions that Binney was involved in, firstly as organising secretary in 1921, and leader in 1923 and 1924, broke new ground in motivation, organisation and attitudes to polar exploring. These achievements included the ground breaking first use of a seaplane in the acquisition of geographical knowledge. Under his leadership the ideas of the age of "heroic " polar exploration, where large sums of money were raised to pay for heavily equipped expeditions in which the role of the leader was paramount, were replaced by a more relaxed and low key, often self-funded type of expedition which were "benevolently monarchical in government and desirous of avoiding heroics."[2]

Binney was reading English at Merton College Oxford, and fell into exploration almost by accident after bumping into Julian Huxley in Blackwell's bookshop.[3] Huxley was at that time a fellow of New College, Oxford and senior demonstrator of Zoology. He asked Binney, in his capacity as the editor of *Isis*, to back an expedition to Spitsbergen and to become its organising secretary. This first expedition was manned mainly by scientists. An ornithological party was led by the Reverend G. Jourdain and a scientific party was led by N.E. Odell. The aim of the first party was to "carry out extensive scientific investigations with special reference to Zoology"[4], whereas the second party was to "attempt to explore and make an accurate survey of the hitherto unmapped regions of the North East of the main Island."[5] It was a good year for weather but due to the constraints and aims of the scientific societies who were footing the bill, Binney was disappointed that more was not achieved in the way of exploration and fresh geographical knowledge. He commented "the sum of our labours was a lean harvest of geographical discovery, quite disproportionate to our crop of excellent scientific work."[6] He decided to organise another expedition with a more overtly geographical emphasis on exploration.

The 1923 expedition had at its core the Merton College rowing eight, along with seven scientists. With this combination Binney hoped to explore North East Land, part of the Spitsbergen Archipelago which was virtually uncharted and with an unknown interior – "a truly arctic country." Professor Baron von Nordenskiold had determined the exact

---

1   G. Hayes, *The Conquest of the North Pole* (London, 1934), p.202.
2   Ibid., p.202.
3   *The Oxford Dictionary of National Biography*.
4   *The Times*, 9th April 1921.
5   Ibid.
6   G. Binney, *With Seaplane and Sledge in the Arctic* (London, 1925), p.23.

position of Spitsbergen in 1868 and surveyed part of North East Land in 1872. A German expedition to North East Land had disappeared in 1912 in an attempt to complete a survey.[7] Schroeder Stranz and two companions had been left on the sea ice between North Cape and Cape Platen in August 1912, hoping to sledge across North East Land and around the north coast of Spitsbergen to Krossfjord. They were not seen again.

Binney's expedition was virtually self-financed, leaving it leeway in decisions about the nature and scope of the exploration to be undertaken. Binney cut down on the number of scientists and relied on what he called his "henchmen"- personal friends who were expected to bear the brunt of the manual labour and assist in the scientific work. Binney, although young at twenty-three, had a mature philosophy about the aims: "my interests had centred around arctic expedition-craft ... and in developing new methods and safe grounds of exploration"[8] W.J. Solas, in his preface to Binney's book on the expedition, commented:

It was not for adventure that that the Oxford expedition set out. Its object was to advance our knowledge of a practically unknown land and to penetrate the secrets of an arctic region.[9]

The expedition sailed from England on 14th July 1923, starting its schedule by stopping at Green Harbour, an established settlement on the west coast of Spitsbergen, and then following the coast to North East Land to find a landing place for the sledging party. Ice conditions prevented a landing on the coast of North East Land so a party was put ashore on the east coast of Spitsbergen in order to make a crossing of New Friesland. On a sledge journey lasting a month from Duym point to Klass Billen Bay, new geographical observations were made. The Mount Newton district was explored; the Loven Plateau was measured at 1,500 ft, Mt Hope and Mt Newton were found to be 5,078 ft and 5,676 ft respectively, and the charting of Merton Glacier which had begun in 1921, was finished. A report in *The Times* announced that the sledge party "has been able to accomplish a survey of the unknown region of east Spitsbergen." New wireless technology was used to send messages from ship to sledging party. This helped greatly the main difficulty of a sledging party, that of arranging where and when to be picked up. Another aim of the radio experiments was to test the range of British broadcasting.

The expedition ship *The Terningen*, hindered by propeller problems, slowly sailed south and then east along the south coast of North East Land. A landing was made at Ulva Bay and the ship rounded North Cape on 13th August. They were able to accomplish a survey of an unknown part of the Spitsbergen coast and found that previous charts of the Spitsbergen Archipelago were often inaccurate.[10] The sledging party were picked up at Klass Billen Bay on 30th August, only five minutes behind schedule. Binney was disappointed that North East Land had been impossible to land on but resolved to organise another expedition, quickly. The expedition had, however, been a success with five landings being made on unknown coasts, with corrections to charts being discovered, and further recording of animal and plant life. According to Hayes "A mixture of Oxford brawn and

7   The Schroeder-Stranz expedition. Binney reported finding a sleeping bag belonging to this party in 1923.
    Ibid., p.26.
8   Ibid., p.21.
9   Binney, *Sledge and Seaplane*, p.13.
10 *The Times*, 6th October 1923.

The North Cape of North East Land, August 1923. (*Sea plane and Sledge*)

brain, tinctured by a Cambridge contingent had proved its capacity for arctic research."[11] Binney had proved that his particular brand of arctic expedition produced results.

Binney wasted no time in organising the next year's expedition. In the foreword to his book on the 1924 expedition he explained his determination to explore North East Land:

> It has not been considered an objective of sufficient importance for a winter expedition and it has been thought too uncertain of access and too big a task for a summer expedition. Thus it fell between the two stools and has been neglected.[12]

Spurred on by the success of the 1923 expedition he planned to rectify this:

> What could be more fascinating than to plan an onslaught on a large scale against the natural defences of the Island, to attempt to explore it 'on the intensive system' during the six weeks when we would hope to find a portion of its shores ice free.[13]

The expedition was planned on a much grander scale than the previous years, utilising two ships, a seaplane and including plans for three sledging parties. The objectives were geographical and scientific. The main aim was to explore the inaccessible isle of North East Land. This was to be achieved by "a successful traverse with sledging parties and conduct an aerial survey with the seaplane."[14] Secondary objectives were to experiment with wireless direction finding and to make a reconnaissance northward towards the pole

---

11   Hayes, *Conquest of the North Pole*, p.206.
12   Binney, *Seaplane and Sledge*, p.25.
13   *The Times*, 10th October 1924.
14   GB 15, George Binney, Scott Polar Research Institute, University of Cambridge.

if time permitted. It was also hoped to beat the existing record for the "furthest north" in navigable sailing which stood at latitude 81° 40'. Binney commented to *The Times* "This would mean that she [the *Polar Bjorn*] would go where no other ship has sailed, and it may well happen that new land will be discovered."[15] This emphasised his opinion that the main objective of this latest expedition was exploration and that scientific objectives were subsidiary to that aim.

The experimentation with aircraft was very topical. The years 1925-1928 would see Wilkins' flights in the Arctic regions, culminating in his flight from Alaska to Spitsbergen in 1928, and Byrd's flight over the North Pole in 1926. Already in 1923 Hammer, the Dutch American aviator, had flown a Junkers aircraft from Green Harbour in a series of flights over Spitsbergen, but Binney considered that Hammer's flights were 'purely aerial', and in view of the fact that they had started and ended in a 'civilised base', that they had not contributed a great deal to the problems of using an aeroplane for arctic exploration. Binney was hoping to "throw some light on the practical value of aircraft for an expedition which is working in the polar regions", [16] and considered that the best way to do that was to take the plane with the expedition wherever it went – "With a sailing sloop as an advanced base the scope of the aircraft work is greatly increased in the Arctic." [17] However, he did not consider the plans for the aircraft as the main objective and was not prepared to let the seaplane's work jeopardise the efficiency of the expedition as a whole.

Letters from Binney to the prospective members included instructions for everyone to bring a gun or rifle to procure fresh meat and they were also advised to "bring your favourite laxative."[18] All members of the expedition signed an agreement which set out the terms of their acceptance by Binney. This amounted to an agreement about their financial contribution, a promise to bring a camera and take photos for the press, and a commitment on behalf of their families that they would contribute to funds for a rescue expedition if it became necessary. [19] Although the style of the expedition was relaxed, they all also had to agree to abide by Binney's decisions.

A member who had also been on the 1923 expedition, Hugh Clutterbuck, contributed £3,000 to its cost and the remainder of the eventual cost of £5,300 was contributed, each according to his means, from the other members. Although it was expected that members contribute to the cost, when Ian Colquhoun wrote saying that he could not come because of an unexpected call on his finances Binney replied telling him that he could pay in instalments and that "We are after men, not money".[20] The Royal Geographical Society and Oxford University supported the expedition and gave small grants. Hayes saw this self-sufficiency as the reason why the expedition has not received the recognition it deserved: "No public appeal being made for funds, the venture attracted little attention and should be better known."[21] The expedition, however, received support from Messers A.V. Roe who built the seaplane, Armstrong Siddeley who lent the engine and British Petroleum who provided the fuel. The total number of explorers was twenty-five. There were eight Oxford

15   *The Times*, 9th June 1924.
16   Binney, *Seaplane and Sledge*, p.30.
17   Ibid., p.97.
18   SPIRI, GB 15.
19   Ibid.
20   Ibid.
21   J.G. Hayes, *The Conquest of the North Pole*, p.206.

The air party – Taylor, Ellis, Tymms. (*Sea plane and Sledge*)

men, three Cambridge men and seven from the services. Most of the personnel were under twenty-four years of age. Binney showed a determination to break with traditional methods by taking with him eight technicians and nine scientists. Usually few technicians were taken and in this the expedition showed itself modern and forward-looking. Key members were C. S. Elton, chief scientist, E. Relf, physicist, surveyor and wireless operator, Lt. J.R.T. Aldous, on loan from the War Office, as chief surveyor, Capt. F. Tymms as seaplane observer and navigator, on loan from the Air Ministry, and Dr H. Florey[22] as medical officer.

The expedition set sail in the *Polar Bjorn* on 19th June, reaching Tromso on the 27th. Binney was glad that it was a Norwegian vessel as he did not think its overloading would have passed the standards of the British Board of Trade. Binney had decided views on the hiring of a professional crew to sail the chartered ship. He considered that those expeditions who ran an expedition ship on an 'amateur' crew were "Allowing pride to interfere with expediency."[23] The crew of the *Polar Bjorn* were experienced sailors, but their expertise was but mainly at coastal sailing, rather than in negotiating arctic conditions, so at Tromso Binney took on a captain, Nicholai Aas, with arctic experience.

During the voyage the navigators and technicians gathered in the main saloon while the base of the scientists was Elton's cabin. The light-hearted atmosphere of the expedition can be gathered from Binney's account of the voyage. Speaking of the navigators group, labelled by the rest as the "cosines" he said "one notes that some lurking despiser of the cosines club has crossed out the word 'Nautical' on the almanac and substituted 'Old Moore's' instead." Of the scientists he says, they congregated in Elton's cabin "surrounded by test tubes, bottles of pure alcohol and formulae. Of course we all know why the scientists

---

22   Later to become famous for his role in the discovery of penicillin.
23   Binney, *Seaplane and Sledge*, p.43.

The *Polar Bjorn* ice-bound in Hinlopen Strait. (*Sea plane and Sledge*)

Caption Florey and Binney (right) after the reindeer hunt. (*Sea plane and Sledge*)

are all so cheerful; we suspected it long ago."[24]

On arrival at Tromso they were greeted with the sad news of Andrew Irvine's death on Everest. The year before, he had been a leading light of the Merton expedition. Binney remembered Irvine as "lion hearted, stalwart and laughter loving."[25] The *Polar Bjorn* followed the by now well-established route to Spitsbergen, around to the west coast and landing at Green Harbour, managed to unload the seaplane, and then set off for Liefde Bay on the north coast which was to be the main base. Binney stayed behind, as the *Oiland* was due to arrive at Green Harbour and Binney and the pilot, A.G.B. Ellis, were to attempt to fly from Green Harbour to Liefde Bay. The plane was an Avro 504 K with a Siddeley Lynx 180 horse-power engine. In place of the observer's seat a small cabin had been added, with windows and a sliding roof. It had been named Athene, after the goddess who had helped Odysseus, but was often referred to as "that ... seaplane."[26] The first test flights were reasonably successful and Binney described the sensation of flying above Green Bay: "There we were looking down on the whole mighty range of Spitsbergen peaks, soaring above glaciers, spying down on a vast country whose secrets are laid bare to the skies alone."[27] However, the plane had been flying without much of the equipment it would usually have onboard and Binney was worried about its sluggish performance even with a light load. A further 150 revolutions would need to be produced, by adjustments to the engine, if the seaplane was to perform well in all circumstances.

Having completed test flights the seaplane set off at 9.45 am on 14th July to join the expedition which was establishing its base at Liefde Bay. Binney described the flight with typical understatement – "our first and worst adventure in the seaplane." At first all went well, with the aeroplane making 70 mph with no strain. However, after 59 minutes of flying, the sudden failure of the engine resulted in a sea ditching. The plane was well equipped for an emergency landing on land, with a month's supplies and sledging equipment. Unfortunately the paddles and collapsible boat had been removed to lessen the weight. Binney and Ellis made makeshift paddles out of ice axes and sledging ration boxes and attempted to paddle for shore. When they had landed they were within a quarter of a mile of the shore, but the seaplane's fixed wings had acted as sails and within ten minutes they were double that distance from shore. Three hours later they had made little progress and were in danger of being swept entirely out to sea. As each headland approached, they paddled furiously for the rocks, but were swept past each time. They were very thirsty and dared not eat for fear of increasing their thirst. They realised that on the increasing swell the plane would swiftly break up.

After hours of paddling with a makeshift paddle, at 11.45 pm when the situation looked hopeless, Ellis announced to the astonished Binney that he was going to get some sleep: "Good night mate. I'm going to turn in." However, at 1.00 am they spotted a small motor-boat struggling out to them and realising rescue was in sight, drank the small amount of brandy they had been saving and smoked their last cigarettes. Their rescuers were Norwegian University students who were working for the Norwegian Government at a weather research station at Quade Hook. As the seaplane had passed Quade Hook, Binney had seen their hut and fired off a few rounds of his gun, but did not realise he had

24   Ibid., p.44.
25   Ibid., p.47.
26   Ibid., p.77.
27   Ibid., p.74.

The *Polar Bjorn* moored to an ice floe off the sledging base. (*Sea plane and Sledge*)

Finding Isis Point. (*Sea plane and Sledge*)

attracted their attention. Ellis and Binney had been adrift for nearly 14 hours and were exhausted. Importantly for Binney's hopes for the rest of the expedition the seaplane was also rescued and proved repairable. One of the piston heads had broken and the cylinder had been badly scored with bits of broken metal. Every part of the engine would have to be dismantled and washed. The experience had been salutary. Binney commented "we were no longer harbouring blind delusions of mechanical perfection in aircraft."[28]

As soon as the aircraft and crew were safely back at Liefde Bay the *Polar Bjorn* and *Oiland* set out to reconnoitre a suitable place to land on the north coast of North East Land. Another near disaster occurred when both ships were caught on reefs off Low Island but managed to get off within 12 hours. The objective was to land at Brandy Bay, but not only was the bay still icebound, there did not appear to be a glacier at the head of the bay from which to launch the sledging parties up onto the ice cap. No suitable landing place could be found on the north coast so Binney turned back and eventually found a suitable place at the entrance to Whalenberg Bay. He explained that a base further inside the bay would have given the sledging parties better access, but that it would have also considerably increased the risk of being frozen in if weather conditions changed quickly, or alternatively being frozen out, and consequently unable to pick up sledging parties.

Binney described the difficulties of summer sledging in his article in *The Times:* "The condition of the ice was all but hopeless. But here is one of the drawbacks of a summer expedition. However soft the snow you must go ahead." He went on to explain how trying to move equipment by sledge was difficult in such conditions: "It is a thankless task dragging idle theodolites through an endless quagmire of snow and water, the dogs worn to mere skeletons, hungry and apathetic."[29] Two sledging parties were landed at Whalenburg Bay on 21st July. The northern party had a wireless transmitting set as well as a receiver, for the first time on any sledge journey. However, the usefulness of this innovation was undermined by the fact that Law, the wireless operator, had been taken back to King's Bay with pleurisy. During this northern journey, no messages were received from inland, due to the fact that the sledgers were not confident of the wireless procedures, and due to the disorganisation resulting from Law's illness, communications from the ship also broke down. Binney commented in his account of the expedition:

> Wireless experiments conducted under favourable conditions ... are of very little practical value ... such experiments can only be of practical value if carried out under the many difficult conditions which face a sledging party during an arduous journey.

The party consisted of Lt. J.R.T. Aldous, RE, leader and surveyor, F.A. Montague, an Oxford running blue, W.B. Carslake, an expert mountaineer, and Lindquist, one of the Norwegian dog drivers. The two sledges, one of nine feet and one of eleven feet, carried 1,350 lbs, which when a margin of 4% is added for the fact that everything was soaked in water, meant a true weight of 1,400 lbs. Due to the poor snow conditions of half-frozen slush, the party only averaged three to four miles a day. Aldous described men hauling the smaller sledge up the glacier to higher ground as "One of the hardest jobs physically I have ever had."[30] Difficulties with the quality of the dogs' pemmican which necessitated

28   Binney, *Seaplane and Sledge*, p.96.
29   *The Times*, 10th October 1924.
30   Sledging diary of Lt. J.R.T. Aldous, 21st July 1924, cited in Binney, *Sledge and Seaplane*, p.119.

A photographic portrait of Binney, date unknown. (*The Conquest of the North Pole*) (1934)

in them having to have double rations in order to keep their strength up resulted in a curtailment of the party's reach. They visited Mount Celsius, a trig point established by a Swedish expedition at which they needed to take readings for their survey and found some Swedish beer bottles, unfortunately empty. Their journey of 25 days had seen 18 days of fog or blizzard. A high point was the view experienced at the top of Snow Hill, where peak by peak the whole of the North Cape Mountains came into view. They returned on 15th August, having seen little but the plateau.

Meanwhile the *Oiland* had returned to Whalenburg Bay from a reconnaissance along the south coast of North East Land, on 5th August, with interesting news about ice conditions of the east coast. Usually the closeness of the polar pack ice to the large ice cliffs on this coast had made landing unlikely but now the *Oiland* reported open water of the east coast. Binney rapidly decided to seize this opportunity and lead a sledging party from the east coast of North East Land to Whalenberg Bay. This would be the first crossing of North East Land. The journey took eleven days, covered 75 miles and entailed Binney leaving the main part of the expedition under the command of Tennant. He reported to *The Times* "as we had no idea what conditions we might encounter in the interior we took three weeks' rations and a packet of playing cards." The first few days involved very hard and wet conditions of soft snow to reach the plateau. Binney described the weather conditions prevailing. "Fog, mist, winds and blizzards are requisites dear to the heart of North East Land. Occasionally the mist would roll away and reveal a vast expanse of snowy waste. There is no uncovered land in the interior".[31] They then came upon the "ice canals" described by Nordenskiold. These were chasms from 39 to 100 feet wide and some 40 feet deep. Binney, with typical understatement and optimism, reported to *The Times* that "as their floor was level they proved excellent places to camp, affording protection from the wind." Two days later they came across an ice field of impassable crevasses. "Perched between two yawning chasms we camped."[32] The glacier that now lay beyond and separated them from their destination of Whalenberg Bay was named Eton Glacier and posed severe problems in crossing it. The sledges had to man-hauled while the dogs were held and gingerly the team picked their way across the glacier. Binney described the Eton Glacier as "The finest feature of the western coast of North East Land." Certainly it provided spectacular views of the coast and the mountains of New Friesland. It was nine miles broad and covered the end of Whalenberg Bay. This third sledge journey was of importance as it enabled a cross-section of North East Land to be plotted.

The central sledging party had meanwhile been surveying along the north coast, a landing at Cape Mohn, their original objective having been impracticable. The party consisted of Frazer, an experienced sledger, Clutterbuck, who was "only really cheerful when circumstances were intolerable", Sandford, the geologist and Schmidt the Norwegian dog driver. They did reach the plateau but encountered very difficult conditions. Torrential rain hindered their return journey and Hayes recounted how "the name of one camping place – 'hell camp' – is an indication not of the temperature but the warmth of the men's feelings."[33] They returned on 15th August and were lucky to do so without serious injury or loss of life.

The seaplane had been repaired sufficiently by 28th July to have a test flight and was moved on 7th August to Treurenberg Bay. A flight was made over Whalenberg Bay to look at ice conditions. A flight on the 13th was hampered by a leaking tank and on the 15th another crash resulted in her being taken to Liefde Bay for repairs. On the 30th the seaplane continued its aerial survey. Throughout the expedition it had taken aerial photos of 100 miles of North East Land coastline. It was the first time that any explorer had transported a fully rigged seaplane on a small ship. Unfortunately it was abandoned, except for the engine, when the expedition parties left as it was in too bad a condition to take home. It had surveyed nearly 100 miles of North East Land taking aerial photographs, and had proved that seaplanes were useful adjuncts to polar exploration. At the time of returning it held the record for the furthest flight north at 80° 14 N. Binney considered that using the aeroplane had been a worthwhile project in that it had:

> Demonstrated that aircraft can play its part in arctic exploration, and that air work can be coordinated with sledging and other scientific interests without monopolising the time or narrowing the scope of the expedition.[34]

On 18th August the members of the expedition who had to return to Britain by the first week of September were taken around to King's Bay to catch a collier ship home. Binney had to decide how best to use the time remaining for exploration and decided

---

31   *The Times*, 11th October 1924.
32   *The Times*, 11th October 1924.
33   Hayes, *Conquest of the North Pole*, p.216.
34   Binney, *Sledge and Seaplane*, p.253.

On the ice plateau. (*Sea plane and Sledge*)

to concentrate on Wahlenberg Bay, especially its base, which had not been explored or surveyed. He considered that as the bay was the most striking feature of the North East Land coastline, as it penetrates inland almost to the ice cap, a survey would be an important addition to the achievements of the expedition. Consequently the *Polar Bjorn* set out on 23rd August and passing Treurenberg Bay on their way south, noticed that the mouth of the bay, which had been ice-free less than a week before, was now filled with ice floes. They anchored on the south side of Whalenberg Bay. Aldous and Clutterbuck managed to get the theodolite to the top of the 1,100 feet high cliffs to take observations while Sandford collected geological specimens and Montague climbed down the face of the cliff to study the Ivory gull colony. The cliffs were named the Clarendon Cliffs. Crossing to the north side of the bay they went inland and discovering a region of Tundra land half surrounded by a lagoon, named it Oxford Peninsula. Unfortunately they did not have time to follow the lagoon as it extended northward into a narrow valley. The large glacier, nine miles wide at the head of the bay, had been seen by the central sledging party and crossed by the southern party, and was now named Eton Glacier.

Preparations were now made for a survey and a hill three miles inland was chosen as the centre of the survey operations. At the end of that day's surveying the captain was anxious to depart as he expected the northerly wind conditions to bring fresh ice. However, the surveying equipment had been left at the top of the hill now known as Carfax Hill, Binney hinted, deliberately. The captain's caution appeared justified as, when a group took the motor boat to the other side of the bay after dinner, they were stranded by some new ice and had to remain there until the following morning when they were able to pick their way through the ice back to the ship. That morning the final observations were taken from Carfax Hill and the *Polar Bjorn* sailed for Leifde Bay. The expedition left Spitsbergen on 1st September and returned home on the 18th. Binney described the moment of departure:

Leaving the aeroplane – our child of many hope and fears – to her lonely vigil of the arctic winter, the *Polar Bjorn* put to sea and from the bridge we stole a last glance at the serene and peerless expanse of Leifde Bay.[35]

The expedition was hailed a remarkable success. According to Hayes, the president of the Royal Geographical Society, "Much geographical work of real value was accomplished."[36] Taking his three expeditions altogether 60 scientific papers were presented. Between the 1923 and the 1924 expeditions North East Land had been nearly circumnavigated and a traverse of the island was completed by Binney's sledge party on the 1924 expedition. Two maps of the island were completed by the School of Military Engineering at Chatham.

The film of the expedition was first shown on 25th February 1925. All the members of the expedition were invited, most replied in the affirmative, but some were apprehensive of the presence of the "panic party". One accepted the invitation but speaking of the "panic party" said "I feel their presence would lead to considerable strain, maybe friction and worst of all plain speaking".[37] It would appear the best-organised and amiable expeditions also suffered from occasional tensions.

The expeditions proved the worth of combined geographical and scientific work and were instrumental in developing the addition of new technologies such as radio and seaplane to the traditional methods. *The Times* commented on the success of the experiments with flight: "The most practical outcome of the venture is the incontestable proof that it has furnished of the value of aircraft in the enterprise of Arctic exploration."[38] The expeditions were well planned, with a successful mixture of "brawn" and "brain". The style of leadership displayed by Binney set the pattern for other inter-war explorers such as Gino Watkins and Sandy Glen. Binney reiterated his faith in his methods when writing in the introduction to his account of the expedition: "This book will have fulfilled its purpose if it fosters the old spirit and points at the same time to beyond the old methods of arctic exploration."[39] It is significant that, as W.J. Solas pointed put in his preface, "the whole party – not a man missing, not even a dog – returned home safe and sound". Binney was awarded the Gold Medal of the Geographical Society of Paris, the Back Award and the Founder's Gold Medal of the Royal Geographical Society for his achievements.

Blockade Buster 1940-44

It was the year of his birth, 1900, that indirectly led Binney to the wartime career which was to continue his contribution to the history of Britain in the 20th Century, by pulling off one of the first major successes of Special Operations Executive. His knowledge of winter ocean conditions and his calm determination, both shown to good advantage on his expeditions, were to be invaluable in the difficult task of breaking the German blockade of Sweden in order to bring vitally needed supplies to Britain. He had narrowly missed service in the Great War, being accepted for a commission on 11th December 1918. He was determined to see action when the Second World War broke out, but at thirty-nine years of age was told he was now too old to receive a commission in the Navy, but he was determined

---

35   Ibid., p.253.
36   Hayes, *Conquest of the North Pole*, p.217.
37   GB 15, Scott Polar Research Institute, University of Cambridge.
38   *The Times*, October 10th 1924.
39   Binney, *Seaplane and Sledge*, p.21.

to contribute to the war effort in an active way.

Binney's exploits in the Arctic in the 1920s had earned him a job with the Hudson's Bay Company and his work in the Canadian Arctic further developed his expertise in arctic living. He wrote *The Eskimo Book of Knowledge* in 1931, which resulted in an offer of promotion to the company's headquarters in Winnipeg, but in 1931 Binney returned to Britain to take up a position developing the exports at United Steel Company.

Britain was depending on supplies of engineering materials and steel from Scandinavia and here Binney saw an opportunity to be of use to the war effort. Sir Andrew Duncan sent him to Stockholm to represent the interests of the British steel industry in Scandinavia, but before leaving Binney also made contact with the Ministry of Economic Warfare and Charles Hambro, who was later to become the boss of the Special Operations Executive in Scandinavia. Binney was asked to use his appointment in the steel industry to keep his eyes open for anything that would help British Military Intelligence. To help him in this task he was made Assistant Commercial Attaché to the legation. He spent the period of the 'Phoney War' travelling around Sweden and Norway, familiarising himself further with the details of the iron ore and steel industries, and negotiating contracts with Swedish companies under the terms of the Anglo-Swedish War Trade Agreement, negotiated in October 1939.

Binney quickly realised that with the occupation of Norway and the collapse of Finland, that the Skagerrak would be closed to shipping and that the Germans would now have control of shipping in and out of Norway and Sweden. Sweden was neutral but dependent on Germany. Binney also realised that it was vital for the British war effort that all the supplies he had been negotiating should get safely to Britain. A message sent to Binney from Sir Andrew Duncan at the Ministry of Supply confirmed that it was of "paramount importance" that the war stores on order in Sweden should be delivered to England[40] and that "any expediment could be used to reach this end."[41] The priorities of the British Ministry of Supply and the Ministry of Economic Warfare were hollow tubes for the manufacture of ball bearings, steel strip, pig iron, bar iron and machine tools. Particularly urgent were the roller bearings for the new strip mill at Ebbw Vale.

Binney's original route to get the goods out via Finnish ports from Petsamo to Kirkenes with the help of France was now useless due to the defeat of Finland by Russia in March 1940. After Germany's attack on France in May 1940, he turned to the idea of moving the material out of Swedish ports via the Skagerrak, despite the obvious difficulties of German shore batteries, Luftwaffe air supremacy and mined shipping lanes. Binney's arctic seagoing experience gave him confidence that things were never as difficult as they seemed. He wrote "automatically we must meet exceptional difficulties with exceptional measures".[42] The flexibility he had shown in adapting to rapidly changing circumstances in the Arctic now became focused on defeating all obstacles to his plan.

Binney's plan now took shape. Realising that the threat of mines was diminished if he kept the ships to the very deep channel in the Skagerrak, the main threat remained from the air. The Luftwaffe were ensconced in bases either side of the Skagerrak, but if the ships could sail in conditions of very bad visibility then that threat was reduced. He decided that the port of Gothenburg would be the assembly point for his ships even though he had no

---

40   TNA FO 371/29424. Report on the Gothenburg shipment plan by George Binney, 12th February 1941.
41   Ibid.
42   Ibid.

intention of departing from there. Fearful that the Swedish Government would impound Swedish ships, he procured Norwegian ships that had been stranded in Sweden after the invasion of Norway. These ships had been put by the Norwegian Government under the protection of 'Notraship', the Norwegian Trading and Shipping Mission based in London, and were therefore Allied ships. Any ships used had to be oil burners as they had to retain an element of surprise for the eventual break out, and coal-fuelled ships took too long to get up steam.

Meanwhile, the fall of France had resulted in the backtracking of support of Binney's plans from the Ministry of Economic Warfare and from the legation staff in Sweden, who were wondering if the war might not be over in a matter of weeks. Binney, who according to Ralph Barker "had been aggressively intolerant of anyone who did not seem to him to be engaged in the all-out prosecution of the War", continued to keep up the pressure, supported by Jack Mitcheson at the legation: "We feel that the question of the delivery of steel to the United Kingdom has passed out of the province of civil servants and is possibly better adapted to the attention of the more adventurous such as Mr Binney."[43] However, by 28th June it was confirmed that Binney should stay in Sweden and continue with his efforts.

The first attempt to deliver Swedish supplies to Britain took place in July 1940 in a fishing boat the *Lahti* and had failed. The ship had been captured by the Germans and taken as prize. When planning the next stage of the operation Binney was convinced that one the reasons for the failure of the *Lahti* was because of low morale in the crew and decided that he should sail with the ships: "He felt that having planned the details he could not fail to take part in the operation."[44] However the voyage of the *Lahti* had given Binney some useful tips in the planning of what had been code named "Operation Rubble". It was apparent that successful blockade running required the cover of long nights and the favour of bad weather. The fact that the *Lahti* had not been blown up by mines and that fishing boats had been operating in the area she was taken in showed that "German minefields, if they existed, enjoyed a greater reputation than their efficiency deserved."[45]

He was now relived of some of the administrative burden involved by Bill Waring, an accountant stranded in Sweden who had been conscripted by the legation. He spoke Swedish and Norwegian and his efficiency was complementary to Binney's more swashbuckling ability to inspire others and get events moving. There were now several problems to be solved before the proposed convoy could convene. The first was the question of crew. The Norwegian masters of the vessels chosen and their crew were reluctant to risk being blown up in the Skagerrak as an alternative to being laid up in a neutral harbour. Binney had been assured that the captains of the Norwegian vessels were enthusiastic about taking their ships to England, but soon realised that that was not the case. They were asking for a British naval escort. Binney explained this could not be provided, at least not until the North Sea. The Royal Navy had learned in the Norwegian campaign the folly of taking British ships too near to enemy shores without adequate air support (see Chapter Seven). He was keen to have the masters on board as they all had the local knowledge vital for the break out in Swedish waters. The masters of the ships were not satisfied with Binney's proposition, saying the risks were too great, but his negotiating skills won the day and although he could

43   Ralph Barker, *The Blockade Busters* (New York, 1976), p.28.
44   TNA FO 371/2924. Report on Operation Rubble by J.M. Addis, Foreign Office, dated 29th January 1941.
45   TNA F0 371/29424. Report on the Gothenburg shipment plan by George Binney, 12th February 1941.

not convince the masters he convinced 31 crew members to join him, including two with Master's tickets, and four radio operators. King Hakon was asked to send a message of encouragement to the Norwegian crews to improve morale in the lead up to the operation. His next attempt at signing up crew was to talk to the British crews of oil tankers that had been captured at Narvik and were in a camp at Halsingmo, free to go in theory but unable to return to Britain. Signing up for Binney's voyage gave them that opportunity.

A race against time now ensued, with the cargoes being loaded swiftly enough to move the ships one by one to Brofjord, an isolated fjord, ready for their breakout. The Norwegian owners were coming under pressure from their owners to get their ships arrested and impounded at Gothenburg, so the planned move became more necessary. By the end of December the five ships were all together at Brofjord, awaiting the right weather conditions to break out into the Skagerrak. There were four large cargo liners and one tanker, with total tonnage of 43,000 tons. These were loaded with Swedish pig iron, special steels, ball bearings and machine tools which, according to Binney, were "Representing a year's supply of Swedish material urgently required by the Ministry of Supply for war production."[46]

The British Government had promised an escort from a rendezvous point at 58° N 03° East. This meant that having emerged from the Skagerrak the ships would still face a hundred miles of dangerous waters before meeting the escorts. The orders were cautious in their estimation of support: "Naval and air support have been promised ... do not think you will be suddenly surrounded by British warships, for such is unlikely, but you may feel something encouraging in the fact that Navy support will be at hand." [47]

On 23rd January 1941 all the captains accepted that conditions were acceptable to sail and that further delay could result in cancellation. The ships were unarmed and not degaussed.[48] Captain Blucher, the pro-ally Swedish head of the harbour police at Gothenburg, had interpreted his instruction on neutrality widely in order to be of help to Binney. Binney remembered that Blucher was constantly on the alert to stop the Germans from planting Nazis amongst the engineering staff. Blucher had used the excuse of a snowstorm to disrupt telecommunications and managed to convey to Binney that there would be little chance of the departure of the ships being discovered until the next day. The first and slowest ship, the *Ranja,* was to go at 14.30 then came the *John Bakke* followed by the *Elizabeth Bakke*. At 16.30 the *Tai Shan*, the last ship, with Binney on board, left. They had all been fitted with sea-cocks which would enable their very speedy scuttling if arrest by the Germans became inevitable. All crews had been issued with Swedish all-over dry suits. The *Tai Shan* was captained by a Norwegian captain and this enabled him to have a Norwegian ship as his flag ship, which he hoped would improve morale and foster a sense of unity between the Norwegian and British crews. The whole operation could have easily been ruined early on by the unexpected presence of the German battle cruisers *Scharnhorst* and *Gneisenau*, who had left Kiel that morning. Fortunately their paths did not cross as the German ships were delayed by ice and were at anchor while the Rubble ships were crossing the approaches to Oslo Fjord.

What was needed was bad weather and poor visibility but by the morning the weather was fine, the ships were in full view of the Norwegian coast and there were still 60 miles to reach the rendezvous. Binney fully expected air attack by the Germans as the weather

---

46   Account of Operation Rubble written by Binney contained in TNA FO 371/2924.
47   Cited by Ralph Barker, *Blockade Busters*, p.60.
48   Ibid.

M/V *John Bakke*

was so good. The expected air support from the RAF did not materialise due to fog at the air bases, but fortunately weather conditions in Norway also delayed the appearance of German air patrols. As the morning hours passed Binney became anxious about the lack of aeroplanes. He had not realised that the main purpose of the RAF in the venture was to protect the naval escort ships, not the Rubble ships. At 11.15 the first of the naval escort ships arrived, the *Niad*, followed by the *Aurora*. A German reconnaissance plane then arrived and though deterred from attacking by the presence of the British ships, kept them all under observation. Binney was worried by the non-appearance of two of the Rubble ships, the *John Bakke* and the *Ranja*.

An RAF Hudson had now appeared on the scene and escorted the *Taurus* and the *Tai Shan* while the *Niad* and *Aurora* went to look for the *John Bakke* and the *Ranja*, who eventually had emerged from the Skagerrak. Meanwhile the Blenheim aircraft escorting the *Aurora* and *Niad* had had an air battle with two Messerschmitt Bf 110 fighters. German intelligence concerning the 'Rubble' ships must have been sketchy because they seemed unwilling the attack the *Ranja* and the *John Bakke* who were sitting ducks for several hours and who appear to have been escorted by German planes. Eventually the German planes realised what was happening and attacked the *Ranja*, fatally wounding one man, but then the *Niad* caught up with her and the attack was driven off. During the hours of darkness the five ships were all escorted to Kirkwall Roads and Binney had the satisfaction of knowing that a year's supply of war material for the British engineering industry had been delivered. Against stiff opposition and facing unlikely chance of success Binney had pulled off a major achievement in terms of materials and morale.

A Foreign Office report written in January 1941 gave Binney credit for the operation's success:

The success of the operation was due to the flawless staff work and the apparent inability of the German machine to function quickly enough. The greatest credit however must be given to Mr Binney, who conceived the plan and pursued it with unfailing courage and determination. He risked his life by sailing with the ships.[49]

On 12th June 1941 *The Times* announced the award of a knighthood to Binney, for "Special services in the supply of valuable war materials". The newspapers, knowing that an embargo had been put on a supply operation, called him "The Mystery Knight". Churchill compared Binney to a seafaring adventurer of Elizabethan times, and gave the go ahead for further blockade running. Binney was offered a job in Washington, but refused, wanting to oversee the next operation.

Naturally, after the success of Operation Rubble, Binney wanted to take advantage of the long nights of winter to arrange another breakout of ships bearing essential materials to Britain. 'Performance', the second operation, was planned for November 1941. The Germans had been annoyed by the 'Rubble' venture and had warned the Swedish Government in no uncertain terms that "connivance in any further operation would be regarded by Germany as an unfriendly act."[50] The procurement of materials from Sweden, was however, still urgent. A "most secret" Foreign office memo on Operation Performance considered that "failure to obtain these cargos would have a very serious effect on tank production—and would retard production of aircraft."[51]

Machine tools for the ball bearing industry, essential to the production of tanks and aircraft, were still desperately required. War materials which were not available from the USA, or those materials which the lack of was causing a bottleneck in the British production line, were eagerly awaited. Another aim was to secure as much shipping tonnage for the Allied cause as possible. The task was obviously to be more difficult a second time. Ten ships were earmarked for the operation. The five tankers were the *B.P. Newton*, the *Rigmor*, the *Buccaneer*, the *Storsten*, and the *Lind*. There were four cargo ships – the *Lionel*, the *Dicto*, the *Gudvang* and the *Charente*, and a whaler factory ship, the *Skytteren*.

The ships and their cargoes were in the harbour at Gothenburg, a mile away from open sea. After Operation Rubble it was also believed that the Germans had mined the North Sea between the Orkneys and the Norwegian coast. The Swedish government, a few days before the proposed departure of the ten ships earmarked for the operation, passed a bill hurriedly through parliament allowing the arrest of the ships. The ships were therefore stuck at Gothenburg while legal battles raged to release them and while telegrams flew back and forth between Binney and the Foreign Office and SOE about the likelihood of Germany declaring war on Sweden if the breakout went ahead. Eventually on 22nd January 1942 Binney received a cable giving him permission to go ahead at his discretion from any time thence.[52] However, the position of the ships in Gothenburg harbour made it very unlikely that an attempt without the support of the Swedish Government would succeed. If the breakout was unsuccessful the Swedish government would arrest or requisition all Norwegian ships in Swedish waters and perhaps reimburse the Germans with equivalent

49   TNA FO 371/2924 Report by J.M. Addis, Foreign Office, dated 29th January 1941.
50   Marcus Binney, *Secret War Heroes: The Men of Special Operations Executive* (London, 2006), p.54.
51   TNA FO371/29424.
52   Marcus Binney, *Secret War Heroes*, p.70.

The whaling ship *Skytteren*

amounts of materials if any ships were successful.[53] By 17th March legal difficulties had been resolved and the ships were free to sail.

While waiting for unseasonal ice to clear the ships were moved to a better position at the mouth of the harbour and German forces in the form of naval and air patrols were waiting outside. Marcus Binney considers that it became obvious that "The performance ships would be driven straight out of Swedish waters on to German guns."[54] Eventually on 1st April the blockade runners slipped out of harbour. Morale was high, with the prospect of sailing at last, and was bolstered by Binney's 'order of the day' in which he assured the captains and crew that he looked "once more to our success, believing that before two days have passed your laughter will resound within a British port."[55]

Their orders were to disperse on different routes and not to act as a convoy. The weather, foggy when they emerged, soon cleared and they were spotted by a German aircraft immediately, with U boats, surface vessels and aircraft in pursuit. It was no longer possible to provide the level of British naval and air support given to Operation Rubble. The three destroyers *Wallace*, *Valorous* and *Vanity* accompanied by three others under the command of Captain Scott Moncrieff, were only able to provide surface protection from about 100 miles from the British coast. Air cover consisted of No. 18 Group Coastal Command and some Mosquitoes from Bomber Command, which would meet the ships off the entrance to the Skagerrak. The RAF put up opposition to air attacks on the ships who made it through the Skagerrak Channel, but they still had 200 miles to go to reach the naval escort.

Six of the ten ships had been lost, either sunk or scuttled. The *Rigmor* and the *Lind* ran into a German patrol boat as soon as they left Swedish territorial waters and on being challenged, returned to the territorial waters. The tankers *Lionel* and *Buccaneer*

53   Ibid., pp.70-71.
54   Ibid., p.78.
55   Cited by Barker, *Blockade Busters*, p.108.

encountered a German armed trawler, who proceeded to open fire on the slowest of the ships, the *Buccaneer*, allowing the *Lionel* to escape. The captain of the *Buccaneer* started to evacuate the crew prior to scuttling the ship, but was prevented from loading the lifeboats by heavy fire across the boat deck. Determined to succeed in denying the tanker to the enemy, he set of explosive charges in the engine room which enveloped the ship in dark smoke. The German trawler, seeing that the captain was determined, ceased fire and allowed the evacuation of the ship. The whaling ship *Skytteren* was challenged by a German patrol boat and also scuttled, her crew being taken on board by the German vessel. The *Storsten* survived hitting a floating mine and an air attack to be finished off by an attack from a German patrol vessel, but the captain succeeded in getting the crew into lifeboats and scuttling the ship. One of the lifeboats was lost without trace. The *Rigmor*, after changing her mind about returning, sailed west and was within 180 miles of the Scottish coast when she was attacked and abandoned, later sinking. Binney aboard the *Dicto* had stayed off the coast of Halo Island, waiting a favourable weather forecast. When the forecast he received predicted that the weather would clear, leaving the escaping ships exposed, he broke radio silence to warn the other ships. Because of a mistake in wiring the sets, the message went out on the wrong wavelength and was never received.

The *Lionel* and the *Dicto* had managed to return to Gothenburg with their cargoes intact and the B.P. *Newton* and the *Lind* had reached Britain. The *Newton* was carrying 27% of the total cargo by value and 45% of the value of the cargo was safely back in Swedish ports on the *Dicto* and the *Lind*. Unfortunately this included some of the most sought after material, the heavy machinery needed for making ball bearings in Britain. The operation was considered a partial success but some criticism was made of Binney by the Norwegians for his overconfidence in the face of many problems, asserting that the success of Operation Rubble had warped his judgement about the second, more dangerous attempt. There was some suggestion that Binney had deliberately hesitated and then returned to port, leaving his fellow ships to sail straight into German attacks. Some doubted the explanation of the mis-sent message, and it was not until the enquiry into the operation reported in August 1942 that the mix up with wiring at Gothenburg harbour could be proved. The Swedish Government were also furious that guns had been smuggled aboard the Performance ships and had been used to defend them, in contravention of laws forbidding the export of arms from Sweden. They alleged that "British officials", using their diplomatic immunity, had smuggled the guns on board the ships.[56] Binney was asked to leave Sweden, which he did. In August 1942 the Foreign office produced the results of its enquiry into the operation. This came up with 16 points explaining why the operation was not as successful as hoped for, and exonerated Binney from the criticisms made against him.

Operation Performance appeared to be the last chance to bring out the vital cargoes still left in Gothenburg Harbour. The Swedish Government were even more nervous of the repercussions of ships leaving and put a boom over the mouth of Gothenburg harbour. The Germans stationed a force of destroyers in Kristiansand in southern Norway and extended their minefields in the Skagerrak. George Binney however had not given up and as the demand for Swedish war material continued, set his mind to alternative plans. He put forward a plan involving the use of converted MGBs (Motor Gun Boats) manned by merchant crews, flying the Red Ensign, which would sail to the Swedish coast and pick

---

56   *The Times*, 25th April 1942.

up the cargos of the *Lionel* and *Dicto,* bringing much needed supplies back for the home armaments industry.

The MGBs were the new D class which had a top speed of 27 knots. The plan was to use ten hours of winter darkness to enable the returning MGBs to be 200 miles west of the Skagerrak at dawn. They were armed with two Oerlikons and power-mounted 0.5 inch machine guns. Binney explained how the gunboats would evade attack:

> Our normal cruising speed will be 15/16 knots. Our maximum speed when loaded will be 22/23 knots but this will be reserved for emergencies. If attacked by E boats we should have sufficient firepower to hold our own. If attacked by armed trawlers we should have sufficient speed to evade. If attacked by destroyers or by the Dutch Gun boats we should have to run into the shallow mined waters off the Danish coast where ships of deeper draft would not follow.[57]

It was suggested that the boats fly the White Ensign to make it less likely that the crews if captured would be shot as *Francs Tireurs,*[58] but Binney insisted that Merchant Navy personnel were ideal for the operation, and flying the Red Ensign they would be entitled to enter Swedish ports. The crews were recruited through the office of Ellerman's Wilson. The complement of each ship was between eighteen and twenty years old, the average age was twenty-five, with all the masters being under forty. As merchant ships were allowed to carry an officer from the armed services to take charge of defensive armaments, this allowed Binney to put an SOE person on each ship as a "Chief Officer".

Three engineers were flown out to Gothenburg to maintain the boats at the Swedish end, and a meteorological specialist taken to be based on the *Dicto* to provide accurate weather forecasts as decisions taken on the timing of journeys would heavily depend on them. The five ships, the *Hopewell*, the *Nonsuch*, the *Gay Viking*, the *Gay Corsair* and the *Master Standfast* had a "working up" period in which the mechanical problems which were to beset the operations were already evident. The operations were to start on 24th September. The crews had instructions to engage enemy E boats or trawlers, but to run for the shallows if they encountered heavier ships. As a last resort the ships were to be scuttled.

However, due to trouble in all five ships, relating to bearing problems, the initial start date was cancelled. As a complete cure for the trouble would involve re-engining the ships resulting in the cancellation of the operation for the winter, Binney decided that "if we could not use all the engines the whole time we must make do by using some of the engines most of the time."[59] The operation had now missed the September no moon period and had to wait until October. Eventually, at 16.45 on Tuesday 26th October Operation Bridford set out from the Humber estuary. By dawn of the 27th the flotilla was at a position of 200 miles south west of the entrance to the Skagerrak. Binney planned to reach the Skagerrak by dusk and be poised for a dash through the most treacherous part of the journey under cover of darkness. It was at this point that it was realised that the *Gay Viking*, who had earlier reported engine trouble, was no longer with them.

They were spotted, and came under brief attack by an enemy patrol aircraft, but after they had returned fire, the aircraft disappeared. When nothing further happened, the flotilla

---

57   TNA ADM1/24 248. Report on Operation Bridford.
58   A. Hampshire, *On Hazardous Service* (London, 1974), p.164.
59   Ibid., p.160.

resumed its course to the Skagerrak. Trouble with the gearboxes in *Nonsuch* and *Standfast* reduced their speed to 15 knots. As they would not be able to reach their destination in darkness, Binney reluctantly decided that they would return to Immingham. When they docked they learned that the *Gay Viking*, after having dealt with her engine trouble had proceeded alone, keeping a close watch out for the rest of the flotilla but not signalling as to not give away his own position. After encountering only a patrolling Heinkel 111, which had not attacked them, the *Gay Viking* proceeded as planned through the Skagerrak at night and arrived at Lysekil at 4.40 a.m., returning without incident with 40 tons of much needed cargo.

On the 31st, Binney set off with two of the flotilla who were unaffected by engine trouble, the *Hopewell* and the *Master Standfast*. *Master Standfast* dragged behind during the passage through the Skagerrak and disappeared, not to be seen again. When the remaining vessel arrived in Lysekil they heard the news that *Master Standfast* had been captured by a German armed trawler and had sustained casualties. After extensive engine repairs *Hopewell* then returned with 40 tons of cargo and six Norwegians anxious to reach Britain and help the war effort. The *Hopewell* experienced further engine trouble on the way home, and eventually limped into port on 2nd December. According to information from the Ministry of War, by the end of December the four voyages of the ships of Operation Bridford were comparing favourably with the airlift operation which had been ferrying supplies from Sweden since July. The total freight had already amounted to 121 tons.[60] Over the next months the trips continued, Binney making the fastest round trip from 15th to 20th February 1944. By March 1944 the operation had brought over a total of 347 tons of steel balls, ball and roller bearings machine tools and electrical equipment valued at £300,000, and had also brought sixty-seven passengers. This compared with the £64,000 of material brought out by air. Andrew Duncan, President of the Board of Trade wrote to Lord Lammers, Minister of War for Transport:

> This operation gives a substantial part of the equipment for a vital new ball bearing factory ... which will enable us to maintain our own supply of ball bearings. There is no need for me to exaggerate the importance of this.[61]

Of the officers and crews of the ships of Operation Bridford, four captains were awarded the OBE along with three of the chief engineers. Nine other officers received the MBE, nineteen crew members the British Empire Medal and others, commendations. All these decorations were given for "gallantry and initiative in hazardous circumstances." Binney was awarded the DSO "for outstanding leadership and skill". The SOE men, Thorneycroft, Reynolds and Ruffman, all received the DSC.

After Operation Bridford, Binney suffered a heart attack, and was therefore only able to act in an advisory capacity to the subsequent exploits of the small blockade running flotilla. Operation Moonshine was set up to supply the SOE and resistance sabotage in Scandinavia and Northern Europe through Sweden. A voyage to Gothenburg on 13th January by the *Nonesuch*, the *Hopewell* and the *Gay Viking* delivered 40 tons of supplies and arms for the Danish resistance.

Binney's achievements and leadership have been considered to be outstanding both by

60   Ibid., p.193.
61   Barker, *Blockade Busters*, p.203.

contemporary commentators and historians. The courage and leadership shown by a man who was officially too old to join up resulted in a significant contribution to the Allied war effort. They were however character traits which had been displayed in full measure in the achievements of the arctic expeditions.

2

Freddie Spencer Chapman

The British Arctic Air Route Expedition 1930-31

During the 1920s there had been much speculation in aviation circles about the possibility of an Arctic air route. The most direct route over the Atlantic Ocean was over Greenland, and proposals were made for a route via Iceland, Greenland and Baffin Island. This was the obvious shortest route if landing places could be reconnoitred and weather conditions could be established. Although the weather systems were supposed to be easier to predict over Greenland, rather than the Atlantic, little was known about the weather in Eastern Greenland and on the ice cap which covered most of the island. There was a theory that the air in the high Arctic was calmer and more predictable that the turbulent air currents of the North Atlantic. The Canadian part of the route had already been surveyed by the Royal Canadian Mounted Police at their outposts in the Canadian archipelago. Gino Watkins, who, at twenty three, was already an accomplished polar explorer, put together a proposal to survey the East Coast of Greenland and also to set up a weather station high on the central ice cap which was thought to reach a height of 10, 000 feet.

The expedition was supported by the Royal Geographical Society and the Prince of Wales, and largely financed by Mr Stephen Courtauld, the textiles magnate. The armed forces provided equipment and personnel and Watkins was given a free hand with his selection of men. Of the 14 expedition members, only Freddie Spencer Chapman and August Courtauld had any Arctic experience, as Watkins placed more emphasis on personal knowledge of his team and also liked to mould their Arctic experience himself. He explained in his introduction to *Northern Lights*, Spencer Chapman's official account of the expedition:

> I have always deliberately chosen amateurs for such expeditions rather than men who have had Arctic experience on expeditions other than my own. Men who have been on other expeditions will have formed their own opinions on the best method of travel, and the best way of living in the Arctic. I prefer that members of my expedition should have gained their knowledge with me, since in that case I always know the exact amount of experience possessed by any member of the sledging party. If anything goes wrong on one of those parties and it fails to turn up at the proper time, I can judge more easily what the leader of the part would do in an emergency.[1]

The interior of Greenland rose to a height of over 10,000 ft above sea level. At its highest point the thickness of the ice cap was between 6,000 and 7,000 feet. Conditions were severe, with the lowest recorded temperature minus 64° centigrade, but in 1931 this information was unknown, the height and depth of the ice cap unmeasured, and large sections of coastal mountains unexplored. No British expedition had overwintered in

---

1   H.G. Watkins in the Introduction to F. Spencer Chapman, *Northern Lights, The Official Account of the British Arctic Air Route Expedition* 1930-1931 (London, 1934).

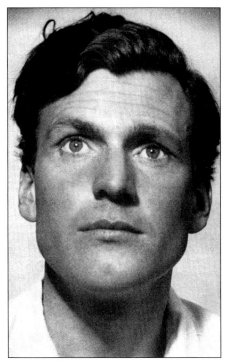

A portrait of Spencer Chapman, date unknown. (Spencer Chapman family)

The British Arctic Air Route expedition team. Gino Watkins is centre,
with Courtauld to his left and Riley to his right. (Riley family)

I. F. Meiklejohn

Q. Riley

J. I. Moore

A. Stephenson

John Rymill

E. W. Bingham

W. L. S. Fleming

B. B. Roberts

W. E. Hampton

Members of the British Graham Land Expedition 1934-37. (*Southern Lights*)

the Arctic for 50 years. Watkins's plans also included the mapping of the coastline from Angmagssalik to Kangerlugsuak, the ascent of Mount Forel and the undertaking of a series of sledge and boat journeys which would add to the knowledge of conditions in Greenland. Two aeroplanes were to be taken to be used in aerial survey, ground support, and the testing of flying conditions. It was hoped that at the end of the expedition a demonstration flight would be made between England and Winnipeg.

Freddie Spencer Chapman, while at Cambridge, had been inspired by Gino Watkins's expedition to Labrador and Spitsbergen, and had organised a small expedition to Iceland in the summer vacation of 1929. The ostensible aim of this expedition was to examine the bird life in northern Iceland and also to collect some plants for Kew Gardens, but writing in his book, *Helvellyn to Himalaya* in 1951, Spencer Chapman confessed: "Actually I wanted to experience again the thrill of setting out on some difficult or dangerous enterprise with

N. A. Gurney

H. Millett

J. H. Martin

R. E. D. Ryder

G. C. L. Bertram

V. D Carse

L. C. D. Ryder

Other members of the expedition. (*Southern Lights*)

friends of similar tastes."[2] He returned unsettled, not altogether willing to start a career as a schoolmaster. His mind was made up for him while skiing at Davos in November 1929, when a chance meeting with Watkins on the slope led to an invitation to become part of the British Arctic Air Route Expedition. It was to be some time before Spencer Chapman appeared in any classroom!

Spencer Chapman joined a team initially consisting of Watkins, himself, J.M. Scott, who had been with Watkins in Labrador, and August Courtauld who had been with J.M. Wordie to Greenland in 1926 and 1929. As preparations for the expedition gathered pace, others were recruited to specific jobs. A. Stephenson was to be chief surveyor, helped by Spencer Chapman, J.R. Rymill and Martin Lindsay, who was on loan from the Royal Scots Fusiliers. The expedition was to take two Gypsy Moth aeroplanes to help with surveying

2   F. Spencer Chapman cited in Ralph Barker, *One Man's Jungle: A Biography of F. Spencer Chapman, D.S.O.* (London, 1975), p.69.

The Quest coming through the pack ice. (*Northern Lights*)

and these were to be the responsibility of Flight Lieutenant N.H. D'Aeth of the RAF and W.E. Hampton of the Royal Air Force Reserve. Flight Lieutenant H.I. Cozens was the photographer, Quintin Riley the quartermaster, L.R. Wager scientist, and Surgeon Lieutenant E.W. Bingham expedition doctor. Watkins later wrote that if he was planning the expedition again he would have made the same choice.

The expedition ship, the *Quest,* a veteran of Shackleton's expedition, sailed down the Thames on 6th July and by 10th July had made the Faroe Islands where J.M. Scott was waiting with the expedition dogs which he had been sent ahead to purchase. On approaching Greenland's eastern coast it took three days for the *Quest* to find a way through the pack ice which is ever present on the eastern side of the island. On approaching the settlement of Angmagssalik the ship was welcomed by a fleet of Eskimo men in kayaks and women in the larger, slower umiaks. Spencer Chapman described how the women had all dressed up for the occasion: "They wore bright red seal skin boots ornamented with the most intricate mosaic of different coloured pieces of seal skin ... a close fitting blouse of some bright coloured material and above that a most exquisite short cape."[3] After a medical examination to ensure that no venereal disease was being brought to the island, the expedition members went ashore, taking with them a portable gramophone. Jeremy Scott, in his book *Dancing On Ice*, described the recollections of his father J.M. Scott of that evening. After increasingly fast paced dancing of the Foxtrot, Cake Walk and Black

---

3   Spencer Chapman, *Northern Lights*, p.16.

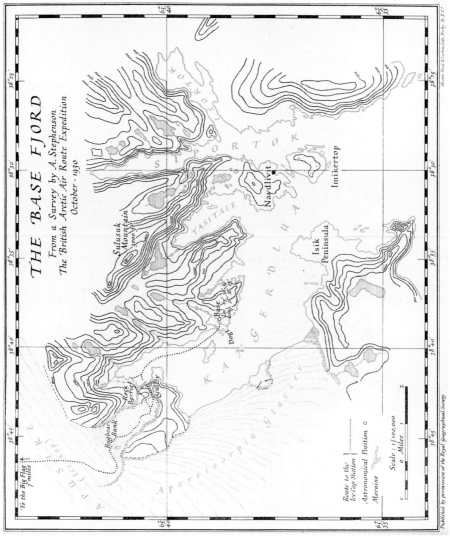

Map of Base Fjord. *(Northern Lights)*

Published by permission of the Royal Geographical Society

Bear helping her cubs onto the ice (*Northern Lights*)

Bottom, Gino Watkins put on a Charleston record: "Wildly exuberant, explorers and Eskimo women danced the Charleston while afternoon become evening."[4]

The next day the serious business of the expedition began with the search for a suitable base. The site of the base chosen had to provide access to a glacier leading to the ice cap. The base had to be in a fjord deep enough for the *Quest* to anchor to unload and there must be some ice-free water nearby for the planes to land and take off. A suitable place was found in the western branch of a fjord 30 miles west of Angmagssalik. This fjord had the advantage of a stony promontory about 100 feet above sea level on which to build the base hut, a shelving beach as a base for the seaplane and a glacier tongue with which to approach the ice cap. The *Quest* was unloaded in a week of back breaking labour, in which the expedition members were divided into two twelve-hour shifts in order that the unloading could continue around the clock. Lindsay commented "Having seldom carried anything heavier than a message, I was surprised to discover that, although exceedingly unpleasant, it is not impossible to take a load of 120 lb."[5]

By the beginning of August the base was completed, the planes unloaded and up and running, much to the wonder and excitement of the watching Eskimos. The aeroplanes were two D.H. Fox Moths with Gipsy 1 engines, made by the de Havilland Aircraft Company. G-AAUR was provided with two undercarriages, one with reinforced floats and the other a

4   Jeremy Scott, *Dancing on Ice: A Stirring Tale of Adventure, Risk and Reckless Folly* (London, 2009), p.59.
5   Martin Lindsay, *Those Greenland Days* (London, 1932) p.22.

standard Canadian style ski undercarriage. This plane also had locker accommodation for rifles and emergency gear. G-AAZR was of standard design, although both aeroplanes had emergency petrol tanks which gave them a range of 560-600 miles in the air. Flying during the summer of 1930 was facilitated by the discovery of an ice-free fjord further up the coast which was named Ice Fjord and formed the base for much of the summer flying operations.

A party under the leadership of Scott consisting of Scott, Rymill, Riley, Lindsay and Bingham set off with the dog teams to reconnoitre to a point 127 miles inland, at a height of 8,000 feet to establish a meteorological station. The route was planned with the help of the first aerial reconnaissance carried out by Watkins and D'Aeth. The aim was to keep observers up at the station for the entire year in order to be able to report on the flying conditions likely over the ice cap throughout the year. It was thought that the weather experienced throughout the whole of north-western Europe may be partly influenced by sudden changes of pressure and temperature occurring over the ice cap. After travelling up the glacier, getting used to handling the dog teams, their way was blocked by a large bank, up which all the sledges and equipment had to be hauled. The reports to *The Times* called this "Bugbear Bank" but Lindsay recalled it was known as "a similar but more Rabelaisian name."[6] Jeremy Scott, in his account of the expedition, calls it "Buggery Bank."[7] This delayed their progress, and when at last they emerged onto the ice cap plateau, fifteen miles from base, it had taken them six days. The second part of their journey was much easier as they had got used to the dogs who were settling in their teams and the men were feeling fitter: "We were by now so fit that that the longest day was quite enjoyable."[8] The members of the party were getting used to living with each other for the first time in the cramped conditions of the tents. Later Lindsay found an entry in his diary recalling an odd dialogue that he had with Quintin Riley after supper in the tent:

A.   Bother. I've forgotten my prayer book.
B.   But dammit, you don't want to say your prayers on the ice cap do you?
A.   Of course I do.
B.   And can't you say your prayers without your prayer book?
A.   Yes. Only I like to remember the saints' days; it makes it so much more interesting.[9]

On reaching the site for the ice cap station, the five men set about erecting the large tent that was to be the basis of the station. This was accompanied by three small igloos for use as storehouses and a latrine. As hot air rises, the entrance to the tent was through a tunnel and up into the tent by a trap door. It was nine feet in diameter and six feet high at the centre. Lindsay described how, despite the cramped conditions for the two men left behind there to man the station, he remembered the time with affection:

Most of the floor space was taken by our two sleeping bags with the current week's ration box between them. Drying on tapes over our heads was always an odd collection of socks and gloves ... this funny little dwelling was a very happy home for us, and Riley and I look back on the days we spent there as being amongst the most enjoyable

6   Martin Lindsay, *Three Got Through – Memoirs of an Arctic Explorer* (London, 1946) p.32.
7   Scott, *Dancing on Ice*, p.78.
8   Lindsay, *Three Got Through*, p.36.
9   Martin Lindsay, *Those Greenland Days* (London, 1932) p.49.

of the expedition.[10]

The meteorological observations were made every three hours between 7.00 a.m. and 10.00 p.m. Lindsay admitted in his diary that he did not like the 7.00 a.m. observation, but continued:

> On the other hand, seven of an evening at this time of year is an hour enchanted. With the setting sun the western sky floods slowly into the most extraordinary extremes of colour – brilliant contrasts of pink, pale blue and orange, purple and gold. Ten o'clock has its delights too, in the beauty of the Northern Lights, a muster of dim lances, close serried, standing erect in the sky.[11]

The rest of the party went in the *Quest* to survey and map the coast north of the base. Their aim was to get into the fjord at Kanderlugsuak, leaving depots of food along the coast along the way and surveying as they went. They could then say goodbye to the *Quest* and work their way back down the coast in a small boat. They discovered a fjord with an ice-free lake at its head which was to prove very useful to the air survey. This was called Lake Fjord and was to become the base camp of Watkins's second expedition in 1933. Surveying from a small boat proved difficult and dangerous and this time saw Spencer Chapman involved in a few hair-raising incidents. Spencer Chapman, Courtauld, Wager and Stephenson had taken the small boat and left the *Quest* temporarily to survey the area around and north of Lake Fjord. One difficulty they experienced was finding somewhere to pitch their tents, as for miles the cliffs came down to the water with no place to land. One night they had to pull all their equipment up a cliff face to find a "heathery ledge" on which to perch, 30 feet up from the sea. Spencer Chapman described the aurora seen one night as:

> More beautiful than I had ever seen it ... It looked just as if a number of cars with green headlights were coming up on the other side of the hills. There were no clear-cut beams: it was as though the lights were showing through a curtain of slight fog. The whole sky was covered with these pale glimmerings, often tinged with crimson or purple.[12]

While surveying a branch fjord separated from another larger fjord by a low col, the party approached the projecting tongue of a huge glacier, which had a large green cave in its ice. As they watched a piece of ice as large as a house crashed off the glacier. Spencer Chapman described what then happened: "To our joy, for it was a spectacle far beyond the description of words, the whole roof of the cave crumbled in and, with a shower of debris and powdered ice, fell into the sea."[13] At one point their radio equipment was waterlogged on a day when they wanted to pick up a reliable time signal to rendezvous with the *Quest*. Having got the time signal they then broke their propeller on an ice floe and had to move themselves toward the meeting point with one oar and an ice axe, pulling them through heavily ice packed water. The sheer pin of an outboard motor would break before any

---

10   Ibid., p.72.
11   J. Scott, *Portrait of an Icecap with Human Figures* (London, 1953) p.31.
12   Spencer Chapman, *Northern Lights*, p.47.
13   Ibid., p.37.

Spencer Chapman seal hunting in East Greenland, 1931.
(*Living Dangerously*/Spencer Chapman family)

serious damage was done to the rest of the engine, but while the pin was being repaired there was no power to avoid ramming ice floes.

Spencer Chapman was responsible for hunting for the boat party and had a very close encounter with a polar bear while trying to photograph it. He had already shot one polar bear that day and on seeing another one decided to try to photograph it, as the boat was too loaded down to kill another one:

> Suddenly I looked up and saw that in an amazingly short space of time the bear with great agility had clambered out on to an ice floe and had turned, snarling, to attack. I dropped my camera into the bottom of the boat and seizing the rifle ... took a snap shot at the bear just as he was about to leap into the boat. We were so near that as he fell forward stone-dead he almost upset the boat with the splash of his huge body. [14]

Having rejoined the *Quest*, which arrived at the mouth of the Kangerdlugssuaq Fjord to pick them up, Spencer Chapman joined Watkins in climbing a hill to get a view of the fjord:

> From the summit we had an unobstructed view down the fjord. It was an exhilarating thought that we were the first white men ever to behold that view. We saw a many

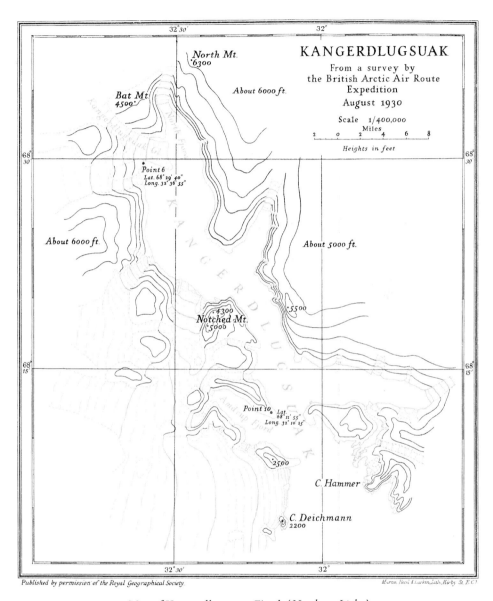

Map of Kangerdlugssuag Fjord. (*Northern Lights*)

The coast between Kangerdlugssuaq and Cape Dan. (*Northern Lights*)

branched fjord about five miles wide flanked by enormous snow mountains, leading up to the largest glacier we had ever seen, whose terminal ice cliffs, several miles wide, projected far out into the water. Behind that the ice cap stretched away to the horizon.[15]

26th August was August Courtauld's 26th birthday and the small boat surveyors celebrated with a meal. The menu consisted of 'bear's tongue soup' as a starter, followed by 'fried fillet of Kangerdlugssuaq trout' and 'theodolite sauce with stewed crowberries'. 29th August brought perhaps their severest challenge. They awoke to find that one end of the boat had become snagged on a rock as the tide fell, resulting in all its contents being tipped into the water. Their petrol supply and food rations had gone, but most distressingly, the instrument box, without which they could not complete the survey, had also vanished. After ten hours of searching they found the box in fifteen feet of water. It was eventually rescued by diving down through the icy water and attaching the boat hook to it so that it could be hauled up. Courtauld then took the theodolite to pieces and eventually made it work again. It was decided that the boat party would complete their survey keeping close to the *Quest* as they had already broken two outboard motors and the captain of the *Quest* considered that returning to base in the small boat was "suicidal". They returned to base on 14th September. Stephenson reported in an appendix to *Northern Lights*, that he considered the surveying and mapping from Kangerdlugsuatsiak to Cape Gustav Holm and in the Kangerdlugssuaq section as accurate to within 500 yards.

---

15   Ibid., p.40.

A few days later, on 21st September, Spencer Chapman was part of the group whose task it was to take up supplies to the ice cap station which had been set up high upon the ice cap to monitor weather conditions. This had been manned by Lindsay and Riley since its establishment on 27th August. Spencer Chapman related an incident which highlights the difficulties experienced in maintaining cordial relationships at close quarters and how easy it is to lose a sense of proportion: " I remember very well I had a fixed idea that Rymill was taking up too much of the tent – It was intolerable and I planned all sorts of scheme for revenge." When Lindsay broached the subject with Rymill "He seemed rather surprised, and replied he had been thinking the same of me ... We measured it found that each of us had exactly half." [16]

Preparations were now in hand for a large party of six men and six sledges to take the wireless set and a large amount of food and fuel up to the ice cap station to prepare it for winter. Spencer Chapman, as the man with the most experience of sledging, led the party. With Spencer Chapman were August Courtauld, Hampton, Lemon and Stephenson. Hampton and Stephenson were to relieve the station and overwinter there until March. Weather conditions, however meant very slow progress. High winds continued and for three or four days a week they were unable to travel. It took them three weeks to cover 30 miles. Courtauld, writing later in his introduction to Spencer Chapman's book *Watkins's Last Expedition*, recalled "The memory will never fade of that little tent we shared, the thoughts we shared, the fears we shared ... on such a journey you get to know the worth of a man." [17] After rendezvousing with Watkins who was returning from a southern sledging journey, it was decided that it would be more practicable if a smaller party attempted to push up to the ice station. Some supplies and the wireless had to be jettisoned to save weight. It was apparent that they would only be able to get enough supplies to the station for one man to overwinter there. Watkins gave Spencer Chapman the task of deciding what to do when the ice station was reached, and whether any one should be left there. His last words to Spencer Chapman were "Do the best you can. You may have to abandon the station. But at all cost you must get the two men out". [18] Eventually on 3rd December, they reached the station. Spencer Chapman now had a difficult decision. Either the ice cap station would have to be abandoned or one man would have to stay, on reduced rations and fuel, until relieved in April. As the meteorological observations at the ice cap were vital to the whole air route expedition, Spencer Chapman was loath to abandon the station. In what Lindsay later described as "a very stout hearted decision", August Courtauld volunteered to stay behind.

As the various parties returned from their expeditions, the expedition members settled down to life at base camp, excepting Courtauld, who was manning the ice cap station. On 19th December the party which had relieved the station and left Courtauld there alone, returned, and there was a "grand dance" at base. On their return they found the base camp highly organised and comfortable, with native Eskimo girls installed to cook and clean. Lemon had spent considerable time that autumn training them when most other members were out on expeditions. The cook was Aprika, Girtrude was the parlour maid and Tina the kitchen maid. One source of possible tension was the fact that Lemon, Watkins and Spencer Chapman had developed relationships with the girls and taken them as mistresses.

16   Ibid., p.73.
17   A. Courtauld, Introduction to *Watkins's Last Expedition* (London, 1938) p.13.
18   Martin Lindsay, *Three Got Through – Memoirs of an Arctic Explorer*, p.46.

Girtrude. (*Northern Lights*)

According to Jeremy Scott, Scott and Lindsay were not comfortable with the arrangement. Lindsay was particularly put out: "He believed what a man got up to in London or Paris was all very well, but in a crowded hut on an arctic expedition he didn't fancy it for himself and objected to it in others."[19] All winter he had an Eskimo woman climbing over him to reach Watkins in the bunk above. Spencer Chapman however seemed not to be worried. He wrote: "I lived with Girtrude more or less as my mistress and spent my time hunting seals or sledging about" and considered "I suppose I have never been so happy in my life."[20] It was at this stage of the expedition that he began to think seriously about his future, but the only conclusion he came to was that he must use his copious diary entries to write a book. This was to be an ambition achieved when Watkins asked him to write the official account of the expedition.

Spencer Chapman described the difficulties of providing for the whole party, their Eskimo servants and the dogs: "There was considerable controversy as to whether it was better to ration the jam and similar luxuries, but most of us preferred to have plenty until they were finished and then do without." In January seal hunting became easier, using techniques learned from the Eskimos. Spencer Chapman described the cramped conditions in the hut: "It became apparent that there was very little room in the base hut ... While Lemon was trying to receive Morse, Stephenson would be repairing a sledge, Wager grinding down rocks to make rock sections for microscopic work, I might be skinning a

19   Jeremy Scott, *Dancing on Ice*, p.86.
20   Cited by Ralph Baker, *One Man's Jungle, A Biography of F. Spencer Chapman* (London, 1975), p.83.

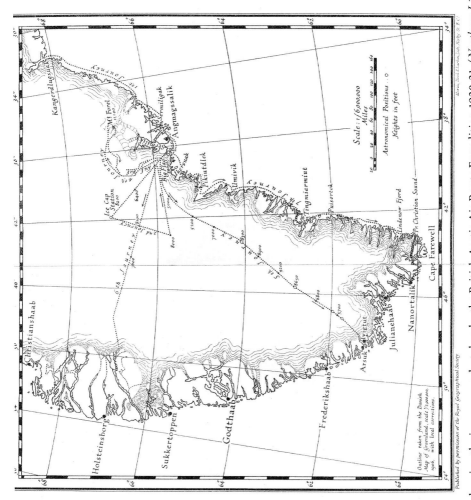

Map showing the journeys undertaken by the British Arctic Air Route Expedition 1930-31. (*Northern Lights*)

bird." [21] He gave the impression that there was very little quarrelling or bad feeling and that on the whole the members of the expedition got on well: "Being young, if one of us thought another any kind of fool he just told him so in no uncertain language, and that was the end of the matter."[22]

On 1st March Scott and Riley set off to make the journey up to the ice cap station to relieve Courtauld, who had been manning the station alone since the end of December. On 7th March the base camp party were astonished to see them return, having run out of provisions and having been unable to reach the ice station due to poor conditions and visibility. They set out again on 9th March and this time managed to reach Big Flag Depot to replenish supplies before arriving in the vicinity of the ice cap station by 26th March. The weather deteriorated and although they were in the area where the station was for three weeks, they could only search on a few of those days, as for days on end they were trapped in their tent by blizzards. By 18th April they were forced back to camp after, as Spencer Chapman put it "The most disappointing journey of the whole expedition."[23] Gino Watkins was not at first unduly worried, as Courtauld had been left with plenty of supplies and was fit when last seen, however he could not rule out the possibility that he was unwell or dead and had allowed the station to be completely covered with snow. Watkins then set out, with Spencer Chapman and Rymill forming another search party.

Courtauld had been left with six ration boxes, 26 gallons of paraffin, two bottles of concentrated lemon juice and one bottle of cod liver oil. He reckoned that one ration box could last, with stretching, one man 24 days. At first he had busied himself by dressing in full kit six times a day to take weather observations. It became increasingly difficult to dig himself out of his tent via his tunnel, and the collapse of the snow house containing his rations meant that he had to dig for several hours to retrieve them. His tent became more and more submerged by drifting snow. He managed to make a ventilation shaft through the roof of one of the collapsed snow houses but on 22nd March the weight of snow prevented him exiting his tent through the tunnel at all. He was a prisoner until the relief party arrived. The only ventilation that remained was a two-inch ventilator shaft in the roof of the tent, the snow having almost reached that point, but other air circulated through the snow walls of the tunnel and side houses. He realised that the Union Flag on its pole protruding from the ice station would signal where it had been covered with snow. With great phlegm he considered that: "There was nothing to worry about as far as my personal safety was concerned." [24] However, by 5th April his diary entry sounded more pessimistic: "Now been here alone four months. No sign of relief. Only a cup of paraffin left and one or two candles. Have to lie in darkness all the time." [25]His food store had become seriously depleted but he comforted himself with the thought that he was using very little energy trapped in the small tent. However by the middle of April: "There was no more light, luxuries had run out, tobacco exhausted". The shortage of fuel made melting water for drinking impracticable, so he sucked on the icicles on the interior roof of the tent. On 5th May his primus gave out and he was left without any heat or light.

Meanwhile, by the last day of April the relief party were close. Spencer Chapman

21   Spencer Chapman *Northern Lights*, p.129.
22   Ibid., p.130.
23   Ibid., p.172.
24   Ibid., p.183.
25   Scott, *Portrait,* p.144.

remembered "A longitude and latitude observation put us only a few miles from the station". [26]The following days were dull and the party thought that they were within two or three miles of the station, but saw no sign. On the evening of 4th May they set out individually by ski, attempting to quarter the area. 5th May was fine, and with the help of the theodolite and the wireless time signal, they confirmed that they were within a mile of the station. Eventually they spotted the Union Flag and went to investigate. Spencer Chapman recalled his feelings of foreboding:

> The whole place had a most extraordinary air of desolation. The large Union Flag we had last seen in December was now only a fraction of its former size. Only the top of the various survey instruments and the handle of a spade projected through the vast snow- drift, which submerged the whole tent with its snow houses and surrounding wall. Was it possible that a man could be alive in there?[27]

Watkins shouted down the ventilation pipe and was answered by Courtauld. They found him thin and pale but otherwise in good condition and remarkably cheerful for one whose last fuel supplies had just run out. Spencer Chapman described his first impressions: "He looked as if he had stepped from Ober-Ammergau. His beard and hair were unkempt and long, and his face stained with smoke and grime."[28] They set out for base, with Courtauld riding on a sledge, and reached base on the 9th after a fast run home, travelling 41 miles on the last day.

On returning to base after Courtauld's rescue Spencer Chapman settled to base life again, learning how to kayak well enough to hunt. After a few summer months of hunting and boating, it was time for the expedition to split up to complete their last planned exploring trips. On 1st July, Scott, Stephenson and Lindsay were to cross the ice cap to the settlement of Ivigtut in south-west Greenland. They were travelling on virtually unmapped ground and were to map and make weather observations. They set out on a beautiful day from base camp. Lindsay described the scene:

> The sun had never shone so brightly, the water so blue or the pieces of floating ice so vividly white. On three sides of us stood dark mountains, silent and impassive, while on the fourth in splendid contrast to them was a high glacier, great pieces from which fell away into the water with a voice of thunder even as we sat there watching.[29]

As they progressed across the ice cap, catching tantalizing glimpses of the mountains of the south west coast they realised that what information they did have was wrong and that the land they could see was completely unmapped. After completing their journey across the ice cap, experiencing crevasses and covering as much as 29 miles per night in the excellent conditions, they reached the head of Ivigtut glacier. Here they had to kill all dogs bar one, Nano, who Scott was taking home. They would have found no one to buy them, as no sledging took place in Southern Greenland.

During his time at base camp and on his journeys inland and on the coast, Spencer

26   Spencer Chapman, *Northern lights* p.174.
27   Ibid., p.176.
28   Ibid., p.176.
29   Lindsay, *Greenland Days*, p.189.

Chapman had taken detailed notes of the bird life of the areas had visited. He gave a detailed description of the birds to be found in summer at base camp, including Arctic terns, Glaucous and Iceland Gulls. At the mouth of the fjord he saw Black Guillemots and Eider Ducks. Flying between the head of the fjord and the lakes were Greenland Mallard, Red Breasted Merganser, Red Throated Diver and Great Northern Diver. Ravens were to be seen in the winter at base and small numbers of Ptarmigan. By March the first Snow Bunting appeared. On the coastal journey he reported Fulmar Petrels, Kittiwakes and Barnacle Geese. Snow Buntings were spotted as far as a hundred miles inland on the journey to the ice cap station and Phalaropes 75 miles inland.

Spencer Chapman was to have undertaken a sledging journey across the ice cap to Holsteinborg on the West Coast with Rymill. However, a glandular cyst in his neck resulted in him returning home earlier than planned, to take care of the British end of the expedition's business and to start writing the official account of the expedition, *Northern Lights*. He arrived back in Copenhagen on the *Gertrud Rask* in September. He had developed an important philosophy on this first expedition to Greenland, which would stand him in good stead in his future adventures:

> Almost all difficulties can be overcome. Mere cold is a friend, not an enemy; the weather always gets better if you wait long enough; distance is merely relative; man can exist for a very long time on very little food; the human body is capable of bearing immense privation; miracles still happen; it is the state of mind that is important.[30]

At the end of the second BARRE expedition to Greenland (see Chapter Three), Spencer Chapman was less upbeat about the results of the expedition. Preparing to leave Lake Fjord he said: "hardly a pang. I am sick of the place. Very different from last year."[31] He also had to say goodbye to Girtrude. Later he heard that Hansie, his son by Girtrude, had died and that Girtrude had married. Despite his pain at leaving her, it is clear that he never envisaged leading a life which she could ever have been a part of. At the end of this second expedition his thoughts were full of his projected career as author and explorer.

Watkins's style of leadership had give Spencer Chapman opportunity to make decisions and take responsibility for them, most obviously in the difficult decision of allowing Courtauld to remain at the ice cap station alone. On the second expedition to Greenland he had opportunity to reflect on being alone for stretches of time, as he was at base camp for a month while Rymill and Riley were surveying. On both expeditions he had faced situations which had made him realise that the human body and spirit was able to endure more than what would be thought possible. He had learned to live off what the country could provide and had developed the resilient attitude epitomised in the quotation from Hamlet that he used when writing of his experiences in Greenland: " .... for there is nothing either good or bad, but thinking makes it so."[32]

The Ascent of Chomolhari 1937

After a spell at teaching at Aysgarth School in the spring of 1936, Spencer Chapman obtained leave to join an expedition to the Himalayas as part of a team led by Marco Pallis.

---

30   Spencer Chapman, *Helvellyn to Himalaya* (London, 1940), cited by Barker p.87.
31   Ibid., p.102.
32   Spencer Chapman, *Watkins's Last Expedition* (London, 1934), p.115.

However he found the atmosphere and organisation of the expedition not to his liking and after an exciting summiting of the Sphinx, which he did admit to enjoying, he accepted an invitation to be the personal assistant to B.J. Gould, the leader of the British Mission to Lhasa. He related the experience in his book, *Lhasa: The Holy City*. One of his biographers, Ralph Barker, considered that the experience in Lhasa had changed Spencer Chapman little, in that he was still undecided both about his abilities and his future. He started to make tentative plans to climb Chomolhari, "The Divine Queen of Mountains", as preparation for a possible inclusion in the 1936 Everest expedition. When his name did not appear in the Everest party list, he decided to press ahead anyway as a last fling before returning to a career as a schoolmaster.

Spencer Chapman now recruited his climbing partner for this venture in April. Charles Crawford was a teacher without a great deal of mountaineering experience, and with only three weeks leave, but who was very enthusiastic about the climb. Spencer Chapman's contacts in Lhasa helped obtain the necessary permission from the Maharaja of Bhutan, and after acquiring three porters the expedition set off for a suitable base camp. On the way they stopped at the Kargyu monastery, where they met the abbot, who told them that they should be very careful in tackling Chomolhari as "She would throw us down the mountain."[33] They progressed up the plain to Phari, passing through a gorge as they approached. As they emerged from the gorge they were treated to an unexpected panoramic view of the mountain, which Spencer Chapman described as "The incomparable pyramid of Chomolhari."[34]

At Phari they were both afflicted by the altitude sickness that was to destroy Crawford's hope of making the summit. On 12th May they set out to reconnoitre the route but met with very poor weather conditions. Spencer Chapman, only half in jest, asked himself whether the Goddess was angry. After failing on one proposed route, the party decided to skirt around three hills and attempt an approach on the mountain's southern ridge. On the fifth day out of Phari, they had good weather and were climbing well into the snow line, but at 20,000 feet Crawford was succumbing to altitude sickness, as were two of the porters. It was decided that he and the porters should return and Spencer Chapman and Passang sent much of the equipment with them and started for the summit. After being forced to bivouac in a blizzard mid-afternoon, and spending the night in a tent with a broken zip door, they set out again in the early hours of the morning. This time things went well: "Passang went magnificently, his cheerfulness and determination never flagging. We could move together and it was possible to achieve a rhythm – a kick, a breath, a pause, a breath – and so on, almost mechanically."[35] After seven hours climbing they were within 500 feet of the summit, which they reached by ascending a snow dome which was relatively easy going. The view from the summit was spectacular and Spencer Chapman was elated: "We had reached the summit of Chomolhari, without offence – it seemed – to the goddess of whom we had heard so much".[36]

Just below the summit, they stopped to allow Spencer Chapman to take some photographs, and as he was doing so, Passang lost his footing and fell past him. Not having time to dig his ice axe in, Spencer Chapman found himself tumbling down the snow slope,

33 F. Spencer Chapman, *Living Dangerously* (London, 1953), p.74.
34 Ibid., p.75.
35 Ibid., p.83.
36 Ibid., p.84.

head first. He described their fall, bumping over ice and rocks, and getting nearer to the 3,000-foot drop where the mountain descended swiftly into the valley. Near to the cliff, he managed to dig his ice axe in and put his weight on it, arresting their fall just in time. It seemed that the mountain was in fact very displeased with them, as bad weather then forced them to remain in their tent on the ice ledge for three days. Spencer Chapman commented later: "I consider myself a connoisseur of uncomfortable nights, but for sheer interminable shivering misery, I have never known anything like those nights in our bivouac tent on the snows of Chomolhari." [37] The Goddess had not yet finished with them, however, as on the final descent Spencer Chapman fell into a wide crevasse and only extricated himself with difficulty, before reaching the safety of Phari once again.

The success of the Chomolhari climb caused a sensation in the climbing world, perhaps resulting in the doubts expressed about the veracity of Spencer Chapman's account. This sort of attitude to the climb was privately current in 1937 but did not escape into the public arena until 1966, when two separate attacks were made on the summit claim, by August Gansser in *The Mountain World* and Rudolf Hannay in *Les Alpes*. Their doubts were based on the fact that the photos of Passang on the summit had been ruined in the fall and that the only other European had been sent back to base. These claims were thoroughly refuted by D.F.O. Dangar and T.S. Blakeney.[38] They looked at the evidence in Spencer Chapman's diary and interviewed Passang, who by then was a veteran Sherpa who had climbed with Sir Edmund Hilary. Ralph Barker considered that, exciting as reaching the summit was, Spencer's most telling achievement was to succeed in bringing the injured Passang and himself safely down the mountain.

The achievement of climbing Chomolhari made headlines in *The Times*: "The ascent of Chomolhari – a Himalayan Conquest – 24,000 feet for £20."[39] Spencer Chapman must have been quietly complacent that the Everest expedition from which he had been excluded had not reached that height, and had cost a great deal more money.

The jungle is neutral 1941-1945

Having joined the Seaforth Highlanders as a Territorial in the months before the war, Spencer Chapman, after taking part in the training for the aborted expedition to Finland (see Chapter Three), found himself part of a the special training centre at Lochailort. He settled at the Commando training centre well and had begun to think that he was to spend the war instructing and not seeing any action. Then, with Michael Calvert, he was sent to Australia as part of No. 104 mission to teach fieldcraft in a newly set up training school in Victoria. Calvert considered him to be unsurpassed in his knowledge of fieldcraft. At the end of 1941 he was posted to Singapore to School of Guerrilla Warfare, STS (special training school) No. 101. During December the Japanese army were advancing through Malaya and Spencer Chapman managed to get to Kuala Lumpur and spend a few days behind the lines observing the advancing Japanese forces. This experience reinforced the idea he had been formulating with his fellow instructor, Sergeant John Sartin, to create 'left behind' parties which would remain behind the advancing Japanese army and harass them by attacking the roads and railways. Each 'left behind' party would be led by an army officer trained in guerrilla warfare and include European civilians who knew the country

---

37   Ibid., p.88.
38   Published in *Alpine Journal* November 1967.
39   *The Times* 26th July 1937.

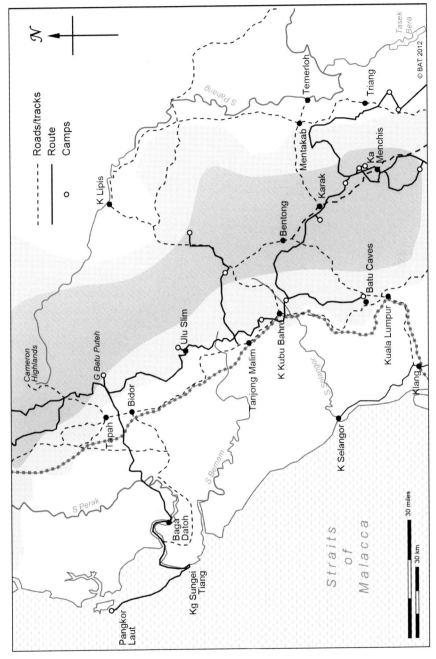

Map showing routes of Freddie Spencer Chapman's movements in Malaya 1941-45. (Barbara Taylor)

and they would be accompanied by selected Chinese, Malays and Indians. On his return he dealt with the delicate negotiations required to recruit young Chinese Communists to help them in their task. Following the sinking of the *Repulse* and the *Prince of Wales*, No. 101 STS recruited Chinese supplied by the Malayan Communist Party. As the advance of the Japanese quickened, it was decided to set up store dumps on both sides of the main range of mountains running north to south down the peninsula.

Spencer Chapman's headquarters were to be at Tanjong Malim on the western side of the range. Leaving a party of four there, led by a planter called Vantrenan, he went back to Kuala Lumpur to finalise arrangements and promptly went down with an attack of malaria. By the time he had persuaded a doctor to let him leave, a day late, the route to Tanjong Malim had been closed by the advancing Japanese. The only way that Spencer Chapman would get to his stores and his men was by crossing the central range of mountains. The journey was fifteen miles, as the crow flies, but the jungle rose to a height of 6, 000 feet. It was thought that the journey would take about five days, and supplies for that amount of time were taken. He set off with Bill Harvey and his sapper sergeant John Sartin. Harvey, who had been ten years in Malaya, seemed convinced that they would be able to shoot and trap wild animals for food, however these did not materialise in the thick jungle, and after eating the tinned supplies that they had set out with, the party was reduced to two spoonfuls of oatmeal per day. They only made about a mile of actual forward progress each day, as much time was spent descending from one mountain range across a swampy valley and climbing up another mountain, sometimes in the wrong direction. Spencer Chapman described the difficulties:

> I had carefully worked out our route from the map, but as soon as we attempted to travel on a certain bearing, we would inevitably be driven off course ... By the end of the day we could merely guess the general direction in which we had been travelling.[40]

They were plagued by insects and leeches, which when bloated, fell off leaving wounds which were still bleeding and likely to develop into jungle ulcers.

After eleven days of struggling through the jungle paths they eventually arrived at Tanjong Malim to find no trace of their comrades or of the food and ammunition supplies. Their situation was serious, with no food, no clothes and no arms and 200 miles from the nearest British lines. Spencer Chapman remarked wryly: "We were indeed a 'left behind' party."[41] Luckily a local Chinese man, Leu Kim, had secreted some of the stores in a cave and they found they had enough explosives to be able to put some of their sabotage plans into action. There then followed what Spencer Chapman called 'the mad fortnight, ' in which the three men set about using their explosives to cause as much mayhem as they could behind the Japanese lines. Refreshed with food and shelter from Leu Kim, they set about this task with a certain amount of relish. As Spencer Chapman enthused "what boy has not longed to blow up trains? ... and if the trains are loaded with enemy supplies and troops, so much the better!" [42] Their first targets were bridges on the railway line just south of Tanjong Malim station, which were despatched with thirty pounds of explosives lodged in the middle of the track attached to a pressure switch under the rail. On another night the

---

40   Spencer Chapman, *Living Dangerously*, p.115.
41   Ibid., p.119.
42   Ibid., p.120.

A wartime portrait of Spencer Chapman. (Spencer Chapman family)

early arrival of a train just after the charge were placed resulted in the three men jumping from the track into a swamp, where they were brilliantly illuminated by the explosion. Their Chinese friends would go out in the day to report on damage, and Spencer Chapman decided that the attacks on the rail system were nor having a big enough effect, as the Japanese were able to repair the damage swiftly, so he decided to switch to the roads

Their main targets on 'Route One', which ran the whole length of the Malay Peninsula, were the convoys of trucks and staff cars that moved at night. Sartin developed a bomb which looked like a bamboo cane on the road, but was actually filled with explosive attached to a wire which could be detonated at a distance by a pull switch. This was used to ambush convoys which would then come under attack from the bombers, who would then melt away into the rubber plantations which lined the road. At first the Japanese reactions were slow. Spencer Chapman had a theory that they kept all their guns underneath the seat of the last vehicle in the convoy, but soon they became alert to the possibility of ambush, and used increasing manpower to pursue their attackers into the jungle, using police dogs to track them.

Reprisals on the local population were increasing. They had little ammunition left, and were exhausted. Spencer Chapman remembered "our muscles and nerves could stand no more," and decided to call a halt. He also thought that the adrenalin and excitement had perhaps made them over-confident and that they were likely to relax their vigilance a little, leading to capture. They had not had the opportunity to make an accurate assessment of the damage they had done, but the local Chinese had and later they learned that the group had wrecked seven trains, cut the rail line in about sixty places, demolished fifteen bridges, and blown up many trucks, usually full of troops. He guessed that they had killed between 500 -1,500 troops. Spencer Chapman also discovered after the war that the Japanese had held back two regiments from the frontline to hunt them down, imagining that there were at least 200 Australian troops in the area.

The group now decided to make their way back to the depot near Tras on the other side of the main range. They avoided their jungle route and took the main road, although it necessitated a journey of 60 miles in which they could only travel by night, hidden in the shadow at the side of the road. On one occasion, they found themselves caught on a barbed wire fence in the headlights of trucks and also spent some time lying at the side of the road while large Japanese convoys went by. When they arrived at Tras they heard that Singapore had fallen to the Japanese and now had to decide on the best course of action. They decided to make for the coast, and obtain a boat in which to sail back to India. Spencer Chapman's idea was that they would then train men to return to carry on the fight behind the lines in Malaya. They were joined at Tras by the remnants of another stay behind party, Pat Garden and Clarke Heywood, and then by the three other members of Garden's group. The eight men set off for the coast, the first group consisting of Spencer Chapman, Heywood, Chrystal and Robinson, on 8th March, and the second group of Harvey, Garden Quayle and Sartin were to follow two nights later. They now reverted to wearing their uniforms and concocted a cover story about being left behind by the retreating British forces. The journey was not a success. Spencer Chapman and Heywood became separated from Chrystal and Robinson. Quayle, from the second party, managed to meet up with Chrystal and Robinson and the three were reunited with Spencer Chapman and Heywood a month later with the help of Chinese guerrillas. However, Sartin, Harvey and Garden were captured at a sentry post. Garden and Sartin were to survive the war as prisoners, but Harvey was executed after a failed escape attempt.

It was now too late in the season to attempt a boat crossing to India, and Spencer Chapman and Heywood, who were now staying at a Chinese guerrilla camp, were coming under pressure to stay in the jungle and train the Communist resistance troops. It was decided that Heywood and Spencer Chapman would be sent to the training camp at the Batu caves. Here they found a large well-organised camp where a hundred young Chinese fighters, including some women, were gathered for training. Four of the men had been to the special training school at Singapore and had been supplied with explosives and ammunition by the school. Also at the camp were six British soldiers who were suffering from Beri–Beri and whose morale was very low. Spencer Chapman nursed them and improved their diet, so that their swellings went down, but he was reminded again of his realisation in the Arctic, that "There is nothing either good or bad but thinking makes it so", as the morale of the soldiers left behind in the jungle depended very much on their attitude to what some of them called "green hell". If they could be persuaded of the positive aspects of life in the jungle and think of it as "a tropical paradise" they usually did better. He summed up his philosophy:

The truth is that the jungle is neutral. It provides any amount of fresh water, and unlimited cover for friend as well as foe- an armed neutrality if you like, but neutrality nevertheless. It is the attitude of mind which determines whether you go under or survive ... The jungle itself is neutral.[43]

Spencer Chapman's biographer, Brian Moynahan, wrote that Spencer Chapman's ability to take a detached attitude which was almost immune from emotional distress sprang from his childhood experiences of losing his mother at an early age. Moynahan considered that Spencer Chapman, in the jungle, thought and felt as little as possible: "Feelings were an encumbrance to a man who each day had to earn his existence among the living."[44] He described the burial of a British gunner who died at the camp only briefly in his diary, but did give some detail of the service. "I could not procure a Prayer Book in order to read the Burial Service, so we had to be content with saying the Lord's Prayer and Fidele's Dirge from *Cymbeline*, after which the guerrillas sang *The Red Flag*".[45]

Spencer Chapman was anxious to obtain news of the war, as he still planned to escape to India and need to know which countries and islands were in Japanese hands, so in May 1942 he set off with Heywood to retrieve a radio that had been hidden at Karak. On the way to Thet they were ambushed by the Malay police and Spencer Chapman was wounded in the calf. On this occasion he was lucky as the wound, although producing a "gaping hole" had not injured the bone and did not become infected as it healed. When they reached the house of a Chinese helper, John, Spencer Chapman went down with acute pneumonia, feeling so ill that he dictated is will to Heywood. Heywood now also became ill, and to compound matters, it was no longer safe in John's house, so they were both moved to a hut on the hillside. When Spencer Chapman emerged from his semiconscious state and delirium he realised that he had not written in his diary for seventeen days. He attributed their recovery to some sulphathiazole tablets he had in his medical kit. They were forced to lay up for two months and Spencer Chapman entertained himself by bird watching. Here his Arctic training reasserted itself as he was most worried that he did not know the names of the birds. "For all I could tell the vivid blue fly catcher or scarlet minivet that I was observing might be the commonest species in the country or entirely new to science."[46] He also started making a collection of dried flowers for Kew Gardens. Throughout this time the local Chinese brought them food, at much risk to themselves.

The Chinese guerrillas now decided that their hiding place was in danger of being discovered by Japanese patrols. As Heywood was still too weak to walk far, the guerrillas moved them to another camp 25 miles away, using a bamboo stretcher for Heywood. Spencer Chapman, although very weak, was able to keep up. They were relieved to find that for the second half of the journey a car had been provided and set out at 9 p. m. on 11th July for the last leg of the journey. However, they had been betrayed and were soon ambushed by a truck containing Japanese soldiers. Spencer Chapman, knowing Heywood was too weak to put up much resistance, took his grenade from him and told him to make for the ditch at the side of the road. When the car stopped, Spencer Chapman created a diversion by lobbing the grenades at the truck, dived under the car and then made for the opposite side of the road, as the Japanese troops were now between him and the left side of the road. In the ensuing firefight Spencer Chapman was wounded in the arm and ear. With Ah Loy, one of their Chinese escorts, he was able to escape down a dry stream bed and with

43   F. Spencer Chapman, *The Jungle is Neutral* (London, 1977), p.115.
44   Brian Moynahan, *Jungle Soldier* (London, 2009), p.157.
45   Spencer Chapman, *Jungle*, p.120.
46   Ibid., p.130.

great difficulty they made their way 14 miles to the town of Menchis, where Ah Loy found a house where Spencer Chapman could dress his wounds and change into native clothes. They reached the camp safely, and over the next week, survivors from the ambush arrived. Apparently there had been 42 Japanese soldiers in the truck, and Spencer Chapman was told that his grenades had killed eight of them. Heywood had been shot in the chest after leaving the car and died immediately. Spencer Chapman was now the only survivor of his left behind parties.

For the next year Spencer Chapman lived with the Chinese guerrillas. He gave a detailed description of life in the camp with its regular and strict regime of training and lectures. Although Spencer Chapman was busy and had enough to eat, he felt frustrated with the lack of action. He realised that, as he had proved, the Japanese were often sitting targets but in view of the fact that there were many Japanese patrols, some looking for him, "it was obviously the wisest policy not only to leave him alone myself, but to preach evasion tactics to the Chinese."[47] In November 1942 he was asked to train guerrilla patrols in Triang, a move he welcome as he had been in communication with two Englishmen called Cotterrill and Tyson who were living with 'bandits', that is non-Communist Chinese groups near Triang, and he very much wanted to find a way of visiting them. Having gained permission, he set off with three guerrillas and walked through the jungle 25 miles, crossing the Sungei Palong River to Johor. On New Year's Day he at last met up with the two British men.

The camp was run by bandits, who Spencer Chapman described as "cheerful and lovable rogues."[48] Any attempt by the Communist guerrillas to train and convert them had been stubbornly resisted, but despite apparent disorganisation, they were well armed. Tyson was suffering from infected leech bites and died a few days after Spencer Chapman's arrival, but Spencer Chapman and Cotterrill enjoyed catching up, talking for hours. He was very tempted to stay at the bandits' camp, but further guerrilla recruits were awaiting training at the camp back at Mentakab, where he returned by early March. Here he received a message that some British men had appeared in the north of the country and were looking for him. On Christmas Day 1943, two years since he had entered that jungle behind the lines, he managed to link up with John Davis and Richard Broome, from STS 101, now called Force 136, who had been infiltrated into Malaya by submarine to find Spencer Chapman's party and to help resistance groups. They had left a radio at the coast, but the Force 136 cell at the coast was attacked and broken up, leaving Davis and Broome unable to contact Ceylon. The February rendezvous with the submarine was missed and in March the submarine did not arrive. It was a frustrating time for the British officers as they had promised to provide arms and ammunition to the guerrillas. There was nothing to do but wait until contact could be re-established.

Meanwhile, Spencer Chapman had become bored, and decided to set out to see if he could find any trace of an anthropologist called Pat Noone, who had disappeared mysteriously. Davis had been instructed to look out for Noone, so was happy to agree to Spencer Chapman's diversionary adventure. He took with him a Chinese guide, and they had been travelling for a few weeks when they fell in with some bandits who kept them virtually prisoner, taking away their guns and ammunition. In *The Jungle is Neutral*, Spencer Chapman described how he escaped by drugging the guards with morphia tablets. Moynahan, Spencer Chapman's most recent biographer comments that this incident

---

47   Spencer Chapman, *Jungle*, p.162.
48   Ibid., p.191.

A wartime portrait of Spencer Chapman. (Spencer Chapman family)

does not appear in Spencer Chapman's diary, in which the escape is reported as "slipping away".[49] He argues that the morphia poisoning incident did not take place. Ralph Barker, in *One Man's Jungle* commented, "Freddie rather skates over the practical difficulties of administering the morphia", but continued in support of Spencer Chapman's version of events, "his ruthlessness, his excess of elation and freedom from any pangs of conscience, are all in character and all ring true.[50]"

Having escaped from the bandits and made two days' progress, Spencer Chapman ran straight into a Japanese patrol, was surrounded and captured, the Japanese shouting "Killy-kollack Killy–kollack." They were obviously looking for the English leader of the guerrillas and asked him if he knew Colonel Chapman. Spencer Chapman had been given the honorary rank of Colonel by the Chinese and was generally known as Colonel Chapman, but his British identity card had Major Chapman on it. Spencer Chapman was therefore able to pose as Colonel Chapman's brother. After an interrogation and surprisingly gentle treatment from the Japanese officers he was put to sleep between two Japanese guards. He had managed to put his diary on the fire, and by judicious wriggling, managed to put some of the Japanese soldiers belongings down the bottom of his sleeping bag. Keeping a close eye on the sentries, at 1.30 he made dash for freedom: "I dashed towards the river below the camp—I went downriver for 100 yards and then up a steep bank on the other side." He was afraid that he would be followed by the sentries, but he remembered: "I never heard a sound

49   Moynahan, *Jungle Soldier*, p.246.
50   Barker, *One Man's Jungle*, p.233.

of pursuit, not a shot, a shout or even a broken stick."[51]

He has escaped twice in as many days, but now had no possessions and no watch, compass or map to navigate with. He used his astral navigation skills learned in Greenland, but still became lost in his attempts to return to the camp where Davis was waiting. He made his way to a deserted hut and lay there suffering from malaria and exhaustion for two weeks, with intermittent visits from some Saki tribesmen. He wrote a message to try and get some supplies of quinine from the nearest guerrilla camp but the Saki tribesmen were too frightened to take it. While lying there he sang songs from his youth and courting days like *The Way You Look Tonight* and *A Nightingale Sang in Berkeley Square*. Just when he had given up and was seeing visions of Nansen saying, on religion: "The thing is not to worry. They are all the same. All you have to do is help people", he woke up to find the fever gone. He eventually made it back to camp on 25th July and had the self-knowledge to realise that he had put himself through much hardship and danger on a whim.

The situation at the camp had not changed, with no radio contact with Ceylon having been established, and no successful rendezvous. Tension soon developed between Spencer Chapman and Davies and Broome because of his intense hyperactivity and his continued habit of diary writing, which they considered to be a grave security risk. Broome commented, rather unkindly, later, "It seemed almost as though Freddie had done all those things in order to write about them afterwards." In January and part of February Spencer Chapman was ill with tick typhus, and when he recovered he found that at last the bicycle generator had ensured a successful transmission with Ceylon. Spencer Chapman heard that he had been awarded the DSO and arrangements were being made for a parachute drop of arms and supplies. The Liberator aircraft that made the drop were operating at the extreme limit of their range and were two hours late over the drop zone. The drop was successful, but everything had to be collected before dawn when the Japanese aircraft would be out searching. Two new officers arrived and two bottles of whisky were drunk. The most important for Spencer Chapman was the arrival of a new anti-malarial drug, Mepacrine.

The British now liaised seriously with the guerrillas about the planned seaborne invasion of Malaya by British troops, codenamed Operation Zipper. As the British came ashore, groups of guerrillas would be attacking roads and railways. Spencer Chapman was on hand to ease the relationship with the recently arrived British officers and the guerrilla leaders, using his three years' experience. It was arranged that Spencer Chapman and Broome should go out by submarine in order to help with the central planning of the operation at Colombo. The journey to the coast took several weeks and involved lying up near the sea to await the submarine. On the night of the rendezvous Spencer Chapman found a beach from which to be picked up. He was to signal to the submarine by means of a white sheet by day or a red torch by night. On 13th May 1945 contact was made with the submarine *Statesman* and Broome and Spencer Chapman were picked by boat after exchanging the password exchange "How are your feet?" to which the reply was "We are thirsty". Spencer Chapman had been behind Japanese lines continuously for three and a half years.

Lord Mountbatten had recommended Spencer Chapman for a Victoria Cross, this was not to be, but he was awarded a Bar to his DSO. The atom bombs dropped on Japan made the invasion of Malaya unnecessary. It was realised that without the cachet of defeating

51   Spencer Chapman, *Jungle*, p.275.

the Japanese, it was going to be hard to restore British rule in Malaya, as the well-organised guerrilla groups were now in an excellent position to rebel. Spencer Chapman volunteered to parachute into Pahang on a goodwill mission to liaise with the guerrillas. He was the first British officer into Kuala Lipis, the capital of Pahang, on 5th September. On 30th September he took the Japanese surrender of forces at Kuantan. By 1948 his erstwhile comrades were fighting the British in the Malayan emergency.

Spencer Chapman had survived being hunted by the Japanese in tropical conditions, causing him hardship, starvation and multiple illnesses, surviving being wounded several times. The practical skills and the psychological strength with which he survived in wartime can be attributed at least in part to his experiences as an explorer, climber and adventurer in his pre-war career.

3

Quintin Riley

British Arctic Air Route Expedition 1930–31

Quintin Riley was born in 1905 and was educated at Lancing College, being a contemporary of Evelyn Waugh, Andrew Croft, and Gino Watkins. He went up to Pembroke College, Cambridge in 1924 and became cox of the college boat. He had a private income of £600 per annum and was therefore able to be somewhat independent and freewheeling. While at Cambridge, his friendship with Gino Watkins brought about contacts with Frank Debenham and James Wordie, who were supportive of the new generation of would be polar explorers. Lancelot Fleming, who was to be a fellow member of the British Graham Land Expedition, said of him, "Quintin was short in stature, dapper in appearance and had a high regard for his creature comforts. On the face of it, he would have not seemed the kind of man to indulge in polar exploration." [1] However, he was asked by Gino Watkins to join the Arctic Air Route Expedition to Greenland, was put in charge of meteorology and was to act as quartermaster. These two jobs became the constant themes of his subsequent exploring career and his expertise in logistics was to be useful in his wartime service. In preparation for the expedition he went to Kew to learn meteorology. He was to become skilled at keeping account of all the stores and materials: "This task suited his neat and thorough approach and it became apparent to everyone that he everything at his fingertips." [2]

Riley's part in the 1930/1931 expedition has been examined in Chapter Two. He developed his meteorological expertise greatly and played a full part in the sledging expeditions. Spencer Chapman was at hand to save Riley when he capsized his kayak whilst hunting, reaching him with his spear and dragging him to an ice floe. During the expedition on 27th October which was his birthday, Riley expressed his satisfaction with life on the expedition and with his first twenty-five years in general:

> My birthday, twenty-five years old, a quarter of a century of my life irretrievably gone. Am I satisfied with it? On the whole, yes.
> 1. I have been extraordinarily happy and lucky.
> 2. I believe in my religion, tho' I might practise it a good deal better.
> 3. I have a wonderful father and a family of whom I am very proud and they of me.
> 4. Here I am in Greenland having a wonderful time and enjoying every minute of it. Really,
> what more could one want? [3]

Riley continued at base tending his meteorological instruments throughout the winter, often under some dire weather conditions. On one occasion there was gale of 140 mph which broke the anemometer. Jonathon Riley, in his research for his biography of Quintin Riley,

---

1   Laurence Fleming in foreword to J. Riley, *Pole to Pole* (Huntingdon, 1989), p.vi.
2   J.P. Riley, *Pole to Pole*, p.20.
3   Q. Riley, *Greenland Diary*, cited by J. Riley, *Pole to Pole*, p.32.

Riley at the ice station. (Riley family)

Greenland 1930 – the start of the first journey. (Riley family)

found detailed accounts in his diary of the culture and language of the Eskimos who visited the base camp hut regularly, as knowledge of the language helped him considerably in his negotiations as quartermaster. In December he went with Watkins, Spencer Chapman and Rymill to visit an Eskimo settlement to stay for a while in the Eskimo winter houses and learn more about their way of life and hunting skills. They stayed in an *ito*, the winter home of some 43 people, who lived communally, an arrangement in which Spencer Chapman described as a state of ideal communism.

Riley's last task on the expedition involved the return of the ship *Gertrud Rask* in early August. He was sent from base to get stores from the ship in case it did not have time to stop at base camp, which would be used by Rymill and Chapman for their last sledging journey to Holsteinborg. From there they would get a ship back to England. Unfortunately after picking up the stores, his journey back to camp along the coast by whale boat, which should have lasted eight hours, took five days due to ice conditions necessitating a long detour. However, the *Gertrud Rask* had reached base camp and Riley arrived back in time to be on board for the trip.

Due largely to Riley's efforts, the expedition had amassed a large amount of meteorological data and proved that the climate of the interior of Greenland was very different from the coastal areas.[4] He reported coastal temperatures of between 63° F. and -3° F., whereas the Ice Cap Station temperatures showed a range of between 29° F. and -64° F. The data showed that depressions moved across Greenland, and therefore climatic conditions varied in different parts of Greenland. He commented particularly on the local nature of the strong gales, up to force nine, experienced at base camp which were not experienced just ten miles away. The faithful recording of the presence and regularity of fog and local gales and the charting of wind and ice conditions all added to the weather picture that Pan Am would be trying to build to aid its decisions about transatlantic flight via the Greenland route. At the end of the BAARE expedition, Riley summed up his experience: "Well it has been a wonderful year, full of interest and I have enjoyed every minute of it. I will not miss any future expeditions that come my way."[5]

Watkins's Last Expedition 1932–33

On the return of the BARRE expedition Watkins planned to head south for an expedition to Antarctica. Unfortunately funds could not be found, as Britain was suffering economically in the world recession. An alternative scheme, to kayak and sledge right around the Arctic, which also did not obtain financial backing, came to nothing. After these disappointing false starts Watkins had eventually acquired funding for a further trip to Greenland. The second expedition was to consist of Watkins, Rymill, Riley and Spencer Chapman. The expedition was very much less well funded than the BARRE and would rely on living off the land by hunting. Stefansson, Arctic advisor to Pan American, had offered £500 toward the costs of a further year of meteorological research in Greenland and the Royal Geographical Society contributed £200. Riley was to be responsible for the meteorological recordings, important in the year 1932-33, which had been designated Polar Year, with meteorological readings being taken simultaneously all around the Arctic. Two large surveying journeys were planned, one into the mountains in an attempt to climb Mount Forel, glimpsed on the previous expedition, the other, by Watkins alone, over the ice cap to Godhaab on the

4   See Appendix F.
5   Greenland Diary, cited by Riley, *Pole to Pole*, p.41.

west coast. From here he planned to send metrological information direct to Pan American airways.

The Danish supply ship, the *Gertrud Rask* arrived in Scoresby Sound on 23rd June, staying for a few days before taking the expedition on to Angmagssalik, where they had a reunion with friends they had made on the BAARE expedition. The ship then dropped them at their base at Lake Fjord. At Scoresby Sound Riley had unloaded his motorboat the *Stella Polaris*, which he had loaned to the expedition, thereby greatly reducing the costs to be incurred. Due to the kindness of the captain of the *Gertrud Rask* in dropping them at Lake Fjord, they were three weeks ahead of schedule, but wasted no time in establishing base camp. Spencer Chapman recalled how, "As we entered Lake Fjord, tranquil and lovely in the mellow sunshine of an August afternoon, we were filled with expectation and joy"[6], but the expedition was soon to experience tragedy.

It was essential that a good supply of meat be put by for the winter, so Watkins, an expert in the kayak, had started hunting on 10th August, while Spencer Chapman went to the river to try salmon fishing. Hunting seals from kayaks is a difficult process, involving harpooning the seal with a float attached, and then landing it successfully. It is not often carried out alone, but with the other members of the expedition busy, Watkins enjoyed going alone, "confidently rejoicing in his own ability and independence."[7] On 20th August Gino went out in his kayak for the day and Spencer Chapman and Rymill were out in the boat, surveying. At 2.40 p.m. they came across an empty Kayak, with Gino's gloves and unfired harpoon on board, but no sign of Gino. After searching up and down the fjord they found his trousers, boots and belt on an ice floe. They then returned to camp, hoping he may have walked somehow back to the base. Riley was at the base and described their arrival "The *Stella* returned. On board was a kayak and I guessed whose it was."[8] No traces of the body were ever found. It is probable that it was eaten by arctic sharks. After further searches of the fjord and glacier Spencer Chapman said, "We definitely realised that he was dead and decided that we must carry on just as before. Gino would have liked us to take no notice, just to behave as if nothing has happened." Sitting under a magnificent Arctic night sky he asked himself "How shall we carry on without his inspiration? I can't grasp the fullness of the tragedy – he might have done so much and now is dead."[9]

The party now travelled back to Angmagssalik to send home news of the death of Watkins and to gain permission from Pan American airways to continue. Messages were sent to Watkins's family, to *The Times*, the R.G.S. and Stefansson at Pan-Am. An obituary in *The Times* called him a "brilliant Arctic explorer" and compared him with Nansen.[10] Having received permission from Pan-Am to continue the expedition, the three remaining members set out in the *Stella Polaris* to continue building their base at Lake Fjord on 31st August. The journey was extremely difficult, and the last part, crossing the mouth of the Kangerdlugssuaq, became a nightmare. Spencer Chapman described it:

> The waves got larger as we approached the fjord mouth, where there were ten or fifteen very large icebergs. Out to sea I watched waves breaking on a berg that must have been

6   Spencer Chapman, *Watkins's Last Expedition* (London, 1938), p.46.
7   Ibid., p. 55.
8   Q. Riley, *Greenland Diary*, cited by Riley, *Pole to Pole*, p.46.
9   Spencer Chapman, *Watkins's Last Expedition*, p.71.
10   *The Times,* 25th August 1932.

The *Stella Polaris* in action. (*Southern Lights*)

over a hundred feet in height ... Quintin was steering his boat now, with a white set face whirling the wheel around trying to keep bows on to the waves. A following wind made the waves break ominously and rushed us furiously towards the point ... At this point we realised we were playing with our lives."[11]

At one point the engine became waterlogged and failed, and their survival rested on Riley's ability to keep the *Stella* away from the bergs just using the sail. The engine then restarted and they reached the shelter of the next bay. They had to wait there until the swell subsided and eventually returned to their base on 3rd September.

The frame of their house was now nearly complete. While Rymill stayed at base and completed the house, Spencer Chapman and Riley went to Angmagssalik and returned with the whale boat, dogs and supplies they needed for the winter. While there they visited their old base from the previous year, and felt mixed emotions, being glad that they had experienced a marvellous year there but thinking about the death of Watkins, the fact that Lemon was dying in England and that most of the members of the previous year's expedition had returned to civilised life. Back at base camp the weather grew colder. The lake above the fjord was frozen by October, but the fjord itself remained clear until November. Despite the fact that they were missing Gino's hunting skills, the party, with the help of the local hunters were getting enough seals and seabirds to vary their diet. As the autumn wore on they were to become more skilled at both fishing and shooting birds. Spencer Chapman

---

11   Spencer Chapman, *Watkins's Last Expedition*, p.81.

was laid up with knee problems for these months and therefore took more interest in the cooking arrangements. He said: "Perhaps the most important qualification of an arctic cook is to be able to serve up seal meat in as great a variety of palatable forms as possible."[12] He recounted the discussions and arguments that they had in the evenings, and described Riley as a "supreme pessimist" and mentioned the trait that Riley was famous for on expedition: "Quintin is happiest when arguing and whatever happens insists on having the last word."[13]

Riley made strenuous efforts to learn the Eskimo language, a difficult task as the vocabulary and verb structure were difficult. Jonathon Riley recounted Riley's efforts to learn the tenses of a verb, helped by an Eskimo woman:

> 'Today the sun shines' said Quintin. Leah gave the word. 'Tomorrow the sun will shine'. Again she gave the word, although it sounded just the same. 'Now', said Quintin, 'yesterday the sun shone. How do you say that?' 'No', said Leah, 'You are talking rubbish. It was snowing hard.' [14]

Riley was also keen to improve his sledging skills. He learned that the best way to drive the dogs was by means of the fan method with traces of equal lengths and that dogs from the same family usually made the best teams.

At the beginning of February the pack ice had solidified and weather conditions were judged suitable for Rymill and Spencer Chapman to sledge to Angmagssalik to buy some more dogs for the winter expeditions and to try and complete a coastal survey on the way. On their return they set off for what Spencer Chapman called "desultory sledge journeys," which penetrated some way into the interior, although not as far as Mount Forel, which they had hoped to climb. By the end of April, Rymill had finished his triangulation for his map of the country around Lake Fjord and had started to fill in the detail using the plane table. Riley was occupied with painting and varnishing the *Stella* and the whale boat, getting them ready for the summer season. On 13th June Riley and Rymill left for Angmagssalik to take equipment there ready to be picked up by the *Gertrud Rask*, and to start making arrangements about the journey back to England. The journey down the coast in the *Stella* had taken three weeks as ice conditions were poor. The boat had almost been crushed by ice twice, and Riley had had to use dynamite to force a route into a more secure bay from which they had to wait several days to escape. Riley had managed to rig a wooden look out platform to the mast of the *Stella* and this proved invaluable while navigating through pack ice. On one occasion they were trapped between the pack ice and an overhanging rock wall...

> ... which towered for a thousand feet above them, when suddenly a shower of enormous boulders, loosened by the summer sun, poured just beside the boat on the ice; another bombardment fell just in front of them, but nothing actually hit the *Stella*.[15]

At this point their plans received a setback in that it proved too expensive to charter the *Gertrud Rask* to pick up stores and equipment from Lake Fjord and to transport the expedition back to England. Luckily a Danish expedition led by Knud Ramussen

12   Ibid., p.127.
13   Ibid., p.129.
14   Q. Riley, *Greenland Diary*, cited by Riley, *Pole to Pole*, p.52.
15   Spencer Chapman, *Watkins's Last Expedition*, p.282.

had arrived at Angmagssalik and offered to take Rymill and his men back to Iceland in September. This meant that they had extra time and could make a more complete survey. Some of this time was spent taking detailed depth studies in Lake Fjord. Spencer Chapman took the opportunity of completing a 20-day kayak journey along the coast to complete ornithological work.

On 20th September the expedition set off for Iceland in the *Nordjstern*. Riley grieved at leaving Gino: "I felt very sad at leaving Gino behind when we passed his cross. My thoughts and prayers are full of him. Now back to the civilised world without him."[16] Riley had been an important member of both Watkins's expeditions, in that his skills as logistics man and quartermaster had made the expeditions more comfortable. His skill at handling the *Stella* had added to the amount of work the expedition had been able to achieve and had on several occasions saved their lives. Although the aims of the expedition had been blighted by the death of Gino Watkins and bad weather, and had not been helped by the need to be providing food by hunting, it can be said that it continued the contribution to mapping and surveying the area started the previous year. In November 1933 Riley was invested with the Polar medal, and was looking forward to going south.

The British Graham Land Expedition 1934-37

During the long winter of the Greenland expedition, Rymill had come up with a plan to explore Antarctica, which on his return he discussed with Professor Frank Debenham and Dr J.M. Wordie. Gradually plans for an expedition, which was to become the British Graham Land Expedition or B.G.L.E., emerged. Quintin Riley's biographer said of the expedition that "it had bridged the gap between the heroic age and the modern era in the evolution of Antarctic endeavour and the technology of Polar travel."[17]

Western Antarctica had not been explored because of its inaccessibility due to pack ice. Shackleton's expedition had come to grief when the *Endeavour* had failed to penetrate the pack ice in the Weddell Sea. However, it was thought the currents prevailing on the western side of the Antarctic Peninsula often left open water near to the shore. Previous expeditions had given some idea of the extent of the peninsula. John Biscoe had made a landing in 1832 on the peninsula at latitude 64° 45° south and named the area Graham Land, after the then First Lord of the Admiralty. Both Charcot in his ship the *Pourquoi-Pas?* (1908-10) and Wilkins and Ellsworth on their recent flights had reported that the peninsula was actually an archipelago of islands, and that channels existed through which the Weddell Sea could be reached. Wilkins flew down the west coast of Graham Land in 1929, reporting a series of islands leading down to mainland Antarctica at Hearst Land. Wilkins was also in the area in a ship in 1935, and reported to Rymill by radio that Lincoln Ellsworth had flown down the coast and had seen a large channel leading west. This was called Stefansson Strait and was thought to be the main sea channel cutting through Graham Land to the Weddell Sea.

However useful aeroplanes were however, they often provided misleading results and were most useful in the way the British expedition planned to use them, in reconnaissance for possible bases and moorings for the ship and for providing advance warning of possible dangers to the ship while navigating down the coast. As Hugh Robert Mills, in his introduction to *Southern Lights* explained, "astronomical observations, without which no

16   Q. Riley, *Greenland Diary*, cited by Riley, *Pole to Pole*, p.54.
17   Riley, *Pole to Pole*, p.90.

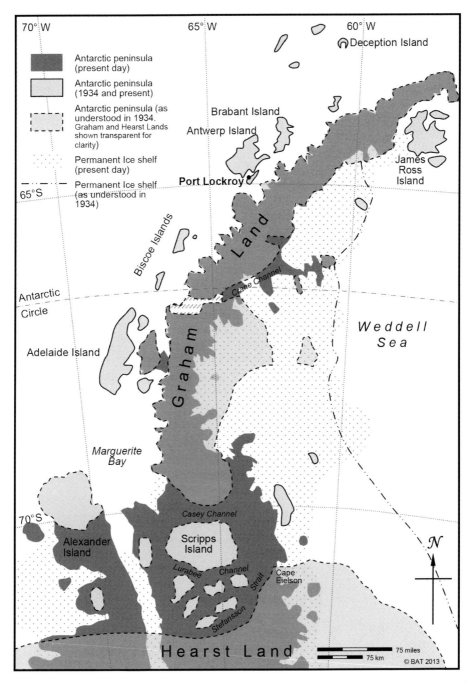

Map showing the discoveries made by the Graham Land Expedition 1934-37. (Barbara Taylor)

useful mapping is possible, must be made from the surface." [18] Before the Graham Land expedition then, very little exploration by sea or land had been carried out in the area to give the party any guidance.

Rymill's plan was to sail down the west coast of Graham Land, from Luitpold Land to Charcot Land, sledge through the frozen channels, and explore the Antarctic coast behind the Weddell Sea. *The Times* in its early reports on the expedition wondered whether it would shed any light on the theory that there were in fact two Antarctic continents, not one.[19] In addition to the geographical aims the expedition had a raft of biological, geological and meteorological aims ranging from research into plankton, mapping glacial movement and, interestingly, in view of future events, the determination of the proportion of the newly discovered heavy water or deuterium oxide, in Antarctic snow. Another feature of the expedition's plans was the carrying of short wave radio receivers in order to pick up radio time signals from Buenos Aries. Comparing this signal with local time, established by astronomical observations, would give a reliable longitude position.

The Times editorial written on 3rd September 1934, mentioned the recent plights of Admiral Byrd and Augustine Courtauld, both of who had been entombed in ice for several months before rescue. It remarked, in considering the Graham Land expedition:

> The experienced explorer takes no heedless risks, but if no risk existed the incentive to conquer the unknown world would not be so strong; Mr Rymill and his companions have taken thought, and as far as possible have prepared for all contingencies. They will not fail for lack of resolution, endurance and readiness to strain mind and muscle to the uttermost.[20]

Rymill was successful in raising the necessary funds, as he had a grant of £10,000 from the Colonial Office and financial help from Salvessens. However, the expedition was always running on a tight budget considering its ambitious aims. One of the consequences of this was the decision to set sail in a wooden vessel, the *Penola*, with only auxiliary engines. This was to cause tension between Rymill plus the shore based party and the captain of the ship R.E.D. Ryder, as we shall see in Chapter Eight. Rymill now started recruiting his party. Quentin Riley was one of the first to sign up, citing his occupation as "gentleman". [21] His extensive experience in Greenland over a number of years and two expeditions would make a very valuable addition to the party. His role was to be one of the two meteorologists and, as in Greenland, to be in charge of stores. Riley said of himself that he had joined the expedition because "he liked housekeeping".[22] He also took his boat *Stella Polaris*, which had proved invaluable in Greenland and was to do so again. Rymill chose initially men who had been with him on the BARRE expedition. W.E. Hampton was in charge of the seaplane, a De Havilland Fox, Alfred Stephenson joined as a surveyor, Edward Bingham as doctor. Others, not from previous expeditions, making up the shore party, were Reverend Lancelot Fleming, joining as chaplain and geologist; Lt. I.F. Miklejohn, of the Royal Signals, in charge of wireless communication; Brian Roberts, ornithologist; and Colin Bertram,

---

18   H.R. Mill, 'Historical Introduction' in J. Rymill, *Southern Lights* (London, 1939), p.20.
19   E.g. *The Times,* 10th August 1934.
20   *The Times,* 3rd September 1934.
21   Richard Hopton, *A reluctant hero – the life of Captain Robert Ryder VC* (Barnsley, 2011), p.57.
22   Riley, *Pole to Pole*, p.59.

Bingham, Riley, Lindsay, Rymill, Scott. (Riley family)

biologist. The ship's company was commanded by Lt. Robert Ryder RN.

On 21st January the long journey to Antarctica via Montevideo and Port Stanley, capital of the Falkland Islands, was complete and the *Penola* had arrived at Port Lockroy, a sheltered anchorage at the northern end of the Antarctic Peninsula. Rymill described the scene as the *Penola* sailed from the southern ocean into the sheltered channels of north Graham Land on the approach to Port Lockroy, observing "the grandeur of the scenery amongst which we should make our home for the next two years."[23] Beyond the ice cliffs of the coast the mountains rose to some 5,000 feet above the sea level and the mountain faces were intersected by glaciers and ice falls. Rymill was particularly impressed by the dead calm sea and the silence: "The only sounds that could be heard were the occasional roar of an avalanche, or a dull grumbling as an ice cliff calved, and perhaps the cry of a Dominican gull going to and from its breeding ground nearby."[24]

By 27th January the Fox aeroplane was assembled and ready to fly down the coast looking for a suitable place for the base camp to be set up. Because of the trouble with *Penola's* engines at Port Stanley the expedition had arrived in Graham Land late in the season and plans for the *Penola* to take the expedition much further south had to be abandoned. Rymill realised that they would have to be content with spending the first winter in northern Graham Land. It was now necessary to find a place for a base further down the coast. Hampton's reconnaissance flights in the Fox resulted in the location of a

23   J. Rymill, *Southern Lights. The Official Account of the British Graham Land Expedition 1934–1937* (London, 1938), p.49.
24   Ibid., p.49.

possible area some 30 miles south in the Argentine Islands. Riley's boat, the *Stella Polaris* now started to earn its keep, as Rymill, Riley and Ryder took it down to the possible site to check its suitability and to plot a course for the *Penola*. Rymill described the *Stella* as "a good sturdy little boat and a veteran of polar work."[25] Riley now also came into his own as quartermaster, providing an excellent lunch for their journey and apologising for forgetting the cigars. Ryder commented in his diary: "It is already an established fact if one is fond of the comforts of life Riley is the person to take along."[26]

The *Penola* had to make two journeys from Port Lockroy to the Argentine Islands. The main creek and anchorage chosen was called Stella Creek, and had a flat stony beach on which Rymill planned to build the base hut. The voyage of the *Penola,* planned to take only a day, was not without possible problems. In the uncharted waters navigation had to be very much by sight. Rymill, Ryder and Riley worked out a system by which, after Hampton had flown over the route, the *Stella* would be used for sounding the harbours and approaches. Ryder described in his diary how useful the *Stella* was in gaining anchorage. "The launch who had escorted the ship down stood by to tow the bows of the ship around the steep and narrow bends.[27]

Construction on the house now began and Riley set up the meteorological station. The hut was finished in early March and Riley expressed in his diary his satisfaction with the result, drawing a detailed layout in his diary and finding everything "extraordinarily comfortable." The journey south by sledge could now begin. Again Riley's role with the *Stella* proved invaluable. With the *Stella* he laid depots for the autumn sledge journeys, towed the aeroplane to suitable landing and taking off places, and ferried other members of the expedition to islands for surveys and seal catching.

It became apparent after air reconnaissance that the expedition could not hope to get up to the plateau to sledge south that winter, so plans were made to sledge down the western coast of Graham Land and to progress further south the following summer. In the meantime, as soon as the sea had frozen over and the ice was bearing in August, several sledge journeys took place down the coast from August to November. Riley beached the *Stella* and gave her an overhaul and then concentrated his attention on his duties as meteorologist and quartermaster. The meteorological instruments were placed in a shelter at the top of the hill near the base, and readings were taken every three hours from 9.00 a.m. to 9.00 p.m. Bingham later described how Riley would go up the hill under cover of his umbrella and then return by ski with the umbrella still up.[28]

On 21st June, Midwinter, a Christmas party was held, which Riley described:

> We had our Christmas tree and distributed gifts from the box sent by Debenhams ... It was an excellent party and we danced afterwards, even the chief! We did not rise very early the next morning."[29]

Life at base camp was busy, even after the sledging journeys were completed. The *Penola's* engines were overhauled and reset in concrete, the dogs, who were being bred

---

25   Ibid., p.53.
26   Robert Ryder, 'Penola', manuscript diary, private collection.
27   Ibid.
28   Ibid., p. 73.
29   Q. Riley, *Antarctic Diary* p.59, cited by Riley, *Pole to Pole*, p.77.

Quintin Riley in the *Stella Polaris* towing the aeroplane into base after a
survey flight, Argentine Islands, Antarctic, 1935. (Riley family)

to produce puppies for the next year's journey, needed much attention. Preparation for
sledging journeys was made, Riley keeping occupied by working out and preparing sledging
rations. Most members of the expedition listened to the B.B.C. and read. Discussions took
place on a wide variety of topics. Riley, who always enjoyed a good discussion, and was
"prepared to be opinionated on almost any topic", [30] took delight in playing devil's advocate.
He would scatter opinions and arguments about until he had succeeded in stirring up a
disagreement and then pursued it with great enthusiasm. He even took *Whitaker's Almanac*
and *Kennedy's Revised Latin Primer* to help him prove his points.

Riley's other preoccupation and contribution to the expedition, especially in the period
before sledging began, was to aid Lancelot Fleming, the official chaplain, in the organising
of the religious life of the expedition and the provision of services. Fleming described
how there was a communion service on Sundays and Saints' days before breakfast and on
Sunday evenings a service, which was followed by a glass of sherry or port. [31] Riley was
himself a devout Anglo-Catholic and his father had presented the expedition with copies
of the *English Hymnal*, which had been in part compiled by his father. He accompanied the
hymns on the voyage out with a piano accordion. Riley, however, disagreed with Fleming
on both the content and the timing of the services. Although he was a firm believer in
sticking to the Prayer Book service, he did not interfere with Fleming's introduction of
a more relaxed liturgy to fit in with his varied communicants, but did draw the line at
proposals that the communion service should be held at any time other than first thing in
the morning. When several members of the ship's company had missed early communion
because of bad weather preventing them coming to shore, Fleming suggested another

30   Riley, *Pole to Pole,* p.77.
31   Fleming's papers, cited by G. Hunt in *Lancelot Fleming, A Portrait* (Canterbury, 2003), p. 7.

communion service in the afternoon, Riley was firmly against the idea: "I talked him out of this. I pointed out that once he had it in the afternoon it would be very difficult to show why it could not be repeated. I am sure I am right about this."[32]

Rymill decided in February to start to move the expeditions base further south as it seemed the best ice-free time for the *Penola* to succeed in moving the expedition would be in March or April. Once again the combination of seaplane, motorboat and Ryder directing operations from the crow's nest, was used to secure a safe route. The *Stella* was used to investigate creeks and inlets to find a secure anchorage where the *Penola* could unload the expedition to establish its new southern base. Rymill described how they worked together:

> Using the *Stella* in this way proved most useful on many occasions, and enabled Ryder to manoeuvre the ship into the most impossible- looking places. He would direct operations from the crow's nest with various flag signals ... I was always amazed that he was able to give the right signals to the right men.[33]

By 29th February a new base was established on the Debenham Islands in Marguerite Bay. By 23rd March the *Penola* was unloaded and a new base established, with hut, aircraft hanger and dog house. Riley spent much time in the next few weeks sealing to build up stocks for the winter, but by 11th April the ice had become too thick to continue and the Stella was pulled up on the beach and covered up for the winter. Reconnaissance by the Fox aeroplane showed a more complex pattern to the topography than expected. There appeared to be an intricate island and fjord system between Charcot Island and the coast. There were no channels visible through to the Weddell Sea and there was no chance of crossing the plateau until south of latitude 69° 30′, below which latitude the glaciers would perhaps give access to the plateau. Rymill now decided that some depot laying journeys should take place in preparation for the main winter journeys. Two parties set out, one on 11th June, and the other the following day. In the first party were Rymill, Stephenson and Moore and the second party consisted of Bingham and Bertram, with dogs, and Riley with the tractor pulling two sledges. However, Moore had to be taken back to base with frostbite and Riley took over his dog team with Hampton looking after the tractor alone. The two parties were now travelling together. Rymill described the scene, sledging on 14th June:

> We had a wonderful view this afternoon. When the sky cleared, the clouds over the Graham Land mountains to the east remained faded into long streamers towards the zenith, where their edge were touched with the reds and oranges of the sunset light from the north. The soft winter twilight made the whole scene look coldly beautiful but rather awe-inspiring. As we sledged along I was impressed by the thought that that here was all this strange grandeur around us, and we – people of the twentieth century who had left an overcrowded land only a few months before – were the first to see it since the world began.[34]

However, the going was tough, with a difficult soft slushy surface. A wind blew up on the night of the 16th and continued blowing. During the night of the 18th the party

32   Q. Riley, *Antarctic Diary,* p.69, cited in *Pole to Pole,* p.74.
33   Rymill, *Southern Lights,* p.89.
34   Rymill, *Southern Lights,* p.121.

Surveying in Antarctica, 1936. Alfred Stephenson with plane table. (*Southern Lights*)

woke up to a sudden vibration of the ice and "two more shocks as if though someone in the distance was hitting the edge of the ice with a heavy hammer."[35] A watch was kept for the rest of the night, using Riley's hurricane lantern which he had brought just in case it was needed. In the morning the party managed, by crossing through the slush and pans of ice and across leads, to regain the shore. Riley commented on the leadership of his dog Salo – "If he stops the whole team stops."[36] The decision was now taken to return to base, but the party had to wait a week to allow the ice to firm up. Eventually on 25th June a journey which took two days over 40 miles on breaking or broken ice took them back to base. At base the winds continued, wrecking the met station.

As conditions prevented further travel south until the ice became more permanent, Rymill decided on some journeys north. Riley, Fleming and Stephenson were sent to the Bourgeois Fjord area to make met observations and examine the geology. Riley's diary for this journey is sparse as he shared a tent with Fleming and spent much time discussing all kinds of topics until late at night. Riley described the benefit of sledging with Fleming: "He has many ideas which lend themselves to long discussions, so pleasant for this kind of weather and beneficial to the intellect."[37]

The discovery of a large sound between Alexander Island and the coast, instead of a narrow fjord as expected from information gathered on flights by Ellsworth, caused Rymill to reconsider his sledging plans. Stephenson, Fleming and Bertram sledged south and west through the newly discovered sound and found that Alexander Island was much larger than expected. Rymill and Bingham, having sledged south by 26th October to meet them, then decided not to explore more of the coast, but in the absence of a channel linking the

35   Ibid., p. 124.
36   Quintin Riley, *Antarctic Diary*, p. 120, cited in *Pole to* Pole, p.83.
37   Ibid., p.106, cited in *Pole to Pole*, p.87.

west coast to the Weddell Sea, to attempt to cross the plateau by sledge. Their journey of 535 miles took 72 days. They reached a height of 7,500 feet on the plateau by 24th November and were expecting to be able to see the Weddell Sea, but instead faced another ridge of mountains. They did not in fact get a glimpse of the east coast and the Weddell Sea until 30th November. Unfortunately they were not able to find a way down to the sea ice.

Riley's last task in the *Stella* was to sail up to Horseshoe Island to meet the returning *Penola* and give her instructions for picking up the party at the southern base and to give Ryder Stephenson's charts. This mission was safely accomplished and the *Penola* picked up the shore party, which left on 12th March. The shore party, including Riley, were taken back to Britain from South Georgia by the *Corona*, an oil tanker belonging to Salvessens. The expedition had mapped the coast of Graham Land from latitude 64° 30'S to latitude 72° 30'S, over 600 miles, and found it unbroken by any channels leading to the Weddell Sea, thereby proving that Graham Land was a peninsula and not an archipelago. This was considered to be a significant geographical discovery. The discovery of the great sound was also a very important contribution to the mapping of one of the last undiscovered regions on earth. It was named George VI Sound in honour of the king who had ascended the throne in 1936.

Riley, with the other members of the expedition, received the Polar Medal, or in his case, the bar to the Polar Medal, its clasp inscribed 'Antarctic 1935-37'. He was one of only five men who were awarded the medal with both arctic and antarctic clasps. Riley had continued to exercise his skills as logistics expert and quartermaster developed in Greenland, and had contributed greatly to the scope and success of the expedition by his deployment of his motor launch *Stella*. These skills, along with his freewheeling disregard of institutional disciple, a result of the influence of Gino Watkins, were to ensure that he had an exciting war.

The Norwegian Campaign 1940

In September 1939 Riley had joined the Royal Naval Volunteer Reserve and spent the first months of the war as the captain of an anti-submarine yacht on the Clyde. However, the Allies were contemplating action to prevent Swedish ore from being shipped through the Norwegian Leads to Germany. They were also worried about the Russian attack on Finland. By the beginning of 1940 the Allies had began thinking of military operations in Scandinavia. It was inevitable that men who had arctic experience would be involved. Riley had already written to *The Times* in January 1940[38] recommending that the Government contact the Scott Polar Research Institute for advice on arctic warfare, concerning travelling, working and surviving in polar climates. Expertise in these fields had been hard won by British Polar expeditions of the inter-war years.

Operations were planned which would be based on two British divisions with air support. A British force was to be trained in mountain and arctic warfare and the 5th (Special Reserve) Battalion Scots Guards was formed. Joined by J.M. Scott, Martin Lindsay and Freddie Spencer Chapman he arrived at Quebec Barracks, Bordon, to join the nucleus of the battalion forming up. Their polar experience was immediately harnessed as they were put in charge of sorting the battalion's equipment. The personnel of the battalion were mustered by a call for volunteers with the appropriate skills. Since many of the 1,000

---

38   *The Times*, 26th January 1940.

5th Scots Guards ski training at Chamonix 1940. (Riley family)

Scots Guards ski training at Chamonix 1940 (Riley family)

volunteers were officers, quite a few had to assume non-commissioned positions in order to take part, but were given the assurance that they would revert to their former rank when they left the battalion. Riley, Scott and Spencer Chapman became Colour Sergeants, while Lindsay, as a regular, kept his rank of captain. In Chamonix, the former explorers overcame logistical difficulties and set about teaching sledging techniques to the officers and NCOs of each company. The battalion was embarked at Glasgow on 14th March to help the Finns in their struggle with the Russians, but at the last minute news came through of the Finn's capitulation and the battalion was disbanded.

The German invasion of Norway began on 9th April. We have seen in Chapter Three how former explorers were involved in the operations at Namsos and how this force was evacuated on 1st May and 2nd. Allied troops had been landed in the Narvik area on 14th April. In order to cover the coastline and to prevent the enemy from setting up submarine or air bases, commando companies had been set up to act as raiding parties. The war diary of MI (R) recorded that 10 independent companies had left with a headquarters consisting of Colonel, later Major-General, Colin Gubbins, Major Kermit Roosevelt, Captain Andrew Croft and Lt Quintin Riley RNVR. According to the war diary "Lt Riley came into say goodbye to Captain Croft not expecting to go to Norway, but he was fired with enthusiasm and left with them four hours later."[39] Riley sailed for Norway on 26th April, sharing a cabin with Croft. Gubbins' Independent Companies had been raised from the second line Territorial Army divisions in Britain. Volunteers had been called for by asking for men "interested in unusual or adventurous training."[40] No mention was made of Norway nor arctic warfare. There was little in the way of training or briefing. Riley recalled that "their map issue consisted of Norwegian holiday brochures."[41]

On arrival at Mosjoen they found themselves taking over the positions left by the French troops who had just been evacuated by order of the French General Gamelin. Their position was untenable as the French troops were to have protected their flanks. After dealing with a group of German cyclists on their way up the main north south road the companies were faced with a large number of ski troops who threatened to encircle them. Gubbins organised a steamer to transport the troops from Mosjoen. Throughout the journey to Bodø, German bombers circled overhead. Lieutenant-General Sir Claude Auchinleck, commander of the British forces in Norway, had his headquarters at Harstad, and after having deployed the independent companies in defensive positions at Moirana, Salt Fjord, Bodø and Fauske, sent the Scots and Irish Guards to reinforce them. The ship that the Irish Guards were on, the *Effingham* was bombed, killing many of the officers. The Scots Guards, according to Jonathon Riley, "proved as unfit for mountain warfare as most of the rest of the force."[42]

The force had very little transport and Croft, on trying to organise some, found that the local police chief was "one of those many rogues or fifth columnists" who would not help. In the face of this intransigence Croft commented, "I had to take a more rugged approach."[43] Riley summed up the situation – "the whole country is riddled with *Quislings* and the Hun knows everything—their equipment, training and speed are infinitely better than ours and

---

39   MI (R) War Diary, 1st May 1940. Croft Papers, private collection.
40   Riley, *From Pole To Pole*, p.102.
41   Ibid., p.103.
42   Ibid., p.105.
43   A. Croft, *A Talent for Adventure* (London, 1991), p.154.

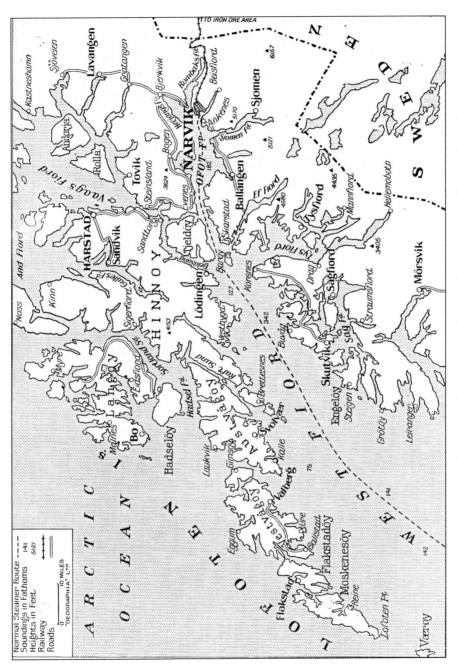

North-west Norway showing the battle of Narvik. (Hutchinson's *Pictorial history of the War*)

they have complete control of the air." [44] It was planned to bring some aeroplanes in from naval aircraft carriers to land on a frozen lake. At this point Commander Bill Fell arrived from Harstad Headquarters with five diesel-powered fishing boats, which became known as "the puffers". Their job was to protect the sea flank and facilitate movement of supplies to the troops further south. Fell was impressed on his first meeting with Riley and Croft: "The first impression in those first moments was of having met two great characters. I sensed tremendous power of endurance. Humour, quick brains and swift decisions, and the gift of using the velvet glove I was to learn about later, but at that moment, I knew I was with two men I could trust anywhere and implicitly." [45] The other functions of the puffers was to transport Riley and Croft on raids downs the coast. Croft explained – "With Bill at the helm we would travel fifty miles south to land in the short hours of darkness behind the enemy lines, creep up on a sentry guarding a bridge, dig position and tamp down our explosives and creep back to watch the resulting explosion from a safe distance, hoping to God that Bill would reappear and take us off."[46]

In between raids, when they would be awake for as much as 50 hours, they would collapse in "Admiralty House", Gubbins's HQ at Bodø, a small white villa in the woods, where Kermit Roosevelt would have scrounged food and prepared it. By the last week in May troops from Rognan and Fauske were being evacuated to Bodø by Fells' puffers and Bodø was coming under increasing air attack. The puffers were operated by Fell, Croft and Riley, with Norwegian crews, some of whom were reluctant volunteers. Riley was able to use his experience of polar logistics and small boat handling to advise on the loading of the men and their equipment. Admiralty House was bombed and destroyed, and Riley, Croft and Roosevelt moved to one of the puffers for their mess. The time had come for full evacuation from Bodø. Riley and Croft went to bring in groups of soldiers from the small islands off the coast. Evacuation started on the night of 28th-29th May when three destroyers arrived from Harstad, taking off 3,500 men on the first two nights and the remaining 2,500 men on the following night. When the last destroyer left, Fell remained with one puffer, as Riley and Croft were still ashore, destroying documents and equipment. The next task of the puffer was to take Croft and Riley to some islands to destroy all fuel dumps and then take them to Harstad, from where the British forces were to be evacuated. The puffers were used then to ferry troops out to the larger ships. Fell remembered that this activity was "driven on by indomitable men like Andrew Croft and Quintin Riley."[47]

Croft described the evacuation of Norway: "Though on a much smaller scale than in France, our force had experienced rugged ordeals, and the final evacuation, with negligible air cover was, like Dunkirk, a triumph of improvisation and nerve."[48] Riley was to comment in later years that it was the first occasion in which the armed services acted cohesively together. Riley was mentioned in dispatches for his work in Norway and had established a good relationship with Gubbins, who wrote to him:

> I am most grateful for all you did in Norway under difficult conditions, and I am afraid with little support from me, as I was too far away to give you a hand. Apart from

44   Riley, *Pole to Pole*, p.105.
45   W.R. Fell, *The Sea Our Shield* (London, 1966), p.56.
46   Croft, *Talent for Adventure*, p.154.
47   Fell, *The Sea Our* Shield, p.72.
48   Croft, *Talent for Adventure*, p.158.

your efforts I enjoyed very much you company, especially during the more critical moments at the end when the rats were beginning disappear and one looked for those one could trust – depend on it, if ever I am lucky enough again to have a naval officer on my establishment, I shall send you a wire.[49]

No. 30 Assault Unit 1941–45

On 3rd June 1940, Churchill instigated the formation of Combined Operations by sending a memorandum to Lieutenant-General Hastings Ismay, his chief military assistant and staff officer. This memorandum set in motion a chain of events which were to lead to the setting up of Combined Operations HQ. He wrote to the chiefs of staff on 3rd June 1940 suggesting the organisation of forces which would take the war back on to the continent and allow some offensive action to take place:

> The completely defensive habit of mind, which has ruined the French, must not be allowed to ruin all our initiative. It is of the highest consequence to keep the largest numbers of German forces all along the coasts of the countries that have been conquered, and we should immediately set to work to organise raiding forces on these coasts where the populations are friendly. Such forces might be composed by self-contained, thoroughly equipped units of say 1,000 up to not less than 10,000 when combined.[50]

He suggested that raiding parties should be organised to operate on the "butcher and bolt principle". In July 1940 Roger Keyes was appointed director of the newly formed Combined Operations. The new companies, which became known as Commandos, were raised initially from the Independent Companies that had taken part in the Norway campaign, and then by calling for volunteers from the three armed services.

Gubbins suggested that Riley's experience at small boat handling would be ideal for the setting up and training of the Commando units which were to be raised to carry out the raids suggested. Troop training began in Arisaig in Scotland, in the West Country, in the Scilly Isles and in Cornwall. Riley was occupied in boat training in Newlyn, operating under a shortage of funds and equipment. He found that some of the trainee boat handlers did not appreciate the need for strict discipline in the boats. He wrote to Commander C.H. Pilcher, his immediate superior:

> I have concentrated on watermanship—It sounds simple enough to shove the cutter off after the shore party has disembarked, anchor the boat, and return when ordered to the beach; but it takes much practice even to carry out a simple manoeuvre such as this, the importance of which is obvious if a raiding party is to be successfully withdrawn. In all the companies the men are beginning to understand the meaning of silence and to realise the need for the strictest discipline, but they have a long way to go before landing and retirement is made without a word being spoken.[51]

---

49 Letter from Colonel Gubbins to Riley cited in *Pole to Pole*, p.108.
50 TNA CAB 120/414.
51 Letter from Riley to Commander C.H. Pilcher, Riley Papers, Liddell Hart Centre for Military Archives, King's College London.

A wartime portrait of Riley. (Riley family)

He had things in hand, however, and reported to HQ of the Independent Companies in August, after commenting on boat discipline: "I have had no difficulties in this respect as I gave each crew a short talk about this before each outing." [52] Riley persevered, and in a few months genuine landing craft, built in 1936, became available. For the crews of these landing craft Riley looked out for men who had been handling small boats as part of their pre-war careers or hobbies, like yachtsmen, fishermen, ex-Merchant Navy men. Riley now recruited another former polar explorer, Andrew Croft, into the training: "You know a great deal about ships' carrying powers, how guns, planes, men etc pack. All your Finnish experience will be invaluable." He continued, persuasively: "The only way we shall beat the Germans is by offensive and for that we have to get put best men in the Combined Ops division – We shall not win the war by keeping people like you in Essex" [53]

Croft and Riley were engaged in the development and testing of the landing craft which would deliver the commando troops from their ships to the raiding targets. After some time with the stopgap craft, Eurekas, they went on to trial the prototypes of the assault landing craft (ALCs), with which Riley was more impressed. After training, the crews were able to manoeuvre the craft ashore quickly. These craft went on to participate in many operations during the war, including the D-Day landings. A letter to Riley from Lord Louis

52   Q. Riley, Report to HQ Independent Companies, August 1940. Riley Papers.
53   Letter from Riley to Croft 20th November 1940. Cited by Riley, *Pole to Pole*, p.114.

Mountbatten in July 1944 passing on a congratulatory message from Churchill, Brooke, Marshall and Smuts to all those who had contributed to making the D-Day landings a success, shows the importance Mountbatten put on Riley's contribution – "This fine tribute is shared equally by all who worked so well at COHQ and I am most grateful for the loyal and devoted service which you gave me"[54] By November 1941 Riley had moved on to Iceland, where he taught winter warfare skills along with a former Greenland Expedition member, J.M. Scott. He had decided views on the prosecution of winter warfare based on his own experiences. He stressed the need for eradicating carelessness. He emphasised that among the things a winter warfare soldier must leave behind him was "casualness – everything must be checked, dependence on others, he must learn to look after himself, carry spare equipment and know where he is." [55] He advised that the arctic soldier adopted experimental mindedness, especially over food. A colleague there later described how Riley had managed to make a lecture on arctic cooking into a hilarious episode which had been "cheerfully arctic rather than grimly military."[56] Obviously Riley was still employing the social skills that had made him such an entertaining tent companion in the Arctic and Antarctic. After returning to England to have a hernia operation, and also to marry Dorothy Croft, sister of his long-time friend and Polar explorer, Andrew Croft, Riley was recruited to a new commando unit which had been set up by R.E.D. Ryder, at the request of Lord Mountbatten. The purpose of No. 14 Commando was to set up bases off the Norwegian coast from where German shipping, Luftwaffe bases, and other military targets could be attacked by canoe. Ryder lost no time in recruiting former polar colleagues, Riley, Augustine Courtauld and Andrew Croft. The commando was to train in Balta Sound, off the island of Uist, the most northerly tip of the British Isles. The boating troop of the commando succeeded in attacking Royal Navy vessels with dummy limpet mines without being detected.

Ryder had developed an ambitious plan to sink the *Tirpitz* as she passed along the inner lead from Trondheim to her base at Altenfjord. The inner lead was sheltered by islands and reefs. Ryder's idea was that small groups of commandos reposition or hide the buoys and navigation lights, thus leading the *Tirpitz* onto a reef.

> An examination of the chart showed that by slewing one of the many sectored lights and moving a buoy, a ship could be led right across a reef – we needed four small parties: one above and one below with radios to give warning; one to swivel the light, one to mask the buoy and set up a flashing light some 200 yards further inshore.[57]

Riley was meanwhile training the boating troop in canoeing skills. Despite some problems with the quality of the canoes assembled and also some difficulties emerging from the mixture of Norwegian, Canadian and British troops, training progressed to a pitch where the troop was relatively efficient in terms of irregular warfare. Ryder's plan progressed to the stage where Sir Malcolm Campbell had managed to get hold of the necessary dummy lights, but was then abandoned as the Admiralty lawyers thought it was against the Geneva

---

54   Letter form Mountbatten to Riley dated 4th July 1944 in the Riley Papers, Liddell Hart Centre for Military Archives, King's College London.
55   'Arctic Warfare', a lecture given by Riley on 13th October 1942 at Chatham House in the Riley Papers.
56   *The Times,* 27th January 1981.
57   R.E.D. Ryder, unpublished memoir, private collection.

Convention. Riley's biographer is of the opinion that opposition from SIS, who had been against the formation of No. 14 Commando, was the reason the idea was abandoned.[58]

However, Riley was now to become part of another operation that Ryder was involved with. 30 Assault Unit was the brainchild of Admiral Godfrey and Commander Ian Fleming. Fleming initially proposed the unit on the 20th March 1942, in part as a response to and in emulation of, the Germans' intelligence gathering success in the Greek and Balkan campaigns in 1941. This had used self-contained units alongside assault troops to gather frontline intelligence and documents. Fleming represented Admiral Godfrey at a meeting of the Joint Intelligence Subcommittee in August 1942 and put forward the idea of an intelligence assault unit whose role would be to move in at the same time, or even in advance of the main invading or raiding force, and to capture enemy material, equipment and documents of importance.

In November of 1942 the value of the assault unit had been proved by its success, led by Duncan Curtis, in Operation Torch. When Riley had returned from his work with No. 14 Commando, Ryder, in overall charge of planning, appointed him to take command of the unit. The unit was divided into three troops, the naval side was comprised of No. 36 Troop, a technical wing of specialist naval officers, No. 33 Troop, a Royal Marine group to act as protection, and No. 34 Group which consisted of army personnel. Riley set about moulding these sections, among which there had been infighting, into a cohesive force. He found that at first "The idea of an inter service unit appeared to be completely lacking". This he put down to, among other aspects, the difference of attitude towards other ranks between the navy and army. He thought it was essential that all ranks were fully trained in the intelligence work they were to be involved in. "The army view is that it is essential to train ORs in intelligence matters and that the value of having ORs who know what to look out for and to conduct a search cannot be overestimated."[59] The navy, he felt, tended to treat their OR marines as bodyguards. However these teething troubles were to work themselves out when the unit went into action in the Sicilian and Italian campaigns.

In the 'History of 30 Assault Unit' he emphasised the sort of man and the sort of training that was required:

> Officers should not only be intelligence-trained but also should be 'jacks of all trades', physically fit to drop by parachute, seize and ride a horse, blow a safe and then live off the country for an indefinite period. Proficiency in languages has always been of paramount importance, initiative and resourcefulness are essential.[60]

Ian Fleming had been busy introducing his own "Instant Agent Course" which included techniques of breaking and entering taught by Scotland Yard, the use of explosives, booby traps and small arms. Fleming himself was in charge of instruction on codes, ciphers, intelligence reports, secret weapons and radar. They were also taught to parachute, drive all sort of vehicles, become expert in wireless and photography. They were required to familiarise themselves with interrogation and techniques and resistance to them, and to identify all enemy uniform and insignia.[61] This panoply of skills was used by Fleming in his

58   Ibid., p.120.
59   'History of 30th Assault Unit', p.3, part of the Riley Papers.
60   Ibid., p.15.
61   A. Cecil Hampshire, *The Secret Navies* (London, 1978), p.181.

later novels. As Jonathon Riley commented they were "the skills which later made James Bond unbeatable." Robert Neville, head of Combined Operations Planning Committee, referred to the unit as "armed and expert looters".[62]

Fleming had also asked for, and received, requests from various sections of the Navy for particular intelligence. The director of anti-submarine warfare was anxious to receive information on, and if possible examples of, U-boat ASDIC equipment, hydrophones and mine detecting equipment, along with papers and documents relating tactics, and log books and war diaries. The gunnery division needed information on ammunition, sights and radar equipment. The director of torpedoes and mines needed examples of torpedo pistols. The list was extensive. High in priority were cipher machines.

Under Riley's command 30 Commando now prepared to take part in Operation Husky, the invasion of Sicily. The unit was to land near Cape Passaro with the Eighth Army's XXX Corps. Riley planned that Huntingdon Whitely would go ashore with the Black Watch Regiment and capture the radar stations at Cape Passaro. Another group under Captain Martin Smith would land further east, Lieutenant Glanville would follow with the unit's transport. Riley's group found that the equipment in the radar stations had been blown up, but valuable documents were recovered. Martin Smith's party had captured a radar station, complete with a set of ciphers and frequencies for the Italian Air Force's homing beacons for the months July to September. Glanville's unit had difficulties with their landing and were dropped in the wrong place, however this proved fortuitous as they found a mobile radar station, complete with technical documents. According to Nicholas Rankin in his book *Ian Fleming's Commandos,* Glanville discovered in the pocket of one of the dead ratings "detailed notes of the long radar course he had just passed and the handbook of the Telefunken T-39 Wurzburg set, identical to the one just 'pinched' at Bruneval."[63]

In his report to the Chief of Combined Operations dated 17th August 1943 Riley complained about the lack of manpower devoted to the unit: "At the initial landing in Sicily, had we had four times as many men than we actually did have (20 all ranks), the large R/D/F stations at Cape Passaro might have been captured intact, or at least protected from further destruction, and looting by Italian civilians and our own troops." [64] There were also difficulties with transport which caused delays sending the equipment back for evacuation. The three units of Riley's force then met up and took over a house in Cap Muro di Porco which became their headquarters. From there two of the units would be searching for intelligence while the third sorted and organised the results so that in accordance with Fleming's original wishes, information would be sent back behind the lines swiftly. On the spot examination of seizures was helped by thy arrival at the beginning of August of four specialist officers in torpedoes and mines. They were able quickly to assess captured material. Information on the Italian homing beacon frequencies helped the RAF to itself take advantage of the system to help it find targets. Riley was annoyed that the Special Raiding Squadron had reached Augusta slightly before 30 Commando, but Riley's men found an Enigma machine which was only slightly damaged, and also found evidence in the form of "bizarre acoustic instruments"[65] that implied that the Italians were not using

---

62   Ibid., p.179.
63   Nicholas Rankin, *Ian Fleming's Commandos: The Story of 30 Assault Unit in WWII* (London, 2011), p.178.
64   Q. Riley, Report to Chief of Combined Operations, dated 17th August 1943, Riley papers.
65   Rankin, *Ian Fleming's Commandos*, p.179.

radar. Riley also reported that "some valuable material was taken from the seaplane base there."[66] By 29th July, ten days after landing, over a ton of documents had been evacuated to C–in-C Mediterranean at Malta.[67] A good working relationship with Eighth Army had been established, enhanced by a visit of Riley with Glanville to Montgomery's Tactical Headquarters, where the unit were given a pass clearing them to work in the Eighth Army sector. Glanville's group were able to enter Catania one hour after the advancing troops. In Riposto and Taormina equipment and documentation was captured, including a new type of mine. After Messina was evacuated by German troops, 30 Commando, after interrogating some Italian prisoners, discovered a torpedo workshop with an 18-inch torpedo under construction. At Messina the unit had to be particularly careful of booby traps left in the deserted buildings and offices. At the commandos' Messina headquarters a fire started under a tarpaulin destroyed all of their personal possessions, along with mortars, ammunition and explosives, resulting in a conflagration that burned down the whole villa which was acting as HQ.

On 9th September 1943, Riley and 30 Commando landed at Salerno after being stranded on a sandbank in their LST, into a fierce battle. A mortar round exploded near to Riley, which permanently deafened him in one ear. As there was no chance of 30 Commando investigating any targets, Riley decided to join in the naval operation to capture the island of Capri. Intelligence had reported enemy signals still coming from Capri and it was the unit's job to investigate. Italy had arranged an armistice with the Allies four days previously and the landing on Capri was not only unopposed, but seemed welcome, the town band playing *It's a Long Way to Tipperary* as the force approached. 30 Commando climbed up to Colonel Salverini's fort at Anacapri, where they found and dismantled the transmitter responsible for the messages. Salverini was the chief of the German post-occupation organisation in the Naples area. In his safe were Italian codes including the cipher for the Italian Fleet, which had not been handed over when it surrendered in Malta. They also found a dossier on fascist party members in Naples, who were planning on continuing the fight. Malcolm Munthe had accompanied 30 Commando to Capri to requisition the house of his father Axel Munthe, the famous author of *The Story of St Michele*. At Munthe's villa, Riley signed the visitors' book: "September 13, 1944 – Liberation by the English" and all the men of the Commando signed their names. The following day Riley moved the Commando to the Island of Ischia, and from a base at the Hotel Roma sections of the commando made raids on the surrounding area. At San Martino, Admiral Minisini, an Italian torpedo expert, was taken into custody, with all his papers, including blueprints. As a result of information from the inhabitants of San Martino, Riley was able to plan and lead an attack on the Monte Cuma area. Information from the papers of Minisini led them to the discovery of a midget submarine with a new propulsion system on the Bala peninsula.

As the Italian front moved north, there were fewer intelligence targets for No 30 Commando. Riley went back to Malta and discussed the future. It was decided that the commando should now be based at Bari, giving it scope for operations in the Adriatic, with a view to helping the Yugoslav partisans. At this time the partisans were divided into followers of General Mikailović's Royalist Chetniks and Josip Broz Tito's Communists. Riley on his first visit, bearing arms ammunition and medical supplies, was able to establish friendly relationships with both factions as he emphasised the non-partisan role of British

---

66   Riley, 'History of 30 Assault Unit', p.4.
67   Ibid., p.4.

A wartime photography of Riley. (Riley family)

forces. However, it became clear that the majority supported Tito. This caused problems for 30 Commando as Sancho Glanville, who had been trying to liaise with the Communists about proposed intelligence targets on which the Commando could carry out small-scale raids. He was helped by Brigadier Fitzroy Maclean, leader of the British mission working underground in Yugoslavia, to put his plans before Tito's staff but received the reply that Tito was not interested. Glanville reported that Tito's decision ruled out working with the partisans. The situation was, however more complicated than it appeared. Tito's intelligence had discovered that Glanville spoke the language fluently, was pro-Croat and had been at one time vice consul at Zagreb. Someone of this nature was not acceptable to Tito, as they knew too much and understood the local situation too well. In his report to the Chief of Naval Intelligence from Yugoslavia, Riley commented:

> On November 3rd I met Major-General Gubbins in Bari who informed me that he had a signal to say that Glanville was unacceptable to Tito. I understand from Brigadier Maclean that anyone who speaks the language and knows the country is unacceptable to Tito.[68]

SOE also had qualifications about Glanville in the region, as it was thought that his personal sympathies would cloud his judgement. Riley was not pleased at the conditions that Tito imposed on the work of the Commando and they were withdrawn to Bari where the army wing of the unit was transferred to the 15th Army Group, and the naval wing

---

68   Report from Riley to Chief of Naval Intelligence regarding situation in Yugoslavia, Riley Papers.

returned to Britain to prepare for the eventual second front.

Ian Fleming and Riley now began to think about reorganising and retraining the unit in the light of the lessons learned in the Mediterranean theatre. Problems of multiplication of command and administrative difficulties were addressed. Riley presented a report and attended a meeting in December 1943 at which it was decided that the title of the unit should be changed and that it should now be known as 30 Assault Unit (30 AU). Riley was not to lead the unit to Normandy, as he was now considered, at thirty-nine, too old. Riley was disappointed, but was then summoned to lead an intelligence assault group that had been requested by Mountbatten, now Supreme Allied Commander in South East Asia, to work in this theatre. Accompanied by Lt. Col. Cass, who had been with Ryder and Riley in the early days of Commando training, he made an exhaustive tour of the front in Burma, taking in Comilla, Imphal and the Yu river. He was then able to come up with the proposed unit. He suggested that training for the unit should be very much along that lines followed by 30 AU, but with the addition of jungle survival and warfare skills. He suggested that Cass commanded the unit, but it was not until March 1945 that Glanville led a detachment to Ceylon to set up the unit. It did however, in the last months of the war in the Far East, take part in missions with the small operations group in Burma, Cambodia and Indochina.

Meanwhile, having organised the setting up of the unit in the Far East, Riley returned to Britain at Christmas 1944. Jonathon Riley commented, "He took with him the personal thanks of Mountbatten, a lifelong aversion to curry and the news that Freddie Spencer Chapman was alive and well."[69] He returned to find that the 30 AU had brought back large amounts of captured enemy intelligence material from their exploits in Normandy after landing at Utah Beach and operating in Cherbourg, Carteret and Le Havre. They were now about to be sent to investigate targets made available by the final push of the allied armies over the River Rhine. Riley was sent to Naval Target Sub Division G-2 at SHAEF to look after the interests of 30 AU and to liaise with SOE, OSS, and SIS. He was able to travel all over Germany identifying targets for the unit. This enabled the 30 AU sections to be immediately behind the Allied advance into Germany. An example of their unexpected finds was the discovery at Frankental of a plant which made propulsion units for chemical torpedoes, parts for V2 rockets and contained information on a fast U-boat fuelled by hydrogen peroxide. Two prototypes of these submarines were later found at Hamburg. A telegram sent on 7th May showed Riley's involvement right up to the end of hostilities: "Lt Commander Riley ... is under orders to proceed to the UK by the fastest possible means STOP He is the bearer of material for the address of the Admiralty which is of the highest operational importance."[70] 30 Assault Unit was disbanded on 1st September 1945. It had made a significant contribution to the war effort and the naval intelligence obtained, particularly, was of use in building the expertise of the post war navy. Riley made the point that units such as 30 AU could have been considered a headache to commanders in the field but argued that their acting as sometime private armies, a law into themselves, meant that they were often more efficient in reaching their targets. Jonathon Riley compared the attitude taken by these groups in the war and the way in which Gino Watkins had led the Greenland expeditions. He argued that in a specialist commando group every member must have the capacity to lead: "such groups ... do not have the luxury of a chain of command or guaranteed reinforcements, and so must live by their wits or perish, just as a Polar party

---

69   Riley, *Pole to Pole*, p.143.
70   Telegram in Riley Papers.

must do."[71]

Like Ian Fleming, Riley did not receive any decoration in the victory honours for his war work. However, he did receive a letter confirming that he was entitled to a silver rosette to go with his Polar Medal and clasp and, in a manner of closing the circle, spent time in 1946 taking part in a study on German polar research during the war.

---

71   Riley, *Pole to Pole*, p.148.

4

Peter Fleming

Brazilian Adventure 1932

"Exploring and sporting expedition, under experienced guidance, leaving England June to explore rivers of central Brazil, if possible ascertain fate of Colonel Fawcett." This advertisement in *The Times* of April 1932 immediately caught Peter Fleming's attention, despite the fact that it would mean giving up a job at *The Spectator*. He was gripped with the possibility of discovering what had happened to Colonel P.H. Fawcett, who had disappeared in the Matto Grosso, searching for a lost city, seven years previously. Having resolved just to find out a little more about it he found himself signed up with his friend, Roger Pettiward. The other members were the leader, Robert Churchward, about whom Fleming had reservations from the start, Noel Skeffington-Smyth, surveyor, and Neville Priestley, both old Etonians. The party was completed by Blunt Mackenzie and Arthur Humphreys. They were to be joined in Brazil by Captain J.G. Holman, who had experience of the interior regions of Brazil.

Peter Fleming had been born in 1907 into a wealthy Oxfordshire family and been educated at Eton and Christ Church College Oxford. His father, Valentine Fleming DSO, had been killed in the Great War. His younger brother was Ian Fleming, later to become famous as the author of the internationally bestselling *James Bond* books. After travelling in America and Asia and a brief spell as literary editor of the *Spectator* Fleming discovered the advert for the expedition to find Fawcett, found the idea irresistible, and signed on. *The Times* asked Fleming if he would be their correspondent on what they grandly christened the 'British Matto Grosso expedition.' There had developed considerable public interest in the fate of Fawcett and *The Times* was looking forward to a scoop. In its article of 7th June 1932 under the heading 'River of Death', the paper described how the expedition would travel via São Paulo to Leopoldina The would travel by boat down the River Araguaia, for about 300 miles, and then, after turning left up one of its tributaries, the Rio das Mortes, the so-called 'river of death', they would make a base camp and trek overland in the area that Fawcett had disappeared. *The Times* described the area: "The River of Death flows through the heart of a region inhabited by the Chavantes, a tribe of Indians whose mastery of the arts of jungle warfare have given them an unenviable reputation in the Matto Grosso."[1]

The latest news of the Fawcett expedition dated from October 1931, when it was reported that a white captive of an Indian tribe had spoken to him. This sighting placed Fawcett in an area of 200 miles of high and unknown country above the Rio Das Mortes. However, an expedition led by Captain Dyott in 1928 had acquired information leading them to think that Fawcett and his party had been murdered. *The Times* commented: "It is with the intention of investigating a tragedy rather than the hope of effecting a relief, that the British Matto Grosso Expedition will strike inland from the river of death."[2] On reaching Rio de Janeiro on 3rd July, the expedition members met Captain Holman

---

1   *The Times*, 7th July 1932.
2   Ibid.

Peter Fleming, 1930. (Peter Fleming Estate)

who was supposedly an expert on the geography and anthropology of the region. At this point Fleming and Pettiward discussed resigning from the expedition as Holman proved reluctant to divulge any information. Eventually he disclosed that new evidence pointed at the region of Kaluene. Holman had a letter which purported to come from the chief of an Indian village on the Rio Kalune, dated 1925, describing how Fawcett had pressed ahead into unknown territory, and how later the villagers had come across "traces of a massacre at what they thought was Fawcett's final camp". This was supported by existing information from a previous American expedition led by Captain Dyott. It was decided to enter the next tributary of the Araguaia, the Tapirapé. As Holman advised that the going would be very hard, they left behind the theodolite, which proved wise but would not allow the expedition to look convincing in a scientific sense. Fleming commented that it "would no longer be able to offset the probable failure of the hunt for Fawcett by brandishing a nice new accurate map."[3] Because Fleming could understand what Holman was saying to the local Brazilians, he gained the impression that Holman was not really interested in the search, but was portraying the expedition as a shooting and sporting one. Later it transpired that Churchward's main aim in setting up the expedition was to further arrangements for setting up a new safari agency with Holman.

In São Paulo the expedition was joined by Neville Priestley, who was to prove an ally, with Pettiward, in enduring the difficulties of the venture. A revolution had just started

---

3   Duff Hart-Davis, *Peter Fleming: A Biography* (Oxford, 1987), p.91.

in São Paulo, consequently the party was delayed. Eventually, after travelling the last 130 miles to Leopoldina in a truck in one day, they sighted the Araguaia:

> A river half a mile wide and more – a river fired and bloody in the sunset: a river that we loved instantly and learnt at last to hate. We gaped at this river. There was exaltation in the air.[4]

Travelling in four boats, two thirty feet clinker-built 'bataloas ', one smaller vessel and a dugout canoe, they paddled down the river for three weeks. Every night they camped on the sandbanks, which in the dry season made excellent camping pitches. They supplemented their diet of rice and beans with game and fish, Fleming's country estate background having made him a crack shot. The natives they encountered were the Carajas, who seemed to Fleming to be "tall, silent and amiable", but he was not looking forward to meeting their neighbours, the Chavantes, who had the reputation of being quite different people. Fleming reported that: "In my opinion the Chavantes represent the only danger in this part of the country that has not been grossly exaggerated."[5]

After reaching the mouth of the River Tapirapé, they camped on the island of Bananal, the largest effluvial island in the world. They were now in a position to travel into the heart of the unexplored area where Fawcett had last been seen. At this stage Holman announced that he was not going any further. Fleming now emerged as the leader of those on the expedition who wanted to continue, and after fierce arguments Fleming and Pettiward threatened to resign from the expedition. Although he was persuaded to accompany them eventually, Holman nevertheless turned back after the first day, leaving the rest of the party to carry on alone with only sixteen days of provisions. It took five days to reach São Domingo, the small settlement which served as a port to the Tapirapé Indians but was actually little more than a series of clearings on the river bank. When they reached it, it was deserted and the party decided to split into two. Skeffington-Smyth, Churchill and Mackenzie would carry on exploring up the river, while Fleming, Priestley and Pettiward would strike out across country in the search for news on Fawcett. At this point the Tapirapé tribe reappeared and Fleming was able to give them the gifts that the expedition had carried with them – necklaces, mirrors, toys, knives and lengths of typewriter ribbon. They were able to negotiate the services of two guides and the next day set out across country. Fleming wrote to the editor of The Times: "Although we may be out of touch for some time, there is no need for any anxiety – as soon as we smell an impossibility we shall turn back."[6]

The first day the party covered fifteen miles over grassland, but at the end of the day, the Indians, who were now quite lost, decided they would return to their camps. Priestley, who had a poisoned foot, decided it would be best if he went with them as not to slow the others up. This left Pettiward and Fleming to continue alone with only Queiroz, a one-eyed Brazilian, to help them. For four more days they struggled on to the south-west, hacking their way through jungle and along an unknown tributary of the Tapirapé, and then wading for two days in the river itself. Their food was nearly exhausted; they were baked by the sun in the day and plagued by mosquitoes at night. In his later write-up for The Times, Fleming declared that the final straw was a thunderstorm which heralded the onset of the

---

4   Ibid., p.93.
5   *The Times*, 30th November 1932.
6   Letter to Barrington Ward, cited by Duff Hart-Davis in *Peter Fleming*, p.98.

rains. As they had food just about enough to make a return to São Domingo, they decided to return. Despite the difficulties, Fleming later described them as the best days he had known.[7] In his diary he wrote: "I felt very sorry to be giving up this ridiculous scramble." Their privations were not yet over. When they returned to São Domingo, they found that the cache of equipment and supplies that they had left there had been taken back down river, making the final leg of their journey out of the Tapirapé river to Bananal a nightmare of hunger and discomfort, cold by night and hot by day: "By day we went naked, for it was very hot ... at night we put on all our clothes against the cold and bandaged the rents in them against the mosquitoes."[8]

After a confrontation with Holman at Bananal, Fleming decided to get back to civilisation as soon as possible so that he could give his version of the events of the expedition before Holman did. This journey necessitated navigating more than a thousand miles of the Araguaia River to Belem on the Atlantic coast. At one stage they had to sell two pairs of dark glasses, a snake bite syringe and a pistol, to hire guides to get them through the rapids of Marabi. Eventually they forced a meeting with Holman and the British Consul at Belem in which the outstanding financial disagreements were resolved and the expedition finally wound up.

In his subsequent book, *Brazilian Adventure*, which became a bestseller, Fleming summed up his journey in a light hearted manner: "In the last analysis, it had been comedy that I looked for, and comedy had been forthcoming – comedy with a faint but stimulating tang of melodrama."[9] In his articles for *The Times* in November he made no great claims for the expedition: "We brought no conclusive proof that Fawcett is dead: but no one who has seen anything of the region in which he disappeared can entertain the possibility of his survival."[10] He also described the expedition as a "foolish and abortive journey" which was "only of interest in so far as it reproduced the conditions in which Fawcett was travelling when he disappeared." Fleming wasted no time, however in producing his book *Brazilian Adventure*, which established his reputation as a travel writer.

According to his biographer, Duff Hart-Davis, Fleming had learned a great deal about himself in the process of the adventure. He realised that he was very physically robust, able to withstand physical discomfort and that in times of crisis he could, and did, display a considerable gift for leadership. But the most important discovery was that he enjoyed adventure in wild places and then writing about it. It was this discovery that was to inform his writing career for the next years before he was able to use his leadership skills to such dramatic effect in the Second World War.

News From Tartary 1933–35

On his return from Brazil, it was not long before Fleming felt the urge to travel again. In June 1933 he set off as a *Times* correspondent to report on the situation in China and the rise of the Communist forces under Mao Tse-Tung in the south, and the battle of the Japanese occupiers against bandit resisters in the north. His adventures in China gave him ample material for his next book, *One's Company*. An idea had started growing in Fleming's mind of a journey from China westwards to India, a journey of 3,500 miles through central Asia.

7   Hart-Davis, *Peter Fleming*, p.99.
8   Ibid., p.101.
9   P. Fleming, *Brazilian Adventure* (London, 1933), p.409.
10   *The Times*, 30th November 1932.

However the province of Sinkiang (the Chinese name for Turkestan), which was directly en route, was closed to foreigners due to a succession of civil wars. However, Peter managed to obtain another contract with *The Times* to travel to China as special correspondent. After four months of reporting on adventures in China, Fleming was ready to start arrangements for his long anticipated trip across Tartary. He explained in his foreword to his consequent book, *News from Tartary*, his motivations: "We wanted ... to find out what was happening in Sinkiang, or Chinese Turkestan. It was eight years since a traveller had crossed this remote and turbulent province and reached India from Peking." He continued that he considered the journey "political if not geographical exploration."[11]

He had met up with a Swiss woman, Ella 'Kini' Maillart, an experienced traveller of the Far East who was planning a similar journey. She was well aware of the political difficulties. She realised that "far more than the inherent difficulties of the journey, it is the politics of men that makes these regions inaccessible."[12] He had met a Russian couple, the Smigunovs, who spoke Mongol, Turki and Chinese, who joined the party, who would guide them as far as Tsaidam, over half the length of their journey. Maillart described how, on hearing about her proposed trip, Fleming said to her: "As a matter of fact I'm going back to Europe by that route. You can come with me if you like." To which she replied: "It's my route and it's I who will take you if you can think of some way you can be useful to me."[13]

With misgivings on both sides, they eventually decided to travel together. Maillart's knowledge of Russian would help with the guides who knew no western language and Peter's British nationality would help when it came to entering India after crossing the Himalayas. As both the recognised routes across Sinkiang to India would have involved them coming up against Russian officialdom and being sent back, their planned route after reaching Lanchow was, as Fleming described ...

> to continue due west across the top right hand corner of the Tibetan plateau. This route would take us through the remoter and not more than nominally Chinese parts of the province of Chinghai, through the mountains round the lake called Koko Nor, and across the basin of the Tsaidam Marsh.[14]

He was hoping that this approach would bring them into Sinkiang at point where it was rumoured that the rebel Tungan armies were in control, who would not require a passport from the central government. He summed up this plan thus – "It all boiled down to bluff."[15]

The first part of their journey was by rail and lorry as far as Lanchow, where their plans received a severe setback. Maillart and Fleming were granted a visa to proceed, but the Smigunovs came under suspicion as Russian spies and had to be left behind. They set off for Sining with three mules. Fleming described their departure: "We were alone. The mules plodded in a small fine cloud of dust along the track which followed the crumbling bank of the Yellow River."[16] Maillart remembered that although she felt dismay at leaving the

11   Peter Fleming, *News From Tartary* (London 1936), p.12.
12   Ella Maillart, *Forbidden Journey – From Peking to* Kashmir (London, 1937), p.4.
13   Ibid.
14   Fleming, *News From Tartary*, p.35.
15   Ibid.
16   Ibid., p.75.

A pass in the Pamirs. (Peter Fleming Estate)

Smigunovs she felt that "carrying it out alone added some suggestion of bravura to our exploit. Our conquest of Tartary would seem all the more fascinating if it were carried out by our own efforts."[17] They reached Sining in five days by dint of marching twelve or thirteen hours per day, but again found official obstacles in their path. While waiting for their visa they visited the lamasery of Kumbum. Although Fleming was sceptical about religion he admitted to a "Tight, chill, tingling feeling which I suppose is something between spiritual awe and physical fear".[18]

Before leaving Kumbum, Fleming and Maillart posted their last letters for Europe, the next opportunity to post would not be until they reached India. The next stage of their journey involved hiring four camels for the price of four taxis from Hyde Park Corner to Hampstead and looking for the Mogul caravan of the Prince of Dzun. On reaching the vast frozen lake of the Koko Nor they caught up with the caravan. After a gift of a small second-hand telescope, the prince agreed they could join the caravan, with which they travelled for seventeen days. Fleming described the atmosphere of the caravan at night:

The wind dropped at night. Outside the iron land froze in silence under the moon. The silver tents were quiet. The watchman moved among them squatly like a goblin ...

17   Maillart, *Forbidden Journey*, p.43.
18   Ibid., p.93.

a wolf barked. A star fell down the tremendous sky. The camp slept."[19]

They continued travelling with the caravan. Turning away from the Koko Nor Lake, they passed through the first mountain pass at 13,000 feet. They came across Kulans – wild asses who cannot be tamed, but whose meat is prized. Maillart described them as "pretty creatures—their proud heads held high and their manes erect like an archaic frieze", and was glad that Fleming did not kill one.

On arrival at Teijinar they met a Russian, Borodishin, who put them up and advised them of the best route to enter the dangerous and remote province of Sinkiang. The most direct route would, he advised, be heavily guarded by the Tungan rebels and would be very dry. He offered to guide them on the first part of an alternative southern route, which was over very difficult terrain and unlikely to be watched, but would have streams for water. They set out with fresh camels to cross what the locals called the 'black cold mountains', with no discernible track to follow. At one stage Borodishin became lost and they camped without water. Two days later they arrived at Issik Pakte where the Russian left them but procured two new guides. They were now in the province of Sinkiang but so far had not seen signs of rebellion. Pushing on to the oasis of Cherchen, in the last few days of May, their camels began to fail. Two had to be left behind as they could not go on. Fleming wanted to end their misery with a bullet rather than abandon them, but their guides explained an animal which was "thrown on the Gobi" may be saved by a miracle. If he is killed his troubled soul would follow the other camels and bring them bad luck. Maillart's horse, Slalom, was now flagging. The following day they decided to leave the horse behind, at a river where there was fresh water and a little grass. Maillart recalled: "now it was time to say goodbye to him—I kissed his nose ... and I went away, leaving my little horse motionless in the solitude behind me."[20] The strain was also beginning to tell on Fleming: "I found that I was crying, for the first time in years "

A few more fourteen hour days brought then to an oasis at Bash Malghun, where refreshed by fresh bread and milk and having acquired three donkeys and a guide, they were able to set out on the six day journey to Cherchen. On arrival at Cherchen Fleming described the abrupt change: "Wonder and joy fell on us as we slipped into coolness and delight as smoothly and abruptly as a diver does. Everywhere water ran musically in the irrigation channels."[21] After some consternation on the part of the officer in charge of the garrison, that their passports were not valid for Sinkiang, their passports were stamped and they were offered a place to stay at the house of the Aksakal, an Afghan village leader who claimed to be the representative of the British Government and had a Union Flag above his door. Now Fleming was able at last to find out the true political situation, which would be a marvellous scoop for *The Times*. He found that the fighting had died down, but that the Tungan[22] rebels, heavily supported by the Soviet government, were in control of all the southern oases. Communist Russia was making a great effort to establish itself as the major foreign power in the area. Fleming described at some length in his book *News From Tartary* the complicated interests of the major powers, including Britain and Russia, he summed up the situation: "If it is untrue to say that at least four powers are watching with the keenest

19   Ibid., p.133.
20   Maillart, *Forbidden Journey*, p.164.
21   Hart-Davis, *Peter Fleming*, p.76.
22   Fleming, *News from Tartary,* p.249.

The Desert Road. (Peter Fleming Estate)

interest the present situation in Sinkiang, it is only untrue because the present situation in Sinkiang is almost impossible to watch."[23]

With his scoop safely in his notebook, Fleming and Maillart now progressed slowly west through deserts moving from one oasis to the next. Whenever they reached a centre of population they stayed with the Aksakal, or British Government representative, most of whom were Afghans. On 23rd July they arrived in Kashgar. Kashgar was five or six weeks travel from the nearest railhead in India, and to most people seemed remote but to Fleming and Kini it was civilisation. They were met outside the city by a man from the consulate called Barlow who said, "I don't know if you drink beer?" As Fleming commented, "He very soon did."[24]

At Kashgar they discovered that their long absence had been causing concern in England and a series of cables were sent to establish their safety. Maillart called Kashgar "the town of our dreams" as they were entertained in colonial-style luxury by the Consul, General Thomson–Glover. They discovered that it was almost as difficult to leave Sinkiang as to enter it. Each one of their muleteers had to have a passport with a photograph and their own passports were only returned to them with Chinese visas after a fortnight. The local officials arranged a banquet for them before they left, after which Maillart confessed to having a severe headache.

The last trek of the journey was over the Himalayas. At the 'Pass of a Thousand Ibex,' the Mintaka Pass, they left China behind them and arrived at the end of their journey at Srinagar. They had travelled 3,500 miles and the whole journey had cost them £150 each. They returned to rumours of war. Italy was attacking Abyssinia and there was talk of the

23   Ibid., p.245.
24   Ibid., p.325.

Suez Canal being closed. Maillart and Fleming decided to return to their respective homes swiftly. Flying over Paris, Maillart reflected that Paris, France and "the white race," counted for nothing "against the magnificent scheme of things we call the world."[25]

In the opinion of Hart-Davis, Fleming's biographer, "the feat that he and Kini had accomplished was one of exceptional courage and endurance."[26]

Flying into Namsos 1940

Fleming had returned from his trip to Tartary "brown, older, tougher." The outbreak of war in 1939 saw him in a position to take on board new adventures and opportunities, and as his biographer commented, "He had a burning desire to fight in the front line, to kill the enemy and generally to emulate the unemphatic heroism for which his father was still remembered."[27] His age, thirty-two, made the prospect of promotion in a front line infantry company unlikely and he was to find that, instead, his skills of travelling, languages and leadership were to be used in intelligence work of a very varied nature. Already in August 1939 his help had been asked for by the War Office to organise a mission to China which would help the Chinese in more effective resistance to the Japanese. Fleming agreed to do this and asked Martin Lindsay to join him. Lindsay, with typical enthusiasm and thoroughness, started to brush up on his Chinese. The proposal, in the end, did not come to fruition. For the rest of 1939 he was in London on the staff of MI (R) and continued to write sporadically for *The Spectator*. During a short illness in March 1940 he wrote *The Flying Visit*, the plot of which envisaged Hitler being shot down over Britain and the consequent dilemmas faced by the Government who in the end decide to parachute him back to Germany. It was a light, humorous fantasy but clearly showed the author's contempt of Hitler and strangely but coincidentally foreshadowed the actual landing of Rudolf Hess in 1941.

It was in April that he had the first chance to see action. Germany invaded Norway on the 9th April 1940, at the same time that Churchill and the British Chiefs of Staff were contemplating an attack on the Norwegian coast. German troops successfully landed and key positions on the Norwegian coast fell into German hands. However the Royal Navy inflicted heavy losses on the German invasion fleet at Narvik on 13th April. Meanwhile the Allies had despatched three expeditionary forces to Narvik, Namsos and Andalsnes. The object of Operation Maurice was to capture Trondheim, the first phase being to establish a base at Namsos.[28]

Although information the War Office had received said that local inhabitants of Namsos had reported there were no Germans for sixty miles,[29] there was some doubt as to whether Namsos was actually under German control. A reconnaissance mission was needed. The War diary of MI (R) recounted how they were asked at very short notice to provide a reconnaissance mission. Fleming managed to hear about this, volunteered, and found himself in charge of "No. 10 Military Mission" which consisted of Fleming, Martin Lindsay, who he had contacted and asked to join, two Norwegian-speaking officers and two signallers. They flew via Kimmel in Orkney and Sullom Voe in Shetland. At this stage

25   Maillart, *Forbidden Journey*, p.300.
26   Hart-Davis, *Peter Fleming*, p.184.
27   Ibid., p.213.
28   TNA, CAB 65/12/25.
29   Ibid.

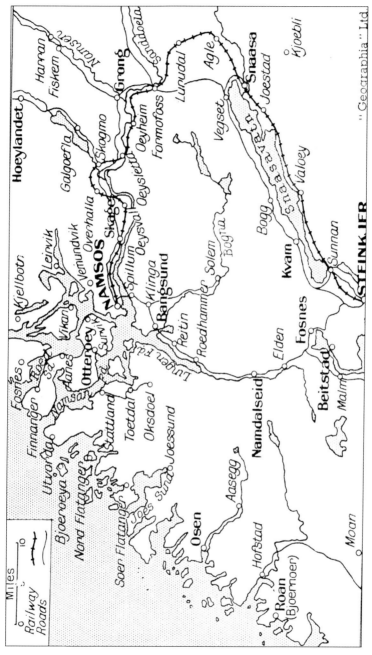

Map showing Namsos area. (Hutchinson's *Pictorial History of the War*, 1940)

Fleming felt very upbeat about the mission and the prospect of landing in Norway: "I feel very glad and the war seems suddenly quite different", he wrote in his diary.[30] However, MI (R) had reservations: "We wished them well in their thankless task as, as until they reached Norway they would not know whether the Germans were already there."[31]

Flying up the Norwegian coast approaching Namsos, Fleming felt that the bomb load that was on the Sunderland was being wasted and signalled for permission to find a suitable German target. Permission was denied; a signal from the HMS *Glasgow* said "Essential to observe complete secrecy."[32] In his diary he described the descent into Namsos:

> Apart from a cat there was no sign of life at all ... No. 10 Military Mission had been ordered to find out who was in occupation at Namsos. Here it was, hovering over the place like a kestrel over a rickyard, and for all it knew Namsos might have been occupied by the Tibetans.[33]

Namsos was, in fact, not occupied, and after a suspicious welcome from the Norwegians, Peter Fleming was the first soldier to be landed in Norway.

The commander of the force to land at Namsos was Adrian Carton de Wiart, a Great War hero, who as Hart-Davis put it had, "only one eye, only one arm and, rather more surprisingly, only one Victoria Cross."[34] He arrived by Sunderland flying boat and on landing was pinned down by heavy fire from an air attack from six Junkers for two hours, in which his aide-de-camp was injured in the knee and sent home. [35] He was welcomed by Peter Fleming and Martin Lindsay and remembered: "On board I found Captain Peter Fleming and Captain Martin Lindsay, and whoever may have been responsible for sending them, I thank them now, for there and then I appropriated them, and a better pair of men never existed."[36] He went on: "Captain Fleming, from being adventurer and writer, turned himself into a general factotum number one and was the epitome of:

> Oh I am the cook and captain bold
> And the mate of the Nancy Brig
> And a Bos'un tight and a midshipmite
> And the crew of the Captain's Gig"[37]

By the time Carton de Wiart had arrived, the marines had landed on the 14th and were holding a bridgehead south of the Namon River. The 14th and the 146th brigades went ashore at Namsos between 15th and 17th April.[38] They were reinforced by troops which had landed at Andalsnes but had been transferred by ship to Namsos. Over a six-day period landings at Namsos were completed during the three hours of darkness and every trace of activity removed before daylight, leaving no trace from the air. As they landed they

30   Duff Hart-Davis, *Peter Fleming,* p.223.
31   War Diary MI (R), 24th April 1940. Croft Papers, private collection.
32   Hart-Davis, *Peter Fleming,* p.223.
33   Diary of Peter Fleming, quoted by Hart-Davis, p.224.
34   Ibid., p.224.
35   TNA, CAB 65/6/39.
36   Adrian Carton de Wiart, *Happy Odyssey* (Barnsley, 2007), p.166.
37   Ibid., p.166.
38   *After The Battle* No.126, 2004.

British troops disembarking at Namsos, 15th April 1940.
(Hutchinson's *Pictorial History of the War*)

moved southwards to Steinkjaer, in transport provided by the Norwegian commander in the locality, Colonel Ole Berg Getz, en route for a possible attack on Trondheim. Fleming had been in touch with the Norwegians at Steinkjaer, and reported that "they were very low in spirits and that leadership was sadly lacking."[39] The War Office also received a report from the troops landed at Namsos that it was under four feet of snow and offered no concealment from the air. It was also considered that "the southward movement of a force larger than one battalion would be slow and conspicuous from the air."[40] Berg Getz also warned that the ice in the fjord would be soon melting, making the road to Steinkjaer vulnerable to naval attack.[41]

The landings continued successfully but the arrival of the French Chasseurs Alpins on 19th April, who were trigger happy and fired on a German aeroplane, gave the game away and the occupation of Namsos by Allied troops was discovered. By the evening much of Namsos had been burnt out as a result of air attacks from the Germans. The minutes of the War Cabinet meeting on 22nd April, however, had a different interpretation of events: "a German soldier who had been taken prisoner stated that the Germans had been unaware of the landing at Namsos until it had been mentioned in a BBC broadcast."[42] An account in *After the Battle* magazine mentions that because the landings had to be achieved in a few hours of darkness, some of the French troops' equipment had to be left on the ships, but that they had machine guns. It described how there was a reconnaissance flight by a German aircraft that morning and that later they returned and bombed the town. This

---

39   TNA, CAB 65/112/26.
40   TNA, CAB 65/12/25.
41   *After The Battle* No. 126, 2004.
42   TNA CAB 65/12/31, 22nd April 1940.

Destruction of a church at Namsos. (Hutchinson's *Pictorial History of the War*)

scenario would seem to give credence to Fleming's account of how the Chasseurs Alpins had alerted the Germans to the presence of Allied troops at Namsos. General Carton de Wiart later recalled the mistakes made by the French troops:

> Although far better trained than we were and experienced at looking after themselves, they did not obliterate the traces of their landings. The next morning the Germans saw that troops had been put ashore and the French made themselves more noticeable by loosing off their machine guns at them, which succeeded in making matters much worse. The Germans responded with more and more bombs and in a matter of hours Namsos was reduced to ashes.[43]

A telegram was received by the War Office from Carton de Wiart on 22nd April, stating that the German aircraft dominated the situation and that his position was becoming untenable and that he might have to evacuate his troops. A message was returned pointing out the "importance of keeping troops in being and informing him of steps being taken to provide air support". The Prime Minister had agreed that "we would have to be guided by the men on the spot and no decision was called for until the situation was clearer."[44]

Carton de Wiart decided to send Fleming back to Britain on 26th April to find out what the government's intentions were regarding Norway and meanwhile hung on at Namsos under air attack. When Fleming reached Sullom Voe he was surprised to be congratulated on being alive, and found out that *The Daily Sketch* had reported him killed in Norway. After being frustrated by delays on his way to report to London, he ended up ordering a special train from Inverness to London at enormous expense to the War Office. He delivered his dispatches to the War Office, had an interview with Churchill

---

43   Adrian Carton de Wiart, *Happy Odyssey*, p.168.
44   TNA, CAB 65/12/31.

and returned to Norway. Carton de Wiart had received contradictory messages about the evacuation of Namsos and later recalled Fleming saying to him "you can really do what you like, for they don't know what they want done."[45] A telegram had been received by the War Office from Carton de Wiart on 22nd April. One of the contradictory orders was to evacuate to Moesjen, about 100 miles north of Namsos. Carton de Wiart was unsure of the wisdom of this and sent Lindsay and Fleming to reconnoitre the route in a car. He recalled: "They took twelve hours to cover forty miles. I believe that the War Office considered me very unreasonable for opposing their suggestions, but I felt at that moment the move only looked feasible on the map."[46] At a cabinet meeting discussing the operations in Norway on 23rd April it was minuted, "Captain Fleming reported that the maintenance of any force at Namsos was dependant on Norwegian cooperation, which was practically nonexistent since Namsos was out of touch with the Norwegian Government and most of the population had fled."[47] Notes Fleming made under the heading "General's requirements", gave an idea of the conditions at Namsos while waiting for a decision to be made on evacuation. "Need signals. No code. No ambulances. Little petrol. No artillery. No military police. Transport unorganised. No pipe. Fourteen days' food supplies. No casualties. NCOs don't exist. No maps."[48]

By 24th April the 'Maurice' Force had regrouped and taken up defensive positions north of Steinkjaer, supported by the Norwegians. Carton de Wiart reported to the War Office that he saw "very little point in remaining in that part of Norway sitting out like rabbits in the snow."[49] At last there was a message to say that the force would be evacuated in one night. De Wiart remembered: "In the course of that last endless day I got a message from the navy to say that they would evacuate the whole of my force that night. I thought it impossible but I learned a few hours later that the navy do not know the word."[50] On 2nd May a fleet of British and French ships arrived at Namsos. Martin Gilbert wrote of how when the Navy arrived it found the town ablaze: "The first ship to reach the quayside was the destroyer *Kelly* commanded by Lord Louis Mountbatten. The *Kelly* took off 229 French troops, ferried them to a waiting transport and then returned for more."[51] The evacuating force were bombed relentlessly. A British destroyer *Alfredi* and a French destroyer *Bison* were both sunk. The War Cabinet were told on 3rd May that the evacuation had been successful and that 6,400 troops had been taken off.[52]

Fleming had displayed future talent for deception by leaving behind a carefully half-burnt document suggesting that a major bridge had been rigged as an ambush for advancing German troops.

General Carton de Wiart summed up his experiences in Norway:

The War Office had done its level best to help us. But they had not the power, the equipment or the facilities to make that help effective. Politically Norway was worth a gamble and I am sure the gesture was important ... I was glad that I had been sent, and

45 Hart-Davis, *Peter Fleming*, p.230.
46 Carton de Wiart, *Happy Odyssey*, p.173.
47 CAB 65/12/32.
48 Hart-Davis, *Peter Fleming*, p.226.
49 *After The Battle* No.126, 2004.
50 Carton de Wiart, *Happy Odyssey*, p.174.
51 Martin Gilbert, *The Second World War* (London, 2000), p.58.
52 TNA CAB 65/7/3.

notwithstanding the debacle, I never doubted the ultimate issue.[53]

Fleming had emerged from the Norway campaign with his first taste of action behind him and a mention in despatches, but was unimpressed by the way the Norwegian campaign had been handled. He commented in his diary "the errors were so gross, the muddles so pervasive and the whole affair over with so quickly that there really wasn't a great deal to be learned from it."[54] Hart-Davis commented that many of Fleming's fellow officers believed that Fleming's report to the War Office on his return contributed to Chamberlain's downfall, but offers no evidence to support this.

Auxiliary Units and Greece 1941–42

Soon after his experience in Norway Fleming found himself in charge of the first active unit of the "Auxiliary Units " who were to be "left behind" to work behind enemy lines if the enemy had succeeded in invading and occupying southern England. He was given a detachment of Lovat Scouts, two aircraftsmen with a wireless and a sapper subaltern, Mike Calvert. With this material he set about forming a secret unit known as XII Corps Observation Unit – the prototype of the "Auxiliary Units". His knowledge of the countryside proved invaluable and he quickly built up contacts with gamekeepers, poachers and foresters who knew every inch of the area. It was thought that Kent would be one of the first parts of the country to be occupied, and that the stop line of defences would be on the southern outskirts of London. Fleming's unit would lay low by day and attack the enemy at night. One of the main tasks of preparation was the construction of underground lairs and laying in stocks of weapons and ammunition. Fleming's unit were also provided with bows and arrows. The idea was taken up over the south and east coasts and by October 1940 more than 3,000 men had been trained for these resistance 'last ditch' operations. Fleming thought that although the units would have had initial success in harassing the enemy, reprisals against the population would have stopped them. In the event their courage and efficiency were never put to the test, and the organisation remained so secret that its existence did not come to light until many years after the war.

At the beginning of 1941 Fleming became involved with a scheme organised by the head of SOE in Cairo, Colonel George Pollock. The aim was to send a small force to Cairo and then proceed to recruit Italians from Italian prisoner of war camps to help in resistance and to form a "Garibaldi legion" to accompany the Allied invasion of Italy. Fleming, although harbouring doubts, raised a small force who were sent to Lochailort for SOE training. This small, almost private army, travelled to Cairo via the west coast of Africa. The scheme collapsed when no Italian POWs could be found to participate, leaving Fleming kicking his heels in Cairo awaiting instructions. Eventually after a meeting with General Wavell, it was agreed that Fleming could take his force to Greece. At this time, the beginning of April 1941, it was felt likely that the Germans would follow their invasion of Yugoslavia with an invasion of Greece. One of the places they were likely to attack was through the Monastir Gap on the frontier between Greece and Yugoslavia. Fleming came up with a scheme to take his small force to this gap, and when overrun, to organise a "stay behind" resistance force similar to the one planned in Kent, going to ground and harassing the German lines of communication. As Hart-Davis pointed out, the plan was both ambitious

53   Carton de Wiart, *Happy Odyssey*, p.175.
54   Hart-Davis, *Peter Fleming*, p.231.

and brave as "no one in Cairo had the slightest idea what conditions would be like in the far north of Greece."[55] Fleming and his men packed into a car and two lorries and proceeded to the Monastir Pass, Fleming sending a telegram back to Baker St saying "AM HOLDING MONASTIR GAP".

However, they had arrived too late to train resistance fighters as the German force was advancing swiftly towards the gap. Fleming decided the best course of action was to join in the retreat and offer his men, arms and explosives to the forces on the ground. His men put their explosives to good use, destroying twenty locomotives in a marshalling yard and setting booby traps after being involved in a successful attempt to get an ammunition train away from Larrissa which was being heavily bombed, to troops further south who were desperately short of ammunition. On their return to Athens, Fleming and his force were asked by General Wilson if they would sever the coastal road between Missolonghi and Navpaktos. Although they did not manage to blow the bridge, they did inflict enough damage to make the road impassable for several days. The Allied forced were now being evacuated through Piraeus harbour and Fleming's last task in Greece was to provide protection for a small group of the wives and children of British officials as they were evacuated on the small yacht *Kalanthe*. The yacht anchored off the coast of Kimlos. The women and children went ashore and Fleming's party manned the yacht's four Lewis guns.

The following evening the yacht was hit by enemy aircraft. Fleming described the scene:

> The first one comes over the hill from the east. He slants down straight for us, lets his bombs go far too soon ... He comes on, machine gunning hard, masthead high and we engage him, eight men standing nakedly to the tall Lewis gun mountings ... then the second bugger comes into the attack. This time he has us.[56]

The yacht had been hit and the people on shore watched as it burst into flames. They rowed out to pick up survivors. Fleming had been wounded by bomb lacerations to the head, shoulder and thigh. The women of the party managed to deal with the wounded without much in the way of medical supplies but within two days a relief expedition from Crete arrived. After a very trying journey by caique they arrived at Crete and the wounded, women and children were taken on board the *Hotspur* and the *Havoc* to Alexandria, accompanied by the entire gold reserves of the Greek banks.

Deception in the Far East 1942-45

At the beginning of 1942 General Wavell was appointed Commander in Chief of the Allied Forces in the South West Pacific and sent for Fleming because of his knowledge of the Far East. By the time Fleming arrived the situation in the Far East had changed and Wavell had established his headquarters at Delhi. One of Fleming's first tasks for Wavell was to fly to Chungking and to start establishing the intelligence links which he was to nurse throughout the next three years. Back in Delhi he applied himself to intelligence and deception against the Japanese, taking over the section GSI (d) whose task it was to devise the deception programmes and carry them out. Fleming described the objectives:

> To make your enemy take – or refrain from taking – a particular course of action, and

---

55   Hart-Davis, *Peter Fleming*, p.242.
56   Ibid., p.250.

thereby to improve your chances of defeating him. Merely to gull him ... is only half the battle: it is not enough, even, that he should 'do something about it'. He must do what you want him to do.

One of the deception ploys directly influenced by Wavell was "Operation Error" in which the Japanese were to be convinced, by documents in a briefcase left behind in the Allied retreat from Burma, that Wavell had been injured. Also in this briefcase was to be a whole raft of false information on Allied strengths and dispositions. To add to its authenticity it had a photograph of Wavell's daughter Pamela, and a letter ostensibly from Wavell to Joan Bright,[57] in Whitehall containing misleading information wrapped up as indiscreet gossip. Fleming was responsible for making up the contents of this briefcase and proposed to drop it at Ava Bridge, fifty miles north of Shewbo, as the Allies were retreating across this bridge. He stage-managed a car crash on the bank of the river and left the car, clearly visible with the briefcase and other corroborating evidence. Although there was never any evidence that the ruse had succeeded and that the Japanese had been fooled into acting on the information contained, Wavell considered that the deception was a significant part of his efforts to save India, as the information was aimed at persuading the Japanese that Allied strength in India was far greater than it actually was, thus making them pause and give Wavell's force time to re-group.

Fleming stayed in Delhi for the rest of the war using it as a base for his intelligence operations. In May 1942 he travelled to Kabul to make contact with a man in the American Embassy who had contact with the Japanese, and was able to pass on false information to them and also to the German Embassy. His most important role was as an unofficial liaison office between the Chinese government and the Allied powers, which involved him in much travelling between Chungking and Calcutta. In May 1942 he came up with what he called the 'purple whales' plan in which the wholly imaginary transcript of a meeting of the inter-Allied conference in Delhi included the information that Britain would be able to invade the continent with ten divisions any time after July and that Tokyo could expect heavier attacks from the air soon. Chinese agents sold the transcript to the Japanese.

GSI expanded its activities in the course of the war. It was renamed D Division in 1944. Fleming remained in charge until the end of the war. Among his deceptions were letters written by female members of his staff, purporting to be Wrens, to imaginary lovers, which contained apparently indiscreet revelations about military affairs in Delhi. He also ran a group of double agents, including the agent known as 'Silver', who helped Germany by smuggling Subhas Chandra Bose out of India to Afghanistan. Imaginary characters such as 'Harry Singh' and 'the inebriated colonels' also contributed to the dissemination of false information to the Japanese. The uncertainty of the Allied operations in the South East Asian theatre posed a problem for Fleming, as often Mountbatten's plans had to be changed and on several occasions Fleming had produced a plan to use as a feint which was uncannily like the plan eventually decided upon in reality. Fleming remarked that it was difficult to tell lies unless he knew what the truth was going to be. Another aspect to Fleming's work was physical deception, which was developed using devices such as the 'pintail', a bomb which would attach itself by a spike to the ground when it landed and then after an interval send up Very lights. Another ruse was to drop miniature paratroopers out of a single

---

57   Joan Bright was running the Commander in Chief's Special Information Centre in the War Office.

aeroplane to simulate unexpected attack. Fleming sometimes invited senior officers to view his physical deception and asked them to say what they had seen, which was often not what had actually happened.

Two information deceptions that seemed to have had some effect on Japanese troop movements were Plan 'Stultify', which aimed to encourage the withdrawal of Japanese troops from Rangoon, allowing the Allied forces to occupy it in May 1945, and Plan 'Sceptical', which suggested an attack on Bangkok, thereby drawing more Japanese troops into the area. Both these plans could have contributed to the fact that no front line units remained in Malaya at the time of the Allied invasion in May 1945. In February 1944 Fleming managed to get himself attached to 77th Brigade, which, as part of Ord Wingate's force, was to land in the Burmese jungle into the heart of enemy territory, and attempt to break the stalemate existing on the Burmese front. The 77th Brigade under Mike Calvert, was to land by glider in a clearing designated 'Piccadilly' in the jungle. Fleming's glider, 15P, took off on 15th March, crossing the Chindwin River an hour later. However shortly afterwards, it made an emergency landing on the dry bed of a river, and Fleming and the soldiers found themselves trapped behind enemy lines and separated from the rest of the 77th Brigade. When it had been established that there had been no serious injuries, Fleming ordered ciphers and all secret documents to be burned. The resultant fire attracted the attention of a lone aircraft that fired on the plane but was later assumed to be a Hurricane. With typical Fleming *sang froid* he made a speech pointing out the advantages of their position. He stated that:

a. That if we behaved sensibly we had practically nothing to fear from the Japanese, who were almost certainly in a greater state of alarm and confusion than were we.

b. That no one was to think of himself as a 'survivor' or an evacuee but rather as a member of an unusually well found fighting patrol, inserted in the enemy's rearward administrative areas and perfectly capable of seeing off the small parties from the lines of communication units which were all we were likely to meet at this stage.

c. That we had been damned lucky so far.[58]

The party had eight days of K rations, which Fleming reduced to half rations to make it last. As they were completely lost, he decided the best course of action was to walk west, cross the Chindwin River and try and rejoin the Allied army in India. During their march across the jungle they came twice into close contact with Japanese patrols that, Fleming thought, were patrolling anticipating Allied landings in clearings across the area. After a close shave avoiding such a patrol, Fleming "took the party inside the jungle and encouraged them to smoke and boast"[59] in the interests of raising morale. After seven days' march and two further escapes from Japanese patrols, the river was reached. Here Fleming was disappointed by the absence of any boats to commandeer or steal. The banks of the river were fifty feet high with steep sides. In order to be able to take their supplies and ammunition across the river, the brigade medical officer, Major Faulkner, made a raft out of the ration boxes. This task was hampered by the fact that they had realised that they were

58   Fleming's diary, cited by Hart-Davis, *Peter Fleming*, p.293.
59   Report by Lieut. Col. R.P. Fleming on loss of glider 15P on 5th March 1944. In Appendix A of Michael Calvert, *Prisoners of Hope* (London 1952), p.262.

Peter Fleming, 1965. (*Peter Fleming, a Biography*)

very near a village so could not make cutting or hammering sounds for fear of giving away their position. However, the raft quickly became waterlogged and the crossing had to be made by swimming, resulting in one casualty of a non-swimmer, Signalman Angus. Some rations were brought over by two officers who returned over the river to rescue them. These men had thus swum the Chindwin five times in one night.

Later that morning they discovered that Allied forces were now in possession of parts of the west bank of the river, after coming across a patrol of the 1st Seaforth Highlanders. They returned with the patrol to the Seaforth headquarters. Their ordeal was over. This experience did not stop Fleming from immediately wangling himself a trip to the jungle airstrips and going on a patrol with a jeep in the jungle.

His biographer commented that although Fleming's report on the incident was full of praise for the high standards and good morale of the officers and men of the 77th Brigade, that several of his fellow survivors made it clear that "without his unshakable courage and determination, their chances of escape would have been infinitely smaller."[60] Fleming attributed their successful escape to good luck and the maintenance of good morale. He attributed this maintaining of morale to the doctrine laid down by Brigadier Mike Calvert, the commander of 77th Infantry Brigade: "The doctrine consists of maintaining a sense of proportion with regard to the Japanese, the jungle and other real or supposed hazards which beset a small isolated detachment in enemy territory. The feeling of being hunted is an unpleasant one and personnel who become oppressed by it are likely to ... act in a foolish or unsoldierly manner."[61]

---

60   Hart-Davis, *Peter Fleming*, p.300.
61   Report by Lieut. Col. R.P. Fleming on loss of Glider 15P on 5th March 1944.

Fleming had in fact behaved irresponsibly by getting involved on an operation which had no relevance to his deception activities and which contained strong risk of him becoming a prisoner of the Japanese with the consequent risk of much of his high profile information becoming available to the enemy. He escaped court martial as his activities were concealed from Mountbatten until much later.

With the surrender of the Japanese in August 1945, D Division was wound up and Fleming, after a tour of Burma, Malaya and Vietnam to assess the efficacy of his deception schemes, returned to Britain. He received an OBE and the Chinese Government awarded him the Cloud and Banner. He felt the frustration of never being sure to what extent his deception plans had succeed, and the feeling that he could have achieved more if D Section had been better resourced. Although the need to make use of his knowledge of the Far East and his talent for deception precluded any prolonged experience of the action he would have liked, it can be seen that his pre-war adventures had fitted him for the occasions in Norway, Greece and Burma when his courage decisiveness and leadership has been instrumental in saving situations and lives. Joan Bright remembered him returning from Crete in 1941 and visiting the War Office.

He walked in as imperturbably as he had walked out of MI (R) for Namsos that evening many months ago. It was always good to see his square face with its wide smile and to straighten out one's own fevers and uncertainties against his calm acceptance of events and tolerance of human frailty. He was a four square, basic solitary sort of person, immune to luxury, to heat or cold, with a rock-like quality that made him the most staunch of friends and a kindness which made him the least vindictive of enemies.[62]

62   Joan Bright Astley, *The Inner Circle: A View of War at the Top* (London, 1971), p.64.

5

Andrew Croft

The Crossing of Greenland, 1933-34

Andrew Croft received a telegram in the summer of 1933 which read: "Would you consider proceeding Greenland fortnight's time?" Rapidly excusing himself from a commitment to a teaching post at Stowe School, he accepted, leading to what he described as "the most memorable winter of my life."[1] The telegram had come from a university friend, Roger Pettiward, and explained that Martin Lindsay was recruiting members for his planned expedition to Greenland. Croft had been head boy at Stowe, and in reply to Lindsay's enquiries about him the headmaster, Roxburgh, had replied that Croft was reliable, had guts, and "what's more, you will like him." Lindsay's comment was: "I knew I had got the right man."[2]

Lindsay had been a member of Gino Watkins's BAARE expedition in 1931/32, and now planned to explore the "new mountains" discovered and named by Gino Watkins on that occasion. Lindsay had the idea of approaching the mountains on the east coast of Greenland from the west coast, crossing the Greenland ice cap in the process. The east coast of Greenland was at that time very inaccessible, with the chance to get thorough the ice pack and land successfully curtailed to a small window of opportunity in the summer, in some years not being possible at all.

Lindsay intended to use dogs to haul supplies across the ice cap, with an average thickness of a mile underfoot, to travel 470 miles in order to survey the mountains which extended 300 miles down the east Greenland coast between Scoresby Sound and Mount Forel, leaving by ship from the east coast before the winter pack ice set in. Croft's role was to travel to Jakobshavn the winter before the expedition, to acquire the best dogs available and to learn how to drive and train them before the other expedition members arrived the following spring. He found himself on the *Hans Egede* on 17th September, along with eleven Danish girls bound for Greenland. Roger Pettiward, who was at that time hoping to be the third man on the expedition, described waving Croft off "with the best looking of the girls at his side." On arrival at Jakobshavn, Croft settled into his winter quarters. Jakobshavn was at that time a settlement of about 650 Greenlanders and some Danish civil servants. Most of the houses were recent wooden buildings, but Croft became aware of the high tuberculosis death rate as a legacy of previous overcrowding in the settlement.[3] Jakobshavn was the centre of the halibut trade, the fishing activities being cantered on the Jakobshavn ice fjord. Croft spent the winter learning how to drive dog teams and acquiring some knowledge of Danish and the western Greenland dialect, which was to prove useful.

Croft, having bought his "twelve superb dogs",[4] engaged the services of a methylated spirit-swilling old hunter, Tobias, whose instruction proved so effective that Croft had soon

---

1   Andrew Croft, *A Talent for Adventure* (Worcester, 1991)
2   Martin Lindsay, *Sledge: The British Trans-Greenland Expedition 1934* (London, 1935) p.20.
3   Andrew Croft, 'Across the Greenland Ice cap', *Geographical*, Vol. 1 (1935), p.269.
4   Ibid., p.40.

Croft in Greenland, 1933. (Croft family)

understood the knack of driving the dogs in the "fan" trace, using local dialect commands. He said of the art of dog sledging: "A good driver uses his voice only to talk gently to his team. He steers the dogs by word of command, aided and abetted by the whip, from which they turn left and right."[5] Despite the reputation huskies had for ferocity, Croft reckoned that this was because the Greenlanders treated them harshly. He became fond of the dogs and commented: "They respond wonderfully to affection and will rarely bite humans except when frightened; in fact I could even take the food out of their mouths and give it to others more timid."[6]

For Croft, the joys of skiing in the moonlit hours of the winter darkness and of watching the displays of the Northern Lights were added to by the efforts of the Greenlanders to stave of the monotony of the winter months by parties and dancing. The sea ice formed by 45° of frost enabled him to make trips to Umanak and also to Godhavn, the capital and wireless station of northern Greenland on Disco Island. He had surveyed the best route to the ice cap in the autumn, so in the spring of 1934 his first job was to take sledges of food up to the plateau to make a depot ready for the ice cap crossing. The dry climatic conditions of northern Greenland mean that there is rarely large snowfall, so sledging and pack carrying the supplies to the depot over the windswept and rocky terrain was hard work. With six Greenlanders and four sledges he managed to take two tons of dog food up to the old moraine of the glacier, at 2,100 feet. His task was made easier by his good management

5   Ibid.
6   Croft, *Talent for Adventure*, p.40.

Croft's dog team in Greenland, 'on the level'. (Croft family)

of his team, as he ate and slept with them and had become fluent in their dialect as well as Danish. Back in Jakobshavn he bought thirty-one new dogs and set about training them in three separate teams. He also made the traces, canvas harnesses and dog boots required for the trip. Lindsay said of Croft's achievements during that winter of 1933-1934: "I have tried hard, but I can think of no other man who would have done all these things so well."[7]

Early in April, Croft was disappointed to receive a telegram from Lindsay, informing him the Roger Pettiward was not well and would not be arriving with Lindsay on the *Gertrud Rask* from Copenhagen. He was being replaced by Daniel Godfrey of the Royal Engineers, who was a qualified surveyor. Croft became less enthusiastic about the trip. He commented later:

> With Roger there the whole adventure would have been enormous fun, without him it became a bit of a slog. Martin was something of a slave driver and Daniel astonishingly unfit. Neither of them ever became much good at driving dogs. [8]

Pack ice delayed the arrival of Lindsay, Godfrey and their equipment the expedition set off on 23rd May. The delay resulted in coping with the conditions of the spring melt. This meant progress was slow, but by 3rd June, they had arrived at "Halibut camp", a depot that Croft had laid in the winter. Lindsay was pleased and relieved at the extent of the depot: "I wondered once more how on earth it had been done, and hid the emotion of

---

7   Lindsay, *Sledge*, p.21.
8   Croft, *Talent for Adventure*, p.49.

Glacier near Jakobshavn moving 62 feet per day. (Croft family)

my gratitude with a facetious remark: 'Andrew, you may have your colours'".[9] Although Lindsay was pleased with this depot, the first of several disagreements between the two men arose as Lindsay insisted on staying there for a week writing reports for *The Times* for their Greenlander guide, Tobias, to take back to Jakobshavn for despatch. Croft wanted to make progress before the thaw caused more problems. The language skills of Croft enabled him to cajole the Greenlanders, who wanted to go home immediately, to wait in order to take the report. On 12th June they struck camp to set out on their journey across the ice cap. Two days before they set out a thirty-six hour rainstorm which washed the snow away from the crevassed ice ridges, but also filled the valleys between them with snow. There were now just the three of them as all the Greenlanders had returned to Jakobshavn. Croft was obviously keen to get going and wrote in his diary:

> I am feeling fairly normal and calm, ready for all emergencies. The probable reason for this is that I have had my problems and excitements all this winter in anticipation of this journey, and now that the time has come, my happy go lucky nature is no longer perturbed.[10]

The first week of their ascent to the ice cap from the depot was, in many ways, disastrous. The men had to relay their loads through morasses of icy water, sometimes waist deep. The dogs lost morale in the poor conditions and Croft thought this did not bode well for later on in the trip. Higher up there were crevasses, which because of the melt conditions were not covered with several feet of snow. One of Croft's best dogs fell down a crevasse and landed

9   Lindsay, *Sledge*, p.65.
10 Ibid., p.74.

on a ledge, thus sparking a quarrel between Croft and Lindsay. Lindsay ordered Croft not to cross the crevasse and to wait until Lindsay had got a rope off his sledge and come over to size up the situation. Croft, however, anxious about his dog, crossed the crevasse in order to get a better view of the dog's plight. Lindsay, being an army man, was furious about this breach of discipline and told him off in no uncertain terms. Lindsay then insisted as that he was leader he would rescue the dog. When Croft objected to this, Lindsay reminded him whose expedition it was: "everything being mine, including the overdraft."[11] However, what might have become a serious argument passed over, mainly because, as Lindsay freely admitted, Croft was too level headed to take offence for long.

Conditions were better above the height of the thaw and during the next two weeks the party averaged about twenty miles a day. Croft related how the dogs started to lose enthusiasm from boredom at the featureless ice cap but that this was resolved by him going out in front, the dogs he had trained being willing to follow him driverless. As they were making their way across the iced cap it became apparent that their sledging rations were not sufficient. In his account of the expedition, Croft went to the length of including a table directly comparing the sledging rations used on Gino Watkins's expedition and Lindsay's. He worked out that they had six ounces per man more on the previous expedition. By 4th July they were half way across the ice cap but suffering from problems caused by hoar frost as they had to shelter in their tent for three days in a blizzard: "Even our breath, let alone any cooking, caused hoarfrost to shower down upon us, soaking every mortal thing including the reindeer skins below our sopping sleeping bags." Croft blamed this upon the fact that Lindsay, who in an attempt to save weight, had not brought a lining for the tent. At times the journey across the vast expanse of ice cap seemed never-ending: "Everything is exceedingly tiring" wrote Croft in a diary entry: "I woke up after only four hours sleep, feeling very decrepit with a headache and my ankle giving me trouble. The other two seem to be in nearly as bad a way."[12]

However on 20th July they were rewarded for their efforts by the sight of mountain peaks:

> Suddenly peaks appeared over the horizon with thrilling rapidity both to our left and right – peaks which no one had ever previously seen ahead of us was a long spur of land, largely covered with snow and ice. Altogether it was an awesome sight ... we hoisted our sledge flags triumphantly.[13]

In crossing the ice cap at 70° North, the party calculated that they had covered 470 miles in just under five weeks. They now had a further 50 miles of mountainous country before reaching the coast, and realised that their food supply was dwindling. They sledged over a series of steep ridges and hollows caused by the nature of the land blow the ice and were able to use their sails on the downward slopes. On 25th July they reached the top of a snow-covered mountain from which they had a superb panoramic view. They could see a mountain range to the south within five miles and beyond that a large glacier. They were then kept in their tents by a blizzard for two days and emerging from their tent, left the primus stove alight. This quickly caused a fire which could have had fatal consequences in

---

11   Ibid., p.78.
12   Lindsay, *Sledge*, p.154.
13   Croft, *Talent for Adventure*, p.58.

Croft, Lindsay and Godfrey, Greenland, 1933. (Croft family)

Lindsay with boiling point hypsometer and Godfrey with theodolite. (Croft family)

terms of their ability to survive without vital clothing and equipment. Lindsay swiftly put the fire out without too much damage being done, but as Croft related:

> Disaster had very nearly overtaken us. The damage was rectifiable though, with only one needle between us, it took some time to sew up the sleeping bag and repair the entrance to the tent. Daniel's anorak was a write off. This was my moment: from the bottom of my rucksack I fished out the spare suit of windproof clothing and then some coffee with which we could steady our nerves! It had been a close shave![14]

By 2nd August, despite bad weather conditions, they had completed a survey of the range of mountains they named the Monarch Mountains and the large glacier running north-east to south-west, later to be known as the Christian IV glacier. Godfrey now came into his own as a surveyor and was kept busy with the theodolite. Croft remembered that Godfrey's brain seemed "seething with computations of all sorts."[15] Lindsay's job was to help with getting the time signals from Rugby and Nauen on the long wave wireless set, and Croft was occupied taking panoramic photographs.

From a camp called "Nunatak camp" they could look down on the two lines of the mountains which formed the arms of the Kangerdlugssuaq glacier. On their descent they encountered the crevasses of the Kangerdlugssuaq basin, "big enough to swallow a battleship",[16] and then came across a new range of mountains which they surveyed in two days of the hottest weather they had experienced. These mountains were later named after Crown Prince Frederick. Lindsay decide to leave a note, couched in the language of epic polar explorers, in a cocoa tin buried and marked by a cairn of stones, for any future travellers in the region to find:

> First Lieutenant Martin Lindsay and First Lieutenant Arrhur Godfrey of his Majesty's Land Forces and Andrew Croft Esquire, Gentleman, having been encompassed by many and great dangers, sojourned on this location from the sixth to the eighth day of August in the Year of Our Lord 1934. Thanks be to God ye scurvy has yet spared us. We depart this day for Angmagssalik with victuals for 32 days and 18 stronge dogges.[17]

There now only remained 200 miles of travelling back to the coast. However, the "great dangers" were not over, as on his birthday, 22nd August, Lindsay fell into a crevasse. Luckily he managed to land on an ice ledge and was able to scramble out. The expedition returned via the 'Big Flag' depot of Watkins's expedition, travelling down Bugbear Bank and arrived back at Angmagssalik in the nick of time to catch the *Jacynth*, the Aberdeen trawler that Lindsay had arranged to pick them up. It says something both for the spirit in which Godfrey and Croft ended the expedition, and their liking for the Greenland way of life, that Croft was able to say: "had we missed the boat Daniel and I wouldn't have minded a bit."[18] Their journey was the longest unsupported sledge journey ever undertaken at that date, their record was only surpassed in the 1970s.

---

14   Ibid., p.61.
15   Andrew Croft, 'Across the Greenland Ice cap', *Geographical*, Vol. 1 (1935), p.274.
16   Ibid., p.63.
17   Lindsay, *Sledge*, p.190.
18   Croft, *Talent for Adventure*, p.68.

Base hut, Brandy Bay, Spitsbergen, 1935. (Croft family)

The Oxford University Expedition to Spitsbergen 1935-36

Croft returned from three months in India determined on the advice of his friends to settle down to a permanent job. Their advice was to be disregarded, as at the lecture that he gave with Godfrey and Lindsay on their Greenland expedition at the Royal Geographical Society, he found himself being persuaded to join Alexander Glen's North Eastland expedition (see Chapter Six) as second-in-command. Glen considered that Croft's Arctic and dog sledging experience would be invaluable to the expedition. He considered that "Andrew is probably the finest dog driver this country has ever produced."[19] He also wanted an efficient second-in-command who had knowledge of Arctic conditions. Glen described him, after the expedition, as "amazingly hardworking and utterly dependable." Croft was able to use his West Greenland contacts to procure some suitable dogs and arranged to have them sent to Copenhagen. He soon ran into problems with transport of the dogs as neither Danish or Norwegian ships would take them to Tromsö. Eventually the dogs were shipped via Bremen and Trondheim. The dogs consisted of two families, which were called the 'Dupilecks' and the 'Blacks'. Sandy Glen recalled how the Blacks gained superiority: "Each team put forward a claim to a sheltered position to leeward of the base but the Blacks secured victory by force."[20] Croft spent much time at the sewing machine, as on arrival it was found that the dog harnesses, which had been made to fit Golden Retrievers in England, were too small around the chest and had to be altered.

19   Alexander Glen, *Under the Pole Star. The Oxford University Arctic Expedition, 1935-6* (Oxford, 1937), p.16.
20   Ibid., p.46.

The tunnel shaft leading to the trap door of the ice station. (Croft family)

Building the ice cap station – the umbrella-shaped dome tent. (Croft family)

After base camp has been established at Brandy Bay, Croft, Godfrey and the dog teams started the enormous task of relaying supplies up to the central ice cap station which was being built by Glen, Robert Moss and Archie Dunlop Mackenzie and which was to be manned all winter. They spent a month transporting many tons of equipment. The route to the first depot was made difficult by summer thaw streams, but once the party had passed through the area of blue ice and crevasses it established a depot. In September five of the party set out for the heart of the ice cap:

> The memory of that period is still very vivid: creeping forward from flag to flag, getting hopelessly lost in blizzards when within a mere mile of our destination, but feeling all the time that we were rarely truly alone. On one occasion I knew there was a third person who guided us to safety.[21]

The route to the ice cap was marked by poles set in the snow every quarter of a mile. However as time went on they became buried. At the ice cap station poles were set out at a 45° angle to the main route in case a sledging party were to miss the station in poor conditions. Glen related in a lecture given to the Royal Geographical Society in 1937 how Croft and Wright once overshot the station and did not find it again for five days.[22]

In order to give the spring survey parties a good start, Croft and John Wright then undertook a journey to lay depots in the path of the proposed survey parties. It was 23rd October, a date when sledging should have finished for the winter, but they succeeded in pushing on through the snow-free and boulder-strewn Rijps Valley to the crevasse zone of the coastal mountains. They were the first party ever to reach Cape Leigh Smith by land. They found themselves in a wilderness of crevasses and had to lie up for three days to wait for the weather to improve but at last, after several narrow escapes over breaking snow bridges, they managed to find their way out of the crevasse field. Glen described their predicament: "Dogs were continually falling into the depths below to be pulled out again by the sudden tug of their traces."[23] Wright's sledge became wedged half in and half out of a crevasse and Wright narrowly escaped falling down the same crevasse when the snow bridge broke.

At one point on the journey back they were stopped by a polar bear that was stood blocking their way. The dogs had to be kept back while Wright approached the bear:

> John went forward to within ten yards of the animal, which nevertheless continued to approach us. John had the presence of mind to retreat slowly backwards but the bear was now only three yards away from him and suddenly got up on its hind legs, towering up in front of us. John had his ice axe ready while I went slightly forward with the spade, fearing all the time that the dogs would bolt past me. A volley of shouts possibly won the day; amazed by such unfamiliar noises and John's remarkable vocabulary, the bear dropped to his feet and lumbered off to the rocks in the distance.[24]

Having laid the depot Croft and Wright wasted no time in leaving the area and

21   Croft, *Talent for Adventure*, p.90.
22   A. Glen, 'The Oxford University Arctic Expedition, North East Land 1935-1936', in *The Geographical Journal* Vol XC No 3, September 1937.
23   Glen, *Under the Pole Star*, p.106.
24   Croft, *Talent for Adventure*, p.95.

'Rocky ground' – sledging in Spitsbergen, late summer 1935. (Croft family)

returning to the northern ice cap station by 13th November. They had travelled 250 miles on this depot-laying journey.

Croft's adventures during the winter included being lost after being swept of his feet by a gust of wind whilst taking instrument reading at the northern ice cap station. Having lost the guide rope and being unable to find his way back to the entrance, he decided to make for the base camp, steering his way there by wind, eventually arriving there sixteen hours after becoming lost at the ice cap station. He endured having a tooth taken out by Dunlop Mackenzie and having been relieved at the ice cap station, arrived back at the main base on Christmas Eve. Meanwhile, Whatman and Hamilton had been at base camp carrying out important meteorological work, including measuring atmospheric ozone, and studying the Aurora Borealis. Their meteorological reports were transmitted three times daily to the Norwegian Government's station at Bear Island and from there to Norway and England. Croft described the Christmas celebrations when at least some of the party were reunited at base camp. A superb lunch of reindeer meat and mince pies was consumed, and then they listened to the message from the BBC. At the end of the Empire broadcast they heard: "The BBC joins with the Arctic Club and relations and friends of the Oxford University Arctic Expedition in wishing them a Merry Christmas, a Happy New Year and a safe return in the autumn."[25] Croft used the winter months at base camp to write a chapter for the expedition book on the dogs and sledging. On 21st January news came through that King George V had died. The expedition sent its sincere sympathises to Queen Mary and received a reply.

The spring brought good skiing conditions and opportunities for hunting to fatten up

---

25   Ibid., p.99.

the dogs, who had lost condition over the winter, at times giving Croft doubts about their continued health. The members of the expedition welcomed the return of the light and improved conditions. Croft enthused:

> The spring is the best time of year in the Arctic. The atmosphere is beautifully dry and invigorating, the sledging surfaces excellent and, owing to the low altitude of the sun, the unforgettable tints and colourings peculiar to the Arctic are at their best.[26]

On 12th May, after the abortive attempt to travel north over the sea ice (see Chapter Six) Croft and Glen set out on a circumnavigation of the North East Land, Glen surveying and Croft taking photographs. Time constraints did not allow for a detailed survey, but they aimed to provide a reconnaissance map which would be at least an improvement on what was known of the area. At Isis Point four of their dogs became trapped on an ice floe whilst eating a seal that had been shot. Despite Croft's efforts of diving into the sea attached to a rope in order to reach the floe, the dogs were swept away. Miraculously by the morning the tides had turned and the dogs were seen being swept the other way, perched high on the ice cliffs of a large floe. Croft jumped from floe to floe, cut steps up to the floe on which they were stranded and one by one brought them down. Bringing the last one down he slipped and both himself and the astonished dog found themselves completing the last seventy feet more quickly than anticipated. Croft then persuaded the dogs to follow him back to shore. South of Isis Point, due to good weather conditions and visibility, they were able to disprove the existence of Nordenskiold's Fjord. They carried on with their circumnavigation of the island via the south coast. They ended their five-week journey exhausted, but according to Croft they were "thankful to have encircled North East Land, surveyed the east and south coasts and studied the various ice caps." He added: "Sandy had made a good beginning with investigating the country's geology." Croft and Whatman spent the last three weeks of the expedition sledging through central Spitsbergen and climbing some of the highest peaks and were picked up at Ice Fjord on 23rd August by the expedition ship, before returning to Britain.

Andrew Croft's knowledge of and expertise with sledging dogs, learned in a hard winter in Greenland, had been of immeasurable help to Glen's expedition, in providing the wherewithal for transport and in making extensive exploration and surveying possible. Speaking at the Royal Geographical Society in 1937 he expressed the view that the dogs had been a significant factor in keeping up the morale of the party and reiterated his opinion that what he called 'dog traction' was the best form of transport in the Arctic regions.[27] His determination and persistence also made him a very capable second-in-command. Both his Arctic knowledge and his strength of character developed on these expeditions were to enable him to make a strong contribution to the theatres of action in which he served in the Second World War.

Escape from Sweden 1940

At the outbreak of war, Croft, then aged 32, applied to join the RAF, but was told the upper age limit was twenty seven. After having failed also to join the Fleet Air Arm, the decision of how to serve was resolved by a request from MI (R) for him to use his language skills and

26   Andrew Croft, 'Across the Greenland Ice cap', *Geographical*, Vol. 1 (1935), p.267.
27   A. Croft, speaking at a meeting of the RGS, 25th January 1937.

Some of Croft's Colleagues in Operation Snow White 1944. (Croft family)

Arctic experience to supply arms to the Finns who had been attacked by Russia in November 1939. He was to be accompanied by Malcolm Munthe. The war diary of MI (R) recorded on 19th December 1939: "Captains Croft and Munthe left by air for Stockholm to hand over military stores to the Finnish government from His Majesty's Government."[28] They set up a line of supply via the port of Bergen, through Norway and Sweden, to the rail head at Torino, on the frontier with Finland. However, throughout the journey of the arms and explosives through neutral Sweden and Norway it was not to become apparent that the supplies were military. This route succeeded in getting military supplies through until the Russian defeated the Finns and an armistice was agreed on 13th March 1940. Croft thought that the supply had been reasonably successful, with 144 aircraft, and a large quantity of hand grenades, anti-tank weapons and machine guns delivered. He did, however, admit that some of the supplies fell into the hands of the Germans in Bergen harbour in 1940 as the Russo-Finnish War had ended sooner than expected. R. Sutton Pratt, the military attaché in Sweden, was impressed by the way that Croft and Munthe had handled the supply of equipment and arms to Finland: "I cannot speak too highly of their services and the way in which they overcame all difficulties."[29] Meanwhile, in January 1940 Croft and Munthe had been recalled to London. Croft was asked to organise the cold weather supplies needed for a planned force of one thousand men to be sent to Finland. The armistice put paid to this idea, and after returning to Torino to wind up the supply mission and after spending some leave with Munthe at Munthe's mother's house at Darlana, Croft and Munthe were asked to report to the military attaché at Bergen, as an agreement was being sought with the Norwegian government to allow British troops to land in Norway to protect the country from German attack. Croft thought such an agreement was "highly

28   Entry for 19th December 1939, War Diary MI (R), Croft Papers, private collection.
29   Letter from Sutton Pratt to Lt Col Holland at MI (R) January 1940. Croft Papers, private collection.

unlikely", but proceeded to Bergen, while Munthe was sent to Stavanger.

Croft was in Bergen when the German invasion of Norway began. He had seen a blackboard outside a fisherman's shop on the evening of 8th April which said "German fleet steaming north through Kattegat", and awoke in the night to find Bergen harbour under attack. Croft went at once to the British Consular shipping agency which still had boats with arms, which had been meant for Finland, in harbour, and helped burn all confidential documents. At 6.00 a.m. the senior naval officer gave the order to disperse. He recollected later: "I still fondly imagined that the Germans might be driven out of Bergen during the course of the next few days and determined to stay as long as possible."[30] He walked to find a view of the harbour and saw four German destroyers approaching the harbour. On returning to his hotel he found that it had already been taken over by Nazi sympathisers but managed to sneak to his room to collect his passport, money and warm clothes. He set out aiming to get to a port on one of the Norwegian fjords and try and find some British naval vessels. After a long trek over the mountains to Sammanger fjord he found that the Germans had arrived before him and so had to press on. By the evening of 23rd April, after having a lift in a Norwegian car and borrowing some skis, he arrived at Bulken. He calculated that since leaving Bergen he had walked 150 miles. After being 'arrested' by Norwegian troops, he was given a lift on a troop lorry to Gudvangen and then travelled by boat and ferry to Alesund on 17th April. In his autobiography, Croft related what happened next:

> Then I had a remarkable stroke of luck. I was standing on the harbour wall looking out to sea when I spotted a British destroyer. The Norwegians sent a signal on my behalf and the ship edged suspiciously towards us. I was escorted out to the ship in a rowing boat and somehow convinced the captain that I was bona fides. He gave me his reserve cabin and I dropped exhausted into the bunk.[31]

The destroyer was the *Ashanti*, which had been taking part in minesweeping operations in support of the British landings in Norway. She had come under air attack on 9th April and was to continue operations in the Norwegian area before returning to Kirkwall.[32] Croft remembered his days on board, spending time helping on the ship's anti-aircraft guns: "most of Saturday we spent potting at German aeroplanes – some twenty or more – but we only winged one."[33] On 24th April Croft travelled down to London and reported to the War Office. Within twenty-four hours of being debriefed Croft was posted to Colonel Gubbins's Independent Companies as chief intelligence officer and found himself on the way back to Norway. His part in the Norwegian campaign has been described in Chapter Three.

Auxiliary Units 1940

On his return from Norway, Croft had a brief spell at the independent companies' training school at Inverailort Castle, sharing a room with David Stirling. Commander Bill Fell, who had been with Croft and Riley in Norway, related a story of how he had visited Arisaig Commando School with Admiral Roger Keyes to inspect a commando exercise. The

---

30   Scrapbook kept by Croft of his wartime experiences. Croft Papers, private collection.
31   Croft, *Talent for Adventure*, p.149.
32   Uboat.net.
33   Scrapbook of wartime service. Croft Papers, private collection.

admiral fell asleep and when he woke up he was faced by Croft and Riley, who had led the attack "landing noiselessly and captured the admiral and all the strong points."[34]

Croft was now to become part of a scheme devised by Colonel Gubbins in response to the possible invasion of Britain. This plan consisted of organising clandestine 'left behind units' which would harass the invading German army from behind its lines. The units were to be organised by intelligence officers who were to be:

> allotted to areas, will reside there permanently, and will work in the closest touch with the military commander and the LDV commander so as to assist in every possible way the selection, training and organisation of these sub units, and the provision and storage of equipment.[35]

These units were to be organised within twenty miles of the coast, and Croft's area of responsibility was to be Essex and Suffolk. He was to choose men from the Home Guard, train them in guerrilla warfare and help them create underground hideouts. He chose the leaders of his group from men from a wide variety of backgrounds. They included a master of fox hounds who had a unique understanding of the local country, fruit growers, farm workers, poachers and smugglers. Croft was on his own ground, and used his father's home as a base, filling the barn behind the vicarage with arms and ammunition.

Croft allowed each patrol leader to choose his own men, based on their local knowledge, and then screened them. The patrol leaders were taken to the auxiliary unit's training school at Coleshill, Berkshire, to be instructed in sabotage and guerrilla warfare. Underground hideouts were constructed. Croft set up twenty-four units in Sussex and Wiltshire and the importance of secrecy was emphasised, so much so that it is only recently that members of these units admitted to having been in them. The resistance units in his areas were optimistic that they would be able to hold out behind German lines indefinitely, but fortunately they were never required to put this belief to the test.

Assistant Military Attaché in Sweden 1941–42

In the summer of 1941 Croft was "greatly surprised" to find himself ordered back to Scandinavia to become Assistant Military Attaché to Sweden. When he arrived in Sweden he became aware of the pessimism of the Swedish population as to the prospects of the Allies defeating Germany. Brigadier Sutton Pratt, the military attaché, commented on how "un- neutral the Swedes were."[36] This defeatist attitude of some Swedes was echoed in the opinions of the British minister at the legation, who was in favour of a negotiated peace. Croft heard that Sir Malcolm Sargent was to speak in Stockholm and managed to persuade him to speak on 'Britain at War'. The musician gave a "splendid address" which convinced the audience of the resilience and determination of the British people and received a standing ovation.

Croft had many contacts with the resistance, and was kept under constant surveillance by the Swedish police. He said of his role in Sweden:

> My job as assistant military attaché was largely clandestine on behalf of all three

---

34   W.A. Fell, *The Sea Our Shield* (London, 1966), p.86.

35   Memorandum to LD Area Commanders unsigned and undated. Croft Papers, private collection.

36   Croft, *Talent for Adventure*, p.164.

A wartime portrait of Croft. (Croft family)

services, to get as much information out of Norway as possible and to help the Norwegians as much as possible. I had a number of safe houses where I used to meet the Norwegians coming across, so I was really 90% SOE.[37]

Some information that Croft received from the Norwegian resistance was to be useful in Allied operations in Spitsbergen in 1941 (see Chapter Six).

However, the relative security and comfort of life in neutral Sweden resulted in Croft "eating my heart out to get back to active service and lend a hand in any way he could."[38] In a break from his duties at the legation, Croft was involved, with Sandy Glen, in air reconnaissance over arctic convoy routes and took part in a resupply flight to Spitsbergen (see Chapter Six). After the Battle of El Alamein, the Swedes' attitude to the British and therefore to Croft changed, as it became apparent the Allies had now a chance of winning the war.

Operation Balaclava – Corsica 1943-44

As promised, Croft was relieved of his duties in Sweden after a year, and found himself drafted to work with combined operations, taking part in training commando units which would be involved in the planned raids on the coast of occupied Europe. His boating and survival skills were particularly in demand. After training activities with canoes, kayaks and

37   File 'Sweden', Croft Papers, private collection.
38   Croft, *Talent for Adventure*, p.166.

follboats Croft was anxious to see action with the men he had been training, but was told that he was forbidden to take part in operations against Scandinavia because of his previous work as military attaché in Sweden. He received a letter from the Lieutenant Colonel who was officer commanding of No. 14 Commando on 13th January 1943 informing him "The commander of SS Brigade has ordered that in no circumstances are you to take part in operations in or against Scandinavia until further notice."[39] Croft wryly commented "penance for an ex-military attaché to Sweden."[40]

After the disbanding of No. 14 Commando, Croft volunteered for operations with Special Forces and was sent to Algiers to serve in the Mediterranean sector, based at the Special Forces centre, codenamed Massingham. He was put in charge of small boat training at Sidi Farouch, instructing on the use of rubber dinghies, two man Klepper canoes and Royal Engineers assault boats. During this period Croft had a break with a number of operations involving the submarine *Seraph*, involving landing an American party into Algeria to sound out the possibility of French resistance support for an Allied landing in North Africa. Other adventures in *Seraph* included landing wireless sets at Porto Fino for use by the Italian resistance, and assisting in the capture of an Italian merchant ship. His Arctic navigating experience was useful in winning a bet with the captain of the *Seraph* that he could navigate the submarine back to Algiers by celestial navigation. In a talk given to a conference on the Italian resistance in 1986 he recounted that while he was on board the *Seraph* she torpedoed a German ship and was attacked with a depth charge by an Italian destroyer by depth charge. In a letter to Croft, the captain of the *Seraph* thanked him for his services.

I am grateful for your splendid contribution and shall always, when looking back at those incredible times remember Andrew Croft as one of the most reliable, straightforward and good chaps it has been my lot to know and to work with.[41]

The next phase of Croft's war service was to stand out in his memory in later years:

If I could relive any chapter of my life during the war, it would undoubtedly be Corsica. From September 1943 to August 1944 I had the fun of running my own show to a large extent unsupervised. [42]

To men like Croft who had been responsible for their own lives and those of their fellow explorers in harsh and isolated conditions, the opportunity to take command and show initiative, using skills that they had already developed, was an opportunity not to be missed. Croft reckoned that the meticulous preparation and attention to detail learned in the Arctic stood him in good stead: "The loss of a torch or a pair of gloves on the Greenland ice cap would have been a major disaster; consequently I left nothing to chance."[43]

Croft was described by Adolphus Cooper, a SOE operative working in the Mediterranean, as ' a splendid man, tall, with finely chiselled features." He continued, "He

39   Croft, scrapbook on wartime experiences.
40   Ibid.
41   Ibid.
42   Croft, *Talent for Adventure*, p.177.
43   Ibid., p.177.

is determined and strong, a man of action, his body so finely tuned and disciplined that he could never understand a man complaining of tiredness."[44] Cooper described how Croft considered tiredness to be a weakness rather than a condition.

The role of the unit which Croft led was to land agents, equipment and wireless sets on the shores of occupied France and Italy. His orders were:

A. You are to set up in Corsica a base from which clandestine operations can be launched on the adjacent coasts of Italy and Southern France by coastal forces and high-speed craft.

B. To reconnoitre an unfrequented part of the coast and there to arrange small boat training.

C. To organise sea transport when required between Corsica, Sardinia. North Africa and Southern Italy either for stores or personnel.[45]

Although the RAF had made progress in the dropping of agents and supplies into occupied France, there was still a shortage of aircraft and crew for these sorties and it was felt that more passengers, store and equipment could be landed by sea. The unit was given the trawler *Serinini* (*MFV 2017*) and set out for Corsica to establish bases there from which to approach the chosen landing beaches. The group which Croft assembled around him, codenamed 'Balaclava', and to which he added as the unit grew, gelled well and went on to fight together in southern France. Balaclava was the first of the clandestine boating units to establish itself on Corsica, its cover being ISSU-6 (inter-service signals unit).

On arrival at the port of Calvi the unit planned to liaise with the 'Front Nationale', who had been the resistance organisation while the island was occupied. They made contact with Ignace Bianconi who helpfully found them a base and a mooring position. Croft later paid tribute to his help: "Ignace Bianconi was the first man this unit met on its initial arrival at the end of September 1943 ... Speedily he established the contacts necessary for the success of this unit and its subsequent Anglo-French Mission." [46] They decided that operations aimed at the Nice coast would leave from Calvi, but that the port of Bastia was more suitable for trips to the Italian coast or Elba. Croft's group set up a base in a villa not far from Bastia which had room to put up agents waiting to be landed and also had space for meetings of the various security operations which would be using the boats based on Corsica. These included the Secret Intelligence Service, SIS, the Special Operations Executive, SOE, the American Office of Strategic Services, OSS, MI9, 30 Commando and the Bataillon de Choc, French "shock troops". These various groups operating out of Bastia and sharing resources and operational ability were under the overall of Rear Admiral Richard Dickinson. Croft was always anxious that his group would remain independent and not be swallowed up in the other security services involved. Brooks Richards, the head of the French section at Massingham, noted later in his official history of clandestine operations in the Mediterranean " the uniquely friendly atmosphere" in Bastia.[47]

---

44   Cited in David Stafford, *Mission Accomplished, SOE and Italy 1943-1945* (London, 2011), p.76.
45   Letter from F.B. Richards to Croft, Croft scrapbook.
46   Typed sheet 'Ignace Bianconi' in Croft Papers, private collection.
47   Ibid., p.76.

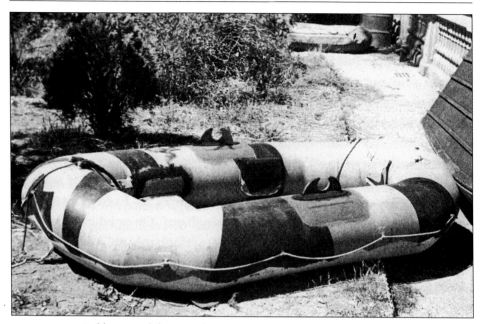

Rubber assault boat used in operations in Corsica. (Croft family)

The boats that would be used were Motor Torpedo Boats, (MTBs), Motor Gun Boats, (MGBs,) Italian *Motorscafi Antisommergibili* (MAS boats) and American Patrol Boats (PT boats). The Italian MAS boats were the fastest option, with a top speed of 42-47 knots. They had the added advantage of a low silhouette. Their disadvantage was their very noisy engines and their slow speed whilst operating on their quieter auxiliary engines. Croft did not trust their Italian crews. And his suspicions proved correct as on one mission to drop some French commandos, the Italian crew took over the boat, murdering one of Croft's colleagues, Lt. Dow, and then defected to the Germans.

The first mission for Croft and the Balaclava team was codenamed 'Valentine' and was to land two agents on the Italian coast north of Spezia. The first two attempts using ML 576 had to be abandoned due to sea conditions too rough to launch the rubber landing boat. On 2nd December a further attempt was made, using MAS 541. Croft was glad of the extra speed of the MAS boat as if they had encountered German E boats, they would have been outgunned and would have needed to make a quick getaway. Two hours out from shore they cut the main engines and proceeded on auxiliary engines only. As they approached an air raid was in progress over Spezia. A few hundred yards from the coast the rubber dinghy was put over the side, with Geoffrey Arnold as armed look out, and Croft rowing. The cliff looked far steeper that the aerial reconnaissance photos had shown and it was forty minutes before a suitable beaching was spotted. Croft guided the dinghy to the tiny beach and the agents were dry landed after Arnold had checked the safety of the immediate area. Later Croft learned that the agents, a wireless operator, Silvio de Fiori, and Pablo Risso, were part of the 'Otto' organisation, an anti-fascist group operating in Genoa.

The rubber dinghies or surfboats use to land the agents and their equipment were about nine feet in area when inflated. They were manned by two men, one in the bow as lookout, who was armed with a submachine gun, and one rowing and handling the boat.

Sometimes Royal Engineer boats were used, but all were equipped with sails, emergency repair equipment and a ration pack. They had to row some distance, in the dark over choppy seas and unknown rocks and reefs to land their passengers, often with bulky luggage and wireless sets, and ensure the security of the landing area. The boats were camouflaged with light green or pink reflective aluminium paint and were invisible at forty metres. Croft remembered:

> On one occasion I watched German troops, alerted by radar, noisily running down towards men while I carefully back-watered out to sea, confident of our camouflage, but with a panic-stricken agent's revolver at my chest. Rather unnecessary I thought![48]

When landing blind without a reception committee in the area, they ran the risk of encountering an enemy ambush. Bringing agents out was even more dangerous. Michael Foot, in his history of the SOE in France, considered that:

> There was always a fearful risk that accident, indiscretion or treachery might betray a prearranged rendezvous to the enemy. In that case ... a warship and its crew might be lost in an attempt to bring out a single and not necessarily a valuable agent.[49]

Most operations took place in the moonless period of the month and in between missions the group practised silent landings at the beach at Calvi, experimenting with the most successful camouflage techniques. They also managed to establish and measure the distance from which the approach of a boat would be invisible to the enemy. Their next mission was to land two OSS agents blind, that is without a reception party waiting for them, at St Tropez. The MAS boat chosen was fast, but unfortunately her speed affected her compass and the boat ended up in a heavily defended stretch of the coast and had to make the last silent part of the journey on its auxiliary engines, which took five hours. Croft and Miles landed the agents successfully in a spot with overhanging cliffs which hid the dinghy's approach, but by the time they had rowed back to the MAS boat it was dangerously light, leaving them vulnerable to attack on the way back to Bastia.[50]

On 3rd January Croft was asked to take part in the landing of four SOE agents, two women and two men, north of Spezia. The practical difficulties of handling a dinghy with six people and the agents' equipment aboard while looking for a landing place which all the party could cope with, proved impossible and the agents had to be re-embarked and taken back to Bastia. Another attempt on 21st January also failed. The situation was then complicated by both the men on the mission, Raneri, an Italian wireless operator and Martin, a Canadian, both falling in love with one of the women, Fiammetta, and the other woman, Anna, becoming ill. Martin then also complained of a weak heart and said he was too ill to carry on. The operation was abandoned and later it was discovered that Raneri was a fascist. The two women had been given Paddy Davies's Room at the villa and were caught amusing themselves by trying on his Naval uniform. Croft commented that if women

48 Talk given by Croft at a conference on Italian Resistance at Bologna, October 1986. Croft Papers, private collection.

49 M.R.D. Foot, *SOE in France* cited by A. Cecil Hampshire, *Undercover Sailors, Secret Operations of World War Two* (London, 1981), p.193.

50 A. Cecil Hampshire, *Undercover Sailors*, p.174.

Croft's usual colleagues on sea operations, Harry and Don. (Croft family)

were to be included in such operations in future that it would be better if they were not accompanied by men.

Croft was involved with another landing involving the 'Otto' organisation on 28th January. This was Operation Tail Lamp and involved landing a man on an Italian mission close to Genoa at Voltri Pier, which Croft described as "probably the best defended port in the Mediterranean"[51]. The first landing failed due to the panic of the crew of the MAS boat who retreated at the sight of some enemy ships on the horizon. A few days later the landing was tried again, using American PT boats, but now with seven agents to deliver. The reception committee did not turn up near Voltri Pier but the agents decided to land anyway, with Sergeant Miles in charge of one dinghy and Croft the other. The agents were found a secure hiding place ashore and the dinghies returned to the PT boats. A second landing, Operation Anstey, took place at Voltri pier on 21st March 1944 when seven SOE agents and three SIS agents were landed. Croft considered that the successful Voltri operations gave him the most satisfaction and sense of achievement.

Croft's unit was now expanding, with the appointment of Ken Carson as administrator and a signals section under the command of Sergeant Collins. For the first time they were able to talk to agents in occupied territory if this was thought necessary. In February fifteen operations were carried out and in March nineteen. However, about half of these failed to complete their missions successfully. The activities of the unit were also expanded by the arrival of Captain Peter Fowler of 'A' Force, charged with organising escapes from mainland Italy of prisoners of war who had managed to get to the coast. On 31st March Colonel John Anstey, Croft's superior officer from Algiers, visited Bastia, and on his return to Algiers sent a congratulatory telegram:

---

51   Croft, talk at Bologna 1986.

MUCH ENJOYED TRIP AND WOULD ASK YOU TO CONVEY TO
ALL RANKS MY HIGHEST APPRECIATION OF A) THE FIRST CLASS
OPERATIONAL EFFICIENCY OF ALL SECTIONS DUE TO THE ABILTY
OF EACH ONE TO SURMOUNT ALL DIFFICULTIES B) THE OBVIOUS
SPIRIT IN THE UNIT C) YOUR HOSPITALITY. EACH ONE OF YOU
BY YOUR ABILITY TO CO-OPERATE WITH OTHER NATIONALITIES
IS DOING THE GREATEST POSSIBLLE SERVICE AND LAYING THE
FOUNDATIONS OF GOODWILL THAT IS SO IMPORTANT NOW AND
WILL BE EVEN MORE IMPORTANT AFTER THE WAR.[52]

As spring approached, the demand for operations increased. Captain Hege, who
was responsible for collecting information about the German defences on Elba, asked for
several missions to take agents in and out of Elba. Just before the French assault on Elba, it
was essential that three agents were landed. Croft took two PT boats and for the first time,
stayed aboard to direct operations while the agents were landed. The island was captured in
two days and on 19th June Croft received a wireless message from the agents on the island.
"Mission terminated – awaiting instructions" and added to his log:

> We have played a major role in the Allied landings on Elba, as the Charles mission
> was put in four times and exfiltrated three times, once with enemy close at heels. In
> addition we have maintained and supplied equipment.[53]

The final sortie took place on 29th July 1944. The air supremacy gained by the Allies
meant that the sort of missions performed by boats were now more suited to aircraft. As
soon as the south of France had begun to be liberated it was planned that the 'Massingham'
headquarters in Algeria be wound up and operations from Corsica stopped. From December
1943 until July 1944 fifty-two sorties had been attempted, of which twenty-four had been
successful. Croft had taken part in twenty-four operations, usually as dinghy handler.
Eighty agents had been landed and twenty-four taken out. Croft considered that this was
an achievement which had gone unrecognised in the official accounts of the war. Ten of
Croft's men received decorations, a DSC, an MC, an MBE, two DSM, two BEM and four
Mentions in Despatches. The citations read: "For exceptional courage, judgement and fine
seamanship during landing operations on enemy defended coasts in the Mediterranean".
It is the opinion of naval historian A. Cecil Hampshire that: "Such sorties to the enemy-
held coasts of Italy and France ... played no inconsiderable part in bringing about the final
downfall of the Third Reich."[54]

Operation Snow White France 1944
Croft had been informed in June of 1944, in strict secrecy, that he would be required to take
part in the invasion of Southern France. The plan was to parachute in west of Montpellier.
He was to choose seven men to accompany him, and with a nod to his Arctic experience
the mission had been codenamed "Snow White and the Seven Dwarves." On 6th August,
Croft, accompanied by Carson, Arnold, Collins, Bourne–Newton, Miles and Chambers

52   Croft, *Talent for Adventure*, p.197.
53   Cecil Hampshire, *Undercover Sailors*, p.144.
54   Ibid., p. 114.

left Corsica to return to Massingham for parachute training. Later Peter Fowler replaced Carson because of illness, and Collins was considered too much of a security risk, so was replaced by two French wireless officers, Lt. J. Lapointe and Lt J. Celigny. Carson was disappointed not to accompany Croft and wrote from Calvi: " I can only say in the words of the old song 'My heart is good but my feet won't let me'"[55]

In his report on the operation Croft enlarged on its objectives. The Allied high command was placing much emphasis on disrupting east–west communications. The job of Croft and his men was to "take steps to deny the enemy the subsidiary roads and rail routes lying to the northward of the N 9 ... Operation Snow White had orders to work on routes 609 and 609, Route Nationale N 9 and corresponding rail routes." [56]The party were parachuted by an RAF Stirling on 16th August and had an enthusiastic reception from the local *Maquis*. After a meal of roast mutton the leader of the reception committee, Jacques, sent a message to the local *Maquis* leader 'Sultan'. He gave Croft a silver medallion from around his neck and Bordeaux wine flowed freely. Croft remembered in his log of the operation: "on reading out operation order he [Sultan] showed obvious signs of delight that his request for arms and help in the Bédarieux-Clermont L'Hérault-Roujan triangle had been realised by our arrival".[57]

Despite the enthusiastic welcome, Croft reported that the *Maquis* were "badly informed, armed, and organised".[58] The local group was called the 'Bir Hakeim' under the leadership of a man called Montaigne. After several complicated meetings in which all the local *Maquis* heads had to be present, Croft's unit set off in convoy with five motorcyclists, three lorries and two private cars. They received a big welcome from the local population, as the *Maquis* had not dared to use the roads preferring, as Croft rather scathingly reported, "their heavily defended villages", but now were organised to begin attacking the Germans. The first demolition exercise carried out by Arnold and Bourne-Newton planned to use the Spanish section of the *Maquis* to blow up a bridge between Bédarieux and Faugerés on the N 609. On the way to the target the car broke down. A replacement car was obtained by hijacking a German staff car, but the sabotage party were too late to successfully lay the charges before it became light. As the charges were being placed in their holes a German patrol arrived and opened fire with a machine gun. The *Maquis* retaliated but were forced to retreat. The incident did, however, according to Croft's report, stop German convoys passing along the road for thirty-six hours as the German troops patrolled the roads on both sides of the intensively, stopping all traffic from using it.

The day of 20th August was spent in sending local people off on motorbikes to obtain intelligence, and handing out arms to some sections of *Maquis* who were leaving their mountain hideouts to engage the enemy. As a result of the information gathered they learned that the German 198th Division was leaving Pezenas and proceeding north with all speed. An attempt to ambush this division failed as the lorry carrying the *Maquis* who were going to assist Croft's men broke down. The ambush had to be cancelled because of what Croft described as "the first of our many transport difficulties in this area." Croft heard the story of why the local *Maquis*, the 'Bir Hakeim', were so demoralised. In May 1944 about sixty members of the local groups had climbed to the plateau of La Parade, south of the

55   Croft scrapbook.
56   Report by Croft on Operation Snow White, TNA HS3.30.
57   Ibid.
58   Ibid.

Gorges du Tarn on the Central Massif, to receive a parachute drop of arms and equipment. They had been betrayed and were ambushed by German troops. Thirty-two were killed and twenty-seven survivors were arrested, tortured and executed. They were very short of arms as a result of this failure, so Croft gave them three PIATs, four Bren guns and twenty-five British rifles.

On Monday 21st August reports were coming in that the German convoys were avoiding the main roads. Arrangements were made for Croft and most of his party to prepare an ambush of Route N109 on the high ground east of Gignac, while Fowler and Bourne-Newton would blow up the bridge on the River Dourbie on the main N 9. Fowler, accompanied by two gendarmes on a motorbike and sidecar, set out to make sure that there was no way for the German tanks to bypass the bridge, while Bourne-Newton went to reconnoitre the bridge itself. As Croft's ambush party was about to set out the news came that Fowler and the two gendarmes had been ambushed by a group of SS trainees on bicycles. The bearer of the bad news was clutching Fowler's beret. He had been shot through the head. Croft's ambush party the set out, arriving on Tuesday 22nd and finding an ideal spot at Capion as a base for their ambush activities.

Having established that the ambush would take place that night, Croft then returned to Mourèze to find that at last good news awaited him. Bourne-Newton reported that he had been successful in blowing an eight-metre gap in the Dourbie Bridge. The important route of the N 9 could no longer be used by German tanks and lorries. Peter Fowler was buried that afternoon at Mourèze, with the whole village and the local *Maquis* attending as well as the Snow White mission. Croft now returned to Capion and set up the ambush for the evening. The German troops were moving up from the south and it was uncertain whether they would travel past the planned ambush, but Croft had also arranged for a group of *Maquis* to ambush the alternative route near Clermont L'Héuralt. In his report Croft described the extent of the ambush:

> The ambush positions on the north side of the Route N109 covered about one kilometre of the road at the eastern side of which was a bridge with three Bren gun positions nearby; at the western end were placed two PIATs, one Bren and a Browning: the troop consisted of six Britishers and thirty Frenchmen.[59]

Croft and his men waited all night at these positions but as Croft reported, "no Germans came, only a lot of rain." The convoy had been warned of the ambush and had taken a long detour. However, the alternative ambush had succeeded in attacking a German convoy on route N69.

Reinforced by a *Maquis* section of fifty men Croft responded to an urgent message from Montpellier for assistance as although that German troop had moved out, the residents were afraid of their return and there was also a lot of looting and pillaging taking place. Packing up all ammunition and stores, Croft's party and the *Maquis* proceeded to Montpellier where they received a tumultuous welcome. Croft reported that "the Britishers were not exactly assaulted, but embraced hundreds of times by both sexes." Croft spent a few days in Montpellier, arranging for patrols and town defences as the town slowly came back to life after the German occupation. Croft remembered how mysteriously spare

---

59   Report by Croft on Operation Snow White, TNA HS3.30.

Croft during the Second World War. (Croft family)

parts appeared from hiding places and the continual faults to the water supply, electricity supply and broadcasting stations which had been a feature of the area under occupation, suddenly disappeared. With the radio station now working Bounin, the Commissaire du Gouvernement for the five local departments, decided to go on air to address that local population. He managed to persuade Croft to make the first speech. Outside the hall, in the Place de la Comédie, a huge crowd had gathered and Croft then found himself on the balcony, addressing them. During that evening huge crowds remained in the square, singing British songs and mobbing the Snow White party wherever they appeared.

However, Montaigne had received intelligence that a German column, travelling north, might turn south to Montpellier, so Croft set out to arrange an ambush and defensive positions at Montferrier. However, the column did not materialise, and Montaigne, in disappointment, handed Croft the control of the French forces. Croft decided to pursue the German column northwards, which they did until it had reached Quissac and came under attack by another *Maquis* force.

Over the next few days Croft was engaged in transferring the British responsibilities to Bounin and his staff. On 2nd September the Snow White mission took part in a huge parade, inspected by General de Lattre de Tassigny. As Croft commented, "that was really the finale". An old friend, Peter Storr, arrived, with orders to transport them to Lyons, where they were once again given a warm welcome and were present when General de Gaulle addressed the crowds in the Place Belville. Croft's main impression of this trip through Southern France was meeting and talking to many heroic survivors of the *Maquis* resistance against their German occupiers.

General Gubbins had decided to keep Croft's team together, and after a series of contradictory and cancelled orders, involving a possible mission to Norway and then the Far East, it was decided in March 1945 that the unit would parachute into Denmark, behind the lines at *Generaloberst* Lindemann's headquarters. This would have been what Croft described as, "the most dangerous mission of all".[60] Thankfully, the lives of Croft and his men were saved "by Hitler's timely suicide in Berlin."[61] Croft ended the war in Denmark, helping sort out the situation after the Germans had surrendered. He acted as a liaison between General Dewing, who had taken the surrender, the Danish resistance, and the Germans.

During his remarkable wartime career Croft had been involved in several of the major theatres of war and had been able to use the skills obtained in his pre-war exploring career to good effect. In recognition of his courage, skills and leadership, he was awarded the DSO on 15th March 1945.

60   Croft, *Talent for Adventure*, p.216.
61   Ibid.

6

Alexander 'Sandy' Glen

Expeditions to Spitsbergen 1933 and 1935–36 – "Those delightful dotted lines"

In early 1933 Alexander 'Sandy' Glen, then a student at Oxford, was on the brink of his pre-war exploring career. It was characteristic of him that in *Young Men in the Arctic* he described how his polar exploration happened by chance: "One morning early in 1932 I had a bath ... it was an epic bath, for I was disturbed half-way through by an explorer."[1] The ensuing conversation resulted in Glen starting to think about organising an expedition. He had determined views on the necessity for Arctic exploration. He conceded that there was more to do on what he called "extensive" exploration, for example, a north to south crossing of Greenland and exploration of the heart of Antarctica, but he had his sights set on "intensive" exploration, that is a more detailed examination in terms of glaciology, detailed mapping and meteorological investigations. He believed that university expeditions were ideally suited to this type of expedition as they were "informally led and versatile"[2]. The keynote was not in strict discipline but in a reliance of every member of the expedition playing his part as best he could.

In the introduction to his book describing the 1933 expedition, *Young men of the Arctic*, Glen gave his rationale for exploration in the Arctic. He stated that mapping was not enough, and that all branches of science must play their part. He emphasised the need for weather research: "The Arctic countries ... certainly exercise very great influence on weather conditions of America and Europe. This naturally affects agriculture and every other trade or industry which is dependent on the weather."[3] The 1933 summer expedition resulted in interesting reports on geology, glaciology, geomorphology, seismological surveys and experimentation with wireless communication (see Chapter Nine). It laid the basis for the larger expedition which was to take place in 1935/36, overwintering on the North East Land of the Spitsbergen ice cap. In the introduction to his account of the second expedition, *Under the Pole Star*, Glen paid tribute to the previous expeditions to Spitsbergen led by Stranz in 1912, Binney in 1924 and Ahlmann in 1931. He was fully aware of the difficulties of surveying and overwintering on North East Land and referred to the 'peculiarly evil' reputation of that part of the Spitsbergen Archipelago which, including the *Nobile* disaster of 1928, had taken the lives of half of those who had set foot on it.

Glen again had clear ideas as to the purpose of this expedition. The possibility of a transatlantic air route had been investigated, and the British Arctic Air Route Expedition of 1930-31 had resulted in a gathering of weather information on Greenland. The establishment of winter ice cap stations, although gathering vital information, had cost the lives of two members of the German expedition led by Wegener, and resulted in August Courtauld being stranded alone in his station for six months whilst participating in the

---

1   A. Glen, *Young Men in the Arctic* (London, 1934), p.23.
2   Ibid., p.29.
3   Ibid., p.16.

Robert Moss

Karl Bengtssen

'Daniel' Godfrey

'Brownie' Whatman

'Sandy' Glen

Expedition members. (Croft family)

British Arctic Air Route Expedition. More work was needed on Arctic survival techniques and Glen planned to establish two ice cap stations as part of the work on North East Land. Strategic aspects were also considered as the Soviet Union had been developing meteorological stations in the Eastern Arctic and looking at ways of exploiting the vast mineral reserves of Siberia as well as looking for an alternative trade route if a war came. But in Glen's opinion the whole plan for commercial exploitation of the Arctic was intimately bound up with the development of air travel. However, he realised that as far as the islands of higher latitudes than 80° degrees north, that "the main importance ... must be their influence on weather conditions in Europe and Siberia."[4] This importance was to be one of the main considerations of operations Gauntlet and Fritham, which Glen found himself involved with in 1942. Andrew Croft, second-in-command of the expedition, in his memoirs A *Talent for Adventure*, was more specific as to the scientific aims:

> Most important of all, however, was to be the continuous research on the ionosphere the region in the upper atmosphere which is responsible for the long distance propagation of radio waves. This particular work in such a high altitude as 80° north

---

4   Ibid., p.3.

More expedition members. (Croft family)

was to prove of such importance to the development of radar – vital in the war that was coming – that all members of the expedition were awarded the Polar Medal in 1942.[5]

The recent discovery of the existence of the ionosphere, a number of reflecting layers about 250 miles above the earth's surface, had given rise to ideas of bouncing radio waves off it to be able to transmit signals around the curvature of the earth. Croft described how the experiments took place: "A succession of radio waves was sent vertically upwards from a special transmitter and each one examined on return from the layers above by means of a special device which enabled them to be seen with the eye and photographed."[6]

Further research planned included the study of the atmospheric ozone, including measuring the thickness of the ozone layer. Research had suggested that solar ultra-violet light radiation was the chief decomposing agent in the depletion of ozone, but that ozone is created mainly by atmospheric electrical discharges in the higher latitudes. It was therefore considered important to measure the thickness of the ozone layer north of the Arctic Circle.[7]

5   A. Croft, *A talent for adventure* (Worcester, 1991), p.81.
6   Ibid., p.99.
7   A. Glen, 'The Oxford University Arctic Expedition, North East Land 1935-1936', in *The Geographical*

The ionosphere hut. (Croft family)

The expedition was backed by the Royal Geographical Society as well as some eight Oxford Colleges and two Cambridge colleges. Significantly, the War Office lent valuable equipment and allowed the secondment of two officers, A.S.T. 'Daniel' Godfrey from the Royal Engineers and A.B. 'Brownie' Whatman, to join the expedition. The potential of the ionosphere research had obviously been realised. Glen then set about choosing his party. He admitted that he "did not set much store by exaggerated physical toughness or an equally exaggerated athleticism". He was looking instead for "something infinitely more valuable, and that is mental stability, which is often found in company with sophistication".[8] Andrew Croft was asked to be second-in-command and in charge of the dogs. Archie Dunlop MacKenzie was the organiser. Richard Hamilton became chief physicist, John Wright in charge of the survey and astronomy, David Keith was the biologist, and Robert Moss was appointed to be in charge of the central ice cap station. Notwithstanding the many scientific and academic motivations for the expedition, Glen and his companions were for the most part young and light-hearted explorers, who set of in 1935 with a full scientific staff and meteorological equipment and with high hopes of filling the gaps in the map of the coast of North East Land "which were still marked on the map with those delightful dotted lines which so stir the imagination."[9]

The expedition set out aboard the sealer *Polar* from Tromso, heavily over-laden with

Journal Vol XC No 3, September 1937, p.199.
8   A. Glen, *Under the Pole Star* (London, 1933), p.11.
9   A. Glen, *Under the Pole Star*, p.6.

Unloading supplies at base camp, Spitsbergen expedition, 1935. (Croft family)

expedition supplies although seven tons had to be left in Tromso to be brought later. At Tromso they had met up with the dogs who had been shipped with great difficulty by Croft from Greenland. On the morning of 1st August the *Polar* reached South Gat Sound on the north west of the archipelago, where their hut and some more supplies had been landed four weeks earlier. Ice conditions were the worst since 1917 and Glen made the decision to place base camp at Brandy Bay on North East Land Island, rather than try to go as far as Rijps Bay, as planned. The base hut was completed on 21st August, complete with a small shack eighty metres away for ionosphere research. The first records from the ionosphere transmitters and receivers were taken on 30th August. In addition to this research, meteorological observations were to be taken regularly at base camp and forwarded to Britain. Research on the features of the Aurora Borealis in that part of the Eastern Arctic, measurements of magnetism and ozone were to be taken. An advance hut then had to be positioned nearer the possible routes to the interior and a site was found near the base of glacier leading to the ice cap at Lady Franklin Bay. On 25th August the *Polar* left for the last time for Norway. All written communication had to go with the ship and from then on wireless would be the only method of communication. The letterbox made by John Wright had written on it: "Collection August 1935 – next collection Summer 1936? Who knows and who cares?"[10], an attitude which showed the optimistic mood of the party. Glen noted that they were all

10   Ibid., p.56.

Expedition hut living room. (Croft family)

Sledging over sea ice north of Spitsbergen. (Croft family)

glad to see the ship go.

Glen intended the expedition to live well at base camp and had planned the food supplies around "the menus of normal life in England. Every variety of food was included and there was a comprehensive range of sweet and chocolate". He chose high quality tinned meats which would not be affected by frost and would supplement the meat obtained by hunting. He felt that there was room for improvement to the sledging rations devised by Gino Watkins which he felt "had proved sound but dull." The expedition was to experiment with the inclusion of cheese, dried vegetables and bacon in the sledging rations.[11]

On 19th August the boat survey party set out to map the north coast from Brandy Bay to Zordragger Bay. The survey was to be approximately third-order accuracy in the ordnance standard. Under the command of John Wright they reached Extreme Bay and climbed to Extreme Hook to check on the beacon set up by a joint Swedish/Russian survey of the west coast 1899-1902. They managed to re-erect the beacon, which consisted of a huge metal drum surmounting a ten-foot iron pole. From there they boated around North Cape to Cape Lindhagen, mapped Scoresby Island and reached Loven Bay. Here Wright travelled inland to investigate a rocky outcrop of nunatak 1,000 feet high. Rijps Bay was surveyed within a fortnight, but as Zordragger Bay had no safe anchorage, they set out back to base.

The ice cap on North East Land was gradually retreating and only in comparatively recent times had the land valley running through the centre become exposed and divided the ice cap in two. Measuring this glacial retreat was one of the expedition's aims and in order to do this it was decided to have two ice cap stations. On 6th September the parties left to set up the two ice cap stations in the interior. Once the site of the central ice cap station had been chosen, Archie Dunlop Mackenzie, Robert Moss and Glen Stayed out to build it while Andrew Croft and Daniel Godfrey relayed all that was needed from base camp. The setting up of the two ice cap station was crucial to the success of the expedition. Glen gave two justifications for attempting such a difficult task:

> If meteorological stations can be established in the heart of the Arctic Lands ... the efficiency of weather forecasting would be greatly increased. Similarly there are many problems of the utmost importance to Geology and Glaciology which can be satisfactorily studied at these stations alone.[12]

He expanded on the aims of the ice cap station in a paper give to the Royal Geographical Society in 1937: He wanted the expedition to continue the glaciological work of Professor Ahlmann on the Swedish-Norwegian 1931 expedition, and in particular to study the effects of the violent winds which were present on the North East Land ice caps. He need to measure the gain and loss of the ice cap over the different seasons and to do this "precipitation, ablation and thaw were to be measured with extreme accuracy ... The action of the wind was expected to be one of the most important factors of removal." [13]

Making the stations involved complex logistical problems. Andrew Croft recalled:

11   A. Glen, 'The Oxford University Arctic Expedition, North East Land 1935-1936', in *The Geographical Journal* Vol XC No 3, September 1937.
12   Ibid., p.116.
13   A. Glen, 'The Oxford University Arctic Expedition, North East Land 1935-1936', in *The Geographical Journal* Vol XC No 3, September 1937.

Croft in the tunnel under the ice station. (Croft family)

To the central station seven and a half tons of food and equipment would have to be sledged; two men's supplies for ten months, while four and a half tons would be required for the four months' maintenance of the northern station – twelve tons in all or at least twenty return journeys for each available dog.[14]

The expedition had taken advice from Augustine Courtauld and Dr Fritz Lowe, who was at the ice cap station of the ill-fated Wegener expedition to Greenland in 1930.

Each station was began by digging down through the 'firn', that is crystallised ice containing air, for about four feet and inserting the tent into the hole. It looked like a giant umbrella, as the outer canvas was placed over eight wooden ribs and the inner canvas was hung from these ribs. This meant that there was a three inch air space which improved insulation. A wooden floor had a trap door which led to the tunnels which were to be excavated underneath, including a tunnel to the main entrance shaft to the ice station. This main entrance was to be located as far as possible to the tent so that its trap door would not be buried in the snowdrifts forming around the tent roof. In the middle of the door was cut a small hole so that if necessary a hand could be used to clear accumulations of snow, thus preventing the occupiers being trapped inside, as Courtauld had been in Greenland. While

14   A. Croft, *Talent for Adventure*, p.90.

Base point. (Croft family)

the 'firn' was quite easy to dig, it was layered with thick ice, which could only be chiselled away very slowly. The meteorological instruments were placed outside within a roped-off area with a guide rope leading to the entrance in preparation for taking readings in the dark of winter. Robert Moss lived at the ice station for ten months, being kept company by other members of the expedition in turn throughout November and December. He continued digging the tunnels underneath further and making twice-daily observations. This routine was replicated at the north ice cap station, which had been built similarly but contained fewer tunnels. David Keith's stay at the central ice station was enlivened by a 'firnstoss' or ice quake: "The effect is exactly that of an express train crashing though an underground railway."[15] At one stage they accidentally entered a large and deep crevasse leading to an underground lake while tunnel building. The crevasse had three galleries; the floor of one was the roof of another. The lowest layer was seventy feet below the surface and contained a lake, which remained unfrozen, except for the month of May when a thin layer of ice formed. Moss swam to explore this lake until the point where it disappeared into the darkness beyond it. Conditions at the stations were comfortable, with the temperatures inside never falling below zero. Between the outside and inside there was sometimes a difference of temperature of 120° Fahrenheit. Boredom was relieved by an exhaustive daily

15   Ibid., p.131.

The Dupileck dogs. (Croft family)

routine of observation and maintenance and also listening to radio talks and dance music from the BBC. The wireless transmitter and receiver were powered by a bicycle attached to a dynamo. Glen remembered that the news bulletins were dominated by "war and threats of war" and was glad to be able to feel detached from this 'other' world.

The long polar nights ended and by 9th April Glen and Andrew Croft were ready to set out on a sledging journey onto the sea ice travelling north. They wanted to travel to as high latitude as possible, to take soundings and study weather conditions relative to those of North East Land. Previous attempts to travel over the Arctic Ocean had included Nansen's Journey from the *Fram* to the Franz Joseph Islands in 1893/4 and Peary's attempts from North Greenland between 1898 and 1909, culminating in his claim to have reached the pole in 1909. Despite the unlikelihood of a successful trip, Croft and Glen were confident of adding to the store of arctic experience and of producing some information which would be of use in further attempts. They took two Nansen sledges, with a combined weight of 900 lbs pulled by nine dogs. The swift onset of blizzard conditions after the first night's camp resulted in a decision to turn back to base. When they were only two or three miles from land, conditions worsened and open leads appeared in the water. Croft fell and injured his head, and then, in attempting to right the sledge, Glen fell against the ice, the result being, as he described it, "complete oblivion". Glen was severely concussed for thirty-six hours, being able to continue his physical movements unaffected, but with no sensation of consciousness or recollection of events. Croft was able to get them to shore and erect a tent in the shelter of an old hut, where Glen recovered consciousness. They were then able to get back to base. On 17th April they set out again, progressing a little further onto the sea ice, but being turned back by pack ice and pressures ridges. Glen considered that the trip had been a failure technically and scientifically, but added: "certainly we probably learnt more in those brief weeks than during the whole of the rest of the expedition. Maybe because failure is the best teacher."[16]

On 10th April, Archie Dunlop Mackenzie and John Wright started the spring journey, a detailed survey of the Rjipps Peninsula and Rjipps valley. On 12th May Glen and Croft set out to journey around North East Land cross the East Ice Cap to get to the east and south coasts to map the coastal areas. They travelled south along the almost unbroken ice cliffs, mapping hitherto undiscovered coast line south of Isis point (see Chapter Four). It had been thought that the coast was here broken by a fjord, but this did not exist. The last survey journey set out on 19th July. Consisting of Richard Hamilton and John Wright, the party planned to survey the north coast from Rasch Island to Dove Bay. This expedition successfully mapped forty miles of complicated coast in four weeks.

The results of the expedition had included a plane table survey of the north coast, and the mapping of the coast and ice edge from Dove Bay eastward by short-base and photographic methods. Glen summed up the geographical achievements in his article in *The Times*, on 1st October 1936 -"North East Land has now been completely mapped and must be considered as part of the best known lands of the Arctic." Of the scientific results, he said: "Almost every branch of science has yielded valuable results."[17] He also commented many years later in his autobiography on the benefits to the participants: "I doubt if at the end any one of us was not rather different from fifteen months earlier, for a life of strange peace in a land of unusual beauty had given more to all of us than we could guess."[18]

Two incidents from the expedition, also related by Glen in his autobiography, form a link from the Arctic to the Second World War. On the occasion of Mussolini's invasion of Abyssinia in October 1935, the expedition party expressed their indignation by sending a telegram declaring war on Mussolini. "We, the inhabitants of North East Land, strongly deprecate your wanton aggression in Abyssinia ... We would advise conciliation. Otherwise we will put at the disposal of the League of Nations our mobile columns under General Ajo"[19](Ajo being the lead dog of the 'blacks' dog team). Glen later found out that the telegram had caused a little consternation in Italy because of the mention of an armoured column under a general. The other incident related to the ionosphere equipment, which Glen found out was more secret than he had appreciated. He had shown the equipment proudly to hunting ship the crew and two German guests of a Norwegian hunting ship that had come to their base towards the end of the expedition and was later told off by the Admiralty who thought that the Germans were spies, who were, however, looking for prospective fuel dumps and safe anchorages rather than evidence of radio wave research. This incident was a precursor of the way in which Spitsbergen would become important strategically in the coming conflict.

Yugoslavia 1940
Glen's exploits in Spitsbergen had brought him to the attention of the Naval Intelligence Division and in 1938 he joined the RNVR. From May 1939 he worked as a meteorologist for Admiral John Edgel. Glen told an amusing story about his incompetence as a meteorologist

16   Glen, *Under the Pole Star*, p.247.
17   *The Times*, 1st October 1937.
18   A. Glen, *Footholds against the Whirlwind* (London, 1975), p.39.
19   Ibid., p.37.

in which he forecast a starlit night with confidence only for twenty-four hours of thunderstorms to arrive. He thought that this resulted in his transfer to naval intelligence but it is probable that his pre-war record had gone before him. He was interviewed by Admiral John Godfrey and told he was to be sent to Belgrade. After some initial confusion, when Glen was under the impression that Belgrade was in Romania, he was directed to swot up on Yugoslavia and Romania. The admiral told him that "the Danube is our special interest and both countries may be key."[20] The interest in the Danube lay in the desire to stop the Germans using the river as a route to supply vital raw materials in the area, such as the oil at Ploesti, up the river to Germany.

At the time Glen arrived in Belgrade, in January 1940, the major Western European influences on the country were traditionally French and British. Germany was aware of the importance of the Balkan countries to its supply lines and according to Glen "had courted Yugoslavia with patience and diplomacy throughout most of the 1930s."[21]After the fall of France, opinion in Yugoslavia swung more to the British, but aware of Germany's military power, she had maintained neutrality, which by the end of 1940 seemed to be more favourably biased towards Germany. Glen's first impressions on arriving at Belgrade seem to have been ones of enjoying the vibrant cafe and social life: "I was rather left to my own resources, partying most nights with the Americans, Belgians, Greeks and my new Yugoslav friends. It was a bit bewildering as to what my own duties were and it was all rather heady stuff." [22] After settling in a flat with Julian Amery, assistant press attaché, however, he settled down to learn as much as he could about the complicated political, religious and ethnic issues which were important in the country which only been a united entity since 1919. Glen described how after getting out and about in Yugoslavia and meeting people in weddings and family gatherings, that it was the Serbs who won his allegiance: "It was the Serbs who seemed to posses the virtues of hard hill folk whom by nature I admire so much."[23] The Serbian Peasant Party was also felt to offer the best chance of resistance under possible future German occupation. Glen in this period met and fell in love with Zorica, a Yugoslav woman who was married to a Belgium and had returned to Yugoslavia via Spain when Belgium was invaded.

The British Government's attitude to Yugoslavia throughout much of 1940 was to encourage its neutrality in order to prevent what historian Sue Onslow described as "a premature explosion in the country".[24] However, according to Onslow this policy began to shift from November, as Britain became worried about growing German pressure on Yugoslavia to join the Axis powers. Meanwhile, the SOE men in Belgrade were making links and providing intelligence from government and other political parties in the country. Reports came from the legation which drew on up to ten separate sources of information.[25] Glen worked hard at establishing links with the Serbian Peasants' Party and its leader and deputy, Milan Gavrilovic and Milos Tupanjanin. He was in at least daily contact with Tupanjanin and in frequent contact with many leading politicians in the Serbian Peasant

20   Alexander Glen and Leighton Bowen, *Target Danube: A river not quite too far* (Lewes, 2002), p.5.
21   Ibid., p.8.
22   Ibid., p.35.
23   Alexander Glen, *Footholds Against a Whirlwind*, p.54.
24   Susan Onslow, 'Britain and the Belgrade Coup of 27th March 1941 revisited", *Electronic Journal of International History,* Institute of Historical Research, University of London, 2005, p.9.
25   TNA HS5 912, 'Report drawn up by Lt Glen on his relations with Yugo-Slavs', 17th November 1941.

Party.

In a report written by Glen on his return to London he emphasised the links he had been able to establish:

> This paper is based on fairly close and continuous personal contact with the leaders of the different Yugoslav Leaders. From July 1940 until April 1941 I was in at least daily contact with Milos Tupanjanin, deputy leader of the Agrarian Party and in frequent touch with many other leading members of the party, Dr Mila Cavrilovic, leader of the party and now minister in Moscow. I also now possess the confidence of the radicals and Dr Groll, Baka Viacic and Dr Kenesvic of the Democrats. I would also add that that while in Belgrade I had in my capacity of Assistant Naval Attaché, a close liaison with the general staff. I met a considerable number of Yugoslav army officers and used to see fairly frequently Major Milhailovic and Colonel Vasic, who are now leading the Serbian and Bosnian guerrillas at the present time.[26]

He arranged for the Serbian Peasant Party to be subsidised. At the same time links with the Slovenes were resulting in minor acts of sabotage to railway stock travelling to Germany. The leader of the Croatian Peasant Party was also a friend of Glen who was able to arrange that this party received a small subsidy from January 1941.

Glen described the feeling in Belgrade at New Year 1941: "It was clear that the crunch could no longer be delayed". On 25th March Prince Paul signed the tripartite pact which aligned Yugoslavia, with the Axis powers. Germany gained full transit right for the army and supplies for Germany. Yugoslavia had avoided invasion. This was only a temporary reprieve, however, as in Belgrade there was immediate reaction to these events. Glen described it:

> In Belgrade as in Serbia there was public uproar. 'No pact, better war' was the chant around the solidly packed streets with young and old, men and women clamouring that national honour and Serb integrity came first, that death was preferable to dishonour.[27]

On 27th March a group of young army officers with support from Serbian army units and the Yugoslav air force carried out a *coup d'état*, arresting Price Paul and setting up a government under General Simovic. The extent to which the British representatives in Belgrade were responsible for the coup has been the source of much discussion by historians. Churchill declared "Yugoslavia has found its soul" and Dalton, head of the newly formed SOE, was congratulated. Onslow thinks that "it was a much needed fillip to the 'upstart' service – SOE."[28] She also believes that at least one of the major players in the coup was in regular contact with SOE representatives. Glen thought that the coup would have gone ahead without the British encouragement given:

> In Serbia the coup represented the will of most. It was a Yugoslav – more accurately Serbian – occasion, a brave if reckless move, in the tradition of people who place

---

26   Ibid.
27   Glen with Bowen, *Target Danube*, p.58.
28   S. Onslow, 'Britain and the Belgrade Coup of 27th March 1941 revisited', p.2.

honour above all else. One which should be remembered as such and not forgotten.[29]

On 6th April Germany launched Operation Punishment and began bombing Belgrade prior to an invasion.

On 4th April Glen had been transferred officially from his role as Naval attaché to the SO2 section of SOE, probably with the anticipation of him working behind enemy lines in event of a German invasion. Glen, with the help of Zorica as interpreter, spent the days leading up to the bombardment driving around Belgrade picking up opinions on the coup and talking to as wide a variety of people of all ages as possible. The atmosphere was one of pride and joy, tempered by the realisation that war was probably inevitable. On the morning of 6th April Glen's instructions were to take Hugh Seton Watson, of the British Foreign Office and SOE, and to try to get Tupanjanin and his son, along with Alexi Gavrilovic, the son of the Yugoslav minister in Moscow, out of Belgrade to Zornick. It was believed that the Government GHQ was to be established there. Seton Watson, Glen and Zorica spent the day collecting the explosives which had been hidden in various safe houses and taking them to be hidden in the swimming pool of a country house outside Belgrade. Tupanjanin's party was ready to leave at nightfall and Glen had been instructed to keep in contact with the Yugoslav Government or the General Staff, but events had moved quickly and as Glen put it "into effective rout and total confusion". The party decided to drive westwards toward Kotor, which involved a journey over the mountains through Sarajevo. The conditions were cold and icy and Glen's car ended up resting on a tree over a cliff with a thousand foot drop below. They were rescued by a peasant with an ox who spoke prefect English, having just arrived back in the country from Manchester. They all piled into the other car and finding the HQ at Sarajevo disintegrating, pushed on for the coast and Mostar. On the outskirts of the town they found that Croat troops had mutinied, and were taking advantage of the confusion to stake their claim to their own country.

Glen realised that the leader of the Serbian Peasant Party and two English officers were unlikely to fare well in custody of the Croats and the party continued through Mostar, only avoiding road blocks by being directed up a mountain side road by a sympathetic Croat officer. Glen described the scene. "He cannot have failed to recognise Tupanjanin, while I was in RNVR uniform and the car had a CD Belgrade number plate. He paused and said very quietly in Serbo-Croat, 'There is a little trouble here. A little way ahead you will find a rough track up to the hills. Take it – it will be better." Glen had no idea why this Croat officer had saved their lives, but did, as he put it "see that this was not just cloaks and daggers, to understand that this was not only the defeat of a Yugoslav army, but the break-up of a country, treachery and betrayal alongside earlier heroism and great courage."[30]

Luckily Glen's party were captured by the Italians and eventually, along with a selection of diplomatic refugees, Yugoslav politicians and some elderly nurses, were evacuated by Sunderland sea plane. Then, after a stay of two months in Chianciano, they were designated as "hostages to be returned to London."[31] Glen thought that this was possibly to gain some advantage if the war did not go Italy's way. Glen's report on his view of the situation in Yugoslavia in 1941 ends with these observations:

---

29   Glen with Bowen, *Target Danube,* p.60.
30   Ibid., p.65.
31   Glen, *Footholds Against A Whirlwind,* p.73.

I have tried to give in this paper a description of some of the elements in Yugoslavia which I have been able to see at first hand. There may be gaps but this record may contribute to a better understanding of the present problems. It is to be hoped that Yugoslavia will again be inclusive of Croatia, Slovenia and Serbia and that there may be greater wisdom on the part of all three in building afresh.[32]

In view of the subsequent support of the British for Tito and the Communist partisans rather than Mihailovic and the Serbian Peasant Party, and the consequent Communist Government post-war, the closing sentence of his report seems almost prophetic: "Our role seems to be to ensure that the foundations are sound and in this work let us not again make the mistake, in seeking to win over and love our enemies or appearing to hate our friends."[33]

Glen seems to have played a useful role in Yugoslavia in 1940/41 making and maintaining contacts with the Yugoslav politicians and army leaders. His exploits in escaping Belgrade after Operation Punishment secured the safety of key figures such as Tupanjanin along with his son and Gavrilovic's son. In his report he made it clear that he considered the information he had been able to bring out of much use to the Allied cause. He gave an analysis of each member of the Yugoslav Government in exile, their strength and weaknesses:

I can therefore claim some knowledge and understandings of how the personnel and actions of the Yugoslav government in London are likely to be regarded in the parts of the country which are still withstanding the Axis and how the policy of the British Government towards the different problems of Yugoslavia is likely to be interpreted.[34]

That Glen's work in Yugoslavia was considered important is confirmed by a letter in the National Archives from SOE to Admiral Godfrey at naval intelligence. The letter is unsigned but expresses appreciation at Glen's role:

The above officer, while serving as Assistant Naval Attaché in Belgrade was, over a period of a year, from April 1940, and with your generous permission, of considerable assistance to SO2. As from the 3rd of April he was transferred to SO2 and from that date and his arrival in Madrid on the 13th June, was under my direct Command. I would like to place on record that during this period he carried out his duties in an exemplary manner and contributed in no small degree to such successes as this organisation was able to achieve in Yugoslavia. I should also mention that from the 6th April he carried out to my entire satisfaction important work at considerable personal risk.[35]

After Glen had arrived back in London, however, a flurry of correspondence in his service record pointed to some concern with the fact that Zorica had accompanied him. A letter in his records detailed the suspicions that Zorica and by implication, Glen, came under:

---

32   TNA HS 5/912.
33   Ibid.
34   Ibid.
35   TNA HS 9/590/3.

Nothing is known to the detriment of this man. In August 1942 he was engaged to be married to the Baroness Zora Cartuvels de Collaert, Yugoslav by birth who became Belgium by marriage to an official in the Belgium foreign office. Her stepfather was Chef de Protocol at the Ministry of Foreign Affairs at Belgrade.

The letter recounted how Zorica had come under suspicion while with Glen in Lisbon, on the way to returning to London. "British passport control was under the impression that he had disclosed to her all he knew." On the couple's return to London Zorica was interrogated. It was soon accepted that Glen had not given her any information nor had she been approached by Germans or Italians for information from Glen. Despite the interrogators commenting on her possibly slightly pro-Italian attitude, she was released. "Our final conclusion was that there was nothing on which to suspect the Baroness of anti-British actions and she was subsequently released."[36]

It was not long before Glen was being recruited for the Spitsbergen operations and he was not to return to the Balkans until 1944.

Operation Gauntlet and Operation Fritham

In August 1941 Glen was in a position to use the knowledge of Spitsbergen he had acquired on his two expeditions and his awareness of the importance of meteorological reports to make a significant contribution to what he called " this curious special war"[37], the events of which were to unfold in 1941 and 1942.

By the autumn of 1940, after the surrender of Norway to Germany in June, both German and Allied planners had come to realise that they needed control of the North Atlantic. Germany needed free access to the Atlantic Ocean through the North Sea and the Allies had to keep open supply routes to America. After Germany had invaded Russia, in June 1941, it was essential to ensure convoys got through to Russia, the new ally. As both sides were heavily dependent on meteorological reports on the northern Atlantic Ocean and ice conditions there, up to date knowledge of ice condition in Barents Sea was essential for planning convoys. It was particularly essential to the Allies to have information on the state of the ice between the North Cape of Norway and the South Cape of Spitsbergen, only 350 miles apart, so that convoys could be routed as far away from German airbases in Norway as possible. Germany needed to know when bad weather was expected to help shield the convoys leaving from the Scandinavian ports. The extent of the arctic ice pack is never constant and changes not only from year to year, extending further south in a bad ice year, but from month to month. The delivery of long-range Catalina aircraft made reconnaissance of the North Atlantic routes more feasible. Checking on ice conditions was not the only reason for the reconnaissance flights. Spitsbergen had become more strategically important in 1942 for a number of reasons. There was a possibility that convoys could use the sheltered fjords on the west coast of Spitsbergen to refuel in summer months and it was also a consideration that if the islands fell under German occupation, that the Luftwaffe could use them as a base to attack the convoys.

The Norwegian and Russian coal miners on Spitsbergen had created settlements at Longyearbyen and Barentsberg, and in the inter-war years had a population of about 3,000.

---

36 TNA HS 9/590/3.
37 A. Glen and F. Selinger, 'Arctic Meteorological operations and counter operations during World War', *Polar Record* Vol.21, 1983.

Destruction of the wireless station at Barentsberg. (Hutchinson's *Pictorial history of the War*)

Norway, by the terms of an international treaty of 1920, had sovereignty of the archipelago, but rights of settlers, like the Russian miners, were respected. The significant coal output of the mines, 500,000 tons, had been continuing to sail to Norway as usual despite the war and in August 1941 Operation Gauntlet had been mounted to evacuate Norwegian and Russian miners from Longyearbyen and Barentsberg and to deny the Germans use of the coal.

Under the command of Rear Admiral Vian, 'Force 3', consisting of the cruisers *Nigeria* and *Aurora*, supported by the destroyers *Icarus, Anthony* and *Antelope,* escorted the passenger liner *The Empress of Canada* to Spitsbergen and evacuated the Russian and Norwegian miners and their families. The operation was manned by 650 troops, consisting mainly of Canadian forces and some British sappers. Also on board were Glen and Lieutenant-Colonel A.S.T 'Dan' Godfrey, a veteran of the 1933 British Trans-Greenland expedition, who had also been on the expedition to Spitsbergen with Glen in 1935. They were to lend their arctic expertise to the enterprise. The Norwegian wireless operators kept up a string of false weather reports coming from the island, which convinced the Germans that the weather was foul over Spitsbergen and consequently bought time for the operation to be carried out.

The operation removed and destroyed most of the vital equipment at the mines and the coal dumps were set on fire. Before Force 3 left Spitsbergen both the director of the Norwegian mining company, Store Norske, Einar Sverdrup and Glen made representations to Brigadier Potts, the Canadian commander, and Admiral Vian, that a small force should be left on the island. Their argument was that this would discourage the Germans from landing and setting up Luftwaffe bases to attack the convoys. This would have allowed Glen and Godfrey to use their arctic survival skills. Glen, after all, had overwintered under the ice cap on North East Land, part of the Svalbard Archipelago. Admiral Vian did not

Norwegian inhabitants of Spitsbergen wait to be evacuated.
(Hutchinson's *Pictorial history of the War*)

Aerial view of the destruction of the coalfields on Spitsbergen. (TNA ADM199/730)

consider that the Germans would use the island because of problems with twenty-four hour daylight, leaving airstrips more vulnerable to discovery and attack. Glen commented years later "I did not think that the senior naval or the senior military commanders seemed to appreciate the strategic importance of Svalbard at this stage." He continued:

> I have wondered since at how such a party we would have fared. What we could not know was that its range would have had to cover all of Svalbard as the enemy could establish weather stations anywhere ... A small compact party might have had a considerable effect on a hit and run basis.[38]

However, the force returned to Britain on 3rd September and the evacuation of Spitsbergen was declared a success.

In the opinion of Ernest Schofield, navigator on the Catalina aeroplane that did most of the reconnaissance flights to Spitsbergen, the Germans did not want to use it as a base, considering that their air bases in Norway were sufficient. F. Selinger, involved in German counter-intelligence during the war, makes it clear that the reason Spitsbergen was so valuable to the Germans was the possibility of setting up weather stations. This is borne out by the fact that no time was lost by both the Luftwaffe and Kriegsmarine in setting up weather stations on the islands as soon as Force 3, Operation Gauntlet, had gone. A Luftwaffe meteorological station, codenamed Banso, was established in late September in Advent Bay. Its presence there was discovered by radio intercepts at Bletchley Park and three mine sweepers were sent to destroy it. The personnel of the station quickly evacuated by air, only to return as soon as the minesweepers had left. Ironically, much of the organisation and planning of the Banso station was done by Dr Erich Etienne, who had been on a Oxford University expedition to Greenland in 1936.

In the spring of 1942, responding to increasing Norwegian pressure to return to Spitsbergen to prevent deterioration of the abandoned mines in the spring thaw, and bearing in mind the need for regular accurate meteorological information of help the Atlantic Russian convoys, it was decided to send a small force to reoccupy the islands. On 4th April 1942 a Catalina aircraft made one of a series of reconnaissance flights from the air base at Sullom Voe over the Svalbard Archipelago. Their task was to gauge the position and extent of the sea ice between Jan Meyen Island and Spitsbergen, and to find out if there were any enemy forces on the island. Glen and Sverdrup were on board, as this flight was in preparation for an operation they were both to be involved in, the purpose of which was to deny the use of the islands to the enemy and to make safe the Norwegian and Russian mines which had been evacuated the previous August in Operation Gauntlet. Over Ice Fjord, the reconnaissance flight was lucky enough to have bright sunshine and the remains of the burning coal dumps at Barentsberg could be clearly seen. Unfortunately they did not fly up Advent Valley as far as Banso, and so missed seeing the enemy weather station that was established there. There had however been some evidence that the Germans were actively pursuing meteorological operations in the Arctic and that there might be a base on Spitsbergen. This information had been obtained from a stolen German briefcase and the information smuggled out of Sweden by Andrew Croft, who was assistant military attaché at the time.[39]

---

38   Ibid.
39   Andrew Croft, typescript memoir dated January 1984, Croft papers.

The operation was codenamed Operation Fritham. As far back as October 1941 Churchill had expressed his opinion on the evacuation of Spitsbergen: "No Germans can be allowed on Spitsbergen, I don't know why we cleared out. Anyhow, intruders should be destroyed."[40] At a meeting on 25th March the joint planning staff met to discuss the pros and con of invading Spitsbergen. Three justifications were given for the reoccupation:

1. It was considered that if the use of the islands was not denied to Germany that they would use them as a base to use for attack on the Allied convoys to Russia.
2. To prevent the enemy establishing meteorological stations which would be of great use to them.
3. To reopen the mines and obtain coal.
4. The committee were also aware of the use to which the Allies could put the island to themselves, as a base for Coastal Command aircraft to hunt down hostile submarines and surface vessels threatening the convoys and to obtain their own meteorological information.

The operation, lead by Sverdrup, consisted of sixty Norwegian troops accompanied by three British liaison officers, Sandy Glen, Dan Godfrey and A.B. Whatman, who had also been on the 1935/6 Spitsbergen expedition. They were to use two Norwegian ships, an icebreaker *Isbjorn* and an old ex-sealer, *Selis*. They set sail from Greenock on 30th April 1942. The reconnaissance flight that Glen had been part of on 4th April, had failed to spot evidence of the weather station at Banso despite the good weather conditions. A reconnaissance flight in a Catalina piloted by Flight Lieutenant Tim Healy set out on 3rd May with Sandy Glen and Dan Godfrey on board to check on ice conditions and to see if there were any signs of German activity, as intercepted radio signals had indicted an base on Spitsbergen. Unfortunately weather conditions made the flight inconclusive and the possible landing of Godfrey and Glen at Cape Linne to await Operation Fritham was abandoned. Glen and Godfrey were flown to Akureyri in Iceland to join the seaborne operation. While the ships were making their way to Spitsbergen, on 12th May, Flight Lieutenant Poitier and his crew flew another reconnaissance over Spitsbergen and came back with some alarming information. They had been flying up Ice Fjord and had seen a Heinkel 111 on the ice. They had attacked and prevented it from taking off in pursuit of them and then returned to give warning of the German presence on the islands to Operation Fritham. The Admiralty sent an urgent message to the *Isbjorn*, which was never received, probably, according to Glen, because of a magnetic storm[41], also possibly because of the antiquated radio equipment on board, and the operation continued, oblivious to the danger. It is unknown what decision Einar Sverdrup would have made if the message had got through, but taking into account his determination to return to Spitsbergen to deal with the deserted mines, it is likely that the operation would have continued regardless.

The *Selis* and the *Isbjorn* arrived at 20.00 hours on 13th May. Because of thick ice in Ice Fjord, they could not penetrate Advent Bay and turned in towards Green Harbour, near the settlement at Barentsberg. They were unable to get near the shore and realised that a long channel would have to be cut towards the harbour by the icebreaker. Two parties were sent off to reconnoitre. The first was to go to over the ice into Barentsberg and another,

---

40   TNA WO106/1996.
41   A. Glen, *Footholds against a Whirlwind* (London, 1975), p.101.

consisting of Glen and Whatman, skied over to the old wireless base at Cape Linne. Glen described his feelings:

> It was good to be back in the Arctic. As the ski slid through the snow we talked contentedly of many things, old days and new ones two ... it was a perfect Spitsbergen day. No cloud, temperature about 0° Fahrenheit and conditions ideal.[42]

On their return to the ship they found that Dan Godfrey had been disagreeing with Einar Sverdrup's decision not to offload men and supplies by sledge to the shore, but to continue the ice breaking operation and to take the ships straight to the jetty to unload. Godfrey was the only experienced professional soldier in the party, and recognising the vulnerability of the ships in the ice, wanted to get everyone ashore as soon as possible. At 5.00 hours on 14th May a Ju 88 flew over and probably observed them. Glen later related to Ernest Schofield, the navigator of a reconnaissance Catalina involved in the operation, how angry Godfrey had been. Schofield commented: "Godfrey forecast accurately what would happen when the German aircraft returned to Norway. The two ships, locked in ice would become sitting ducks for enemy bombers."[43] At 20.00 hours the confirmation of this appeared in the form of four Focke Wulf Condors over Green Harbour. The *Selis* and *Isbjorn* were, after fifteen hours of icebreaking, not yet at the harbour. The attack lasted half an hour and at the end of that time the *Isbjorn* had been sunk and the *Selis* was on fire. Some men were thrown onto the ice by the blast and Glen described what happened to him:

> Einar Sverdrup, Daniel Godfrey and I were standing together on the bridge of the *Isbjorn,* both Oerlikons were firing, the next thing I remember is lying on the ice with a few yards away a great hole of black water into which the *Isbjorn* had disintegrated.[44]

Whatman thought that Godfrey and Sverdrup had been dragged down the stairway by the blast and had gone down with the ship. The survivors quickly scattered and made their way to the shore, about twenty-nine minutes away over the ice. Glen recounted later how he had lost his spectacles with the initial blast but that they were blown back to him by the blast of one of the next bombs. Thirteen men had been killed and nine wounded, of whom two subsequently died. The sixty that were left had lost their leader, their supplies and all their equipment. In their favour, however, was the fact that all the men were all skilled in arctic life and conditions.

At Barentsberg the accommodation was still habitable and a certain amount of supplies were found, including the frozen carcasses of the pigs slaughtered during the evacuation of the settlement the previous August. German aeroplanes returned over the next days and there was further bombing and strafing. The survivors, however, lay low and there were no further casualties. Command of the operation was now assumed by Lieutenant Ove Lund, Sverdrup's second-in-command and he decided to send out two parties to gauge the strength of the Germans on the island, as the intervals between departure and return of the enemy aircraft suggested that there might be German units in Advent Bay and King's

42   Ibid., p.106.
43   E. Schofield and R. Conyers Nesbit, *Arctic Airmen: The RAF in Spitsbergen and North Russia 1942* (London, 1987), p.105.
44   Ibid., p.102.

Bay. Glen led parties travelling from hut to hut, disguised with a motley assortment of white camouflage such as bed sheets and doctors' coats. Observation of the Banso airstrip and weather stations caused them to overestimate the strength of the force there, but the reconnaissance parties returned to Barentsberg satisfied that the Germans did not possess a strong enough garrison to attack the survivors' party overland. Glenn was very appreciative of the calibre of the men who made up the party of survivors: "I retain the highest respect for the Norwegian soldiers, so recently coal miners, who held their place in Svalbard in those lonely months of 1942, in a situation which could have well broken professional soldiers."[45]

It was expected that eventually a search party would respond to the fact that nothing had been heard from Operation Fritham. On 25th May a Catalina was sighted and the preparations that Glen had put into readiness to communicate with a rescue flight were put into operation. Glen, Whatman and Skribaland, a Norwegian wireless operator, waited in a hut at the entrance to Green Harbour with an Aldis lamp. Glenn had used his experience of being on the previous Catalina flights, and a conversation with Tim Healy prior to setting out, to guess where the most likely place would be for the rescue flight to begin looking for signals from survivors.

Catalina P for Peter, manned by Tim Healy and his crew, had been given instructions to search for the missing ships in the area of Ice Fjord and Barentsberg. Messages intercepted at Bletchley Park had shown that two ships had been sunk in the area, but Healy and his crew were unaware of this when they set out on 25th May to find out what had happened to the party. According to Schofield, on arrival over Spitsbergen there were jokes about what to expect: "If he stands to attention and salutes, he'll be one of us, if he waves to us he'll be Norwegian, if he shoots at us he'll be German, if he has snow on his boots he'll be Russian."[46] The flight set out, and after reconnoitring Advent Bay and Longyearbyen, noting the wreckage of a Heinkel 111, returned via Green Harbour and saw the long lead cut in the ice with a hole at its end. The signal from Tim Healy to 18 Group on his return to Sullom Voe describes what happened next:

> At 0035 coasted to Advent Bay. Reached at 0100. Saw wreckage of the HE 111 Attacked by N/210 on 12th May obviously abandoned ... At 0118 an Aldis lamp flashed from the entrance to the fjord position 78° 05° North, 14 10° East ... first flashed 'Fritham' then passed message "Ships sunk. Nothing saved. Survivors here. Germans Advent Bay ... help essential".

P2/10 responded: "Recco when weather ok. Will organise help. God bless."[47] During the next ten days, a further four flights were made by Healy and his crew to resupply the survivors and to rescue the wounded. The flight on 28th May carried Tommy guns, ammunition, medical supplies and morale boosting items such as cigarettes, jam and chocolate. In order for the already overburdened Catalina to get to Spitsbergen with the supplies and with enough petrol, the aircraft had to be stripped down to the bare minimum of weight including crew parachutes and bunks. The first trip dropped the supplies and attempted to ascertain, by Aldis lamp, the needs of the survivors and advice on how and

---

45   A. Glen and F. Selinger, 'Arctic Meteorological operations and counter operations during World War', *Polar Record* Vol. 21, 1983.
46   Ibid.
47   TNA WO106/1996.

where to land to pick up wounded. On the flight which took off on 6th June the Catalina was at last able to land in open water at the entrance to Green Harbour. A close watch was kept for enemy aircraft, and the Catalina was prepared to take off in the space of a few minutes, leaving the shore party. No attack came, however and a detailed report from Sandy Glen, and six of the wounded, were taken back to Sullom Voe. Sandy Glen was most impressed by the achievement of Tim Healy and his crew in flying four sorties, each of twenty-four hours, in bad weather conditions and at risk of enemy attack. Tim Healy was awarded the DSO, and in Glen's opinion "It is no overstatement to say that it is entirely as the result the efforts of Tim Healy and his aircrew that the garrison in Spitsbergen was once again place in an offensive position."[48]

By 14th June, the British and Norwegian planners were ceasing to regard Operation Fritham as a complete disaster and wanted Glen home to discuss the ideas that the joint planning committee were having about sending a force to set up a Norwegian garrison on Spitsbergen. Glen was picked up on 15th June and went back to London to discuss plans for what was to become Operation Gearbox. The cruiser *Manchester* and the destroyer *Eclipse* were to sail to Spitsbergen to reinforce the garrison. Prior to this, Glen and another old Arctic explorer friend, Andrew Croft, who had been temporarily seconded from his posting as naval attaché in Sweden, were to accompany Tim Healy on a reconnaissance flight flying from Akureyri in Greenland. The aim of this flight was to map the southern limits of the drift ice between Iceland and Spitsbergen so that the Atlantic convoys could chose the most northerly route possible to avoid the German aircraft based at airfields in Northern Norway. They were then landed at Barentsberg to take much needed supplies to the small force that was still maintaining a presence on the Archipelago there and to prepare for the main force of Operation Gearbox. Croft enjoyed the three days spent flying with Glen, piloted by Squadron Leader Tim Healy: " To see Greenland again gave me intense pleasure ... We completed our task in a few days .., on one occasion remaining airborne for as long as twenty seven hours."

Operation Gearbox landed at Barentsberg at 12.30 hrs on 2nd July and took six hours to take ashore 116 tons of equipment and land fifty troops to become the garrison force. Ernest Schofield said of the operation: "By brilliant planning, organisation and performance, the operation had been completed successfully. Barentsberg had been reinforced without the enemy being any the wiser."[49] Meanwhile the Germans at Banso weather station were making plans to abandon their manned station, leaving in position a remote weather machine, the Krote. When the *Manchester* moved round to Advent Bay the Germans had departed, leaving in a great hurry. Although the German and Allied forces had been only a small distance apart on the island all winter, the conditions had made it impossible for each to ascertain each other's strength. They had no armed land confrontation, the Germans contenting themselves with bombing the survivors at Barentsberg. Both the Allies and the Germans achieved, in some ways, their objectives. The Norwegians had re-established sovereignty of the Svalbard Archipelago and maintained a presence there until the end of the war, but the Germans also maintained manned and automatic weather stations in Spitsbergen until 1945.

The most interesting elements of the Spitsbergen operations were the way in which men of vast arctic experience like Glen and Godfrey were able to use their peacetime skills

---

48   Glen, *Footholds against a Whirlwind*, p.106.
49   E. Schofield and R. Conyers Nesbit, *Arctic Airmen* (London, 2005), p.164.

in time of war, and the development of the ability of the RAF in using Catalinas to increase their range and competence in arctic flying. It is also interesting to speculate what would have happened if Spitsbergen had been permanently evacuated and the Germans allowed to establish a greater presence there.

Albania and Yugoslavia 1944-45

A year after the break-up of Yugoslavia two main resistance groups achieved dominance in a complicated situation in the country, with civil war between Serbs and Croats, exacerbated by the actions of the fascist regime of the Ustache in Croatia. The Communist partisans were under the leadership of Tito and the Chetniks under the leadership of Mihailovic. By 1943 the partisans had become an increasingly effective force and were tying down twenty-three divisions of German and Italian troops in Yugoslavia. Glen stressed that this was largely without foreign help and that the partisans had achieved this position on their own, despite civil and religious war, and without supply of weapons from outside. It was only in spring 1943 that the first British liaison officer, Captain Deakin, reached Tito's headquarters. With the gaining of control of the southern Italian coast after the surrender of the Italians, the opportunity came to resupply the partisans if areas of the Dalmatian coast could be secured by them.

Glen's assignment was to land on the island of Korucula to rendezvous with Fitzroy Maclean and give him a new transmitter. Landing on the island with the transmitter and a can of peanut butter for Maclean, he was under the impression that the island was still under enemy occupation. After being despatched by an MTB and landing from a dinghy, Glen and his colleague crawled painfully up the beach, keeping under cover. Glen recalled: "We crawled on gallantly until challenged by a Detroit-born partisan guard who asked 'are you guys doing this for dooty? There ain't a German on the Island'"[50]. Glen remained in Albania for the next few months, reconnoitring safe beaches for supplies to land on from Italy. By mid-November the Germans had retaken much of the Dalmatian coast and the partisans retreated. During the window of opportunity, however, over 6,000 tons of weapons and ammunition had been delivered to Yugoslavia.

Glen said of the time spent in Albania that, "as a contribution to the war effort, the value must have been exactly zero".[51] In *Footholds against a Whirlwind* however, he gave an upbeat account of his experiences, including the riotous companionship of Anthony Quayle. The powers that be in Naval Intelligence were also doubtful of the value of Glen's presence in Albania, as a message from Lt. Commander Giles to HQ Special Forces Bari shows: "It is not considered that the present situation in Albania justifies the retention of Lt. Commander Glen DSC, RNVR, as BNLO. His work is mainly concerned with static intelligence which would be equally valuable and more easily obtained in a few months' time when weather improves." The message went on "It has been suggested that Lt. Commander Glen should be sent to Yugoslavia with the object of attaining intelligence on enemy shipping on the Danube ... it seems that detailed reports on the Danube shipping might be of use to the strategic air force in Italy ... Request your approval for Lt. Commander Glen to be withdrawn from Albania to discuss the project."[52]

Glen's last exploit in Albania was to rescue a group of American nurses who had crashed

---

50   Glen, *Footholds against the Whirlwind*, p.147.
51   Ibid., p.152.
52   TNA HS 9/590/3.

in Albania. They had been moved from military mission to military mission across Albania, evading capture and reaching the partisans' sea base. An MTB from Bari came to collect them and Glen, as the only naval officer in Albania, escorted them. When challenged by a flotilla of British destroyers, Glen recounted his reaction: "With the authority of the President of the United States behind us we replied 'Proceeding on most secret duties.'"[53]

When Glen had originally been sent to Yugoslavia in 1940, Admiral Godfrey had told him of the plans to stop the Danube being of use to the Germans, and had told him "cause havoc on the Danube." The efforts of the SOE had some success, with the sabotaging of boats and bribing of experienced pilots away from working on the river, but Glen had had little part to play in this before the coup and invasion. He was now to be plunged into the heart of Allied activities concerning the Danube. The two major preoccupations of the Naval Intelligence Department were the mining of the Danube to deny German access, but also consequently to warn the Russians of the mines when they arrived at the river, and to provide Allied liaison to help them find them and sweep them. Glen was parachuted into Yugoslavia on 28th June 1944. His role was to gather intelligence about the river and to get through to the Russian forces, aided by Tito's partisans, to warn them about the mines and to offer the service a of a minesweeping unit which was standing by under the command of Commander Vladimir Wolfson RNVR. Glen was summoned to see Admiral Cunningham in Naples and told:

> The Danube mining is of the highest importance and we want as much on the spot intelligence as we can get. Soviet Forces will need the use of the river ... We are counting on you to make early contact with the Red Army, get through to their high command, inform them of the mines, of our wish to help and of course find out whether they will accept that help.[54]

Glen and a wireless operator parachuted into partisan lines near Citluk village to be part of the Twilfit mission. Glen commented on the ease of the transport arrangements: "It has always seemed to me that the most civilised method of transport is by parachute. No passports, no customs, on the spot delivery and lots of drink to celebrate."[55] They were welcomed and whisked to bed within three hours of leaving Brindisi. Glen and his wireless operator, Sergeant Turner, joined the 23rd Partisan Brigade and worked their way north to the Danube with them. They received information about the success of the mining of the Danube which was second- or third-hand but turned out to be mainly accurate. During July and August they moved with the brigade, marching by night and resting by day. It was at this period the Glen had his spectacles eaten by a pig, and after several days of marching nearly blind, had a replacement pair parachuted in, much to the annoyance of the partisans, who were expecting a supply drop. They were joined by a steady stream of recruits to the partisan movement, who Glen described as being from every age, gender and background. By the time the Dolphin Mission, led by Captain Dickie Franks, arrived in Yugoslavia to join Glen on 15th September, their sabotage plans had been overtaken by events, in that the mining operations had been proven successful. However their other main objective, that of supplying reliable information about the river, was carried out very well. Glen had

---

53   A. Glen with L. Bowen, *Target Danube*, p.71.
54   Ibid., p.72.
55   Glen, *Footholds against a Whirlwind*, p.160.

requested, from the field, the inclusion in the Dolphin Mission of former Danube pilots Ralf Navratil and Jaroslav Vrana, who were now serving in the British armed forces, as Sub Lt. Ralph Turpin and Flying Officer Peter Bing. Their local knowledge and linguistic skills would be invaluable. The fourth member of the Dolphin Mission was Sgt. Roberts, experienced in behind the lines work, a wireless operator and a linguist.

Glen and Turner now joined the Dolphin mission and left the partisans they were with to join the 25th Partisan Brigade. Their main aim was to inform the Red Army about the mined area of the Danube. By the end of August they were near the Red Army and heard that a partisan delegation was to set out to make contact with the advancing Russian troops. Glen and Dickie Franks asked to go along but were not allowed. Glen recalled: "We were told firmly but politely that this sacred communist occasion could not be sullied by the presence of two communist lackeys."[56] It was just as well, as this delegation was imprisoned by the Russians.

On the morning of 26th September Glen and Franks discovered an abandoned German motorbike and sidecar. Five of them managed to get on the motorbike and sidecar and went haring down a road to run suddenly into a road block which was manned not by Germans but by Russians. Luckily, as they were on a German vehicle, it appeared that the partisans had warned the Russians not to fire on partisans or "lunatic Brits". Glen remembered the eventual meeting with Russian troops was emotional: "We threw ourselves into each other's arms, caps in the air, tears streaming down our cheeks". He believed that it was the first meeting of forces fighting Germany from the East and West, and writing in 1975 had no reason to doubt this.[57] They were quickly taken to the Russian battalion HQ in Klokosevac where they found the commanding officer, Colonel Sucharnikov. The urgency of their mission was established and a promise of transport given, but then it was time to celebrate. A signal was sent to Admiral Cunningham and he sent a personal reply which was the cause of further celebrations which went on all day. Glen remembered: "even now, almost sixty years later I remember the exaltation we shared that day."[58]

The journey to the Russian HQ was complicated by the fact that German troops were regrouping and still in the area. The *troikas* they were travelling in came under attack and Glen and his party escaped by following a Russian sergeant down a ravine with heavy pursuing fire. The sergeant then identified heavy gunfire in the near distance as Russian and guided Glen and the others back to the Russian lines. Bing was captured by Chetniks in German uniform but managed to escape and rejoin the party at Turnu Severin.[59] Only when he had escorted them across the River Danube by ferry to the divisional headquarters at Turnu Severin did the Russian sergeant leave them.

The first few days at Turnu Severin were anxious ones for the group. As Dickie Franks said, "If a bunch of ruffians claiming to be Russians without papers landed on a British HQ, I bet no one could understand them and they would be shot."[60] One evening, Franks overheard a conversation which he took to mean that their Russian 'minders' were planning to divide up their possessions. However they were allowed limited freedom of movement and Bing and Turpin met up with some old Danube workmates who gave them valuable

56   Glen, *Footholds*, p. 67.
57   Ibid., p.168.
58   Glen with Bowen, *Target Danube*, p.87.
59   TNA ADM/1/6849, Report on the activities of the Dolphin mission to the Danube.
60   Glen with Bowen, *Target Danube*, p.83.

evidence as to the success of the mining of the river.[61] It was then decided by the Russian command that Glen's group was to be moved to Vidin. On the journey the mission had opportunity to observe further damage to the shipping on the Danube. At Prahova the river had been blocked by four warships and four or five barges sunk in a line across the river.[62] At Bregova, Glen was asked to address a special guard of honour of 100 Red Army soldiers. Franks described it as "One of the most peculiar moments of his [Glen's] war." Even though he was speaking through an interrupter he managed to mystify his audience, by among other gaffes, congratulating them on all being Christians". Glen attempted to explain the difficulty: "That was quite an experience among a people whose reactions are rarely quite what they seem." [63]

On arriving at Sofia, Glen reported to General Zeitov, from whom he had a cool reception. Although the Russian command were interested in information on areas extensively mined, they were suspicious of the motivation of the British party. Franks, in his report said: "During discussions with the Soviet Corps HQ and General HQ the impression was very strong that whilst technical assistance would be welcomed by the Red Navy, Soviet preparedness to accept British naval parties would be limited by suspicion of their political intentions."[64] Whilst staying at Sofia Glen had a meeting with an NKVD colonel who gave a chilling assessment of the fate of the returning Soviet troops who had been able to experience life and conditions outside the Soviet Union:

> There are several categories. Most of the men will pass through, loot, rape, enjoy and forget. Then there are those who may be influenced; they will go to re-educational units, two, three or five years should suffice. Then the third category, those who draw conclusions. They will not see the Soviet Union again.[65]

Glen, Franks and the entire Dolphin Mission were ordered to return and be airlifted to Bari on 15th October 1944. Their mission to Yugoslavia had arrived too late to bear fruit in sabotage, but they had found out important information about the extent of the mining operations on the Danube. Franks summed it up in his report.

> It is therefore submitted that the Dolphin party has achieved a twofold result. Firstly it has collected sufficient accurate information to enable departments to assess with fair reliability the effects of the economic disaster sustained by Germany on the Danube over the period of the last six months. Secondly it has been able to appraise the present situation on the river and supply certain details as to the organisation being set in motion there by the Soviet forces, as well as to present some indication of their intentions.[66]

Glen considered that compared with the minelaying on the Danube and the destruction of the Ploesti oilfields, the Twilfit and Dolphin missions were 'pygmies'. However he did

61   ADM1/16849, Report on the activities of the Dolphin mission to the Danube.
62   Ibid.
63   Glen with Bowen, *Target Danube*, p.110.
64   Ibid., section of Frank's report entitled 'General Conclusions'.
65   Glen with Bowen, *Target Danube*, pp.97-98.
66   ADM1/16849, Report on the activities of the Dolphin mission to the Danube.

point out that they were afforded the opportunity to observe at close quarters the Red Army, from generals and assault troops to low quality holding troops, and that there was a certain amount of criticism of Stalin and the Communist Party present. He concluded:

> It was for our seniors, and now for historians, to assess what our two missions achieved or failed to achieve in the context of the Danube. For us it was very simple: an experience which in the richness of events one could ever hope to share.[67]

Glen had experienced much since his first expedition to Spitsbergen. Edward Crankshaw, in his foreword to *Footholds Against a Whirlwind*, considered that Glen's vitality and determination shown in his exploration adventures served him well in the unusual activities he volunteered for in the war. He considered it fortunate that Glen, although "a successful man of action", was both "articulate and contemplative", [68]allowing us to benefit from Glen's stirring accounts of his activities in peace and war.

---

67   Glen with Bowen, *Target Danube*, p.100.
68   Edward Crankshaw in foreword to *Footholds against a Whirlwind*, p.9.

7

Martyn Sherwood

The voyage of the *Tai Mo Shan* 1933-34

In the spring of 1932 five young naval officers at the South China Sea Station decided to return to England on leave by means of an ocean voyage which would take them back to Dartmouth via Japan, the North Pacific, the west coast of America, through the Panama Canal and across the Atlantic. The route was an ambitious one, with its object of taking a small boat against the prevailing winds and covering fresh ground by taking a northerly route via the Aleutian Islands. In applying for leave to do so from the navy they explained that they were eager to collect metrological data and plot winds and currents. Part of their route also lay among uncharted waters near Ganges Island, the existence of which was unproven and they proposed to spend no more than fourteen days looking for it.[1] They were also interested in exploring the archipelago of the Kurile Islands, which lay between the north of Japan and the Kamchatka peninsula. They made the case strongly that as young naval officers the experience would be beneficial to their future naval careers. The voyage already had the potential to be exciting and dangerous, but papers released on the death of R.E.D. Ryder in 1986 led to speculation that the officers had also undertaken to spy on possible Japanese naval positions.[2]

In 1934, Martyn Sherwood, one of the crew members, wrote an account of the voyage. Sherwood had served in the Royal Navy in the Great War and had seen service in the Baltic in 1919 in defence of the White Russians against the Bolsheviks. He was the oldest of the expedition at thirty years old. Although a submarine specialist, just prior to the voyage he was serving on the aircraft carrier *Hermes*. Whilst serving on the *Hermes*, Sherwood was awarded the Lloyd's Medal for Saving Life at Sea. In November 1931, he was involved with other crew members who faced dangerous conditions collecting survivors from the Japanese steamer *Ryujin Maru*, which was wrecked on the Tan Rocks near Foochow, in which nine men were saved. Three officers received the Silver Medal, and six ratings the Bronze Medal. This Lloyd's medal had only been awarded seven times since 1907.[3]

Robert Edward Dudley Ryder, whose papers disclosed another side to the voyage, had attended Cheltenham School and entered the navy in 1925. As a Lieutenant he served in the submarine HMS *Olympus* of the 4th Flotilla in China from 1930 to 1933. He was the only in one of the party to have had experience of ocean racing at the Fastnet and Santander races and was therefore made sailing master and navigator on the voyage. He also had the main input into the design of the yacht. Her designers were Edward Cock, chief manager at the great shipyard, and H.S. Rouse, Vice-Commodore of the Hong Kong Yacht Club. Martyn Sherwood described the *Tai Mo Shan* as "a vessel of exceptional grace and beauty."[4]

---

1   Richard Hopton, *A Reluctant Hero: The Life of Captain Robert Ryder VC* (Barnsley, 2001), p.16.
2   *The Times* 25th August 2007 carried a story examining the evidence from Ryder's papers.
3   Dix Noonan Web, Medals Auction Site. http://www.dnw.co.uk/medals/auctionarchive/viewspecial collections/itemdetail.lasso?itemid=60285. Consulted 15th January 2011.
4   Martyn Sherwood, *The Voyage of the Tai –Mo- Shan* (London, 1935), p.11.

The crew of the *Tai Mo Shan*. (*The Voyage of the Tai Mo Shan*)

The decision to manage without an engine was made on the grounds that it would increase the weight of the vessel too much and also take up too much space. The dimensions of the boat were: "displacement 23½ tons, length 54 feet overall and 42 feet designed waterline. Her draft was 8 ft 5 inches and in ketch rig she had a sail area of 1,040 square feet."[5] Her name translated as "high hat hill" and referred to the highest mountain in Hong Kong.

The crew members consisted of four submarine officers and a Lieutenant Surgeon. Lt. Martyn Sherwood was the cook and member of the starboard watch, the other being Lt. George Salt, who was bo'sun and in charge of the finances. The port watch consisted of Lt. Philip Francis, in charge of wireless communication, and Lt. Surgeon Bertie Ommanney-Davis, ship's doctor. *The Times*, in a review of Sherwood's book, commented on the possibility of there being "too many cooks for the navigation but too few in the galley."[6] Sherwood had thought of this dilemma and before sailing had taken a course in cookery with the Hong Kong and Shanghai Hotel Company, who had responded to his advertisement in *The South China Morning Post* asking for cookery lessons.

The speculation in the clandestine purposes of the voyage has been engendered by the planning notes for the voyage and correspondence discovered in Ryder's papers, which were used in articles in *Classic Boat* and *The Times* in 2007. The article in *Classic Boat* described one of the aims of the voyage as "a search for advance UK and US submarine bases for attacks on the Japanese navy in the Kuriles and the Aleutians." In his planning notes Ryder wrote of the crew's intentions "to produce an intelligence report on all places visited, in particular Ganges Island, if discovered" and their intention to observe "any possibilities advanced base for submarine operations or as a W/T or WF/T station in event

---

5   Ibid., p.10.
6   *The Times*, 26th April 1935.

Ryder the navigator. (*The Voyage of the Tai Mo Shan*)

of hostilities against Japan or between Japan and America."[7] The *Tai Mo Shan* was provided with powerful wireless equipment at the expense of the British Navy, who made sure that Francis was trained to use it, with Sherwood also receiving training as his deputy.[8]

On Wednesday 31st May 1933, the *Tai Mo Shan* was ready and set off for Japanese waters. After initial bouts of sea sickness, the crew settled down to life at sea in the yacht. Sherwood expressed his sense of satisfaction and relaxation.

> Time was our own. we had no masters; clothing was mainly conspicuous by its absence, and there was none to draw attention to the fact that that it was wrong to eat your food out of a bowl with your feet on the table.[9]

The Japanese Government had refused permission for the *Tai Mo Shan* to land on the Kurile Islands and the Commander in Chief had ordered the proposed search for the Ganges Islands to be abandoned due to the risk of typhoons. The *Tai Mo Shan* made her first port of call after five days, averaging 101 miles per day. Their destination was Keelung on the island of Formosa, which was under Japanese control, having been ceded to Japan in 1895 after the first Sino-Japanese War. They were boarded early the next morning by representatives of the Japanese army, navy, customs and medical services. In his account of the voyage Martyn Sherwood says, rather disingenuously in the circumstances, "they seemed rather surprised, when as a result of their enquiries we explained that we were doing the trip solely for pleasure."[10] The intelligence support signed by all the crew and submitted to naval intelligence from the *Tai Mo Shan* on 7th January described how the yacht's arrival in Keelung coincided with a large-scale landing operation by the Japanese navy and also told

---

7   *Classic Boat*, September 2007.
8   Ibid.
9   Sherwood, *Voyage*, p.28.
10   Ibid., p.30.

A heavy sea north of Japan. (*The Voyage of the Tai Mo Shan*)

of their attempt to observe the fortifications at the port.[11]When they arrived at Yokohama, twelve days later, they had an even larger reception party and were again interrogated as to their purpose in going north. This time the crew were able to reassure the Japanese officials who did not speak English, by showing them a natural history text book and explaining that they were a party of botanists. On walks ashore the crew were sometimes tailed by a Japanese police officer. At a brief stop in Nemuro, on the northern coast of the island of Hokkaido, they were once again interrogated and seals (which did not work) were put on their cameras. The crew then set off on the Northern pacific route towards Vancouver, via the Aleutian islands.

Sherwood described how they had decided to pass by the Kurile Islands, a long chain of small islands stretching from Hokkaido to Kamchatka. He described briefly the history of the islands and their ecology, but also warned of the thick fog that was around the islands in the summer months, when the cold current from the Arctic meets a warm current from Japanese waters.

The only hint Sherwood gave of anything unusual about this part of the voyage in his book was his comment as they passed the Kurile Islands: "At this period of our voyage we had a great feeling of suppressed excitement." However, the intelligence report explained that their protracted interrogation at Nemuro made it "obvious that the Japanese has something of a secret nature in the north Kuriles" and that "further evidence of possible fortifications at Paramishir came from Russian vessels who were, it was subsequently learned, captured in the main Kurile Strait". They were able to report that the Kuriles were patrolled by the fishery protection vessel the *Shinkatsu Maru*. This report related how a "nocturnal visit" to Paramishir was considered, but abandoned because of the ever-vigilant presence of the *Shinkatsu Maru*.[12]

---

11   Intelligence report to the Admiralty signed by the crew, Ryder Papers, private collection.
12   Ibid.

The next part of the voyage was marked by weather conditions which slowed the progress, with little wind and overcast skies. Ryder, however, as navigator, managed to get enough result from shooting the sun, when it appeared, to continue to fix the ship's position. After experiencing their first rough weather in the *Tai Mo Shan*, the result of a monsoon that had passed into the Bering Sea instead of curving over Japan as usual, they reached harbour in Attu on a perfect summer evening.

> When we rounded the eagerly awaited point we caught our first glimpse of Attu. High hills covered with wild flowers, except where numerous valleys bore traces of their winter covering, for deep drifts of snow still remained, formed the background to a most attractive little bay.[13]

The Times described how from Attu two expeditions were carried out by Ryder and his crew. One, by foot, crossed the mountains in three days to reconnoitre Massacre Bay while the other set out in the small boat carried by the *Tai Mo Shan* to survey Holtz Bay. The journey was carried out by oar-power as the party had not had room to bring an outboard motor, and subsequently returned as the wind was too fresh to continue the survey.[14] Sherwood mentions the overland journey casually: "One party went off for three days waking and camping" but *The Times* report commented on the difficulties of mountain travel without any means of transport and described how they set out with "ten days provisions and camping equipment on their backs."[15] Despite the difficulties Ryder produced a sketch survey of Holtz Bay that was later commended by the Royal Geographical Society in 1936.[16] After a day or two of the rough passage from Attu across the Bering Sea apparently Ryder was the only crew member who did not suffer from seasickness, and demanded regular feeding from the cook, Sherwood, who was struggling. However after a few days all had once again regained their sea legs. Within six days they had arrived at Dutch Harbour, where they were entertained by the American Coast Guard Service. Proceeding through the Unimack Pass they had good weather and Sherwood was impressed by the spectacular scenery.

> Saturday the 26th August was ushered in with a fine golden sunrise which was reflected over a clear sky; the sea was in the serenest of moods. Glistening in the rays of the early morning sun, Shishaldin volcano reared its pointed cone, which was covered with snow, the gleaming whiteness of which completed the most perfect view I have ever enjoyed.[17]

They entered the Pacific and were able to pick up their first American radio station playing *Who's Afraid of the Big Bad Wolf.* On Tuesday 12th September they arrived at Victoria Harbour, British Columbia, having done the 1,732 miles in twenty days. At Victoria they stayed at the Royal Canadian Naval Barracks.

The crew had been looking forward to their arrival at San Francisco. Arriving

---

13   Sherwood, *Voyage*, p.60.
14   *The Times*, 13th July 1934.
15   Ibid.
16   Hopton, *A Reluctant Hero*, p.43.
17   Sherwood, *Voyage,* p.84.

at night on 6th October, they saw the lights of the work in progress on the new bridge "which is to span the harbour mouth and of which the people of San Francisco are rightly proud."[18] Once again they received copious hospitality at the St Francis Yacht Club and the University Club. Prohibition was still in force but the crew managed to visit several "speak easies". On meeting the manager of one club they were informed that "he was known to have had at least four people bumped off."[19] On leaving San Francisco they were thrilled to see the US Naval dirigible *Macon*. This craft, built by Goodyear, had been commissioned in July 1933[20] and was taking up her moorings in San Francisco for the first time. At San Pedro harbour, Wilmington, after a week of very light winds and slow progress, they had an opportunity to visit Hollywood and saw scenes from various films being shot. They met and were photographed with Bette Davies and were also introduced to John Barrymore, Alan Mowberry and Maureen O'Sullivan. Martyn Sherwood met Larry Kent, an actor and yachtsman who offered to be of use in his yacht *Audacious* by sailing with them down to Acapulco. The *Audacious* would offer a tow to the *Tai mo Shan* if she was becalmed. Their stay in Acapulco included a hair-raising flight over the mountains to Mexico City in an old Fokker plane. Sherwood described passing over the twin mountains of Popacatapetl and Ixtaccihuatl, or "the sleeping woman", before landing and being shown Teotihuacan, including the temple of the god Quetzalcoatl and the pyramids of the sun and the moon.

The crew accepted a tow from the *Audacious* down to the Panama Canal, although they had reservations as they could not have claimed to sail the whole route. However, after arrival at La Libertad, Kent announced that the towing was taking too much of a strain on the *Audacious's* auxiliary engine so the *Tai Mo Shan* sailed down to Balboa. Ryder had not wanted to accept a tow in the first place and expressed relief when they were under their own power again. He remembered, "it was with a considerable feeling of relief that we weighed (anchor) at 15.30 to rely on the wind and not the vicissitudes of Larry Kent."[21] On arrival at Balboa, the port at the eastern end of the Panama Canal, the party were spared the expense of hiring a tug to take them through the canal as they managed to hitch a lift moored securely to a diesel lighter which was transporting a load of bananas through the canal. Here they met a variety of adventurers including the one-eyed captain of a Glasgow-built steam pinnace and treasure hunters on their way to the Cocos Islands. Setting sail for Jamaica, they arrived after eight days sailing, averaging ninety miles a day. They met up with friends on the HMS *Danae* at anchor there and were also entertained at Government House.

The decision to stop at Crooked Island proved the beginning of the most frustrating part of their voyage. After a day or two moored outside the reef and making the acquaintance of the Island's small Seventh Day Adventist community, the *Tai Mo Shan* became beached on 12th February. *The Times* reported the circumstances: "While weighing during the night the boat dragged anchor and stranded in shoal water. Attempts to kedge off failed, so the *Tai Mo Shan* was hauled up above the low water mark on soft sand under the threat of strong westerly winds."[22] The vessel was listing to port so the decision was made to unload most of her moveable items onto the shore. The entire island community helped with

18   Sherwood, *Voyage,* p.95.
19   Ibid., p.97.
20   US Navy Blimps and Dirigibles, http://bluejacket.com/usn_avi_lta.html.
21   R.E.D. Ryder's typescript memoirs, cited by Hopton, *A Reluctant Hero*, p.41.
22   *The Times,* 13th July 1934.

The *Tai Mo Shan* at Panama. (Ryder family)

manual labour, but would not lend their shovel to help dig out around the keel as it was the only one they possessed and they did not want to impair its ability to dig graves. A passing steam yacht, the *Vagabondia*, refused to tow the boat off but did lend her launches, with jacks to assist, but the ship remained stubbornly beached. On Tuesday 20th February Ryder hitched a lift with the local mail steamer *Alisade* to Nassau where he would try and arrange assistance if it proved necessary. On 25th February Sherwood was still confident that they would release the *Tai Mo Shan* by their own efforts: "Red has a tug ready at Nassau. I am confident that this will not be necessary now." On the night of 26th February the ship was eventually refloated with the help of men and equipment from the schooner *Louise* and a message sent to Ryder that all was well. The repairs and payment of labour had cost £120 pounds and Sherwood reflected that the purchase of a small engine at the start of their trip would have saved them from getting into difficulties in the first place.

Sherwood described the physical condition of both ship and crew members on arrival at Nassau as "pitiable", Lt Francis had a broken ankle, so by the time he had had an operation and convalescence the other members of the crew had recovered somewhat. At Bermuda the ankle needed further attention, but the crew members were determined to wait for Francis, even though this meant that the Atlantic crossing would start later. They enjoyed the hospitality of several British ships at harbour there and also spent time resting in the gardens of Admiralty House. As Sherwood commented on leaving, "what a month that was!" After a good start, after ten days the *Tai Mo Shan* was half-way across the Atlantic and the possibility of a twenty day crossing was mooted. However as *The Times*

The *Tai Mo Shan* approaching Dartmouth. (Ryder family)

described, by 8th May the ship was hove to in an 80 mph gale.[23] The winds then died and light or nonexistent winds hampered progress. At noon on 30th May the crew sighted land. Once docked at Dartmouth they experienced a rapturous welcome from friends, relations and naval top brass. The King, George V, sent them a telegram – "H. M. the King wishes to welcome the officers of the *Tai Mo Shan* on their safe arrival home after their eventful voyage from China."[24]

The voyage of the *Tai Mo Shan* has been called "One of the greatest blue water voyages of the inter-war years."[25] It achieved its objects of sailing half-way around the world against the prevailing winds without an engine and showed the determination and courage of its crew members, who in contrast to some other expeditions of the thirties got on well throughout and remained friends. *The Times* of 9th July 1944 contained an interview with Ommanney-Davis in which he remembered "they were a grand crowd, and I think it is a great tribute that we were all as good friends at the end of the trip as we were at the beginning."[26] Ryder's biographer, Richard Hopton, has dismissed the speculation that the trip was a cover for some espionage, arguing that the plans which included the visit to the Kurile Islands and the investigation of Ganges Island were merely a way of persuading the naval authorities to take the planned journey more seriously. However, in the planning for

23   *The Times*, 13th July 1934.
24   Sherwood, *Voyage*, p.226.
25   *Classic Boat*, September 2007.
26   *The Times*, 9th July 1944.

Operation Chariot in 1942 Ryder was to show much talent in misleading everyone and maintaining cover for the Raid on St Nazaire (see Chapter Five). It is possible that he was using the idea of the young officers' 'stunt' as cover for more secret purposes. In a letter to the shipbuilder Mr Cock in 1933 he had said :

> The yacht is required for an expedition which is to explore and chart certain anchorages in the Aleutian Islands, which matter we are endeavouring to keep confidential ... I should like to emphasise that the *Tai Mo Shan* is not being built to sail to England as a stunt as is commonly supposed and would ask you to treat her real intention as confidential.[27]

It is clear from both Sherwood's account and Ryder's papers that there would have been an attempt to land on the Kurile islands if the Japanese had not been so keen on preventing them. There is no denying the fact that the navy installed wireless equipment and trained the crew in its operations. The intelligence gathered may have been of little consequence but this does not detract from the willingness of the spirited young crew to place themselves and their yacht in danger if necessary.

The *Cape Passaro* Trawlers at Namsos 1940

Sherwood retired from the Navy later in the year and after a spell as an unsuccessful silver fox farmer, learned Russian, obtained a job with a British Steel Company and ended up working in Australia. At the outbreak of war in September 1939 he was anxious to rejoin and contribute to the war effort, stating "I was naturally anxious to get back into uniform and to join in the fray at the earliest possible moment." His first task was to help choose suitable merchant ships to form a Q ship force. He travelled to Glasgow and chose *The King Gruffydd* and *The Willamette Valley*, which subsequently sunk with Sherwood's old pal 'Red' Ryder in command. The Q ships or 'mystery ships' were armed merchant ships with concealed weaponry whose purpose was to lure enemy submarines into surface actions and then attack them with their concealed weapons. In World War One they had had some success, accounting for 10% of all U boats sunk and were considered to be a valuable part of the anti-submarine campaign.

The King Gruffydd became Sherwood's first wartime command. Inside her, hidden from enemy eyes, were 100 depth charges. She had three 4-inch guns on each side, covered by removable panels which would expose the guns when needed, and four 21-inch torpedo tubes. The pair of machine guns were regarded by Sherwood as a pitiable form of defence against air attack and as a result of a disagreement with a senior naval officer over the lack of such defence against air attack, Sherwood found himself removed from the Q ships and on an ASDIC course to learn the rudiments of this anti-submarine device.[28] ASDIC is a system similar to sonar whereby the ASDIC beam is sent out from an oscillator enclosed in a dome underneath the ship's hull and the returning wave of sound is plotted by a stylus on iodized paper, giving an idea of what is in the sea surrounding the ship. After this training Sherwood was put in charge of a group of four trawlers who were tasked with defending from submarines the approaches in the Bristol Channel to the ports of Swansea, Cardiff and Bristol. In his autobiography *Coston Gun* Sherwood related several incidents about

---

27   *Classic Boat*, September 2007.
28   Martyn Sherwood, *Coston Gun* (London, 1946), p.173.

Martyn Sherwood, c.1940. (*Coston Gun*)

the early use of ASDIC, including the problems of 'non-subs' – previous wrecks which, moving in the current, mimic the sound waves of submarines and were sometimes attacked by mistake, [29] but Sherwood considered that ASDIC was a godsend: "It was entirely on this instrument that our good service as an anti-submarine service depended."[30]

In February 1940 Sherwood was posted to take command of the *Cape Passaro*, a White Sea trawler recently launched in June 1939 and which was now to be converted and used by the Royal Navy. She was, according to Sherwood, "the very last thing in fishing trawlers"[31], but had actually never completed a fishing trip to what should have been her hunting grounds in northern Norway, the White Sea and Bear Island. She was designed to withstand the toughest weather conditions. Some trouble with her degaussing coil necessitated a stop on the Tyne which was enlivened by a brief audience with Queen Elizabeth. The *Cape Passaro* sailed to Scapa Flow as part of a small force of trawlers. The other group accompanying them was led by Commander Geoffrey Congreve.

The 15th Anti-Submarine Striking Force was made up of the *Cape Passaro*, under the command of Sherwood, who commanded the force, the *St Goran*, commanded by Lt. Commander William McGuigan, *St Kenan*, under Lt. Jimmy James and the *St Loman*, with Lt. Cambridge commanding until replaced by Lt. Warwick. After the German invasion of Norway in March 1940 the 15th and 16th striking forces were given orders for Norway. Lt. Warwick was given command of the *St Loman* as its captain had received his

---

29   Ibid., p.191.
30   Ibid., p.184.
31   Ibid., p.183.

Men on board a trawler sweeper preparing to cast the otter float overboard
during minesweeping. (Hutchinson's *Pictorial history of the war*)

desired MTB command. Warwick remembered plenty of 'Dutch courage' being delivered
to the ships and various farewell evening parties. He remembered "The most notable host
being Martyn Sherwood on the *Cape Passaro*"[32] and also considered Sherwood to be "a
somewhat legendary character."

The trawlers of the 15th and 17th striking forces were to support the landings at Namsos.
The *Cape Passaro* was given an Oerlikon for defence against air attack. The force set out on
the evening of 24th April and made their way to the Namsen Fjord. The trawlers had orders
to keep the mouth of the fjord clear of submarines. When they arrived at the mouth of the
fjord, troops were transferred to them from a troop carrier that had brought them so far
and the *Cape Passaro* took them to the pier at Namsos on 28th April. The trawlers steamed
the twenty miles "through the mirror-like waters of the fjord"[33] and began unloading men
and ammunition at the piers at Namsos. Sherwood described how, when an aircraft flew
overhead while they were unloading, all lights were doused and "we crouched where we
were, and never a moment was there".[34] On this occasion the aircraft flew on unaware
of the landing operation being completed in the half-darkness of the short Norwegian

32   C. Warwick, *Really Not Required* (London, 1997), p.9.
33   Ibid., p.13.
34   Ibid., p.200.

night. However, the next morning, Tuesday 30th April, an air attack on Namsos started. Sherwood received an order at 8.00 a.m. for all ships to cast off from the jetty because of an imminent air attack. Sherwood described how they ignored this order at first as "nobody ashore wanted to be parted from their ammunition. We were equally eager to be rid of it." But as the aircraft approached, the trawlers cast off from the pier and started to head down the fjord. The *St Goran* and the *St Loman* went to minesweep at the fjord entrance and the *Cape Passaro* and the *St Kenan* completed their unloading once the air attack was over.

During renewed air attacks the *Cape Passaro*, the *St Goran* and the *St Loman* ran for the cover of steep cliffs at the side of the fjord which fortunately ran down to deep water close to the shore. They were now under heavy air attack but managed to get the *Cape Passaro* under the cliffs and roped to some boulders. Meanwhile the *St Goran*, under the command Lt. Commander W.C. McGuigan RNR, was further out in the fjord and came under heavy air attack from Heinkel He 111s.[35] The *St Goran* was also manoeuvred into the cliff shore, but sustained heavy damage. Lieutenant Alan Reid, RNVR, of HMT *St Goran* described the damage in the subsequent report to the Admiralty:

> A fire, which subsequently transpired to be bedding, broke out in the mess deck and the magazine was therefore flooded. This fire was afterwards extinguished. The ship was found to be in the following condition. The A/S Bridge was completely shattered, the steering gear was out of action, the Oerlikon gun and two of the Lewis guns were damaged by shrapnel. The topsides in the mess deck were punctured in several places and she appeared to have a slight list to starboard.[36]

Reid now decided to land the wounded men, as there were no British ships within the area with sufficient anti-aircraft power to resist a further attack. At this point the HM Trawler, *Arab,* caught them up and the wounded were transferred to her. After a consultation with Commander Congreve on the *Arab* the rest of the crew of the *St Goran* were landed at the fjord side. They later came under renewed air attack as did the deserted *St Goran*.

Sherwood took a borrowed motor boat and went to look for the *St Goran*. He found her deserted with only the three dead left by the wheelhouse. One was the captain, 'Mac', who was a friend of Sherwood. Sherwood put the dead on the motor boat and headed out for deeper water to bury them. He described the service:

> I did my best, it probably was not very like the proper burial service but we talked of our Friend, who was always a Friend to fishermen ... Tears rolled down the cheeks of these honest rugged men.[37]

The other fatalities from the *St Goran* were picked up by fishing boat from the shore and buried from the *Cape Passaro* the following day. Lt Reid made the decision to scuttle the St Goran as it was impossible to make it seaworthy under the circumstances and he was afraid that her ASDIC equipment might fall into the hands of the enemy, and therefore reluctantly decided that the only course was to sink her. The sea cocks were opened about

---

35   Trawlers lost at Namsen Fjord, http://www.royal-naval-reserve.co.uk/namsen-fjord/default.htm.
36   Report ADM 199/478, pp.223–226.
37   M. Sherwood, *Coston Gun*, p.204.

Gun crew of converted trawler (Hutchinson's *Pictorial history of the war*)

02. 00 on Wednesday 1st May. The *St Goran* however proved reluctant to go to the bottom and the *Cape Passaro* had to help with gunfire.

The trawlers had been sheltering in the fjord trying to disguise themselves with branches of trees, but the attack on Namsos was continuing and the trawlers now tried to finish landing supplies and ammunition. Sherwood was summoned to the flagship of Admiral Vivian and was surprised to find that the Allied forces were now planning to evacuate Namsos. British and French troops were loaded on to the *Cape Passaro* by the light of the burning fires of Namsos and under constant threat of air attack, and were ferried to the troop ships waiting off shore, which then steamed off down the fjord to exit. According to Sherwood's account the trawlers were the last ships left in Namsos. Captain Richard Stannard, in command of HM Trawler *Arab*, was awarded a Victoria Cross for holding his ship close to the jetty for two hours to extinguish a fire, thus saving part of the jetty which was essential to the evacuation. Sherwood's remaining trawlers, the *Cape Passaro*, the *St Loman* and the *St Kenan* were now given orders to proceed to Narvik. Admiral Vivian had said "you are to go up north near Narvik. It should be much quieter there."[38]

The *Cape Passaro*, *St Loman* and *St Kenan* were now sent to a rendezvous anchorage at Skelfjord. Colin Warwick remembered that because of the evacuation of the Allies from Namsos, the Luftwaffe were "concentrating their attention to the British ships in the fjords."[39] The 'beat' assigned to them was through Skelfjord, past the Lofoten islands and Lodigen to Harstad, which was their base. They took troops off a transport near Lodigen at the head of the Vest Fjord and delivered them to Harstad. The *Cape Passaro* was able to deliver vital cutting equipment to HMS *Eskimo* stranded in elfjord and unable to proceed until damage to her bows had been cut away. Her next task was to tow some landing craft sixty miles down the coast to Narvik in preparation for the coming attack on it. As the

---

38   Sherwood, *Coston Gun*, p.207.
39   Warwick, *Not Required*, p.20.

Corvette attacking enemy submarine sea raider. (Hutchinson's *Pictorial history of the war*)

trawler altered course to reach Boden Bay it grounded briefly on a shoal and lost the ASDIC oscillator. As Sherwood was considering how to retrieve it at the same time as refuelling one of the landing craft, the *Cape Passaro* came under air attack. Despite zig-zagging and returning fire, particularly with the Oerlikon, the engine bed was fractured, the 4-inch guns destroyed and the machine guns lost when the bridge was hit. A third direct hit caused the bows to plunge and the stern to lift high into the air. Sherwood gave the order to abandon ship and when the men were in the boats, his coxswain 'Sunshine' and himself jumped in. He remembered "It was too choppy to be pleasant. It was hard to see over the crests of those icy waves ... I caught a glimpse of the cliffs that edged the shore. 'I don't think I can do it' I decided." However his shipmates picked him up on a raft and they made it to shore. They were still not safe from air attack, huddled at the side of the fjord and were relieved to see the cruiser *Cairo* return fire and then send a boat to rescue them. Four men from the *Cape Passaro* died. Three bodies were found floating near the wreck, but the 'Sparks' was missing. When he had recovered Sherwood took a boat to search the sides of the fjord, but he was not found.

In total the Norwegian campaign in the spring of 1940 saw fourteen trawlers sunk with the loss of twenty-seven personnel of the Royal Naval Patrol Service. The editor of the *Royal Naval Patrol Service Association Newsletter*, writing in 2010, commented that one of the reasons for the failure of the Norway campaign was the inability of the Royal Navy to "contest command of the air off a distant shore". He quoted Captain Harrison-Wallace, the Extended Defence Officer in Norway, in his report to the Admiralty, 4th May 1940.

Unless command of the air is obtained, the use of the trawler type of A/S Craft is impracticable. I wish to bring to your notice the high standard of courage, endurance and devotion to duty shown by all ranks in exceptionally trying circumstances. Incessant bombing and machine gunning practically for 20 hours in the day with little or no means of retaliation is trying for the most experienced men and steady nerves. Many of the crews are inexperienced fishermen on war service. This experience was evidently telling, but fine leadership of the officers maintained the morale at a high standard.[40]

Sherwood was taken back to Greenock and then sent to Aberdeen for re-kitting and then sent on leave to await appointment. He was sad to leave the trawler anti-submarine force and commented on the city of Hull as being "a city remarkable for the men it breeds". On 16th August 1940 he was awarded the DSO for his service in the 15th Striking Force: "For bravery and devotion to duty in certain of HM Trawlers employed on the coast of Norway."[41] A fellow officer concluded that "all of us in trawlers would have gladly followed Martyn Sherwood to hell and back."[42]

Corvettes in the Mediterranean 1940-42

In July 1940 Sherwood was given command of a group of 'Flower class' corvettes. After a brief convoy duty escorting a group of seventy ships, with the help of only one trawler, to fifteen degrees west, the group were sent to the Mediterranean. In the rush to get them ready in Liverpool the ventilation shafts necessary for the Mediterranean were left to be finished on arrival. This resulted in the seas pouring in the unfinished shafts and making the mess decks and sleeping quarters very wet. Later, Sherwood was criticised by the Flag Officer for "splicing the mainbrace" half way across the Bay of Biscay, but when he explained the conditions, he was excused. He commented, "I heard no more. Most senior naval officers are brought up to be human."[43]

Sherwood's group of Corvettes were the *Peony,* the *Hyacinth,* commanded by Hopkins, peacetime commander of the P & O Liner *Cathay,* the *Salvia,* commanded by a former British India Captain, and the *Gloxinia,* commanded by Pomeroy, a member of the RNVR in peacetime. They arrived at Gibraltar on the 23rd and were deployed as close escort for SS *Clan Forbes,* SS *Clan Fraser* and SS *New Zealand Star* for the passage to Malta, covered by ships of Force H (Operation Collar).[44] As this convoy consisted of fast ships, the corvettes were unable to keep up and had to rejoin the convoy at Malta where it was joined by HM Cruisers *Manchester, Southampton* and *Coventry* and HM Destroyers *Defender, Diamond, Gallant, Greyhound,* and *Hotspur* as Force H had left to engage the enemy.

Having arrived safely at Suda Bay in Crete, Sherwood was questioned closely by Admiral Cunningham about magnetic mines, which were only then making their appearance in the Mediterranean. The *Peony* was sent to Benghazi harbour to deal with the mines there. On arrival Sherwood found the harbour full of wrecks and remembered wryly his instructions: "Go to Benghazi and sweep around in ever widening circles."[45] His comment was "had we trawled around in circles our fate would almost certainly have been sealed."[46] The difficulty in Benghazi harbour lay in the shallowness of the water, as the *Peony's* degaussing equipment did not protect it from mines under ten fathoms. The problem was solved by dragging the

40   *Royal Naval Patrol Service Association Newsletter* 2010.
41   DSO, *London Gazette* 16th August 1940.
42   Dix Noonan medal auction site. http://www.dnw.co.uk/medals/auctionarchive/viewspecialcollections/itemdetail.
43   Sherwood, *Coston Gun,* p.223.
44   http://www.naval-history.net/xGM-Chrono-20Cor-Flower-Gloxinia.htm.
45   Sherwood, *Coston Gun,* p.224.
46   Ibid., p.224.

copper electrode of the minesweeping equipment, cased in rubber and made buoyant with tennis balls, astern of the *Peony* and clearing a small section into which the ship moved and then repeating the procedure. This was a slow process but cleared enough water for supply ships to be able to berth at the harbour. While in Benghazi harbour Sherwood rowed out to the mooring of HMS *Terror*, a monitor ship that had been supporting the Allied attack in Libya by bombarding the shore and acting as a water carrier for the advancing army,[47] to investigate a suspected parachute mine. Sherwood and a demolition officer succeeded in blowing up the mine safely. However, the *Terror* was sunk on 24th February on her departure from the harbour.

The *Peony* was now deployed on convoy duty from Alexandria to Tobruk and the return journey. Sherwood related the sinking of the Polish tanker *Warzawa* attached to one of his convoys and his surprise on picking up survivors, finding the medical officer was a rather glamorous woman who commented "we've been wandering round the Med for two years unescorted and now this happens."[48] At the beginning of April 1940 Sherwood was sent to Piraeus harbour to take command of minesweeping operations. The harbour was full of wrecks and covered with oil due to the explosion of an ammunition ship. The harbour needed to be used as part of Operation Lustre, landing Allied troops on Greece in response to the German invasion. Sherwood assured them that he could clear the harbour of mines in forty-eight hours, which he did under difficult conditions as the harbour was full of oily corpses and the oil was constantly getting all over their equipment and the men operating it.

Sherwood was at Athens when the evacuation of Allied troops was taking place and stayed behind when his corvettes sailed to help General Freyberg and Field Marshall Sir Maitland Wilson in order to help with the Allied evacuation.[49] A message came through that more evacuation ships would not be arriving for four days. When the German forces were in sight from his rooftop, Sherwood managed to commandeer a car and driver, but had to put on a khaki private's uniform over his naval whites to attract less attention. Sherwood remembered: "Those days of furious driving along that mountain road with high cliffs towering above us on one side and a sheer drop on the other will live in my memory."[50] He had received orders to go to Kalamata to help with embarkation but met a car coming the other direction who told him that Kalamata had been taken. When hiding in a deep ditch for the driver to sleep, Sherwood met a Greek girl who gave him food and a crucifix which he carried for the rest of the war.

At length they arrived in Monemvasia and after being rescued from anonymity among a group of soldiers by General Freyberg set sail on HMS *Griffin*, one of the last ships to leave Greece. In a personal handwritten account found with Sherwood's medals he recounted:

> I was in Piraeus blowing up magnetic mines as the Germans came closer and closer. We got twenty-four ships with supplies for the Allies, but, alas, too late. I then helped with plans for the evacuation of Commonwealth troops, and, finally, with my young Army driver, was the last to leave Athens with the Germans close on my tail and

47   Uboat.net.
48   Sherwood, *Coston Gun*, p.229.
49   Dix Noonan Medals site, http://www.dnw.co.uk/medals/auctionarchive/viewspecialcollections/itemdetail.
50   Sherwood, *Coston Gun*, p.245.

certainly above it. We did just get off in a British destroyer [the *Griffin*] arriving at Monemvasia.[51]

Sherwood's somewhat laconic retelling of the events is belied by the fact that he was awarded a bar to his DSO "for the withdrawal from the beaches of Greece under fire and in the face of many and great difficulties of many thousands of troops of the Allied armies."[52]

The Corvette group was now sent back to convoy duties along the North African Coast. On Christmas Day, 1941 the *Peony* noticed an oil slick and went to investigate. They found one Chinese man in the water dead and later found out that the *Salvia*, their sister corvette, had been sunk after picking up enemy prisoners of war from the sinking of the *Shuntien*. The *Salvia* had gone down with all hands, including Captain Sherwood's old friend, John 'Dusty' Miller.

Landing Craft to Algiers 1943

After the success of the Italian human torpedoes on the *Queen Elizabeth* and the *Valiant* at Alexandria Harbour, Sherwood volunteered to be one of 'the charioteers' to man a similar revenge attack, but was told that at forty-three he was twenty years too old. In May 1942 the *Peony* was sold to the Greek Navy and Sherwood was given a new task by Lord Louis Mountbatten. He was to go to America and bring back over the Atlantic 150 landing craft, LCI, delivering them to Algiers by June 1943. This was the first time that flat bottom boats had been taken across the Atlantic and as Sherwood said, "you cannot simply shove off into the Atlantic with craft as small as these unless the most careful preparation have been made."[53] Most of the men who were sailing in them apart from the officers sent to navigate them had never been to sea. Sherwood remembered that the engineers did a particularly good job with the engines. On each of the three voyages that it took to get all the landing craft over the Atlantic, the average speed remained at 11 knots. The vessels, whose captains were not used to such high power and speed, got them involved in many collisions, and as they were welded not riveted they needed constant repair. Once safely in North Africa, the landing craft were taken over by combined operations ready for the assault on Sicily.

D-Day and after

In the run up to D-Day Sherwood commanded the sloop *Hart* and found the pre-D-Day pressure stressful: "Never again would I like to experience that pre-Normandy strain. It was plain hell. The paper work was colossal. Keeping to oneself the multitudinous secrets involved was one of the most trying feats imaginable."[54] The *Heart* completed thirty-five crossings to Normandy once the invasion had commenced. After this he asked to be relieved and found himself as Staff Officer Operations at HMS *Ferret* in Londonderry. Very quickly tiring of a shore-based office job he reapplied for a command in October 1944. He was assigned command of the destroyer HMS *Highlander* and carried out escort duty across the Atlantic. In April 1945 he dropped depth charges on what was thought to be a submarine but was actually the wreck of an ammunition ship which had sunk with her cargo unexploded. There was an enormous explosion astern of the ship which

---

51   Dix Noonan auction site.
52   *London Gazette,* 3rd June 1941.
53   Sherwood, *Coston Gun*, p.245.
54   Sherwood, *Coston Gun*, p.283.

could be heard in Bristol, 100 miles away. On 15th April the *Highlander* sustained major damage from a collision with ice and had to be towed into St John's Newfoundland.[55] An Admiralty communication quoted by Sherwood said: "A degree of blame is attributable to Commander Sherwood. He is to note and return."

Sherwood ended his war in Penang, where on 6th October 1945 he took the surrender of 4,000 members of the Japanese navy, as senior naval officer in Penang. He was presented with a Japanese officer's sword which he sent to the Royal Naval College at Dartmouth. He had been also present at the surrender of the German navy's high seas fleet in 1918. In a letter accompanying the sword he gave his impression of the ceremony, with long lines of Japanese officers waiting in the sweltering heat to ceremonially give up their swords. He suspected hidden hatred and dreams of revenge lay hidden beneath their inscrutable faces and said "Never again must power pass to those under civilised people again, or our empire will surely be the target for revenge."[56]

Sherwood's naval career had spanned the era of two world wars. He bore no enmity to Germans and in his memoir *Coston Gun*, several times bemoaned the stupidity of war. His two books on his life experiences, *The Voyage of the Tai Mo Shan* and *Coston Gun*, were written with modesty characteristic of his generation of adventurers. The title for *Coston Gun* derived from the gun that was used for 'shooting a line' from one ship to another so that items could be transferred. In the preface to *Coston Gun* Sherwood said that in the book "I shoot my own line", but the result was a fascinating tale of a life spent at sea, with many adventures in peace and war.

55   www.naval-history.net.
56   Sherwood, *Coston Gun*, p.289.

8

R.E.D. Ryder

The Voyage of the British Graham Land Expedition Ship *Penola* 1934-37
We have seen in Chapter Five that R.E.D. Ryder played a major role in the planning and execution of the voyage of the *Tai Mo Shan*. Towards the end of the voyage of the *Tai Mo Shan*, however, Ryder was beset with doubts about the worth of the voyage in terms of adventure and exploration. He felt that they had, in accepting some tows, not covered the whole voyage under their own power, but also felt that they had not achieved much in the way of visiting out of the way places and completing surveying. That this opinion was not entirely justified we have seen in the previous chapter, and was expressed before the adventures experienced on Crooked Island, but Ryder felt dissatisfied, a feeling which was not improved by the prospect of returning to a routine life struggling up the promotion ladder in the Royal Navy. His adventurous spirit was shown in a letter to his sister from Attu in August 1933: "I have been wondering to myself if I shall ever be able to settle down pacing the quarter deck of some battleship. The feeling of freedom and of being one's own master grows on one"[1]

He was therefore delighted to hear of an opportunity to be the captain of the expedition ship of John Rymill's British Graham Land Expedition and was determined to get on to what he described to his father as "the biggest show ever".[2] *The Times* carried an article in April 1934 which reported the request in the Admiralty fleet orders for volunteers from which there could be appointed a captain for the expedition ship.

> The expedition needs one Lieutenant, R.N., who must be capable of commanding and of navigating a three-masted top sail schooner ... experience on ice is not necessary.[3]

Despite the fact that there were over 200 applications, Ryder was appointed. We have seen in Chapter Three that the expedition was short of money and the most immediate indication of this was the choice of ship. The *Penola* was a Breton fishing schooner, 112 ft long and 24ft wide and able to carry 200 tons. Rymill, the leader of the expedition, explained his reasoning:

> The most expensive parts of an Antarctic expedition are the buying, outfitting and maintenance of a ship. These I proposed to cut down to a minimum by buying an old sailing ship with auxiliary power and running it with amateurs except for the captain and chief engineer.[4]

---

1   Richard Hopton, *A Reluctant Hero, The Life of Captain Robert Ryder VC* (Barnsley, 2011), p.49.
2   Ibid., p.149.
3   *The Times*, 28th April 1934.
4   John Rymill, *Southern Lights, The Official Account of the British Graham Land Expedition 1934–1937* (London, 1938,) p.29.

R.E.D. Ryder. (Ryder family)

Ryder described the *Penola* "a heavy lumbering type ... with a large carrying capacity for her length", but commented that when sailing against the wind her performance was not good. Ryder and his crew set about making modifications to make the *Penola* more suitable for Antarctic seas. She was sheathed from forward to amidships with greenheart to protect the hull from the ice, and the bow was stiffened to withstand the shock of collision with ice. The modifications, however, "undeniably reduced further her capabilities as a sailing ship."[5] The auxiliary engines were only of any real use in calm seas and with no wind, when they could achieve a top speed of five knots. Ryder's experience under sail was to prove essential, as the *Penola's* engines were inadequate for her size and were out of action for much of the voyage. Verner Case, one of the sailing crew, told Laurence Fleming in 1985 "under power with a clean bottom the ship could make five and a half knots in a flat calm. She couldn't beat to windward; a headwind stopped her dead."[6] He also revealed that the *Penola* had gone aground nine times on the voyage, though most people were only aware of two of the occasions. With such an unreliable and poorly performing ship, Ryder would be accepting the responsibility of transporting the expedition safely through Antarctic waters. Differences of opinion about the necessity of making the ship as safe as possible were a feature of the disagreements between Ryder and Rymill during the expedition.

A former Guards officer and sea adventurer, with experience in Canada and the Arctic, James Martin had been appointed as first mate, but Ryder was allowed to chose his elder brother Lisle, who was also an experienced sailor, to make up the crew. The three other members of the six-man crew were Lt. Commander Hugh Millett, a Royal Navy Engineer, Colin Bertram, a veteran of two Cambridge University expeditions and the youngest

5   A lecture given by Ryder (undated) in his papers concerning the expedition.
6   Giles Hunt, *Lancelot Fleming, A Portrait* (Norwich, 2003), p.34.

member, Norman Gurney, who had applied to join the expedition at the end of his first year at Cambridge. The crew of the *Penola* were to take the whole of the rest of the expedition, consisting of the shore party, dogs and equipment, deep along the unexplored coastline of the Antarctic Peninsula.

The ship was loaded at St Katherine's Dock, London between 1st and 10th September 1934. After a blessing from the Bishop of Gibraltar the ship set off, laden with twenty-five tons of excess cargo loaded on deck. As there were only six crew members the scientists and shore party were expected to take their share of work and watches on board. Ryder's strict enforcement of naval routine and discipline caused some resentment among the non-crew members of the expedition, who consisted of Cambridge scientists, used to going their own way, and former members of Gino Watkins's expeditions who were used to a much more relaxed expedition style. Quintin Riley commented on the disagreement as early as 25th September:

> There is too much naval discipline (Captain's Sunday inspection) but if you have a N.O. to run your ship you must let them have their way, of course. In actual fact it only amuses the rest of us, who don't take it too seriously.[7]

However, the situation seemed not to have improved by 12th January 1935, en route from the Falkland Islands to the Antarctic Peninsula. Ryder wrote in his diary:

> The scientists requested again to be excused scrubbing and cleaning the ship. They are fully prepared to do the work necessary for the safety of the ship but they feel that their scientific work is more important than mere cleaning The request has been turned down as it is hardly possible to differentiate between all the various sorts of work on board. [8]

Riley's biographer, Jonathon Riley, however considered that if the Gino Watkins's style of leadership had prevailed on board, that it was probable that either things would have been left undone or a few people would have done everything. Later Ryder was to admit that he had been a little overzealous and that when required to work hard the shore party were prepared to put in very long hours to achieve specific tasks.

Penola's engines failed as soon as she left the Falkland Islands. The engine beddings were made of unseasoned timber which had split, resulting in the engines shifting and stopping. This was the cause of disagreement between Ryder and Rymill, as Rymill wanted to make progress to the Antarctic while Ryder was anxious about the safety of the ship in Antarctic seas without reliable engines. After a return to the Falkland Islands to inspect damage it was decided to proceed under sail. On 21st January the *Penola* arrived in Port Lockroy. Ryder was impressed by the scenery in the run in – "the magnificent scenery and novel surroundings into which we had so suddenly come will remain vividly in my mind for many years."[9] The *Penola's* first major task was to ferry the expedition to its first base camp on the Argentine Islands. As we have seen, Ryder flew down the coast with Hampton in

---

7   J. Riley, *Pole to Pole*, p.62.
8   R. Ryder, unpublished typescript diary, private collection.
9   A lecture given by Ryder (undated) in his papers concerning the expedition.

Lisle Ryder. (Ryder family)

order to reconnoitre a suitable base and then went with Rymill and Ryder in the motorboat *Stella* to make sure that the anchorage spied from the air was suitable for the *Penola*. The two journeys needed to transport the expedition to 'Stella Creek', the new anchorage, took four days and the first journey back to Port Lockroy was quite hair-raising, with Ryder directing operations from the crow's nest. This was a strategy which he was to adopt frequently in Antarctic waters: "up in the Crow's nest one is very snug and the sight of the ship twisting and turning below in accordance with one's hand signals is pleasing to watch." [10] In a lecture later in life he explained the difficulties of the Antarctic Peninsula coast:

> For a ship of our power the navigation of this coast is not easy. The wind from the west and the south-west which brings the fine weather is unfortunately a headwind and may bar further progress in these confined waters for anything up to a fortnight.

He also described how, in examining the various inlets and possible anchorages, the *Penola* sometimes ran briefly aground, "the disadvantages of not being able to go astern always added a certain zest to the proceedings."[11]

By 5th March the hut at the base was complete and the shore party moved in, leaving conditions less cramped on board. However, this separation did not encourage close relations with the crew and Ryder made sure that the ship's crew visited the hut as often as possible. As winter approached it was necessary to build up food stocks by a sealing expedition. Ryder's participation in this exercise gave him his first experience of the discomfort of camping in polar conditions. Strangely, for a man used to conditions at sea,

---

10   Ryder Papers.
11   A lecture given by Ryder (undated) in his papers concerning the expedition.

The *Penola* anchored at Port Lockroy, British Graham
Land Expedition, 1935. (*Southern Lights*)

he complained about getting wet as a result of melting snow while sleeping in the tents.

By 5th May Ryder reported that winter was "slowly and steadily settling in". Later in May he went for a walk with his brother Lisle and described his surroundings:

> The scene of the coastal mountains ... and grotesque shapes around one, the smooth snow slopes of one's own islands bathed in the wonderfully clear moon light are beyond the description and almost beyond imagination. They seem to be infinitely more wonderful than anything else in the world.[12]

On 7th June Rymill started teaching Ryder the art of sledging. Ryder commented in his diary: "Sitting on a little hard summer sledge one is close to the ground and appears to be going at a sound speed. Great rocks of ice are missed by inches." he continued, describing crossing the thin ice across the tide crack, "which bends visibly under our weight". He soon picked up the skill: "With shouts of 'Huit Huit ' and with a roll of the whip, off I went ... the dogs following the previous tracks and then, after, loud cries of 'Ah –Ah' brought them to a standstill at once." [13]He was initiated into polar travel skills, Stephenson giving him lessons in adapting his sea-based navigation skills to those required for sledging. He used his confidence in crossing ice and skiing to complete some surveying. In the winter months Ryder spent much time tending to the ship's engine and mending sails but was also enthusiastic about training up his dog team. His diary entries for June and July contain detailed comments on the varying abilities of the dogs and the decision that it was " a great

---

12   Ryder, diary entry 15th May 1935.
13   Ibid., 7th June 1935.

Deck cargo of the *Penola* on the way to the southern base. (*Southern Lights*)

improvement having Spot out front." [14] In July Brian Roberts was suffering with acute appendicitis and at one stage it looked as if Bingham would need to operate. Ryder recalled being asked if he was prepared to give the anaesthetic: "As may be imagined, the prospect was not welcome and one was strongly inclined to shirk the responsibility. As however, someone has to do it, I accepted."[15] In the event his anaesthetic skills were not needed.

Ryder was pleased to be chosen to participate in a sledge journey which, after a frustrating wait for the weather to be cold enough for firm ice, set out on 18th August. By the second day they were in previously unexplored country. Rymill explained: "No one had, to the best of my knowledge, ever landed anywhere on the mainland south of a point opposite the Argentine Islands." [16] By 21st August they were fifty miles south of base. Here Rymill decided that Moore, who was suffering from frostbite, should be taken back to base, so Moore, Rymill and Martin turned around, leaving Ryder and Bingham to continue alone. After a good run of twenty miles on 22nd August, they were prevented from reaching their planned destination, Adelaide Island, by poor ice conditions. After a survey of the ice conditions from a high point on the chain of islands on the north side of Pendleton Strait, they decided to return to base as Ryder considered that the ice was unreliable and that it was inadvisable to continue or to camp on it. His opinion was confirmed by Rymill, who flew with Hampton in the Moth for a rendezvous with Ryder and Bingham on the group of islands north-east of Cape Evenson. It was decided that Ryder and Bingham would work their way northwards surveying the coast and outlying islands. This plan did not work out

14   Ibid., 30th June 1935.
15   Ibid., 6th July 1935.
16   Rymill, *Southern Lights*, p.70.

well, as not only did they have to wait for the Moth to return with surveying equipment, they were forced to lay up for four days after only one day of surveying. However, according to Bingham's diary, between 1st and 4th September Ryder made progress: "Ryder spent the entire day taking observations of every possible kind, while I booked his bewildering maze of figures."[17] On 2nd September Bingham took Ryder to Jagged Island where Ryder climbed to the highest point to take some angles. On 11th September Rymill turned up by sledge and together they made a very difficult trip back to Stella Creek by 16th September. Ryder and Bingham had travelled the furthest south the expedition would achieve that year.

Brian Roberts's condition had deteriorated and Bingham, the expedition doctor, had decided that it was necessary for him to be returned to the Falkland Islands to have his appendix removed. It was also advisable that the *Penola's* engines should receive a refit, which also meant going back to the Falkland Islands. Rymill now worked out new plans which depended heavily on the *Penola*. The ship was to visit Deception Island to pick up some wood to build the second expedition hut and return to Stella Creek, pick up the shore party and take them all to a new southern base. After disembarking the shore party of the *Penola* would then depart for the Falkland Islands to over-winter there and be repaired. Ryder, although seeing the necessity for the voyage, was disappointed, as this ruled him out of any major sledging journey in the second winter of the expedition.

There now followed extensive preparations to make the *Penola* ready for sea and to extricate her from Stella Creek. This involved removing sixty tons of snow and ice from her deck, repairing rigging, loading stores and equipment and cutting a channel out from the creek to open water. After using the motorboat *Stella* to scout out a passage out to sea, on 3rd January the *Penola* weighed anchor and began its journey to Deception Island. When they arrived at Deception Island on 5th January the island was deserted. Ryder described the island a "being a breached volcanic crater". He continued, "the south-east side has a navigable channel one cable wide with high cliffs either side, The sand is a kind of volcanic ash and steamed constantly."[18]

The *Penola* stayed a week bagging up timber and coal in deteriorating weather conditions. Their voyage back to the Argentine Islands was beset with difficulties, the most dramatic being the encounter with an iceberg. It was, as Ryder remembered, a "heavy great sod [that] came slowly at us on the tide and ground around the side but three of us shoved him along"[19] Ryder spent much of the last stretch of the voyage navigating the ship from the crow's nest in snow storms that destroyed visibility. It took seventeen days for the shore party and all its equipment, including seventy six dogs, to be loaded on to the *Penola*, but on 16th February, after a reconnaissance flight by Hampton in the Moth, the expedition set out to find a southern base. Ryder realised that the route would become more hazardous as they sailed south, but following a channel spotted from the air and using the *Stella* to scout ahead, negotiated islands and reefs successfully. Marguerite Bay was found to be ice free and the *Stella* was used to search for an anchorage. Ryder directed the difficult passage into the anchorages from the crow's nest, using different colour flags to signal to Riley, the engineer and Martin, who was looking out at the bow.

At length the *Penola* had disembarked the expedition and all it stores at its new base in the Debenham Islands and was ready to sail to the Falkland Islands to deliver Roberts for

---

17   Bingham's diary, cited by J. Rymill, *Southern Lights*, p.77.
18   Ryder, diary entry, 6th January 1936.
19   Ryder diary cited by Hopton, *Reluctant Hero*, p.73.

The *Penola* in full sail. (*Southern Lights*)

his operation and to have the *Penola* overhauled. The voyage of 997 miles was accomplished in twelve days. There then followed an acrimonious dispute between Ryder, the London committee of the expedition and Rymill, which made Ryder's winter in Port Stanley "a worrying and unhappy time."[20] The estimate for the repair of the engines was much more than anyone had expected and Ryder received, to his consternation, cables from London and Rymill objecting to the costs and forbidding action on repairs. However Ryder was not prepared to take the ship back to the Antarctic without the necessary work being done and threatened to resign his command. Eventually, in July, the money was forthcoming and Ryder sailed the *Penola* to South Georgia to be refitted in the dock at Stromness with the help of the Vestfold Whaling Company. Ryder and his crew, assisted by the Norwegians, worked hard to complete the refit by 2nd October, when the *Penola* returned to the Falklands. After enjoying Christmas festivities on the islands, the ship set sail for Antarctica on 29th December.

As if difficulties of the winter had not been enough, the voyage back to Graham Land was enlivened by a 'mutiny' by Roberts, who was annoyed that his ornithological activities were disrupted by having to change his watch, due to a dangerous imbalance in the performances' of the respective watches. Ryder asserted his authority and after ordering Roberts below Ryder turned the *Penola* around to head back to Port Stanley. Roberts apologised and was reinstated, but valuable time had been lost. Poor weather conditions and more encounters with icebergs meant that the expedition ship did not arrive at the

---

southern base until 23rd February. Even then Ryder's troubles were not over, as on the way into the anchorage the *Penola went* aground near a calving glacier face and had to be towed off by the *Stella*. Ryder recalled: "The following morning the *Penola*, having been towed to safety, the glacier did calve."[21]

The expedition shore party was now re-embarked and on 14th March the *Penola* set out for her first homeward port of call, South Georgia. The shore party returned to Britain from here in the Salvesen Tanker *Canada*, leaving Ryder and his crew to take the *Penola* home via the Azores. They arrived at Falmouth on 4th August 1937. Ryder now had a period of time in the *Warspite* to complete his big ship training. His part in the BGLE was praised at a meeting of the Royal Geographical Society in November 1937 and he won the society's Back Prize, "for the reward and encouragement of scientific geographers and discoverers." In October of 1937 he received the Polar Medal.

Ryder's voyages on the *Tai Mo Shan* and the *Penola* had shown him to be man of determination and initiative, who could cope with prolonged adverse conditions and with unexpected problems. Just three years after the BGLE Britain was at war and he would be given the opportunity to use his undoubted skills and determined personality in the service of his country.

Q Ship Captain, 1940

At the beginning of September 1939, Ryder returned from service on the *Warspite* to take up an invitation to command a Q Ship. In 1939 the main exponent of the use of Q ships in the First World War, Vice Admiral Gordon Campbell, was brought out of retirement to oversee the use of the tactics of Q ships in a new war and it was he who had asked Ryder to transfer from the *Warspite*.

Aware of the different conditions present in the new conflict at sea, and also aware that enemy submarines would now be more cautious of approaching lone merchantmen and convoy stragglers, Campbell decided that his Q ships should also try to ensnare the German ships that were being deployed as "commerce raiders". He requisitioned nine ocean-going merchant ships, none of whom were in their first flush of youth. They were fitted with 4-inch guns capable of penetrating a submarine's pressure hull, which were concealed in hinged flaps on the ships side. They carried four twenty-one inch torpedoes, depth charges and were defended by four Lewis guns. They were also equipped with ASDIC. There was a larger crew than usual so that if the ship was hit, then a 'panic party' could be sent off in lifeboats, making the enemy think that the ship was abandoned, whereas the ship would actually remain manned in preparation for attacking the enemy ship or submarine as it closed to investigate.

The ships were renamed and were officially called 'Admiralty Freighters'. They were manned by regular or reservist Royal Navy officers and the ships companies were a mixture of navy personnel and reservists based at Plymouth. They were to wear merchant naval uniform or plain clothes. The ships were to fly the red ensign unless they were in a neutral disguise, and fly a blue ensign on entering port. Their sailing orders were:

> When satisfied that H M Ship under your command is in all respects ready to engage
> the enemy, you are to sail twenty miles astern of an outward bound convoy. Your

---

21   R.E.D. Ryder, typescript memoirs, cited by Hopton, *Reluctant Hero*, p.84.

Wartime portrait of R.E.D. Ryder. (Ryder family)

prime object is to engage and destroy the enemy wherever he may be found. You are not to return without special orders.[22]

In his book *On Hazardous Service*, A. Cecil Hampshire was of the opinion that additions to this order were given verbally by Campbell to the effect that the captains were to allow their ships to be torpedoed in order to lure the enemy ship near enough to be attacked.[23]

Ryder took command of HMS *Willamette Valley*, which was to masquerade as a Cardiff tramp steamer *Edgehill*. He brought with him a colleague from the *Warspite*, Michael Seymour, as 1st lieutenant and James Martin, his first mate on the *Penola*, also joined the crew, becoming adept at the ways in which the ship's appearance could be disguised. Lt Commander Thompson, who had been transferred from the Merchant Navy to the Royal Navy, was his navigating officer, and passed on his experience of merchant ships to Ryder. Thompson could tell the nationality of a ship long before the name of flag could be spotted. On one occasion, Ryder asked him how he could tell a certain ship was from Liverpool: "four guard rails" Thompson replied, "they only give you three in Cardiff."[24] The *Edgehill* could be disguised in a number of ways. She had a ten-foot funnel extension which could be added to alter her silhouette, which could also be changed by extending the bridge with canvas screens and stowing the derricks vertically instead of horizontally. Her appearance could also be changed by overnight painting in various colours.

The *Edgehill's* initial cruise began on 25th February 1940. The wide-ranging nature

22   A. Cecil Hampshire, *On Hazardous Service* (London, 1974), p.33.
23   Ibid., p.34.
24   Ibid., p.56.

of the task suited Ryder's independent personality and he was later to consider his time in the *Willamette Valley* as well spent. After cruising along the North Atlantic traffic, Ryder decided to move the ship to the Gibraltar channel routes. After searching the Azores Islands unsuccessfully for a suspicious vessel which had been reported as 'probably a submarine', the *Edgehill* headed for Bermuda to take on more fresh water. They arrived in mid-March after twenty-four days at sea. Ryder was concerned about security on two counts. Firstly there were already two fleet auxiliary ships at harbour, who in the tight knit world of the navy, might well have realised that *Edgehill* was not a fleet auxiliary ship; secondly, because of the freedom of access to Bermuda from the United States. He recounted in his private log: "Bermuda is a tricky place as far as tourists are concerned for the USA permits them to visit the island without check. It would be easy therefore to send agents down and information can be quickly transmitted from the United States". However, the crews of the real fleet auxiliary ships said nothing and Ryder was pleased to note that "the armaments supply officer evidently was not aware of our identity."[25]

By 30th March the *Edgehill* was under way again, impersonating the SS *Boulton Hall* by dint of painting the lower half of the funnel and setting up a jumbo derrick and two Samson posts. This transformation was achieved in the hours of darkness. During April the ship went south, crossing the equator and sailing parallel to the Brazilian coast before setting course for Sierra Leone. For a week at the end of April they shadowed a convoy from Freetown to Gibraltar. In May they sailed around the trade routes from Gibraltar and the channel, but despite reports of submarines operating in this area they failed to locate any. On 18th May a cruiser and two destroyers were sighted ahead. Ryder wrote: "we at once went to action stations for receiving a search party and in a few minutes everything was ready. The force was identified as French. The nearest destroyer *Boulanais* came to intercept us and signalled for our identity and voyage. We replied '*Edgehill* – Freetown to Plymouth'".[26] This satisfied them and Ryder commented on how easy it would be for a disguised merchant raider to evade detection.

On 11th June the *Edgehill* left Gibraltar on a west-north-westerly course. The ship was disguised as the imaginary Greek ship, *Ambea* of Piraeus. Ryder recalled: "I painted her name in proper Greek characters on the bow and the stern and on the lifeboats and later on two large Greek flags on the side"[27] The advantage of being disguised as a Greek ship was that they did not have to sail in convoy, but it could not zig-zag and were restricted to the normal traffic routes. In the light of the fact that several Greek ships had been sunk recently, Ryder decided to steam without lights at night. He considered this as a necessary part of his policy of avoiding action with submarines at night. As part of the preparation for action with submarines Ryder had decided to use two calls signs for his submarine report. One was if needed in a genuine attack when assistance was required, using the normal call sign and the name *Edgehill*, the other, using a disused call sign SVVH, would be used to simulate a call for assistance in order to entice a submarine to investigate. When on the fifth day out they picked up a distress call from the SS *Yarraville*, it was decided to close on her, but at the same time Ryder recalled "we advertised the fact by wireless *en clair* that we were 160 miles to the west and proceeding to her assistance in hope that it might draw the enemy."[28]

25   Ryder log, IWM papers.
26   Ryder log.
27   Report of an interview with Lieut Cdr R.E.D. Ryder, 20th July 1940. IWM papers.
28   Ibid.

They discovered only oil and wreckage at the last reported position of the *Yarraville* and on Friday 28th June received orders to proceed to Halifax. The ship had not been zig-zagging in the day and the degaussing equipment was defective. Ryder called the crew to action stations, as was customary after dark, for an hour to an hour and a half. Ryder described what happened next in his official report:

> We were struck by a torpedo on the port side just forward of the bridge. This could not have happened at a more inopportune moment. It was too dark to see if a submarine were on the surface and he was in a position to shell us silhouetted against the afterglow, as we then would be, without out being able to see him. Furthermore he could overtake us and torpedo us again.[29]

The ship's ASDIC equipment had been knocked out in the attack so no retaliation could be given with depth charges. Ryder briefly considered making smoke and getting away as the engines were not damaged but decided to follow procedure in the hope that the enemy submarine would come closer and shine a searchlight, giving the ship's guns opportunity to attack. The panic party were ordered to leave and the ship was stopped. After the boats had been away for twenty minutes, one returned as it was badly damaged. Just after their return a second torpedo struck: "There was a screeching of flying metal and a blinding flash and the engine room was set on fire badly."[30] Attempts were made to fight the fire and move the ammunition away from it, at the same time as keeping one gun port operating. However the whole ship was now alight and Ryder later thought that the submarine, seeing the men fighting the fire, realised that the ship was not abandoned and decided to finish it off.

A third torpedo struck and it was then obvious to him that "this was final". He ordered "all hands on deck". An attempt was made to lower the other small two boats, but almost immediately the ship sank by the stern, rolling through at 90° as she went. About half an hour later she sank. Ryder was thrown off the bridge into the water, and after having given a lifebuoy he had grabbed to a man floating next to him, managed to cling to some wreckage. He kept hailing any crew that might be near and was answered for a while but after 1.30 a.m. he heard "nothing more".[31] At dawn he was still clinging to the wreckage. He was covered with fuel oil, which had got into his eyes, and as the sun grew stronger it became very painful, blinding him. In an interview in July 1940 he admitted that he had thought to "slip off and finish the struggle", but after having bathed his eyes with his handkerchief he felt better and resigned himself to waiting to be picked up. On the fourth day the SS *Inverlithy* picked him up in a much weakened condition. Only twenty officers and men were saved from a ship's complement of ninety.

The Q ships were not considered by naval strategists to be a success. Cecil Hampshire quoted some opinions of Q boat captains – "too late, too slow, too old and outdated" and "I would call it a farce from beginning to end."[32] Churchill said "these decoy ships have

---

29   Most Secret Report on the Sinking of the HMS *Williamette Valley* compiled by Commander R.E.D. Ryder 27th January, 1941. IWM Papers.
30   Ibid.
31   Ibid.
32   Hampshire, *On Hazardous Service*, p.90.

been a great disappointment so far in this war."[33] It was decided in spring of 1941 that the four remaining ocean-going vessels should revert to the white ensign and become armed merchant cruisers.

The Raid on St Nazaire 1942

On 25th February 1942, Ryder, who had been engaged in staff work as Naval Liaison Officer to General Alexander's staff at Wilton House, was ordered to attend a meeting at Combined Operations Headquarters. In his memoirs and in Lucas Phillips's account of the raid, we hear of how he slipped into the meeting fifteen minutes late, noticed plenty of combined operations "top brass", and then found that he had been appointed to be naval commander of the raid on St Nazaire. There is contradictory evidence as to the reasons for his selection, Ryder being of the impression that he was chosen because no one else was available, but it was clear that a man of first class ability was needed. Lucas Phillips related how John Hughes-Hallett, a senior officer involved in the initial planning of the raid, had enquired at the Admiralty in search of a first class officer to lead the raid. On being told that such men were in short supply Hughes-Hallett emphasised the importance of the job: "you can count on a VC for him if that's a guide ... obviously there's no guarantee but that's the size of the job."[34] After the war it emerged that Sir Dudley Pound, in 1942 First Lord of the Admiralty, had pressed for his appointment. The prospect of leading a raid on enemy occupied territory raised Ryder's morale. "I felt that all I had done previously led up to this. I knew what I wanted. I could picture the whole action and had complete confidence in my ability to lead this force."[35]

The aim of the strategic planners in early 1942 was to prevent the battleship *Tirpitz* from breaking out into the Atlantic and wreaking havoc with Allied shipping. Since such a breakout was dependant on the *Tirpitz* and other large German ships being able to use the ports on the French Atlantic coast it was important that all should be done to prevent this. The dock at St Nazaire was the only one large enough for the *Tirpitz* to use for berthing or repairs and if it was not available it would have been unwise of the German navy to allow the *Tirpitz* into the Atlantic. The dock was therefore regarded as a target by the enemy and consequently became very heavily defended. Ryder also pointed out that the quality and range of the enemy 's radar had improved, and that in the St Nazaire area there was known to be a radar station on Point le Croisic and possibly on Noirmoutier Island also. He emphasised that "the extreme accuracy of the enemy's fire controlled in this manner had already been established at this time elsewhere. The undetected approach of an expedition such as ours was therefore very problematical."[36]

The port at St Nazaire had become one of the most important centres for shipbuilding in France, and in 1935 the *Normandie* was built there, necessitating the building of the enormous structure which could act as a dock for refitting and repairs, or a lock connecting the Penhoet Basin directly to the river. The dock was 385 yards long and 55 wide and could accommodate a ship of more than 85,000 tons. St Nazaire itself is situated at the mouth of the River Loire before the river opens out to become an estuary containing shoals and mud flats. The main dredged channel 'le Charpentier' was close to the north shore and heavily

---

33   Ibid., p.89.
34   C.E. Lucas Phillips, *The Greatest Raid of all* (London, 1958), p.55.
35   Ryder papers on the St Nazaire raid, IWM.
36   R. Ryder, *The Attack on St Nazaire* (London, 1947), p.2.

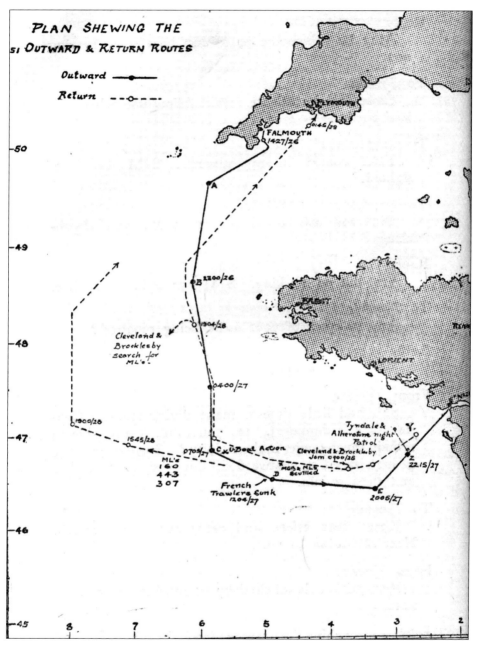

The outward and return routes of the raid on St Nazaire. (By permission of the Ryder family)

HMS *Campbeltown*, showing the protective armour
plating added to the bridge. (Ryder family)

defended by coastal batteries, patrol boats, and minefields.

Churchill had intervened by memorandum and a personal meeting with Sir Dudley Pound, demanding action on neutralising the threat of the *Tirpitz*. However, as the problem of the *Tirpitz* was one of high priority to the Admiralty, the naval planners were already formulating a plan which would attack the dock by sailing up the estuary over the shoals and mudflats, thus avoiding detection by the shore batteries. By studying the tide tables Captain John Hughes-Hallett had ascertained that vessels drawing less that twelve feet would be able to negotiate a route away from the channel. The plan was to concentrate on the destruction of the dock, using an expendable ship packed with explosives. The ship would carry commandos who would disembark, after the ship had rammed the lock gates and before it exploded, and who would attack dockyard objectives including eight lock gates, six power installations, four bridges and six gun positions.[37] A flotilla of motor launches would then take off the commandos and the crew of the expendable destroyer and return them home. It was decided that the *Campbeltown* and her task was the prime consideration. Ryder, in his report on the operation emphasised "we envisaged sacrificing, if necessary, everything in order to get the *Campbeltown* in."[38]

Ryder now set about the organisation of the naval part of the plan. After some difficulty and delay a suitable ship was found, the HMS *Campbeltown,* and on 3rd March Ryder and Lt. Col. A.C. Newman presented their plans for approval. As the attack was to take place during the last few days of March, to ensure suitable tides, they then started preparations flat out. Ryder and Newman worked out a list of modifications to the *Campbeltown* in "less than an hour". The ship had to be lightened in order to have a shallower draught. Her normal armaments were replaced by eight 20mm Oerlikons. Four rows of bullet-proof

---

37   C.E. Lucas Phillips, *The Greatest Raid of All* (London, 1958), p.47.

38   Ryder Papers, IWM, 'general description of the operation'.

The dock at St Nazaire before the raid. (Ryder family)

plating were placed on deck to protect the soldiers who would be laying there on approach. The bridge was protected by bullet-proof plating. The two after funnels had been removed and the two front funnels were raked to give the ship a passing resemblance to a German torpedo boat.[39]

Ryder now turned to the organisation of the flotilla of accompanying motor launches and motor torpedo boats. The force which was assembling at Falmouth consisted of sixteen motor launches. Four of these were designated to carry the extra commandos and four were equipped with torpedoes, at Ryder's request, to form a spearhead during the outward trip in case of unforeseen opposition nearer the Loire River. The convoy also included a motor gunboat, MGB No. 314, which became the headquarters ship at St Nazaire. Motor torpedo ship no. 74 was given the task of torpedoing the lock gates if the *Campbeltown* failed to arrive. The key remaining naval personnel had been chosen. Lt. Commander Sam Beattie became captain of the *Campbeltown*, Lt. Bill Green was navigating officer and Lt. Verity, beach master. Lt. Nigel Tibbits was in charge of the explosives on the *Campbeltown*. The decision had been made to scuttle the destroyer after the commandos had disembarked and before the explosive charge went off.

Ryder now showed an advanced version of the talent for subterfuge and security that

39   R. Ryder, *The Attack on St Nazaire*, p.28.

he had displayed on the voyage of the *Tai Mo Shan*, by creating an elaborate cover story to explain the build up of what was obviously a naval task force. He invented, and put himself in command of the 'Tenth Anti–Submarine Striking Force', which, it was put about, was to conduct long-range sweeps into the Atlantic. This also explained the fitting of extra fuel tanks and the improvements to armaments. He also later claimed to be the first person to think of deliberately and misleadingly applying for tropical kit for his men to imply a false destination. The dress rehearsal for the raid, named 'Vivid', took place on the night of 21st March at Devonport, where the King George V dock gates were very much like those at St Nazaire. The *Campbeltown* did not take part, as her captain maintained that ramming dock gates was not something you could practise. In Ryder's own words Vivid was "A hopeless failure as far as the attackers were concerned."[40] However lessons were learned, including the necessity to deal quickly with any offshore patrol vessels before they gave the game away and the difficulty of landing in the glare of searchlights. The subterfuges to delay the enemy opening fire which were to be used to such good effect on the real raid were also developed as a result of the exercise.

As the weather on 25th March had been good for five days Ryder asked for permission to set out with his convoy a day earlier than planned. This was agreed to and at 14.00 on the 26th the raiding party, HMS *Campbeltown*, two other destroyers, *Atherstone* and *Tyndale*, and 16 motor launches, set out on their fateful voyage to St Nazaire. Ryder in his published account paints an evocative picture of their departure:

> As the sun set on the evening of 26th March a pilot of a single Hurricane fighter was orbiting a small convoy of three destroyers and a number of coastal craft. He probably had little idea that for many it was their last voyage. He may have wondered why he was ordered to keep below 100ft but he was probably more concerned with the haze ... Presently he banked sharply and flying between the columns, sped away to the north ... To the pilot this was the end of his spell of duty ... To those left below the departing machine represented the last link with the homeland they had left six hours before. Much lay ahead and even the least imaginative of the company present, alone with his thoughts, must have speculated about his future.[41]

Ryder set a course to the south-west, keeping clear of the Lizard and the fleet took up its 'cruising order no 1', a formation resembling a broad flat arrowhead which would give the impression of a flotilla engaged in a submarine sweep. Ryder's thoughts on entering the Bay of Biscay were that now he was in the hunting ground of Hawke and Cornwallis. At night the speed of fourteen knots was maintained so that in the day speed could be lessened to reduce the chances of the ships' wakes being seen by aircraft, and so an average of 11½ knots could be maintained to keep on schedule. At dawn the German ensigns were hoisted in the destroyers and the white ensign lowered on the motor launches.[42] Despite the sighting and pursuit of a German submarine, the U-593, and the distinct possibility that the convoy had been spotted, Ryder decided to continue as normal, except by taking the precaution of taking *Atherstone* and *Tyndale* back to the convoy by a circuitous and misleading route. He signalled to *Tyndale* after *Tyndale's* captain had fired unsuccessfully on the submarine "in

40   Ibid., p.34.
41   Ryder, *Attack on St Nazaire*, p.39.
42   Ryder's report, IWM.

one hour's time consider that a sighting report may have been made. Unless this is followed up by reconnaissance aircraft and further fighting, intend to continue with operation."[43]

The U-boat had, in fact, seen the motor launches as well as the destroyers. This information was reported, but as the destroyers *Atherstone* and *Tyndale* had been last seen heading west, it was a assumed that they were heading for Gibraltar. An unexpected sequel to this potentially disastrous sighting was the fact that the four ships of the 5th Torpedo Boat Destroyer Flotilla, who had been reported tied up at St Nazaire, were sent to patrol off the coast that evening, thus removing them from the defence of St Nazaire. The raiding party also met up with trawlers and as it was suspected that trawler crews had German agents on them, *Tyndale* and *Atherstone* went to deal with them. However, after removing the men and all charts and papers off the two trawlers and sinking them, Ryder decided that there were too many trawlers around to deal with in such a manner, and that it was necessary for the success of the mission to ignore further trawlers and take the risk that those they met would not or could not report their presence. He later justified this decision: "It seemed quite clear from these two trawlers that none of them carried a radio, so I did not consider it necessary to investigate any of the large number that were subsequently seen."[44]

At the mouth of the Loire, seventy miles away from its target, the flotilla altered course and adopted its battle order and the headquarters transferred to MGB 314. At 22.00 the submarine HMS *Sturgeon* arrived in its prearranged position in order to act as a beacon so that the navigator, Bill Green, could check their position. The submarine was close enough to converse by loud hailer with the *Atherstone*. This had a morale-boosting effect on Subaltern Carron Purdon, who remembered in a BBC documentary:

> It made you feel that Britain ruled the waves. In spite of the German Navy and the German Luftwaffe and so on here was this British submarine with a very British captain waving and shouting British messages to us.[45]

At 00.30 the flotilla passed the buoy which marked the area of mudflats and shoal waters in the estuary. From the flak activity over the port Ryder realised that an air attack was in progress. Part of their plan was that the port would be attacked by an air raid, but what Ryder could not know was that very few bombs had been dropped due to weather conditions and that the main effect of the air raid had been to ensure that all available enemy flak stations and batteries had been alerted and were fully manned. At the time he considered that "the presence of an aircraft greatly encouraged us."[46] At 00.45 they could see the distant northern shore of the estuary. Unknown to Ryder at the time, at this point the *Campbeltown* briefly grounded twice on the mudflats, but pushed on over them without losing speed. At 01.00 the deserted tower of Le Morées was passed. Ryder described the elation felt at this point that they had remained undetected. They now had nearly two miles to the dock gates and were twelve minutes to target. Suddenly, however, something alerted the shore batteries and the searchlights on both sides of the river were switched on. Ryder recalled "every detail of every craft must have been clearly visible to the enemy."[47]

---

43 Lucas Philips, *The Greatest Raid of all*, p. 43
44 Ryder's report.
45 Hopton, *Reluctant Hero,* p.148.
46 Ryder, *Attack on St Nazaire*, p.46.
47 Ibid., p.48.

The assault on the old entrance, St Nazaire. (Ryder family)

Two German signals were now flashed at the British boats. It was now that the abilities of the bilingual Able Seaman Pike were employed to instigate the bluff that had been prepared to delay enemy fire for as long as possible. To the signalled challenge from the harbour post Pike signalled a bogus German call sign and told them to 'wait'. He followed this by a plain language signal, the gist of which was: "Two craft, damaged by enemy action, request permission to proceed up harbour without delay". Firing from this post ceased and Pike then replied to the other challenger on the port beam, but before this could be completed, the ships came under fire from the north shore. Quickly Ryder ordered the international signal sent by Aldis lamp for vessels being fired on by friendly forces and the firing stopped once more. Ryder commented later "these were tense and exciting moments – it does not fall to everyone's lot to find them." [48]The signals sent by Pike, in German, had obviously caused some doubt in the defenders' minds as to the identity of the intruding ships. It is uncertain who exactly the Germans thought the British flotilla were, but the ruse certainly gained them precious minutes and further progress up the river. In six minutes the *Campbeltown* was expected to reach the dock gates. There were now no heavy batteries to pass, but increasingly heavy fire from shore showed that they had been identified. *Campbeltown* and the MLs now ran up their white ensigns and returned fire. Ryder described the scene – "for about five minutes the sight was staggering, both sides losing off everything they had. The air was full of tracer ... flying horizontally, and at close range." The gun layers on the MLs, manoeuvring their short range weapons on slippery decks, managed to produce a slight lessening of enemy fire, which did not last long but which coincided with the *Campbeltown's* approach to the dock gates.

48   Ryder's recollections 35 years later, 'Folder A', IWM.

As she approached the gates, the destroyer increased her speed to twenty knots. Under continuous fire, First Chief Petty Officer Wellstead and then the quartermaster, were wounded at the wheel, and Tibbits stepped in to guide the ship in. At the last moment Beattie saw the dock gates illuminated by a searchlight or incendiary and gave the order to ram the gates. As the *Campbeltown* hit, her bows were crumpled back thirty-six feet and her fo'c'sle protruded over the inner gate of the lock. The commandos, still under heavy fire, scrambled ashore. Beattie now gave the order to abandon ship. The sea cocks were open and the scuttling charges set. The *Campbeltown* was now in the perfect position to demolish the lock gates when the main explosive charges in the bows detonated. The first half of the plan had been executed successfully, albeit four minutes late.

The MGB headquarters ship now manoeuvred into the old entrance, as Newman and his headquarters staff were desperate to get ashore and join the commandos who had disembarked from the *Campbeltown*. After landing Newman's party, Ryder's boat picked up survivors off the *Campbeltown* and then Ryder went ashore, accompanied and guarded by Able Seaman Pike to satisfy himself that the destroyer was firmly set in position. He heard the scuttling charges detonate and saw that the *Campbeltown* was settling by the stern. Satisfied that all was well and that the torpedoes from MTB 74 would not be needed, Ryder returned to his boat, and finding Wynn, captain of the torpedo boat, there alongside and awaiting orders, told him to fire his torpedoes into the outer lock gates of the old entrance and then return to Falmouth.

Meanwhile, the two columns of MLs had not fared well. They had approached the last few miles up the estuary under withering fire. Of the MLs on the starboard column, only one, ML 177, managed to land its troops successfully. During the six minutes after the *Campbeltown* had struck, most of the starboard column MLs were out of action. Lt. Rodier in ML 177 had taken off survivors, including Beattie and Tibbits, from the *Campbeltown* and they set off for the open sea at 01.57. The MLs in the port column had been told to land their commandos at the old mole. The only one to succeed in this was Lt. Collier in ML 457.

After picking up survivors from the *Campbeltown*, Ryder and the MGB headquarters ship moved out of the old entrance to find a nightmare scene before them. Ryder recalled "up and down the river, there seemed to be 7-8 blazing MLs."[49] By now the MGB was the only motor vessel left and was consequently attracting fire. Unable to communicate with Newman and the shore party, Ryder was only able to try and work out what was going on in the battle on the quay. The MGB was hit repeatedly as Ryder, Curtis and Green the navigator decided what to do. The possibilities of the MTB being of much further help seemed hopeless. The two planned re-embarkation points at the old mole and the old entrance were both still in enemy hands, and the MGB was full of wounded, out of ammunition and with only a few able bodied crewmen left. Ryder regretfully decided the MGB should leave without attempting to re-embark any of Newman's party: "It was unlikely that we would survive another five minutes with the fire that was being concentrated in our direction."[50] After dropping a smoke float as a decoy, the remaining motor launch sped down the estuary. It was a difficult decision for Ryder to make. In a BBC documentary filmed in 1974 he remembered "we'd been working closely with the commandos and Charles Newman ... and to leave them behind was very sad but we were faced with the fact that the only two possible places for withdrawal were in enemy hands."

49   Hopton, *Reluctant Hero*, p.156.
50   Ryder's report.

Retreating down the estuary the remaining motor craft had to face fire from both sides of the estuary and from the heavy coastal batteries past the Les Morées tower. The MGB was the last to leave the port, but overtook ML 156. When safely out of the shore batteries' range, Ryder reduced speed to see if any other MLs would catch up. It was here that a German patrol vessel appeared and fire was exchanged before the MGBs superior speed affected her escape. Slowly the remaining motor craft assembled and met up with the *Tyndale* and *Atherstone*. The crew of ML 156, which was sinking, and the wounded of the MGB and the other three MLs, were taken on board. When the destroyers *Cleveland* and *Brocklesby* arrived, Ryder relinquished command to Commander G.B. Sawyer. As the convoy of four destroyers and three small boats set out for home, it was decided to scuttle the motor craft as they were slowing progress and the wounded needed to get to treatment at home. *Atherstone* and *Tyndale* arrived at Plymouth at 02.30 on 29th March. Three remaining MLs made their way back alone, the only small vessels to return out of the eighteen that had set out.

The *Campbeltown* exploded on the morning of 28th March, destroying the gates of the Normandie lock and putting it out of action for the rest of the war. The commandos that had arrived in the *Campbeltown* had succeeded in the demolition of their objectives, the pumping house, the winding house and detonating charges on the inner caisson gate. The few commandos who had been landed from the motor launches had no realistic chance of success and although they fought their way into the port they were rounded up and arrested, although five did escape and managed to get to Spain.

In his remarks and recommendations after the raid, Ryder said: "The plan we attempted seemed to me reasonably sound and in fact we achieved the main object, though it must be admitted the cost was high." [51] In his analysis of the casualty figures for the raid, he later commented "the numbers killed were small compared with many operations which took place later and achieved less." [52] A longer-term result of the raid was the increasing efforts of the German army to defend the long Atlantic coast, using a disproportionate number of men and resources in constructing the Atlantic Wall. The raid also provided a distinct boost for British morale at a bleak time in their fortunes of war, and also for French morale at a time when German occupation seemed to be unending in prospect.

When the news of the St Nazaire raid broke in the press, Ryder became somewhat of a national hero. On 21st May his citation for the Victoria Cross appeared in the *London Gazette*:

> For great gallantry in the attack on St Nazaire. He commanded a force of small unprotected ships in an attack on a heavily defended port and led HMS *Campbeltown* in under intense fire from short-range weapons at point-blank range. Though the main object of the expedition had been accomplished in the beaching of *Campbeltown*, he remained on the spot conducting operations, evacuating men from *Campbeltown* and dealing with strong points and close range weapons while exposed to heavy fire for one hour and sixteen minutes, and did not withdraw till it was certain his ship could be of no use in rescuing any of the Commando ships still ashore. That his Motor Gun Boat, now full of dead and wounded, should have survived and should have been able

---

51   Ryder's report, 'Remarks by Naval Force Commander', 1942, IWM.
52   Ryder, *Attack on St Nazaire*, p.93.

to withdraw through an intense barrage of close range fire was almost a miracle.[53]

Ryder had felt a sense of destiny when appointed as naval commander of the raid on St Nazaire and had said "It was as if I had been waiting for it".[54] His previous experiences on the *Tai Mo Shan* and the *Penola*, added to his naval experiences, had produced a character which had been able to achieve the accomplishment in action noted in the citation for his Victoria Cross.

Following the raid on St Nazaire, Ryder was employed at Combined Operations Headquarters where he took part in the planning of the Dieppe Raid. He was to have led the party which was to capture enemy barges and attack dockyard installations once the harbour entrance had been captured. However, since the harbour entrance remained in enemy hands throughout, Ryder's part in the raid was aborted. We have seen in Chapter Three how Ryder was instrumental in the setting up of No. 14 Commando and 30 Assault Unit. In both these operations he was able to call on the expertise of former Polar colleagues, such as Andrew Croft, Augustine Courtauld and Quintin Riley. In May 1943 Ryder was appointed to 'J Force', whose object was to provide a permanent naval force to supply protection to assault troops. He was to work at arrangements for providing covering fire from a variety of vessels and adapted landing craft which would accompany assault troops' landing craft and provide covering fire.

On D-Day Ryder's task was to successfully land the Canadian regiment, the Queen's Own Rifles at Bernières, followed by the LCTs with the DD 'swimming' tanks aboard, followed by the LCRs and the artillery.[55] The amphibious tanks, nicknamed 'Donald Ducks', did not fare well on D-Day generally, the most notorious instance of their problems being experiences at Omaha Beach. Ryder decided that the sea was too rough to launch the DDs and so they were landed straight onto the beach. Ryder later went ashore to check on progress. Ryder's biographer Richard Hopton discovered that despite the difficulties in landing that the Canadian 3rd Division made better progress than any other Allied division on D-Day. Ryder was mentioned in dispatches for his part in the D-Day landings, and again in August when in command of the destroyer HMS *Opportune,* in operations against German E-boats in the Channel. From September 1944 to April 1945 the *Opportune* served on the destroyer screen on the Russian convoys, Ryder visiting Russia five times.

Ryder was the only man to receive a Polar Medal and a Victoria Cross. These awards symbolise his amazing career as both Polar explorer and sailor. The same qualities of bravery, resilience and determination characterised his achievements in both fields.

---

53 *The London Gazette* 21st May 1942.
54 Ryder memoirs, IWM.
55 Hopton, *Reluctant Hero*, p.179.

9

Lancelot Fleming

Iceland 1932

Lancelot Fleming entered Westcott House Cambridge for his ordination training on October 1931, after reading Geology and studying at Yale University for two years. He had made the decision to be ordained although a promising academic career as a geologist had been a serious and viable alternative. In May 1932 he was invited to go on a short expedition to Iceland led by Brian Roberts, a biologist. After gaining permission from the Reverend B.K. Cunningham, Principal of Westcott House, who had a liberal understanding of training for ordination, he travelled with the party on a Hull trawler to Iceland. There the expedition travelled by pony, crossing fast flowing rivers, to the Vatnajokull ice cap, which Fleming described as being about the size of Yorkshire. At the edge of the ice cap they sent the ponies back and transferred their equipment onto two eleven foot sledges. At this point they discovered that the seismograph did not work and deposited it to pick up on the way back. This was an early blow to the programme of the expedition as one of their aims was to measure the depth of the ice cap.

The party sledged across the ice cap, each making discoveries in their disciplines of geology, biology and botany. Fleming had his first experience of man hauling, which he remembered made him feel decidedly 'mule minded' as he was convinced that he was the only person pulling any weight and then discovered that everyone else thought that also of themselves. The beauty of Iceland made an impression on Fleming: "the colours of the sky were unlike anything I have seen elsewhere and as the sun rose parts of the ice cap glowed with a rose colour while in the south the horizon was a deep indigo."[1]

On the journey across the ice cap, which took 15 days due to poor weather, Fleming became acquainted for the first time with sledging rations. The twenty-six ounces a day per man was made up of 6 ounces of biscuits, 8 ounces of Bovril pemmican, 4 ounces of butter, 4 ounces of chocolate, 4 ounces of sugar and two drinks of cocoa. He remembered in later lectures on his Arctic exploits that "a plate (of pemmican) in the evening after pitching camps gives you the impression you've had a five course dinner. The great thing is to go to sleep before you discover you haven't"[2] While they were laid up in the tent with four days weather, Fleming read extracts from the Book of Job in order to encourage the virtue of patience. On 14th July they reached the site at Kverkfjöll, at a terminal moraine overlooking a small ice-damned lake from which they were to complete fifteen days of mapping and surveying. Fleming concentrated on a geological exploration of the area. Further plans were put aside because of continuous rain and the party returned along their outward route to find that the trawlers had moved further north following the fish. Following a hair-raising voyage along the shore to the Westermann Islands in a chartered leaky motor boat with a drunk captain, they managed to arrange to be picked up by a steamer out of Reykjavik bound for Hull, and arrived there on 22nd August.

---

1   Lancelot Fleming's diary, cited by Giles Hunt, *Lancelot Fleming, A Portrait* (Norwich, 2003), p.22.
2   Donald Lindsay, *Friends for Life, a Portrait of Lancelot Fleming* (Seaford, 1981), p.57.

A pre-war Portrait of Lancelot Fleming. (*Young Men in the Arctic*)

The Oxford University Expedition to Spitsbergen 1933

Although the next opportunity for exploration came just as he was preparing for his ordination as deacon, again Fleming was fortunate to be given leave. The last days before his ordination were spent preparing to take part in Sandy Glen's first expedition to Spitsbergen. The expedition established base at Klass Billen Bay, but Fleming and the other members of sledge parties A and B were taken around to the north of the island to Treurenberg Bay to establish a base and depot to enable them to climb up to the ice cap. Fleming was to lead a sledging team which consisted of J.M. Edwards, an Oxford biologist, Carrington Smith, a Royal Engineer and Ordnance Survey expert and A.S. Irvine (brother of Sandy Irvine who had been killed on Everest).

The task of sledging parties and A and B was to travel by different routes over the ice cap and return down the glaciers to the southern base. In order for the two sledging parties to be able to complete their surveys, it was necessary for three men to lay a depot on the southern side of the inland ice. On 13th July Fleming, Binney and Smith left with two sledges, each weighing 450 lbs. The summer heat made the snow very soft and it was difficult. Once on the Duner Glacier, the going was easier but halfway up they met a succession of stagnant pools which necessitated long detours. Because of the melting pools the only way up to the head of the glacier was along its steep western flanks, where the going was slowed down by a series of crevasses. Travelling by evening and nighttime they progressed to the head of the glacier. Fleming estimated that they "generally sledged from six to eight hours a day, covering a distance which varied between three and fourteen miles according to the surface and the gradient."[3] At the head of the glacier a magnificent view

3   Ibid., p.61.

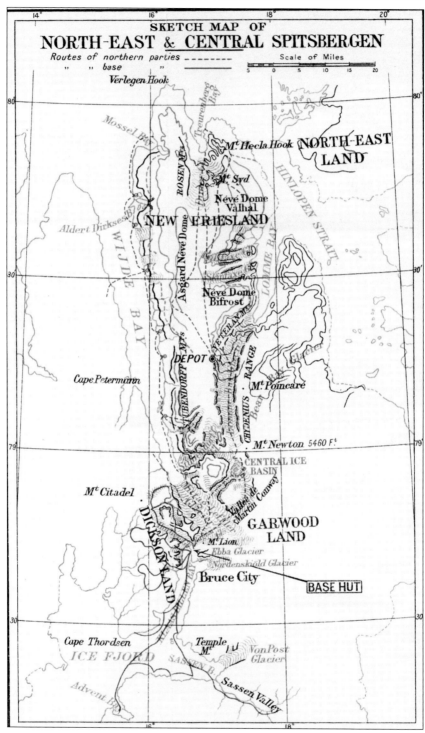

Map showing the route of the northern survey parties, 1933. (*Young men in the Arctic*)

The highest mountain in Spitsbergen, Mount Newton, 1933. (*Young Men in the Arctic*)

of the southern mountains greeted them. They could see in the distance Mount Newton, the Ivory Pyramid, Mont Poincare and further west the purple peaks of the Stubendorff Mountains above the Lomme Bay Glacier. Fleming wrote:

> The realisation of the beauty of Spitsbergen was never forgotten by us. It was so sudden and unexpected. In silence we continued and the same scene, ever changing in tint and hue, remained with us.[4]

Having found a suitable depot site, they unloaded the six ration cases, eight gallons of paraffin, a hundred pounds of dynamite and a pair of spare sledge runners. Three days sledging with a very much lightened load brought them back to Treurenberg Bay. After an overnight camp and catch up session in which sledging teams A and B were reformed, the teams set out on their different routes onto the ice cap the next morning,

Their first overnight stop on 3rd August was at Valhal Dome, one of several broad-arched domes on the ice cap interspersed with valley-like depressions, which correspond with valleys in the sub-glacial land. Smith and Irvine went off to survey Mount Hecla Hook, while Fleming and Edmonds went out to 'geologize' on the Duner Glacier. A second journey by Smith and Irvine to Hecla Hook resulted in them being stranded overnight by poor weather conditions in a hut which had been built for the Russo-Swedish expedition of 1899. Reunited, the sledging party had what they termed 'Valhal Feast', which consisted of a lemon juice aperitif, 'Gull with Pemmican and Worcester Sauce,' 'Valhal Pudding'(porridge and raisins) followed by 'Biscuits and Syrup', washed down by tea.

Three weeks were spent on the inland ice, with mixed success in photography and geologizing and the party arrived at the depot in the Veteran Mountains on 23rd August,

---

4   Alexander Glen, *Young Men of the Arctic* (London, 1934), p.74.

Start of the depot-laying journey, Spitsbergen, 1933. (*Young Men in the Arctic*)

Smith and Fleming outside Glacier Camp, Spitsbergen, 1933. (*Young Men in the Arctic*)

as planned. They now had to make their way back down to the main base at Petunia Bay. Progress onto the glacier was slow, because of the many lateral moraines, but progressing across the Lomme Bay glacier, the fog cleared and once again they were able to appreciate tremendous views of Mount Newton and the Chydenius range of mountains. Having reached the depot laid by the base camp party, Fleming and his companions were confident of reaching the expedition base in a few days. However the journey took six days, and as Fleming commented, they "learnt more of glaciers and their difficulties than ever before."[5] A mistake caused them to descend too early and they found themselves in two previously unnamed glaciers, struggling through a maze of ice hummocks and crevasses. They called the glaciers many unmentionable names but finally christened them 'fantastique' and 'formidable' after their sledges. They reached base camp on the evening of the 10th September where a feast was waiting. Roast pheasant, fried potatoes, fruit, biscuits and jam were consumed while reading *The Times* and listening to dance music from Daventry. Fleming remembered "finally the stories of the other parties [were] told and re-told until the darkness of the Arctic night had turned into the cold pink of morning."[6]

On his death one of Fleming's companions on the sledge party was of the opinion that the obituaries of him did not do justice to one aspect of his character, his courage: "the obituaries … all miss what I think about him, as a Lancashire lad, that is, that he really had guts and courage both mental and physical."[7] Glen praised him for his leadership skills on the ice cap journey. When Fleming was appointed to the bishopric of Portsmouth Glen wrote to him:

> Everyone who has had the privilege of knowing you, Lancelot, had had no doubt that you were cast for important duties. This I remember feeling so clearly as your party was coming down the Ebba Valley after crossing the ice cap. One of those odd striking moments one never forgets.[8]

His biographer, Giles Hunt, argues that the Spitsbergen expedition was good preparation for leadership in the church.

The British Graham Land Expedition 1934-37

On his return, Fleming took up his duties as chaplain at Trinity Hall, Cambridge, but was asked by John Rymill to join the British Graham Land Expedition (see chapters three and eight), which was to set out in the summer of 1934. From the start Fleming was attuned to the tensions existing between the ship's company and shore party, and was particularly aware of Ryder's dissatisfaction with the *Penola* and his worries about the amateur crew, which were, in Fleming's opinion, justified : "only a minority of our party knew which rope to pull and this made the task of the captain and two mates doubly anxious."[9] Fleming became good friends with Ryder, later becoming Ryder's daughter's godfather. Fleming did his best to mediate between opposing sections of the expedition and was to some extent successful, being given credit by the expeditions members for keeping relations harmonious

5   Ibid., p.94.
6   Ibid., p.99.
7   Hunt, *Lancelot Fleming*, p.26.
8   Lindsay, *Lancelot Fleming*, p.65.
9   Hunt, *Lancelot Fleming*, p.31.

'A' sledge party, Fleming first left. (*Young Men in the Arctic*)

as far as possible.

Before setting out, Fleming had received the blessing of the Archbishop of Canterbury, who said that as far as he knew a chaplain had not accompanied an expedition of this nature, and wished him well. Fleming took his duties as a chaplain, as well as his duties as a geologist, very seriously. He asked the Bishop of Gibraltar, as bishop responsible for any part of the world not covered by another Anglican bishop, to bless the expedition at St Katherine's dock before it set out. Lancelot's godfather, Reverend William Holland, was present at the blessing and described the "beautiful prayer of commendation for the ship and all who sailed in her.[10]" He also mentioned that underneath his robes, Fleming was dressed in a dirty blue shirt and torn flannel bags.

During the voyage out he held services on board accompanied by Riley on the piano accordion. Colin Bertram later described how one of Fleming's sermons was seriously disrupted by the first sighting of penguins swimming in the Southern Ocean. At Port Stanley in the Falkland Islands, he preached twice in the cathedral. As he was preaching regularly to a group of educated men, Fleming had to take time and trouble over his sermons. He also had difficulty in pitching his theme to "meet the spiritual needs of an argumentative Anglo-Catholic, a keen Wesleyan, a Presbyterian, a Christian scientist and one or two others who do not know whether they should call themselves Christian or not."[11] Fleming considered that two of his 'congregation' who called themselves scientific agnostics were unable to accurately describe themselves as such by the end of the expedition. Once established at base in the Argentine Islands he worked out a routine for daily and

10   Lindsay, *Lancelot Fleming*, p.72.
11   Hunt, *Lancelot Fleming*, p.49.

Sunday services. At Easter he invited all members, whether they were confirmed or not, to participate in Easter Holy Communion. Writing about his role as chaplain to Professor Frank Debenham in February 1936, he commented "I am more grateful than I could tell you for having been asked to come, and have had opportunities as a parson I particularly value."[12]

While the expedition was based at the Argentine Islands in the winter of 1935, Fleming found the area interesting geologically, with rocks to be collected and analysed, and work on ice samples from different depths to measure the rate of growth or decay of the sea ice. When they moved to their new base at Marguerite Bay the following year, he made some interesting discoveries among the rocks and fossils of Alexander I Land that were described as 'major geological finds'. He was also able to make glaciological observations, which combined with Stephenson's meteorological readings to show a picture of receding ice in the recent geological timescale. This discovery was to prove valuable to later work on global warming and ice cap melting.

In September 1936, Fleming set off as part of a sledging party consisting of himself, Bertram and Stephenson who were to proceed south, turning east when they found a possible channel to the Weddell Sea. They first had to climb and cross the col and were delayed for eight days by poor weather, but then descended to the ice shelf of the sound. They moved south down the sound, travelling between 20 and 25 miles a day. By 19th October they had reached Latitude 72° and in the absence of any sign of a channel running east, decided to turn around and examine Alexander I Island on the way back.

In two days they had crossed the sound and were the first men to visit Alexander I Island, which been charted from the sea by Bellingshausen a hundred years before and named after the Russian Tsar. Stephenson, in his account of this part of the expedition, described how they approached the Island at 71° latitude: " the approach was very easy, as the shelf and land ice merged into a smooth slope, up which the dogs raced, being brought to life again by the sight of rock close at hand."[13] Fleming wasted no time in establishing the nature of the rocks as sedimentary and fossil-bearing.

Fleming described in his report to *The Times* how the geology on the Alexander I Island side of the strait was different to that found on the Graham Land side, with stratified sedimentary rocks bearing many fossils of invertebrates which he considered to show evidence of "a bygone age when the climate of Antarctica was very different."[14] At Alexander I Island Fleming was excited by the fossil finds, including a large shell which indicated that the bedrock of that part of the island was Middle Jurassic. More recent research has found that the rocks to be found on this coastal field of Alexander I Island date from the early Jurassic to the mid-Cretaceous period. The party camped on what they called 'ablation camp', in a bowl-shaped basin, nearly a mile across, surrounded by 100 ft ice cliffs. The rocks had been broken up by frost action, leaving black specks of fine dust which had absorbed the sun's rays, causing a localised excessive thawing. Here they collected some more fossils, mainly brachiopods and belemnites. Stephenson commented that he would have not been surprised to see coal seams in some of the shales near the camp. John Rymill, in his account *Southern Lights*, described Fleming's main geological findings as discovering

---

12   Letter from Fleming to Frank Debenham dated 6th February 1936, cited by G. Hunt, *Launcelot Fleming*, p.59.
13   Rymill, *Southern Lights*, p.193.
14   *The Times*, 12th December 1934.

the difference between the sedimentary rock of Alexander I Island and the volcanic rocks of Graham Land. He added "Fleming spent much of his time studying and interpreting the glacial topography of the country." He remembered that "the narrowing fringing glaciers of the coast and the remnants of a once more widespread ice shelf" were of special interest to Fleming.

As they now only had 22 days food left, it was decided reluctantly to leave Alexander I Island and make a return journey which had taken them 32 days on the outward journey. Moving back up the sound they found that the hard surfaced ice had become deep soft snow. Fleming recorded in his diary: "Our skis would not slide and became caked with clinging snow ... The dogs were having a really hard time of it."[15] At one stage Fleming had the heart-stopping experience of seeing Bertram and Stephenson disappear. They had mistakenly believed that they had reached the bottom of the drifted side of a large ice rift, and fell 30 feet. From where Fleming was waiting with the dogs, it seemed as if they had disappeared into a crevasse. Through his head flashed the awful prospect of having to return to base alone, which he felt would be an unlikely achievement. Luckily they landed on soft snow and were not injured.

They continued to be delayed by bad weather and food supplies were very low. They were forced to kill six of the dogs, to reduce dog food consumption and to feed the remaining dogs, but by 11th November the weather improved and they managed to get as far as Terra Firma Island, where Rymill had left a depot. Fleming remembered that he had "an orgy of porridge, margarine and chocolate". When the base had been regained Fleming realised that they had been close to meeting the same fate as Scott and his party 25 years earlier. The readers of *The Times*, for whom Fleming was 'special correspondent' for the duration of the expedition, however would not have recognised this from Fleming's underplayed report:

> For the latter half of the journey rations had to be slightly reduced and it was becoming necessary to punch additional holes in belts. But at Terra Firma Island, where a depot had been laid, a seal was killed and this inconvenience was happily remedied.[16]

Fleming, Stephenson and Bingham had travelled 600 miles and mapped 500 miles of coastline, 450 miles of which had never been seen before.

The members of the expedition were all back at the southern base at Marguerite Bay before the *Penola* arrived from her repairs in South Georgia. They said farewell to the base on 12th May, after Fleming had been taken up in the Moth to obtain some pictures of the *Penola* returning. The shore party of scientists were taken back to Britain on a whaler from South Georgia, so Fleming arrived back home at the end of May, two years and eight months after setting out from St Katherine's dock. His first curacy had entailed being in charge of five and a half million square miles, with the pastoral oversight of 15 men in unusual circumstances. Bertram remembered "in Lancelot Fleming we had a man who exerted a great influence for good." At the time of Fleming's death, Robert Runcie, Archbishop of Canterbury, described how the experience of the three years in Antarctica had moulded Fleming's character and his style of ministry. His friend and biographer, Donald Lindsay, quoted Bishop Hensley Henson's dictum, that "no one can be respected as a priest who is

---

15   Fleming copied out parts of his diary for friends and family. This entry is cited by Hunt, *Lancelot Fleming*, p.66.
16   *The Times*, 12th December 1936.

HMS *Queen Elizabeth* (Hutchinson's *Pictorial history of the war*)

not first respected as a man" and commented "the years of polar exploration ensured that Lancelot had won respect as both."[17] This pastoral role and his knowledge of the sea and seamen was to stand him in good stead in his wartime career.

Wartime Naval Chaplain

On his return from Antarctica, Fleming took up the post of Dean of Trinity Hall, Cambridge and found time to produce two papers for the *Geographical Journal*, one on 'Relic Glacial Form on the Western Seaboard of Graham Land' which was published in August 1940, and one on "Structure and Flow of Glacier Ice: A review", published in 1938. On the outbreak of war, despite having harboured, like many of his generation of clergy, pacifist views, he decided that the lack of hardly any students left at Trinity Hall made his position there untenable, and volunteered as a naval chaplain. It was the service that appealed to him most as he agreed with the naval premise that chaplains should have no rank, and possibly it appealed as a result experiences at sea as an explorer. He was accepted and joined in June 1940, being posted to the shore training establishment HMS *King Alfred* at Hove. The building was a recently designed swimming and leisure complex, but was requisitioned on the outbreak of war by the RNVR as a training base. Fleming was the first full-time chaplain to the shore base there. During the war years 22,500 officers of the Royal Navy Volunteer Reserve were trained here. The original pools were boarded over; one sports hall was used as a mess room and the other as a drill hall. The underground car park was used as the dormitory. Fleming was gratified to discover the importance the navy gave

17   Lindsay, p.92.

Sunday service aboard a destroyer. (Hutchinson's *Pictorial history of the war*)

to the Christian religion. King's Regulations and Admiralty orders from Samuel Pepys' time stressed the requirement of the captain to make sure Sunday services were held and that the chaplain was not expected to take on other duties which would "interfere with his being regarded as a friend and advisor to all on board." At HMS *King Alfred* trainee officers passed through very quickly, giving Fleming little opportunity to get to know them, but he insisted, on joining, on taking the course that the prospective officers had to take himself. He also asked that he might address each new course of officers in their first week, in order to attempt to get to know them better. After five months in the shore establishment he calculated that he had met and got to know half of the RNVR officers in the Royal Navy.

In 1940 Fleming was posted as chaplain to HMS *Queen Elizabeth* at Rosyth. The ship had been commissioned in the First World War and was the lead ship of the new super-dreadnought class of battle ships, which were oil fired. At the outbreak of war she was undergoing an extensive re-fit, which was being completed at Rosyth, where Fleming joined her.

Fleming's Biographer, Giles Hunt, has described Fleming's first few weeks on the battleship as "probably the most difficult time of his life"[18] Notwithstanding his experience on the *Penola,* most of his 1,200 strong new parishioners were not men of the type he had been used to ministering to. His essentially quiet personality and demeanour made it difficult for him to mix well. However, the evidence is that he made a good job of gaining the respect and even friendship of the 'lower decks'. He rarely wore uniform, preferring instead a suit, worn with a crumpled hat, necessary for the acceptance of salutes.

In the Antarctic, Fleming had learned to be phlegmatic about enduring rough conditions and privations and had picked up a smattering of naval language from Ryder and his crew. When he wore his uniform, his Polar Medal both engendered a degree of respect

---

18   Hunt, *Lancelot Fleming*, p.90.

Fleming emerging from a 15-inch gun on the *Queen Elizabeth*. (Giles Hunt, *Lancelot Fleming*)

and created opportunities for conversations. He also worked hard at knowing all the men and kept extensive records of them and information on their families. He wrote letters for men to their families, and apparently successfully proposed marriage by letter on behalf of one of the crew members. One Leading Seamen commented on the role he played in keeping morale up, having open house in his cabin, serving cocoa and biscuits and mainly "listening to our beefs and making the odd comment and generally cheering us up."[19]

In February 1941 the HMS *Queen Elizabeth* accompanied the HMS *Hood,* and was involved in an attempted intercept of the pocket battleships, the *Scharnhorst* and the *Gneisenau,* who were still at large in the North Atlantic. Admiral Tovey was watching the northern exits of the Atlantic carefully and deployed some of his battleships and cruisers in the search for the German raiders. On 20th February the German battleships were spotted off Finisterre and the HMS *Queen Elizabeth* and the HMS *Hood* joined Admiral Tovey's *Nelson*. Neither ship was actually battle-ready at this time, the *Hood* having just started sea trials after a refit and the *Queen Elizabeth* had not had her guns calibrated after refit and rearmament, but their presence was justified by the circumstances. Stephen Roskill, the author of the official history *The War at Sea*, explained that "the urgency was considered such as to justify the employment of ships which were unlikely to develop their full fighting capacity if an action were to take place."[20] Fleming's ship was therefore steaming to a possible action in which the odds would be stacked against her. He preached a sermon on Sunday 26th February as the ship sailed south. His theme was, appropriately, "Be not

19   Ibid., p.91.
20   S.W. Roskill, *The War at Sea* Volume I (London, 1954), p.378.

anxious for your life."

After respite being berthed at Freetown in West Africa, the *Queen Elizabeth* was next involved in an attempt to take a swift-moving convoy straight through the Mediterranean, as part of Force H, to take tanks to the Army of the Nile. The convoy succeeded in getting four of the five merchant ships through to Alexandria. The ship now joined the Mediterranean fleet at Alexandria. In May she took part in the battle for Crete. The main job of the navy was to prevent enemy landings on Crete and to keep the army supplied. Admiral Cunningham signalled to all ships "stick it out. Navy must not let the army down. No enemy forces are to reach Crete by sea." None did, but only at the cost of British ships being involved in what Corelli Barnet described as "the death ride" on the coast of Crete and in the Eastern Mediterranean.[21] On 25th May the aircraft carrier *Formidable,* the *Queen Elizabeth* and the *Barnham* set sail to attack the German airbase on Scarpento Island to try and reduce the pressure of air attacks on the ships operating off Crete. After initial success caused by surprise, enemy dive bombers attacked the three ships, damaging the *Barnham,* which then returned to Alexandria. From the beginning of September, HMS *Queen Elizabeth* became Admiral Cunningham's flagship following the damage sustained by the *Warspite.*

On 24th November the *Queen Elizabeth* sailed with Admiral Cunningham's force to support his cruisers who were hunting an Italian fuel convoy. German U-boat U-331 managed to avoid the destroyer screen and attacked the *Barnham,* which sank with much loss of life in a few minutes.[22] Admiral Cunningham described the scene.

> The ship rolled nearly over on her beam ends and we saw men massing on her upturned side. A minute later came the dull rumble of a terrific explosion as one of her main magazines blew up. The ship became completely hidden in a great cloud of yellowish-black smoke ... When it cleared away the *Barnham* had had disappeared. There was nothing to be seen but a bubbly, oily patch on the calm surface of the sea, covered with wreckage and the heads of swimmers. It was ghastly to look at, a horrible and awe-inspiring spectacle when one realised what it meant. [23]

Fleming, preaching a sermon just after the war, described how fewer than 500 survivors out of 1,200 crew had been eventually picked up and how that evening he had prayers broadcast throughout the ship. He used as one of his prayers, "That while we pass through the changing things of time we should not lose the things eternal." He felt that every crew member had had the opportunity to be united with their shipmates in their fears and hopes and that this had brought them closer to God, as he put it "into touch with the living God."[24] There is no doubt that the spiritual guidance that he was able to give in such times brought him closer to the seamen he ministered to.

On 19th December the *Queen Elizabeth* and the *Valiant* were attacked by what the official history called "a clever and determined attack at source". Three Italian 'human torpedoes' managed to enter Alexandria harbour when the submarine nets were open to allow traffic, and attached delayed action mines to the hulls of the two battleships. These

21   Correlli Barnett, *Engage the Enemy More Closely: the Royal Navy in the Second World War* (London, 1991), p.356.
22   S.W. Roskill, *The War at Sea* Volume I (London, 1954), p.534.
23   Admiral Cunningham, cited in Barnett, p.375.
24   Hunt, *Lancelot Fleming,* p.96.

mines detonated at 6 a.m., seriously damaging and flooding both ships. The full extent of the damage to the *Queen Elizabeth* was not realised by the enemy, as her hull settled on the bottom and she was able to be refloated in an upright position by a floating dock. By May 1942 she had been repaired enough to make the journey to the United States naval dockyard at Norfolk Virginia, where it took 13 months to repair her. During this time Fleming devoted much time and energy to arranging a holiday with an American family for each crew member.

The *Queen Elizabeth* returned to Britain on 8th July 1943, and Fleming's commission with her ended. Captain Berry, commanding officer for the time Fleming spent on the ship, marked him highly on his officer's report and added the comment "my idea of a real Christian"[25] After a brief spell on HMS *Ganges*, a shore establishment, Fleming was appointed as director of Service Ordination Candidates, thus officially ending his naval service. He was impressed with the strong sense of vocation and Christian conviction showed by the candidates, who were from all backgrounds and all styles of churchmanship.

In Autumn 1946 Fleming returned to work as Chaplain of Trinity Hall. This he combined with three years as director of The Scott Polar Institute and he also served on the council of the Royal Geographical Society and the Falkland Islands Dependencies Scientific Committee. He became Bishop of Portsmouth in 1949, which was appropriate for a man who had spent much of his life at sea in one capacity or another.

---

25   Lindsay, p.122.

10

Augustine Courtauld

The Cambridge University Expedition to Greenland, 1926

Courtauld was a member of the Courtauld textile family and therefore from a rich and privileged background. His story in many ways epitomises the careers of young men with an upper class background and public school education who had missed the Great War and, with no pressing need to earn their living, ended up expressing their individuality and need for adventure by becoming part of the cohort of inter-war polar explorers.

Following a disappointment at having been rejected for naval training when he was thirteen, Courtauld followed a conventional path of school at Charterhouse and university education at Trinity College Cambridge. At Charterhouse he disliked games and concentrated on rifle shooting. At Cambridge, he had 'few academic pretensions'.[1] He spent his 21st birthday in the summer of 1935 at sea off the North Cape of Norway on a visit to the Lapland areas of Norway and Finland and during his time at Cambridge was given by his father his yacht *Duet*. According to his biographer, on leaving Cambridge, and being disinclined to enter the family business, he made a decision that by some means he would travel to the Arctic.

He joined an expedition to Greenland being organised by James Wordie, who had survived being stranded on Elephant Island in the Shackleton expedition of 1914-1917. Wordie was a fellow of St John's College and was becoming a father figure and mentor to a new generation of polar explorers. His 1926 expedition was following on from an attempt in 1923, which had had to be abandoned because of severe ice conditions off the East Greenland coast. Wordie and his party had narrowly avoided repeating history and emulating the fate of the *Endeavour* of being frozen in and crushed by the ice pack. Conditions were considerably better in the summer of 1926 and the team were able to land for a few weeks of hectic work, utilising the twenty-four hour daylight of the summer season.

Courtauld was not seasick and spent much of the voyage looking out from the crow's nest. He was impressed with the change of conditions when the *Heimland*, the expedition ship, entered the pack ice: "no longer ocean but not quite land. The surface of the sea flattened, filed with floating ice.[2]" After dropping off two scientists at Sabine Island, the ship surveyed the coast and Courtauld was introduced to the art of surveying, the use of plane tables and azimuth calculations. Wordie then proceeded to sail into Franz Joseph Fjord, which had not been looked at since its discovery by Professor Nathorst in 1899.[3] Courtauld enjoyed taking part in the mountaineering forays to assess the depths of the range of mountains in the hinterland of a mountain they called 'Petermann Peak'. As the ice-free window was closing in, Wordie had to reluctantly return to the *Heimland* leaving the mountains for future explorers. Courtauld spent his 22nd birthday on the way back to Reykjavik and arrived back in Scotland on 8th September 1926. He had caught the

1 N. Wollaston, *The man on the ice cap: the life of August Courtauld* (London, 1980), p.37.
2 Ibid., p.45.
3 M. Smith, *Sir James Wordie, Polar Explorer* (Edinburgh, 2004), pp.176-177.

224

Pre-war portrait of August Courtauld. (*Northern Lights*/Spencer Chapman family)

polar exploring bug, or as his biographer put it, "just as surely, like a ship in pack ice, his imagination was caught."[4]

Journey in the Sahara Desert 1927

In May 1927, Courtauld was invited to share in a very different expedition. Francis Rodd, diplomat, stockbroker and explorer, was returning to the Sahara to examine again the Air region and the Tuareg people. The party consisted of Rodd, his brother Peter, who was a contemporary of Courtauld, and Courtauld, who was responsible for mapping and surveying. They sailed to Lagos and then took a train north to Kano. They then travelled by car to Katsina on the border of Nigeria and French West Africa. With the help of the Emir they organised their caravan of twelve men and thirty-two camels and set off into the scrub just as the rains broke on 29th May. In early July they had reached the beginning of the desert and after an anxious few days when the only water to be obtained necessitated nineteen hours of digging, arrived in a watering place for the tribes with a deep pool in a gorge with bushes and palms surrounding it. Rodd planned to revisit the village of Auderas, in the mountain region of Air, one of the Saharan mountain groups. He had visited Auderas five years previously and the party received a warm welcome. An old Tuareg friend, Tekhmedin, had heard of Rodd's arrival and travelled 150 miles to see him. Tekhmedin was one of the most famous guides of Air who had fought against the French and knew the Sahara intimately.

Courtauld thoroughly enjoyed the weeks spent at Auderas. He wrote home describing the scenery of the area: "it is more mountainous than Scotland. Great crags and precipices

---

4   Wollaston, *The man on the ice cap*, p.52.

Peter Rodd, Courtauld and Francis Rodd, Sahara Desert, 1927 (*Man the Ropes*)

go all around."[5] He was happy with his allotted task, which was to take theodolite readings from the summits of the peaks in the region. Peter Rodd and Courtauld set off to climb the highest peak an adjacent range of mountains, the Todra range, but were defeated by some un-climbable blocks of rock in their way. Courtauld tried an alternative route a few days later and succeeded in surveying from the top. As they had now mapped 400 square miles of unknown country, Rodd decided it was time to move on to explore the northern Air region. While saying at Iferuan, waiting for permission to move on across the Sahara, Tekhmedin was arrested for sedition and had to be bailed out of prison. Unfortunately the required permission to cross the Sahara to the Mediterranean was refused, leaving the explorers with two options – to return southwards to Nigeria, retracing their steps, or to travel westwards across 500 miles of desert to the River Niger, and on via Timbuktu to the Atlantic coast.

While they were deciding, an opportunity arose to make themselves popular with the French authorities and the local population by stepping in for a missing patrol which was supposed to be protecting the autumn trade caravan from Air by scouting part of the route and warning of possible raiders by looking for suspicious tracks in the desert and making sure the watering holes were safe. The Rodd brothers and Courtauld formed the 'Tarazit Patrol,' along with some members of Tuareg bands. When they returned, they found that their fame had spread and that there were now willing volunteers to accompany them on the next step of their journey.

By 12th November they had dropped down from the Air region and were travelling

---

5   Letter to Mollie Montgomerie, cited in Wollaston, *The man on the ice cap*, p.62.

across the sand. They were following a guide, Khayer, but Courtauld was also plotting their route with a compass and a chronometer. However, he soon realised that the Tuareg man had navigated the caravan for 100 miles without any deviation. When they arrived at the oasis at Battal they unpacked their wireless and aerial and now started taking star observations and checking their position by wireless signal. With this equipment and their growing expertise at celestial observation they were able to fix the water holes for the western desert. Wollaston described how the whole of Air had to be moved several miles east on the map as a result of their calculations.

Their journey westwards was made unpredictable by the loss of confidence of their guide, Khayer, now far from home. After experiencing some hostility Rodd managed to acquire another guide who led them through the part of the desert called the Belly of the Negress, as far as the River Niger. There their Tuareg friends left them to head for home. After some sumptuous hospitality in Timbuktu, the party hitched a lift on a wood-burning river steamer for the eight-day journey to the coast.

The Rodd brothers and Courtauld returned to Britain to be congratulated on the results of their expedition by the Royal Geographical Society. They had drawn seventeen maps while exploring unknown territory, taken meteorological readings and rainfall measurements. They had photographed the rock drawings and writings found and collected a host of botanical, anthropological, geological and historical material. The expedition had been quite different to any others that Courtauld had, or would, experience, but added to his experience and skills set as well as providing, in Rodd, a model of leadership which Courtauld much admired.

The Cambridge University Expedition to Greenland 1929

In Courtauld's absence, J.M. Wordie had been planning another expedition to Greenland, to continue surveying and to attempt to climb the Petermann peak. The party was of a different composition than the previous one, and, apart from Wordie only Courtauld and another man, Forbes, had experience on ice. Wordie chose the Trömso boat the *Heimland*, which had just returned from an unsuccessful search for Amundsen, who had disappeared whilst searching for Umberto Nobile, the lost Italian explorer. The ice conditions were not as favourable in 1929 as in 1926 and it took the *Heimland* nearly a month to push through the pack ice to reach the coast. This delay meant that they landed at Mackenzie Bay late in the season, with only a few weeks to complete their agenda before there was a danger of being frozen in for the winter. Courtauld was one of the six-member team who then set out for Mount Petermann.

The men worked their way towards the peak for five days, completing the map started in 1926. The major obstacle in their way was the Nordenskiold Glacier, but having crossed that they camped at the foot of the mountain. At this point the weather was closing in and Wordie decided that there was no point in waiting for it to clear. If the attempt was to be made it had to be done immediately. All their surplus gear was left at 7,380 feet and after a mug of hot tea the party, minus Varley, who had broken his boots, set out for the summit. They arrived at the south-west crest at five and within two hours had reached a ledge fifty nine feet beneath the summit. By now a strong gale was blowing and Fuchs reported that at this stage his boots were frozen solid and his face had lost all feeling. Wordie thought that the conditions precluded all members going on to the summit as he felt that this final stage of the climb was too dangerous with less than three men roped together. Courtauld and

The view south-westwards towards inland ice from
Petermann Peak. (*Conquest of the North Pole*)

Fuchs were left behind on the ice ledge while Wordie, Forbes and Wakefield cut ice steps to
the top. They reached the summit at 10.30 on 15th August and left a note in a tin, as there
was no space to build a cairn. The light was too poor to take photographs. While he was
waiting, Courtauld measured the altitude by getting out the primus stove and melted ice for
the hypsometer. He measured the height of Mount Petermann at 9,650 feet, not as high as
they had guessed but still the highest discovered peak in the Arctic.

The trek back to the shore was arduous in the extreme, over soft snow which they sunk
into, or black ice swept with snow. Strong winds and freezing temperatures added to their
problems. They were rapidly running out of food and were cold, hungry and exhausted.
Courtauld was carrying a tent, the primus, a plane table, the theodolite legs and the
hypsometer as well as his own personal equipment. He slipped over under this weight quite
often and one of the other members commented later on his rather frail body: "I didn't
think he was going to last out ... anyone less courageous and determined wouldn't have done
so."[6] Wordie now made another difficult decision to cover the last few miles in a single day
as food supplies were almost exhausted. It took fourteen hours, punctuated by small breaks.
Wordie remembered, "if we sat down, we were too tired to get up." As it was they nearly
missed the *Heimland,* whose captain had become concerned about being trapped in ice and
was on the verge of leaving. After a difficult journey back through the ice pack, they arrived
in Aberdeen on 9th September. The expedition was praised for its successes in opening up
new territory to the west of Franz Joseph Fjord and challenging some preconceptions on
East Greenland's geography, and particularly the ascent of Petermann Peak. Vivian Fuchs
described the expedition as "a memorable baptism of ice." [7]

---

6   Cited by Wollaston, *The man on the ice cap*, p.87.
7   Vivian Fuchs, *A Time to Speak: An Autobiography* (Oswestry, 1990), p.60.

The BARRE base in winter, Bugbear Bank in the background.
(*Northern Lights*/Spencer Chapman family)

British Arctic Air Route Expedition 1930-31

Courtauld's twenty-sixth birthday was spent at a precarious fjord-side camp in the Kangerdlugssuaq Fjord, where himself, Spencer Chapman, Wager and Stephenson were surveying this fjord as part of coastal survey from a small boat (see Chapter Two). Courtauld's job was to be in charge of the theodolite observations. Following a mishap in which the theodolite became submerged in deep water, Courtauld took the instrument apart, washed each part with fresh water, cleaned them with petrol and reassembled it. The theodolite belonged to Francis Rodd, and Courtauld noted in his diary: "Francis will be interested to know that in two days I took the theodolite completely to pieces and got it going again."[8] It was decided because of the lateness of the season to complete the survey from the *Quest* as it went back down the coast but Courtauld and Stephenson continued to survey as much as possible and made use of the darker nights by making many astronomical observations.

We have seen how the ice cap station had been manned since its creation by two men, firstly by Lindsay and Riley, who had been relieved by Bingham and D'Aeth. On 26th November Spencer Chapman as leader set out with Stephenson, Hampton Lemon Wager and Courtauld. The plan was to leave Stephenson and Hampton at the ice station to relieve Bingham and D'Aeth. The journey was very difficult and we have seen how Courtauld volunteered to man the ice cap station alone as there were no longer enough rations to support two men throughout the worst part of the winter. Spencer Chapman wrote in

---

8   Ibid., p.110.

his diary, "Courtauld came into our tent this morning and suggested he should stay alone at ice cap station ... Courtauld says he is used to being alone and is very keen to try the experiment in such conditions. With so many books, a good supply of tobacco and ample food for one man he says he will be perfectly happy and is most anxious to do this."[9] When they reached the ice cap station, Spencer Chapman had to decide what to do. Bingham and D'Aeth, the most recent occupants, were against one person staying behind and Bingham's status as doctor added weight to his arguments. Spencer Chapman however was convinced by Courtauld's arguments He wrote, "Courtauld is determined to stay and eventually we gave in. I must say that it would be a thousand pities to abandon the station now, since it had been established and maintained with so much trouble."[10] The following morning, on 6th December, Courtauld waved the other members off: "it was bitterly cold and I didn't watch them long. Coming out an hour later I could just see them as a speck in the distance. Now I am quite alone. Not a dog or even a mosquito to look at." Courtauld wrote a description of his time at the ice cap station in Spencer Chapman's official account of the expedition, *Northern Lights*. He described how the first few weeks he was kept busy with housekeeping chores and with the necessity to get fully dressed six times a day to complete the meteorological observations. It became difficult for him to dig himself out of the tunnel leading from the floor of the tent to the outside, because of the increasing drifting of snow in the gales of increasing ferocity. Much to his relief Courtauld solved this problem by making a hole in the roof of the snow house which was connected to the tent (see diagram), and fashioning a trap door out of a packing case lid.

At Christmas he discovered that four gallons of his paraffin had leaked away, and he could now only use the primus stove for cooking. He allowed himself some reminiscing about Christmases past and also a hint of loneliness was apparent in his diary entry: "How jolly to be at home or even at the base. I suppose they will be having a blind and finishing the last of the alcohol." He continued with his worries about the snow house above his tent. "Hope it isn't going to fall in – if only I could put the clock on to next Christmas."[11] He was expecting a visit from the Moth plane in January, but was not overly concerned when it did not turn up, except he decided that it was time to bring the spare paraffin and food into the ice house. It took him several weeks to locate the extra rations, dig them out and bring them in to the snow house. To pass the time, he designed a new yacht and then moved on to turn his attention to new designs for meteorological instruments. By 15th March he had less than two gallons of paraffin left, and had reduced his food ration to 1lb a day, and was only able to light his lamp for brief periods.

On 19th March a gale from an unusual direction blew snow through his trap door entrance in the snow house, filling it up and blocking any exit. Courtauld now excavated another tunnel to the roof of the other snow house and managed to make a packing case door. He explained the problem with this:

> The shaft was too long to reach up from inside, and to allow me to pack snow around a box covering the hole, as had been done by a previous exit, so the shaft was shortened by digging a hollow from outside. As I feared, a gale immediately started blowing, and drifted up the hollow, thus putting a weight on the closing box. More than it was

9   Ibid., p.123.
10   J.M. Scott, *Portrait of an Ice Cap, With Human Figures* (London, 1955), p.98.
11   Wollaston, *The man on the ice cap*, p.138.

possible to move.[12]

Courtauld was now trapped underground, and further attempts to reach any remaining rations or make observations were impossible. He recounted that it was at this stage he began to be worried about his safety for a number of reasons. He was worried that the air quality would decline as the only exit for air was the two-inch ventilator in the roof of the tent house. He found that fresh air found its way in through the snow walls of the tunnels and side houses, and there remained a good up-draught to the ventilator. He was also concerned that eventually the walls of the tent would collapse under the increasing pressure of snow. A pressing worry was that the relief party would not be able to find him buried under the snow, but he remembered that the Union Flag was on its pole above the tent and trusted in his friends' ability to find it.

Courtauld had been assuming a date of about 15th March for his relief and had not been operating a rigorous rationing system: "I prefer, in fact, to eat my cake rather than have it. 'Carpe Diem' was a tag which served as an excuse whenever I felt hungry."[13] Throughout the first part of April his stores declined rapidly, with no fuel being expended on light, except for making brief diary entries, and all the tobacco was gone. The stove was used to warm oatmeal for breakfast, but all meals taken later were uncooked pemmican, biscuit and margarine. On 20th April he had almost no paraffin, only one candle left, a little pemmican and a few drops of lemon juice. On the day, 5th May, that fuel for the primus ran out Courtauld heard the eventual arrival of the relief party above him.

D'Aeth and Chapman had set out in the Moth on 8th February with the aim of dropping off mail, presents and luxuries to Courtauld. They could not find the ice cap station, however, in a bank of fog, and returned with their load. Another attempt by Cozens and Scott to find the station by aeroplane failed on 25th February. On 1st March Scott and Riley left for the ice cap station to attempt to relieve Courtauld, even the weather conditions were still severe. The ground beyond Big Flag Depot was very difficult, and they were force to turn back. The next attempt, supplemented by Lindsay and another sledge, suffered similar setbacks and returned within three days. Eventually on 26th March, Riley, Lindsay and Scott arrived where they had estimated the ice cap station to be. They then spent a fortnight in atrocious weather conditions crossing and re-crossing the area, hunting for the Union Flag that marked the ice cap station, but to no avail. They had decided not to take the time signal wireless set to be able to fix the longitude as well as their latitude, as it was heavy and would have easily been out of action if involved in sledging incidents. At times, Courtauld in his underground nest must have been very close to them. Scott as leader decided to abandon the attempt and return to allow a fresh party to make another attempt. The conditions were atrocious. Gordon Hayes examined their meteorological records for his book *The conquest of the North Pole* and considered that "the conditions approached the limits of human endurance"[14] Scott's party returned on 17th April and on 21st April Watkins, Rymill, Chapman and three sledges set out, this time taking the wireless time signal equipment.

Meanwhile concern was mounting in Britain. Despite reassurances from Watkins and then Lemon by wireless that the situation was under control, both Courtauld's parents and

---

12   F. Spencer Chapman, *Northern Lights*, p.182.
13   Ibid., p.184.
14   J. Scott, *Portrait of an Ice Cap*, p.153.

Watkins finding the ice cap station, BARRE, 1931. (*Northern Lights*/Spencer Chapman family)

the Royal Geographical Society were becoming anxious. Despite reassuring those at home that all that was possible was being done to find Courtauld, the message from Watkins ended "there is always the possibility that Courtauld is not alive, or unwell, in which case the station is probably completely covered."[15] This elicited a flurry of questions from the expedition committee which Lemon answered with as much information as was available. By 3rd April the Committee had released information to *The Times*, who had press rights of the expedition. This resulted in an article in *The Times* under the headline "Anxiety for the safety of Mr Courtauld".[16] Following this report other papers took up the tale with more sensational stories such as "Marooned on an Ice Cap." The Committee now chartered a Swedish plane, fitted with floats and ski and flown by Captain Ahrenberg to fly from Sweden via Iceland to the expedition base to assist in looking for the ice station or assisting the sledge party with reconnaissance. He set out on 2nd May but was turned back by fog. He landed eventually at Angmagssalik at 1.30 a.m. on 3rd May.

Watkins relief party was making good progress in the meantime. The weather was better, bright but very cold. On 5th May they obtained a fix with theodolite and wireless time signal which put them a mile north-west of where they expected the station to be. Watkins, Rymill and Spencer Chapman set out on skis with a dog each who they hoped would show some sign of excitement if they smelt any trace of a human being. They spotted

15   Ibid., p.152.
16   *The Times,* 24th April 1931.

Courtauld just after emerging from the ice cap station, BARRE,
1931. (*Northern Lights*/Spencer Chapman family)

the Union Flag and hurried towards it with some misgiving, seeing only some instruments and the hands of a spade sticking out of the snow drifts. Courtauld was lying beneath, on his last drop of paraffin, speculating on the chances of relief on this, his 150th day on the plateau. Suddenly he heard what he described as a sound like a bus going by, followed by the sound of yelling, and realised that his long wait was over. "I realized the truth. It was somebody, some real human voice, calling down the ventilator. It was a very wonderful moment."[17]

The rescue party lost no time in digging Courtauld out, and found that despite his privations he remained remarkably cheerful. Having donned the darkest pair of goggles available he emerged, and was surprised to find he could walk. After a night in a tent and a large bowl of porridge for breakfast, he was put on the sledge and after gathering the meteorological records from the ice cap station the party started out for base. As he was being pulled along the ice cap, Courtauld wrote in his diary "it is more wonderful than words can express to be free, out of that dark place under the snow and to be really going home".[18] As they progressed they were surprised to see Captain Ahrenberg's aeroplane, which dropped them unneeded food supplies and letters and messages. It was the first time that they had heard of the furore that had been going on in the press and of the various

17   Wollaston, *The man on the ice cap*, p.166.
18   Ibid., p.168.

Rymill, Watkins, Courtauld and Spencer Chapman on their return to base camp after
Courtauld's dramatic rescue, BARRE, 1931. (*Northern Lights*/Spencer Chapman family)

rescue plans. Courtauld described the fuss over his plight as "absurd hysteria".

In the chapter he wrote in the expedition book, *Northern Lights*, Courtauld reflected
on his experience and on the justification for subjecting a lone human to such an experience.
He thought that there was no reason why a man could not be left alone, provided he had
volunteered, that he was certain of arrangements for his food supply and eventual relief,
that he had plenty to occupy his mind and that the outside worlds were provided with
information on his safety. He added "I consider that a man for this purpose should have
an active, imaginative mind, but not be of a nervous disposition".[19] Although Watkins and
Courtauld played down the danger that Courtauld had been in, it was evident that relief
had arrived in the nick of time and that Courtauld had been very lucky. That same year the
German Greenland party had lost its leader, Alfred Wegener and an Eskimo, Rasmus, on
their way back from their own ice cap station, 'Eismitte'.

Despite imagining that he would stay at base and take it easy until returning to Britain
in August, Courtauld found himself involved in the last adventure of the expedition,
the open boat journey from the base to Julianehaab, 600 miles away on the south coast
of Greenland. Watkins had several plans to fulfil before the expedition left for home. In
July, Scott, Stephenson and Lindsay were to travel over the ice cap to the Settlement of
Ivigtut (see Chapter Two) on the west coast and Rymill and Hampton were to travel across
to Holsteinborg. Watkins asked Lemon and Courtauld to accompany him on the boat

---

journey. In his autobiography, Courtauld described this request:

> Gino asked, 'I say August, would you like to come with me on the boat journey?' Now
> I had heard about the boat journey and had decided that nothing would induce men
> to go. For one thing I thought our whale boats would never make the 600 miles to
> Julianehaab ... for another I was supposed to be getting married when I got home.[20]

He did however agree to go, and commented on Watkins's style of leadership: "Gino
never gave orders, he just asked you to do something: You always did it."[21]

The purpose of the journey was to try and fulfil a remaining aim concerning the air
route. An attempt to chart the coastal mountains to the south of the base from land had
failed, and Watkins now saw an opportunity to chart them from the coast. Watkins hoped
to improve the only existing map of the coast, made in the 1880s, and to obtain details of
the height and extent of the coastal mountains over which any proposed arctic air route
would have to cross. The plan was to take an eighteen-foot whale boat powered by a three
horse-powered motor. Courtauld was not impressed with the arrangements, arguing that
that the amount of fuel to be carried would leave no room for food, and that in the event
of anything happening to the boat, they would be stranded. Watkins agreed that two boats
would be advisable, but said that the party would not need to take much food, as they
would hunt and live off the land. One of the subsidiary aims of this part of the expedition
was in fact to see if it was possible to live off the land as the Eskimos did. He did however
agree to take an extra boat, and on 15th August Courtauld, Lemon and Watkins set out
with two whale boats, loaded with three kayaks, guns rifles and revolvers. They carried
sledges in order to walk out if shipwrecked, and also survey instruments and a wireless.
The only food they carried was suet, oatmeal, tea and sugar. The Danish Government had
given permission for the journey only when Watkins assured them that they could all roll
their kayaks and that they were taking no natives. The opinion of the authorities as to the
wisdom of the coastal journey can be seen in Lemon's comment: "It is curious how reluctant
governments are to give leave for an undertaking which savours to them of 'hara-kiri'" [22]

After surveying the coastal mountains the intention was to travel swiftly around the
tip off Greenland to Julianehaab. Lemon recalled that they divided the duties of the voyage
between them. Courtauld was to take the astronomical observations and cope with the
boat handling, Lemon was to supervise the plane tabling, operate the wireless and maintain
the engine. Nicodemudgy, an old Eskimo hunter who had helped them previously, had
agreed to take his family to winter at Umivik and he took twenty-seven gallons of petrol
on ahead for the group. For the first ten days the boats made good progress down the coast,
calling in briefly at the Eskimo settlements at Shernegoy and Kajartalik. Here the survey
was started, Lemon and Courtauld surveying and Watkins hunting from his kayak. At
Pikiudtlek they met up with a settlement of Eskimos, some of whom they knew well from
the previous winter. Here they were delayed by a storm, initially, but then accounts diverge
as to the reason they stayed in the camp for nine days. Lemon reported that the delay was
caused by continued bad weather and said that "the delay was very annoying and tedious."
But according to Courtauld the delay was caused by Lemon and Watkins settling down to

---

20   A. Courtauld, *Man the Ropes* (London, 1957), p.66.
21   Ibid.
22   Spencer Chapman, *Northern Lights*, p.229.

enjoy life with their friends. He commented "He [Watkins] said we would be here for two days and we have been five already."[23] This tension was not reported by Courtauld in *Man the Ropes*, but he did comment on Watkins's attitude towards Eskimos, which showed his understanding of Watkins's desire to spend more time ashore: "he thought they were better people than we were, and I think he was right ... What he wanted to do above all was to study their hunting methods and way of life."[24]

The weather improved for their surveying of the coast down to Umivik, where they found Nicodemudgy's settlement and stayed another week, Watkins hunting by day and enjoying conversation with the Eskimos in the evening. As the major part of their survey was now complete Courtauld began to be impatient with the willingness of Lemon and Watkins to embrace the native lifestyle and began to suspect that they would not be averse to being frozen in for the winter. When they left, the good weather had broken up and they faced a difficult passage further down the coast. There seemed to be no belt of pack ice to protect the water nearer shore and when the gales and rain started they whipped up the waves against the boats, soaking everything and damaging the instruments and radio. Luckily they found a small sandy beach on which to land and sit out the storm. Courtauld became alarmed at further talk of overwintering by Lemon and Watkins. When they resumed their journey it was in one boat, which was overloaded. Watkins made the decision to continue down the coast, as opposed to overwintering or abandoning the boat and sledging back to base but if they could get no further by the beginning of October that they would stop for winter. After ten more days of rain they suddenly made good progress, on 1st October covering fifty miles. It was essential they reached Prince Christian Sound, the channel that would take them through to the west coast, cutting off the most southerly tip of Greenland, before it froze up. They entered the sound on 6th October and arrived at the first Danish settlement to a warm welcome before continuing up the coast to Julianehaab. Courtauld's return to Britain was further delayed when it was realised Hampton and Rymill had not arrived at Holsteinborg, where they were supposed to complete their ice cap crossing. Thankfully they arrived four weeks late and the remaining members of the British Arctic Air Route Expedition were reunited and boarded a ship for Copenhagen.

His fellow polar explorer, Lancelot Fleming, said of Courtauld and his experience on the ice cap "it was evidently a spiritual experience as if he had been an ascetic meditating in the desert, which is very much where he was." In his autobiography Courtauld quoted the lines from Masefield which were hung up in the expedition hut and which summed up his accepting attitude towards the excitement and danger experienced:

> The power of man is in his hopes,
> In darkest night the cocks are crowing,
> With the seas roaring and the winds blowing,
> Adventure. Man the ropes.

Return to Greenland 1936
On his return to Britain, Courtauld married his fiancée Mollie and settled down to married life, satisfying his desire for adventure by sailing his yacht *Duet* off the British coast and in the waters of north-eastern Europe. However, in 1936 he decided to investigate 'Watkins

---

23   Wollaston, *The man on the ice cap*, p.178.
24   Courtauld, *Man the Ropes*, p.75.

Mountains' on Greenland which had been seen from the air but has still not been explored and climbed. He mounted an expedition of seven Englishmen and three Danes. He also decided that married men could bring their wives. The voyage was Mollie's first taste of arctic travel, and it proved exciting enough, the *Quest* being held fast in pack ice and being swept towards some dangerous icebergs. At one point it was thought that the ship would have to be abandoned, but after passing perilously close to two icebergs, the ice cleared and the *Quest* reached clear water. As they passed the fjord where Gino Watkins had disappeared they stopped the engine and dipped the ship's flag as a gesture of respect.

On 5th August they arrived at Irminger Fjord, where the *Quest* was to anchor and an expedition base set up. As it was late in the season the men set off immediately for the mountains, man hauling their food and equipment. They travelled through mountains, passes and glaciers not seen before by man. At what Courtauld considered the half-way point they depoted a sledge and some equipment and moved on to the Watkins range, guarded by the King Christian Glacier, which was twelve miles wide and a 100 feet long. Having established a camp on the glacier, the next day they set out for the mountain and that night camped under the summit of the peak they had chosen to scale. On the 26th they reached the summit and spent some time establishing the height and taking photographs. The peak turned out to be 12,250 feet, 3,000 feet higher than Mount Petermann. They continued to explore the mountain area for a week, surveying and recording and then reluctantly returned to the fjord. In their absence, the *Quest* had been away collecting material for a hut, as two members of the expedition, with their wives, were to overwinter there. Although Courtauld had been to Greenland several times before this was his first time as leader. He was later to be praised by Wordie for his handling of the expedition and its success. As the ship pulled out of Irminger fjord Courtauld was leaving Greenland for the last time.

Wartime service in the Royal Navy

Just before war broke out Courtauld was involved in a British intelligence operation to survey the northern European coasts and collect information which might be useful in time of war about harbours and landing places. With a group of skilled and like-minded amateur sailors he surveyed the coasts of Norway, Sweden, Denmark, Holland and Belgium.

When war broke out Courtauld was thirty-five. In the years before the war he had developed an organisation called the RNVSR – the S standing for supplementary, which consisted of groups of sailors who were prepared to volunteer themselves and their ships in time of war. With no money or encouragement from the authorities they had organised themselves and carried out training exercises. Now, when Britain was at war, they found that their contribution was not required. Having previously volunteered and being turned down for the RNVR, Courtauld now found himself travelling around England on behalf of the same shadowy intelligence organisation that he had surveyed the coasts for. He was then given a job in the Admiralty in the Naval Intelligence Division starting work on Admiral Godfrey's staff in Room 39. It did not please him overmuch, but at least he felt he fitted in with the motley assortment of recruits that he found there, including a barrister, a classics don, an insurance agent and a royal duke.

To a man of action, it was tantalising to be summoned and asked his advice on such matters as ice conditions off Greenland. He was in fact, instrumental in establishing the vital and hitherto unknown information that the area between Greenland and Iceland was passable in winter and that the inner lead between the coast of Norway and the island was navigable by large ships. When the Norwegian campaign started, he was put in charge of the Norway room and commented "luckily I had a set of my own Norwegian charts and a German atlas. There seemed to be no atlases in the Admiralty". [25] Generally he found his work in the Balkan department and the Scandinavian department boring and routine. At length he escaped to a course for executive officers at Greenwich Naval College, which also proved boring to Courtauld as he knew much of the navigation and seamanship skills he was being taught. He achieved the rank of Temporary Lieutenant at the end of the course and was able to wear his polar ribbon on his uniform. He was sent to HMS *Hornet* at Gosport on a coastal forces course before joining an MTB. The fast boats of coastal defences, the MTBs should have been an exciting prospect, but Courtauld had the misfortune to be posted as First Lieutenant to an elderly Royal Naval Lieutenant Commander who did not allow him much scope to use his initiative. While out in the Solent in the MTB, he witnessed the first raid on Portsmouth by the German air force: "the whole town seemed to be covered in dense smoke, and there were explosions. We opened fire on the enemy planes with our 0.5 machine guns without much effect." [26]

However, when he was given command of a MAC 2, an MTB striped of its torpedoes and one of its engines, he was sent to HMS *Wasp* at Dover. Here, during the autumn of 1940, his boat was required to go to the rescue of both enemy and British aeroplanes which had landed in the sea. Sometimes he returned with an RAF pilot or a German prisoner, but quite often he brought back a corpse, and often saw nothing but wreckage. The crew of the MAC 2 had some very bellicose ideas of what they would do to a downed German airman, but the first time they picked one up they made him a cup of tea and gave him a bunk to sleep in until they reached Dover. Courtauld remembered that they were quite indignant when the German flier was marched off under guard on their return to port. After a while the MAC 2 moved to Ramsgate. Courtauld considered that the reason they did not have much success in picking up downed British airmen, was that, unlike their German counterparts, they did not have self-inflating lifebelts. He also thought that the rescue boats were given poor information about the location of the crashes, resulting in the victims being swept away by the fast tidal currents before the boats arrived.

In July 1941 he was given the command of his own, new, MTB and commenced working-up trials at Weymouth. The boat was then posted to Great Yarmouth and Courtauld became second-in-command of an MTB flotilla. Their task was to defend British merchant ships that were suffering heavy losses from German E-boats in what had come to be known as 'E-boat alley', the passage along the Suffolk and Norfolk coast. The work was demanding, with bad weather making lying in wait with engines cut very unpleasant. The MTBs were frequently breaking down and Courtauld's boat was out of action during the first months of 1942. He became commanding officer of the flotilla and his sometimes eccentric personality and dress sense often caused raised eyebrows. His biographer, Wollaston, recounts an incident which sums up Courtauld's attitude. A member of the House of Lords remembered, as a junior able seaman, seeing Courtauld's flotilla sailing through the harbour mouth where the Port Commander, an austere one-eyed character, stood sternly waiting to take the salute, while "on the bridge of the leading boat Lieutenant Courtauld in a purple silk dressing gown fired his Very pistol at a seagull." [27]

---

25   A. Courtauld, *Man the Ropes*, p.108.
26   Ibid., p.109.
27   Wollaston, *The man on the ice cap*, p.221.

A wartime portrait of August Courtauld. (Riley family)

In October 1943 Courtauld was called unexpectedly to the Admiralty by R.E.D. Ryder, who he knew from exploring circles, and was heartened to hear that at last some of his skills would be used. He was to become part of a top secret 'arctic commando'. His first job was to take landing craft from Fort William through the Caledonian Canal and up to Shetland. He was encouraged by the fact that he had to take his Polar ribbon off to maintain secrecy. After a breakdown in Orkney he joined the unit in Shetland in some rigorous commando exercises, which he found invigorating. He was part of Andrew Croft's boating section of 14 Commando and found himself in the company of other old Arctic friends such as Quintin Riley. Courtauld had a period of time training near Loch Carron, where they practised attaching mines to ships and escaping undetected, but as we have seen in Chapter Three, for a variety of reasons the unit was disbanded in March 1943.

Courtauld's next job in what was to be turning out to be a varied war service was to travel to America, to the US Navy base at Norfolk Virginia. He was to command an infantry landing craft to be delivered to North Africa in preparation for the invasion of Sicily. While in Norfolk he bumped into Lancelot Fleming who was with the HMS *Queen Elizabeth* while she was undergoing repairs (see Chapter Nine). The summer passage turned out to be calm and trouble-free, with the opportunity for Courtauld to do some deep sea navigating. The landing craft were 300 tons, could carry 200 troops and proceeded at roughly eleven knots to Bermuda and then on to Gibraltar along Latitude 32°. On his return he found himself posted to HMS *Garth*, a destroyer working on convoys in the North Sea. He was delighted. He described the *Garth* as a 'grand ship', well organised and with a pleasant and efficient crew all younger than himself. Although he felt that his position had improved he could not help comparing it with his exploring days: "How much one feels descended in the scale of humanity since those days. Then, freedom and responsibility now narrow restriction and complete subordination of body and soul."

In December 1943 he attended a first officer's course at Portsmouth harbour and was duly posted to be First Lieutenant on a corvette which had not yet been finished. After the working-up exercises, the *Tintagel Castle* took up convoy duty in the Atlantic where she remained all through D-Day and the last year of the war. Courtauld was removed from the corvette to be the watch-keeping officer of HMS *Agamemnon* on a long voyage across the Atlantic, through the Panama Canal to deliver her at Vancouver. Courtauld then travelled to New York by train and got a passage home on the HMS *Nelson*. His last job during the war was that of a First Lieutenant of the naval party in charge of disarmament in Denmark. He remembered "while I was there they tried to make me Lieutenant Commander. I told the Admiral's secretary I would rather not, as it would be such a bother to change my uniform."[28] On his forty-first birthday an order came through that Lieutenant Courtauld RNVR was to go on leave awaiting release.

In his early fifties, Courtauld was crippled by multiple sclerosis and perhaps knowing that the end was near, arranged a grand reunion of the members of the British Arctic Air Route Expedition supplemented by some other old explorer friends and the captain of the *Quest*. A sumptuous dinner was translated into Eskimo on the menu, sledge banners covered the table and Courtauld brought his tattered Union Flag that had flown above the ice station. The evening went splendidly with many toasts, including one to Gino Watkins. The fact that transatlantic flight was now commonplace was wondered at.

Courtauld, unlike many of his polar colleagues, had not had the opportunity to use his skills and character to any great extent in the Second World War, admitting to often having been bored. In some ways it might be true that his heart remained in Greenland among "the clear skies and happy people of that gaunt land". He had recommended in 1934 "throw away your job, your friends, your cares, beg a quarter of the money you will need, and buy an eighth of the food you will eat, learn the language and go there ... to learn from these people something of their way of life". Perhaps he did, in some way, always remain 'the man on the ice cap'.

---

28   A. Courtauld, *Man the Ropes*, p.131.

11

H.W. Tilman

H.W. 'Bill' Tilman was sixteen years old when the Great War began in 1914, and determined to take part, passed the examination for The Royal Military Academy at Woolwich with the aim of becoming an artillery gunner. He was commissioned as a regular officer on 28th July 1915. In January 1916, a month short of his eighteenth birthday, he was sent to France and took part in the Battle of the Somme. In January 1917 he was wounded and won a Military Cross. In August 1917 he was awarded a bar to the Military Cross. By the end of the war he had defied the statistics and survived as a subaltern for three years. The experience was to give him a high degree of self-sufficiency and remain an influence on his future life and career.

After the war, still only twenty-one, Tilman chose to settle in Kenya, first at a soldier settlement and then acquiring a coffee farm at Sotik. In 1929, Tilman read an account of the ascent of Mount Batian in Kenya by Eric Shipton, a young coffee planter, and wrote to him to ask his advice on mountaineering in Kenya, thus beginning one of the most famous climbing partnerships of the twentieth century. They pioneered the smaller lightly equipped two-man expedition which has become the norm in Himalayan climbing. Their approach was much simpler than the normal pre-Second World War mountaineering style which involved much expense in hiring guides and porters. Following some climbs on Kilimanjaro and the nearby peak of Mawenzi, Shipton asked Tilman to accompany him on a climb on the twin peaks of Mount Kenya, Batian and Nelion. They accomplished this, Shipton teaching Tilman many of the mountaineering skills he was to use in his climbing career. A further expedition to the Ruwenzori range, referred to as the Mountains of the Moon, confirmed to Tilman that he was dissatisfied with the life of a planter and farmer. He sold his farm to a friend, making enough money to pay off his debts and enough spare for a passage back to England in 1932.

Across Africa by Bicycle 1933

At this stage he had no firm plans other than the increasing desire to climb mountains. A climbing accident in north Wales, in which a friend, John Brogden, died and a female climber accompanying them was seriously injured, resulted in a pause in his plans. He had to crawl for four hours back to the hotel to find help, as he had injured some vertebrae and could not walk. Having been told by his doctors that he would never climb again, he set out for the Alps to see if they were correct. They were not, and he returned fit. His niece remembered how bent he was before he left and how he returned 'ramrod straight'.[1] His next move was to return to Africa to prospect for gold in the Kalamega goldfields, both panning for gold in the Yala River, and following gold-bearing seams in the rock face. When this venture did not produce his fortune, he decided to return to England via a bicycle trip through Africa, starting on the east coast and cycling to the west coast. He

---

1   J.R.L. Anderson, *High Mountains and Cold Seas* (London, 1980), p.109.

241

H.W. Tilman as a cadet at Woolwich. (*High Mountains and Cold Seas*)

decided to travel through Uganda, the Belgium Congo, French Equatorial Africa and the French Cameroons, a ride of approximately 3,000 miles. He had ruled out travelling by car, as he did not have the necessary skills to mend the engine and thought walking would take too long, so settled on the 'ubiquitous bicycle'. As this method of transport ruled out the Sahara, he decided on aiming for the west coast. He explained his reasoning in *Snow on the Equator*: "I had two very good reasons, namely, to get home and see the country, for ever since gazing down on the Congo from Ruwenzori I had longed to travel in it.[2]"

Tilman purchased a bicycle in Kampala for six pounds, and having also bought two spare inner tubes, decided to travel light, with no other bicycle spares, with no tent and just a sleeping bag. He took enough food to last a few days and then trusted to luck, a staple food on his journey being the plantain banana, two of which, he considered was "enough to give you the sensation you had dined."[3] The roads in Uganda were good, and within a week he had ridden through the papyrus swamps of eastern Uganda and the Ankole highlands, and he had entered the Belgium Congo, part of his journey for which he had no maps. After pushing his bicycle for a while along the road, which consisted of broken lava, he broke his self-imposed rules and accepted a lift from a lorry as far as the Lake Kivu to Stanleyville road. He stayed at a hotel for one night at Lake Kivu, but generally slept outdoors away from huts and rest houses as a precaution against relapsing sickness, which was carried by a tick found in human habitations. Relapsing sickness was more serious than malaria and in pre-antibiotic days was difficult to treat. Tilman considered the risk from wild animals as he slept in the open preferable to the risk of becoming ill with relapsing sickness.

Leaving Lake Kivu he found the road led up the Kabasha escarpment of the Great Rift Valley, rather than directly westwards. It took him two days, mostly pushing his bike,

2   H.W. Tilman, *Snow on the Equator* (London, 1937), p.180.
3   Ibid., p.186.

Mount Kenya. (*High Mountains and Cold Seas*)

to climb the escarpment but then had the pleasure of coasting twenty-five miles down hill on the other side. One more line of hills had to be climbed before he left the highlands. As he looked down from the highlands he could see the jungle of the Congo below him, "a smooth expanse of dark olive green stretching away into the distance, flat and unbroken like the sea. It was the Congo forest, reaching westwards to the sea and extending to four degrees north and south of the equatorial line."[4]

Later that day he entered the jungle, in which he was to remain for two weeks. He described the atmosphere as "that of a hothouse sapping the energy of both the mind and body."[5] The only road stretched before him and he felt "as though I had been doomed to ride endlessly along the bottom of some enormous trench out of which it was impossible to climb."[6] He described coming into contact with the pygmies who lived by hunting and came to trade their okapi skins at the roadside villages. The existence of okapi was only discovered by these Ituri forest pygmies bringing the skins out of the forest to trade. The first large river he came to, the Ituri, was crossed by a pulley canoe ferry. Tilman found not being able to bathe during his time in the jungle trying, but he was afraid of picking up the Bilharzia parasite, which led to usually fatal disease. He also took the precaution of drinking nothing but boiled water. After twenty-one days he arrived in Stanleyville at the head of the Congo River. He described entering Stanleyville:

---

4   Ibid., p.208.
5   Ibid., p.208.
6   Ibid., p.209.

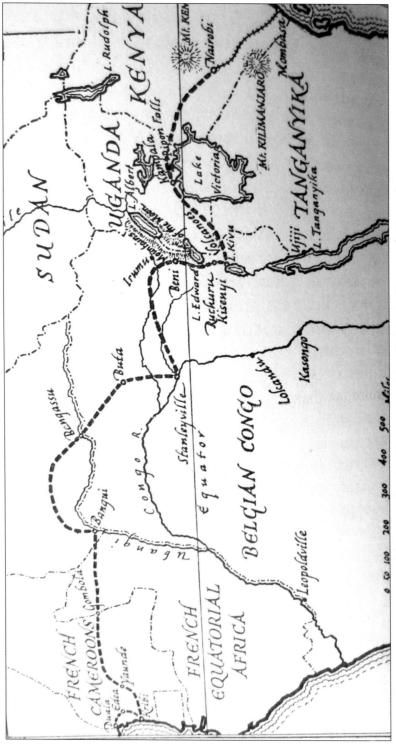

The route taken by Tilman across Africa by bicycle. (*Snow on the Equator*)

After twenty-one days on the road I rode into Stanleyville on a blistering hot afternoon, endeavouring to assume an air of nonchalance, as though riding in from close by for an afternoon's shopping. The effect was rather spoilt when I fell off in the main street with the bicycle on top of me. I was very tired.[7]

From Stanleyville he could have reached the coast by steamer but did not have the necessary fare of one thousand francs. He decided on a route through French Equatorial Africa towards Bangassu. Travelling north and slightly west he found the forest gave way to grassland and more cultivated areas. Leaving Bangassu he set out for Bagui, enjoying the hospitality of some missionaries and some French gold prospectors along the way. On reaching the French Cameroons he began hearing the coastal 'Pidgin' English spoken. After a fifty-six day journey he reached the West African coast at Karibi and caught a ship home, with his bicycle, from Douala. Tilman had come 'out of Africa' and paid tribute to the land he had first come to from the trenches of the Great War: "For fourteen years ... Africa had been my task mistress, and now I was leaving her. If she had not given me fortune, she had given me something much better – memories, mountains."[8]

The ascent of Nanda Devi 1934–36

In January 1934, with no further specific plans, Tilman received an invitation to accompany Shipton to spend five months in the Himalayas. Their objective was Nanda Devi, a pyramid peak which rose out of a basin surrounded by a ring of steep cliffs between 17,000 and 21,000 feet, situated in the Garhwal Himalayas, source of the River Ganges. Several attempts had been made on the mountain but the precipitous cliffs surrounding it are only broached by steep gorges made by glacier streams. In 1905 Dr T.G. Longstaff had reached the top of one of the surrounding cliffs and looked down into the Nanda Devi Basin, but had got no further. Shipton planned a two-man attempt on the peak using only three Sherpas and some local porters. In a break with established mountain convention, the Sherpas went on equal terms with the British men, all being regarded as mountaineers. The Sherpas chosen were Angtharkay, Pasang Bhotia and Kusang. Shipton paid tribute to them:

> Sharing with them our food and our tent space, our plans and our problems, we came to know their individual characteristics and to appreciate their delicious humour and their generous comradeship in a way quite impossible on a large expedition.[9]

On 22nd May they had reached the pass from which they hoped to access the place where the River Rishi joined the Rhamani, in order to progress through the Rishi gorge. They made a base camp on a small beach at the bottom of the gorge and from there their porters returned. Luckily they were able to cross to the southern side of the gorge by means of a huge boulder that had become wedged across it. The cliff at the southern side of the gorge was easier to negotiate and they were able to find a series of ledges which led them, after nine days, to climb down a precipice into the basin, or the 'sanctuary' as Shipton described it. "It was a glorious place and of course that fact that we were the first to reach it lent a special enchantment to our surroundings." He continued:

7   Ibid., p.221.
8   Ibid., p.265.
9   Anderson, *High Mountains and Cold Seas*, p.125.

Several long glacier valleys ran down from the great circle of mountains between 21,000 and 23,000 thousand feet high surrounding the basin. In the centre of this mighty amphitheatre standing 13,000 feet above its base was the peerless spire of Nanda Devi, ever changing in form and colour as we moved.[10]

They were the first explorers to reach this point. At this stage they had three weeks food with them, so spent the time surveying and plane tabling the basin before retreating in the first monsoon rains to their base camp in the gorge. They returned in August to finish their survey and also climbed a little way up the south-eastern ridge of the peak itself. Hugh Ruttledge, district commissioner in the Indian civil service and a mountaineer himself, described the exploration of the Nanda Devi basin as "one of the finest exploits of mountain exploration ever preformed" and paid tribute to the way in which it had been achieved: "A lesson in organisation, handling of men, travel on small resources, courage and the highest mountaineering ability."[11] Tilman was now becoming recognised as one of his generation's outstanding mountaineers.

A sudden decision by the Tibetan Government to allow an expedition to Mount Everest in 1935 and 1936 put paid to plans to return to Nanda Devi in that year, as Shipton was asked to form a team to make an exploratory expedition in readiness for a full attempt in 1936. He asked Tilman to be part of the team. Members of the expedition reached the North Col and spent two months reconnoitring the Tibetan side of Everest. Tilman was not chosen to go on the 1936 Everest expedition, so decided to go back to Nanda Devi and finish the job started by himself and Shipton. His climbing partner was W.F. Loomis, from the USA. By 16th June Tilman, Loomis and Tibetan hill men or Bhotias had carried 900 lbs of food through the Rishi Gorge to the Nanda Devi basin. They then returned to Ranikhet where they made final preparations and were joined by the other members of the party – Graham Brown, Noel Odell, Peter Lloyd, and the other Americans, Arthur Emmons and Charles Houston. Adams Carter, who had been delayed, joined them later at base camp.

The journey back to the basin was fraught with difficulties as it was now monsoon season and it rained continually. The party were only able to cross the swollen River Rhamani because Tilman managed to swim across with a rope which the rest of the party could hang from to cross. Graham Brown, in his account in *The Times*, described how Tilman "in a fine piece of work managed to cross the torrent safeguarded by a rope which was thereafter fixed at both sides of the 'ford'".[12] The thirty-seven porters that were not Bhotias refused to go any further at this point. This necessitated cutting the amount of food that could be carried further and it was decided to cut supplies to forty days food, which were carried up to advance base camp by the climbers, Sherpas and the Bhotias. At this camp in the basin the Bhotias were paid off and returned home. The first 3,000 feet of the lower rock face consisted of rotten rock and was difficult to climb. At camp one they had to dig platforms on the rock face with entrenching tools. Camp two was no more than a ledge to bivouac at and camp three was only achieved after climbing over snow-covered rock with an area of deep snow in between. As soon as all the climbers had reached camp three at 21,000 feet all the Sherpas became ill with dysentery and had to return to base. The

10   Ibid., p.126.
11   *The Times*, 2nd November 1934.
12   *The Times*, 24th November 1936.

party carried on to camp four, which was in a much better position for an attempt on the summit. The first attempt by Odell and Houston had to return as Houston now was sick and Tilman stepped in to take his place. Setting out from a bivouac at 24,000 feet on 29th August, Tilman and Odell looked up to see a snow slope leading to a rock wall of about 700 ft. They decide to traverse the slope westward in order to reach a snow rib which seemed to form a ramp against the wall. They started up the snow slope. Tilman described their progress: "It was like trying to climb up cotton wool and every step made good cost six to eight deep breaths."[13] Reaching a point just below the summit ridge, they decided to take the shorter route to the summit, via a corridor of snow, rather than the longer but seemingly easier route to the left. As they started, a large slab of snow fell off the corridor and the snow fell away from where they were standing. Tilman commented: "the corridor route had somehow lost its attractiveness and we finished the climb without further adventure, reaching the top at three o'clock."[14] The summit was a solid snow ridge, stretching for 200 yards and there was room to walk about and admire the view. Nanda Devi was, at 25,645 feet, the highest peak climbed by man at that time and was achieved without the new techniques and technology which were developed after the Second World War, leading to the eventual scaling of Mount Everest. Tilman felt a tinge of sadness, however standing at the top of Nanda Devi: "After the first joy of victory came a feeling of sadness that the mountain had succumbed and that the proud head of the goddess was bowed."[15]

Attempt on Mount Everest, 1938

In November 1937 it was announced that Tilman was to lead the 1938 Everest expedition. He chose Frank Smythe, Shipton, Peter Lloyd, Odell, Warren and P.R. Oliver and decided upon a small-scale operation which could move quickly, unencumbered by large amounts of porters and supplies. He explained in his account of the expedition: "it should be clear that the fewer men to be maintained at each camp and the less food and equipment they need, the easier and safer it is for all concerned."[16] The 1936 expedition to Everest had been very expensive and had only reached 23,000 feet, and Tilman commented on the 1938 attempt: "by general consent the expedition was organised on a more modest scale."[17] He hoped that seven climbers would give him the flexibility to keep together as a complete party, or to split into two or more parties if necessary. He took the experiences of Watkins and Lindsay on their polar expeditions into account on deciding on a ration of 2 lbs per day and realised that "the whole art lies in getting the most value for weight."[18] Although Tilman disapproved of the use of oxygen when climbing at high altitude, some equipment was taken for medical use for the treatment of frost bite and pneumonia and "for the rather cowardly reason that if we encountered perfect conditions on the last two thousand feet and were brought to a standstill purely through lack of oxygen ... we would look uncommonly foolish."[19]

Tilman and Shipton travelled to India in February 1938 and recruited Angtharkay, Kusang Namgyal, Pasang Bhotia and Tensing as Sherpas. Good weather helped their walk

---

13   Anderson, *High Mountains and Cold Seas*, p.141.
14   Ibid., p.141.
15   Ibid., p.142.
16   H.W. Tilman, *Mount Everest 1938* (Cambridge, 1948), p.5.
17   Ibid., p.13.
18   Ibid., p.18.
19   Ibid., p.22.

in to the Rongbuk glacier and they arrived at its base on 6th April, ten days earlier than the earliest of previous expeditions. The weather conditions started off favourably, and camp three was established under the North Col. However, the weather became very much colder and as several of the party were ill with colds and flu, Tilman made the decision to retreat to the Karta Valley to rest before proceeding, but not without some misgivings." Looking up at the mountain, seemingly in perfect condition for climbing, it was impossible not to feel some misgivings at turning our backs on it ... but the cold was sufficiently intimidating to banish all regrets "[20]

Tilman's party were back on the mountain by 14th May and by the 18th had regained camp three. However weather conditions had changed dramatically. The monsoon season had started early and the mountain was now covered in snow and the temperature had risen. On the 20th they started moving equipment and food up to the North Col. On the slope leading to the col an avalanche knocked one party off the slope, but they were all roped and no one was injured. Tilman was annoyed that this incident was reported sensationally in the press, but according to his biographer, he only had himself to blame as he was notoriously spare with information to the press – "if Tilman had sent fuller stories then there would have been less inaccurate reporting – but if he had sent fuller stories he would not have been Tilman."[21] Because of the likelihood of more avalanches in the prevailing snow conditions, Tilman decided to approach from the west flank of the col. Camp four was established on the col and Odell, Oliver Warren and Tilman spent three days waiting for the weather to improve. Camp five was then established at 25,800 feet and camp 6 at 27,000 feet. From here Smythe and Shipton were to attempt to reach the summit. Having stayed at camp Five on 7th and 8th of June they set off for the summit on the 10th. Despite the fact that Shipton know the chances of success were slim, with the mountain covered in snow, he wrote in his diary account:

> The party was fit and full of hope that we were going to be granted a chance for an attempt on the summit which had been denied us for so long ... Conditions on the ridge as far as camp five had led us to hope that the recent fine weather and cold winds the snow on the upper slabs might have consolidated.[22]

However, the snow was soft and powdery and progress was slow. At 4.15 p.m. Shipton and Smythe pitched their tent on the North-east Ridge below the yellow band and their sherpas returned to camp five. Early next morning they started up the yellow slab through hip-depth soft snow. They continued until they realised that on the steeper sections, in the snow conditions prevailing, they were at a distinct risk of avalanche. Shipton continued: "We returned, completely convinced of the hopelessness of our task— the glittering summit looked tauntingly near."[23]

On their return to camp five they met Tilman and Lloyd on their way up the mountain. Tilman, after speaking to Shipton and Smythe, realised that a summit attempt was unlikely for him and Lloyd, but wanted to examine the summit ridge and possibly take a look at the second step. They set out from camp six at 8 o'clock the next morning but found conditions

20   Anderson, *High Mountains and Cold Seas*, p.156.
21   Ibid., p.158.
22   Ibid., p.83.
23   Ibid., p.84.

Tilman in 1939. (*Snow on the Equator*)

too cold, returning and making tea until trying again at 10'clock. They tried several ways of climbing the rock and ice wall but then returned to camp four. Tilman now decided that the attempt to climb Everest for that year should be abandoned. The early onset of the monsoon season had resulted in heavy snow, which made climbing on the highest parts of the mountain impossible. Tilman, writing to his sister, said "it has been a dim show and I am disappointed, but the weather never gave us a chance."[24]

According to Tilman's account of the expedition in *The Times,* he had been warned by what he called a 'candid friend' that whatever happened on Everest 'not to blame the weather.' But he did explain that the decision to eventually abandon the attempt was made with the advice of his colleagues regarding the weather: "Shipton and Smythe, who have had much more experience than anyone else on the mountain in fair conditions and foul, are convinced that in such conditions as we had to battle against the summit was unattainable". He explained in his article, however, his optimism that the mountain would be conquered:

> What is wanted, therefore, is a succession of yearly expeditions. An expedition smaller probably than the present one should in my opinion, come out to the Himalayas every May. A favourable season will occur sooner or later and I believe that we have mountaineers capable of taking advantage of it.

He ended his article by saying that such a course "seems most likely to meet with early success."[25] A year later the beginning of the Second World War put such plans in abeyance

24   Ibid., p.162.
25   *The Times*, 4th July 1938.

until the 1950s.

The members of the expedition were fulsome in praise of Tilman's leadership. A discussion of a meeting of the Royal Geographical Society was included in Appendix A of Tilman's book on the expedition. In this discussion Shipton commented: "I am very pleased to have this opportunity of congratulating Tilman on the way in which he ran the expedition, not at all an easy matter from all points of view." Lloyd expressed the opinion that "If I ever go to Everest again I very much hope it will be under his leadership." Several members of the expedition, including the doctor, C.B.M. Warren, and N. Odell raised concerns about the provisioning, saying that not enough food had been taken, particularly food which might be appealing at high altitude when eating is difficult. The pros and cons of oxygen use were discussed. Dr Longstaff moved a vote of thanks to Tilman saying: "I think that he has proved that small party has a good a chance as any of climbing Everest. He took two climbing parties of men 27,000 feet in the monsoon, in powder snow and got everybody away without frostbite. A very fine performance indeed."[26]

Artillery Officer 1940-43, SOE in Albania 1943

Tilman knew exactly what course of action he would take, if and when war broke out. He wanted to rejoin as a regimental gunnery officer despite the fact that he could probably have found a job as a mountain warfare specialist, training troops. His climbing plans in 1939 were governed by the need to return to Britain swiftly if necessary, and he turned down an invitation from Shipton to climb in the Karakoam Mountains. A trip to the Assam Himalaya in the early part of 1939 was not a success due to the illness of himself and his Sherpas, and in August 1939 Tilman returned to Britain for a short refresher gunnery course and was posted to 32 Field Regiment RA with the same rank, that of lieutenant, as he had in 1919.

Following the declaration of war, on 3rd December Tilman's regiment was sent to France, to the Lille sector, and Tilman was promoted to acting captain. The quiet period of the phoney war ended in May 1940 and Tilman was involved in providing artillery support for the withdrawal to Dunkirk. The unit destroyed their guns on being pushed back to Dunkirk and fought on as infantry. Tilman was evacuated safely from Dunkirk with 338,000 others. A period of home defence in Suffolk resulted in promotion to acting major and command of 120 Field Battery. In January of 1941 he sailed with the 32nd Field Regiment Royal Artillery to India.

Tilman's letters to his sister Adeline showed his discomfort at the style of soldiering he found himself part of in India: "This is a most demoralising existence – waited on hand and foot by silent slaves."[27] He was pleased when he was moved to sail as part of the 8th Indian Infantry Division to Iran as commander of 107 Battery. Following a brief spell on the Iraqi border the division moved into Iraq and moved up the Tigris valley to Syria. After being attached to a column of troops which entered some Syrian towns without resistance, Tilman returned to Mosul where, as he described it, the unit proceeded to "dig ourselves in against the arrival of the Germans ... it serves as an excuse for digging, which kept us occupied for the rest of our stay in Iraq."[28] Tilman managed to climb two mountains during his time in Iraq and attempted to sow a garden around his tent, but he was getting

---

26   Appendix A in Tilman, *Mount Everest 1938*, pp.116-126.
27   Anderson, *High Mountains and Cold Seas*, p.174.
28   Ibid., p.173.

increasingly frustrated with being in what he considered to be a backwater of the war.

However, in June 1942 the regiment was ordered to join the 8th Army in the Western Desert, to help reinforce the Allied troops who were being driven back across the desert towards Alexandria, and the strategically important Suez canal. Tilman found himself and his battery serving as part of a 'Jock column', units which roamed around the desert to find German tanks and guns and destroy them with their 25-pounder guns. It was not long, however, until Tilman's column was needed to join the brigade group in stemming the German advance. Throughout July Tilman saw action nearly every day. He wrote home comparing this period with his weeks in retreat in France: "We always seem to be where the British Army has its backs to the wall." At this time he was in an armoured car that was blown up by a mine, but was uninjured.

The Battle of El Alamein was the decisive moment in the desert war, and by early November the German troops were retreating. Tilman was engaged in mopping up operations in the wake of their retreat, finding prisoners, vehicles, guns and ammunition. He had spent six months as acting C/O of his regiment during which time the British forces had advanced to Tunis, but in June the new C/O arrived and Tilman reverted to second-in-command, a role he disliked, wishing to be back as a battery commander rather than being at regimental headquarters. An advertisement in routine orders was asking for volunteers for special service and Tilman volunteered, on the grounds that it was 'better to reign in hell than serve in heaven'. A story exists that as acting C/O of the regiment, he recommended his own application. Despite his age, forty-five, he was accepted. His war was about to change course completely.

The initial training at Haifa was strenuous and Tilman discovered that most of the intake was half his age. In August he moved to Derna in Libya where the squadron of Halifax aeroplanes that was dropping supplies to partisan movements was based. Tilman was to command a three-man mission to Albania, code named 'Sculptor'. He was accompanied by a w/t operator, Corporal Gerry Dawson, and Sergeant Butterworth, a demolition and paramilitary expert. Peter Kemp, who was parachuted in at the same time in Operation Stepmother remembered: "By far the eldest and the toughest of us was Major Tilman." Tilman apparently told Kemp that he had volunteered to keep himself fit for his next Himalayan attempt. His reputation as a mountaineer went before him, but he quickly established his fitness and tenacity in his new role. As SOE staff officer, B. McSwiney remembered: "We were all in awe of him."[29]

Tilman and his men were met by Captain David Smiley and Major David Maclean, who had been in Albania for three months and who had established links with the partisans. Tilman was delighted to be back on European soil: "My principal feeling was one of intense satisfaction at having at length got back to Europe, even if it was enemy occupied, after so long in the wilderness. I could have almost hugged the ground."[30] The aim of the British mission which Smiley and Maclean had set up was to try and ensure that the two main resistance movements worked together and to provide supplies and support to resistance efforts. The two main partisan bodies were the Communist-dominated Levizja Nacional Clirimtare, or Nationalist Liberation Movement, and the Balli Kombetar, or National Front. The LNC, although Communist-dominated, was open to all and its main

29   Interview, cited by Roderick Bailey in *The Wildest Province: SOE In the land of the Eagle* (London, 2008), p.75.
30   H.W. Tilman, *When Men and Mountains Meet* (Cambridge, 1987), p.106.

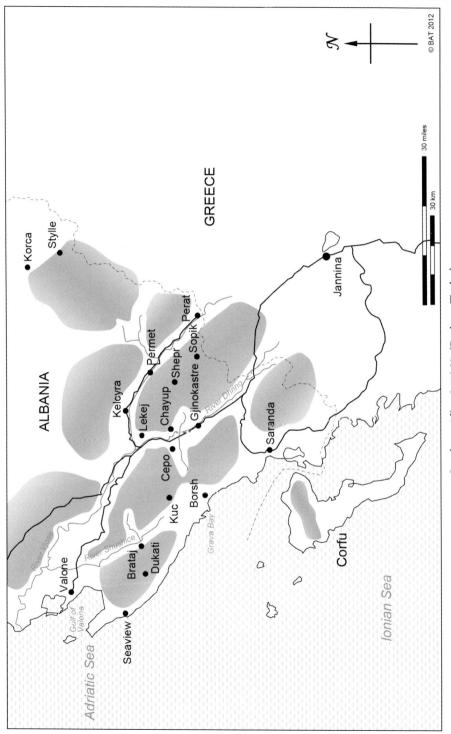

Southern Albania 1943. (Barbara Taylor)

Village house in wartime Albania. (TNA H3/36)

aim was to wage war on invaders. The Balli was anti-Italian, but its main philosophy was to safeguard Albania's borders and to ensure the survival of its pre-war political structure. The LNC was a far more effective fighting force than the Balli, but the Balli had much local support. After the replacement of the Italian occupying force by the Germans, following the Italian armistice, the Bali would sometimes collaborate with the Germans against the LNC. When Tilman arrived, there was suspicion, but not open hostility, between the groups. The British Government placed liaison officers with both the partisan bodies, but Tilman commented:

> It was the peculiar tragedy of Albania that this well-meaning policy was persisted in after it had become clear to most observers that these differences were fundamental and even when only one of the parties was fighting and suffering. [31]

However, at the time of Tilman's arrival in Albania, the work of the British mission in helping the Albanian partisans was progressing well. By September more than twenty tons of weapons, ammunition, grenades and uniforms had been parachuted in and given to the partisans. In his description of Albania, Tilman reported that there were no railways, and then, in an amusing aside which shed some light on the efficiency of the organisation in the early days of missions to the country, he said "the fact that there were no railways in Albania was not as well known as it might have been, for base were in the habit of sending

---

31   Ibid., p.109.

us explosive charges designed specifically for blowing them up."[32] Tilman's operation was one of several that had been dropped to expand the British mission further into Albania. Tilman was briefed at the British Headquarters at Stylle. He remembered:

> In the week I spent in Stylle it became evident to me that the LNC alone had war aims similar to our own and were ready to go to all lengths to attain them. Accordingly I elected to go the Gjinokastre area, which promised to become the centre of the LNC area.[33]

Consequently he departed with his two NCOs to support the LNC in the Gjinokastre area, necessitating a forty mile trip across two mountain ranges and into the Vjöse Valley. Gjinokastre, with a population of 12,000, was the headquarters of the Italian army's 151st Perugia Infantry Division. The villages surrounding it had between fifty and a hundred houses. The people were of mixed origin; those with Greek affinities were in the south and near the coast, and in the valleys were a mixture of Christians and Moslems. Tilman established a base at Shepr, about six hours' journey, down a steep gorge to the Dhrino valley, from the Italian forces at the garrison. He found the local partisans lightly armed, with few machine guns and no artillery. The LNC wore red stars in their caps as a sign of their admiration for the Russian Army and to distinguish them from the Balli. Their greeting was "death to the fascists", to which the reply was "liberty to the people"[34] The garrison at Gjinokastre numbered 5,000 men, including a pack battery of eight 75mm guns but Tilman reported "the partisans had little fear of them and were constantly harassing the roads."[35] He soon got to know the local partisan commander, Islam Radovicka, and as he was introduced over time to different groups, commenting "the spirit of camaraderie in all ranks was noticeable as was the *esprit de corps* of the various *checkas* and battalions."[36]

Tilman's first action with the partisans was to attack an outpost of fifty Italian soldiers at Libhuvo, a town across the river from Gjinokastre. Tilman's job was to prevent reinforcements from arriving from Gjinokastre, but he was assured that it was very unlikely that the Italians would leave their garrison at night. Tilman described this as "a bold but futile effort" as the Italians responded to the partisan's rifle and machine gun fire with machine guns and mortars from behind their defences. Six partisans were killed in the attack. Tilman noticed that as the partisans advanced through the town they set alight some houses belonging to the Balli.

Tilman settled down to life in Shepr, which was not too uncomfortable. He got on well with the partisans although he was not popular with his bodyguards. This was due to the fact that "every morning before breakfast he climbed to the top of the local mountain ... and the wretched bodyguard had to climb it as well."[37]

The situation for the British Mission changed on 7th September 1943 when the Italians surrendered to the Allies. Within hours, British officers in Albania were seeking surrender terms from the local Italian commander. However the German army had been

---

32   Ibid., p.107.
33   Ibid., p.109.
34   Ibid., p.115.
35   TNA HS5/128, Report by H.W. Tilman, 1944.
36   Ibid.
37   Letter from Colonel Smiley to J. L. Anderson cited in Anderson, *High Mountains and Cold Seas*, p.192.

Partisans on parade (TNA H3/36)

prepared for this eventuality and soon German units were entering Albania. The garrison at Tirana surrendered to the Germans and the 11th Brennero Infantry Division left for the coast and escaped by boat. On 14th September Tilman approached the commander of the Perugia Division, General Chiminello, to ask for his surrender, or alternatively to attack the Germans. Chiminello would do neither and would not permit his troops to be disarmed. As Tilman did not have sufficient partisan strength to force the surrender, he cut off the water supply to the garrison at Gjinokastre. Chiminello and his troops then departed for the coast at Saranda, about 25 miles away. When Tilman caught up with them it was agreed that the partisans could have the Italian artillery but that the soldiers would keep their rifles for their protection. The partisans then moved the artillery arms and ammunition as fast as they could away from the port to Kuc and Cepo. Some of the ships that got away from Saranda carrying Italian troops were then dive bombed by German bombers and sunk. General Chiminello and his staff were taken prisoner by the Germans. Roderick Bailey, in his history of the SOE in Albania, describes persistent rumours that they were in fact shot by the Germans and thrown into the sea or that Chiminello's head ended up on display at Saranda.[38] Many Italian soldiers who had escaped capture by the Germans joined the partisan or worked on farms in return for food. Tilman praised the Albanians for their attitude: "the Albanians deserve all credit for not only tolerating, but saving the lives of their late opponents."[39]

During the winter of 1943-1944 the Germans arrived in Albania in strength and did everything they could to court favour with the Albanian people, especially the Balli Kombetar, by declaring greater Albania independent and by placing four prominent Albanians of different backgrounds and religious beliefs as regents. Many of the

38   Note 60, Chapter Three, Roderick Bailey, *The Wildest Province.*
39   TNA HS 5/128.

A nationalist chieftain in wartime Albania (TNA H3/36)

establishment figures in Albania were won over. The tension between the LNC and the Balli Kombëtar degenerated into open war. Tilman was of the opinion that reconciliation was impossible because of the "attitude of the respective sides towards resisting the Germans."[40]

Gjinokastre was taken by the German forces in November. The LNC was committed to resist the German occupation but for much of the time the German troop concentrations were too strong to be attacked by guerrilla forces. The partisans did attack supply routes but often came off the worse. Tilman was present when a smaller force of Germans passed an ambush and were attacked. The German troops called for reinforcements and these arrived with mortars and artillery. Tilman took control of the partisans' heavy guns and succeeded for a while in holding the reinforcements back, by keeping the road blocked, but then his guns were silenced. Tilman's guns were in due course spotted and destroyed by heavy mortar fire. Throughout the winter Tilman became disillusioned by the enmity between the Albanians, particularly the setting alight of villages who were suspected of helping the LNC. The organisation of the LNC in the south was, however, improving and the Balli were being forced into a more overt alliance with the Germans. The LNC at partisan headquarters were also criticising the British Mission to Albania. Constantine Tashko, member of the Central Council and former Albanian minister in New York, criticised their "impartial attitude to the BK who were palpable enemies of the Allied cause."[41] This impartiality, he insisted, encouraged the BK to resist the LNC. He also considered that the

40 Ibid.
41 Ibid.

An old Turkish bridge in south Albania. (*When Man and Mountains Meet*)

air drops brought in not enough for the partisans and too much for the mission personnel.

In November Tilman went down to the coast to the SOE base at "sea view" to visit Commander Alexander Glen to see whether a landing place could be established for sea access to Albania, as he considered that owing to the difficulties experienced with air drops due to the weather and the shortages of available aircraft, this was essential to keep up a good level of supplies. He arranged with Glen for a reconnaissance to take place along the coast to find a suitable place, but this was not arranged until the spring.

In January, it became evident that the Germans were launching an offensive against the partisans in the north and west and on 11th January the partisans and the British in these areas moved south to the Vjöse Valley, near Tilman's headquarters at Shepr. By 24th January German troops had arrived in Tilman's valley and the British retreated further, to mountains west of Korça. In the spring the partisans fought back and made large territorial gains, their numbers swollen with fresh recruits. The 6th Brigade managed at last to take a bay at Borsh and supplies were then able to be brought in by sea and on 22nd May Tilman was brought out by this route back to Bari. Back in Italy he added his voice to those critical of British policy of not denouncing pro-fascist groups working against the LNC and actually continuing to supply and support them.

I was convinced as I left as I had been for some months previously that our policy of backing the LNC was honest and expedient, they being the only party in Albania with the same war aims as our own who are willing to make sacrifice for them ... They

Shecket Razi, commander of the 5th Brigade, partisans, with
Tilman at Premet. (*When Man and Mountains Meet*)

realised that we were doing our best to help them materially, but the good effect of
that was more than offset by our helping equally other parties, if not with money or
material, then with encouragement.[42]

Tilman's biographer, J.L. Anderson, although admitting that British wartime policy in
Albania was tortuous and conflicting, posed the question of "whether the post-war history
of Albania would have been happier if the victorious communists had come out of the war
with a more solid faith in Britain?" Tilman's comments seemed to imply that he thought
that the LNC partisans deserved more loyalty. "The fact remains that that the partisans of
the LNC fought, suffered and died for professed aims and by so doing helped us."[43]

SOE in Italy 1944-1945

While waiting in Bari to be returned to Albania, Tilman seems to have made his views
known on British policy too vehemently with the result that he was not returned and spent
several months in Bari waiting for a posting. He wrote to his sister Adeline: "If everything
else fails I shall go back to the army. Even CO/2 of a regiment would be preferable to
rotting in Bari."[44] He was refused a posting to Special Operations in the Far East on the
grounds of age and rank, but in the second week of August, 1944 was posted to Special

---

42   TNA HS1/28.
43   Anderson, *High Mountains and Cold Seas*, p.195.
44   Ibid., p.196.

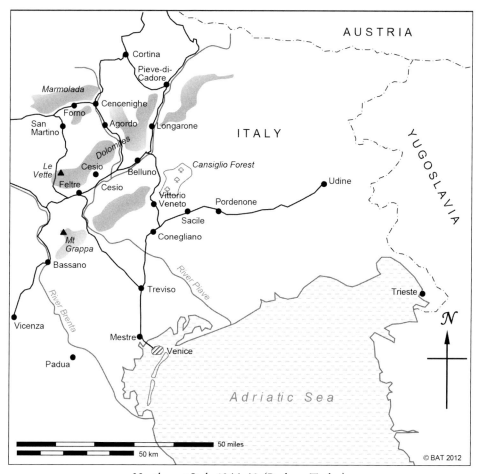

North-east Italy 1944-45. (Barbara Taylor)

Operations in northern Italy, where the Italian Partisans were harassing the German army, which was still entrenched there despite the surrender of the Italians. German resistance was still strong and British and American forces were both sending missions into northern Italy to obtain intelligence about German troop movements and to drop and organise the distribution of arms and supplies. Tilman's mission was called 'Simia' and was destined for the Belluno region. His W/T operator was 'Marini', an Italian ex-submariner whose real name was Antonio Carrisi. The interpreter who had been working with the Long Range Desert Group was an excellent Italian and English speaker called Tito Vittorio Grozer. His second-in-command was Captain John Ross, also an ex-gunner who had met Tilman at a parachute school near Brindisi and who had gone climbing with Tilman when they were waiting to be posted. Although happy with his colleagues for the mission, Ross was taken aback by the briefing received at headquarters in Monopoli :

> The staff there knew nothing about the area were going to work in ... and they had very little knowledge of what the resistance movement was doing and they had very little idea of the geography. They had dreadful maps and sort of pre-war picture postcards of the attractive areas but nothing much else, so as a briefing it was useless.[45]

Conditions on the ground in northern Italy were different to those Tilman had been operating under in Albania. The Italian resistance groups were operating in a geographical area less remote, and the groups were isolated from each other by good motor roads and efficient communications which benefited the Germans in seeking out the Italian partisans. However, the divisions between political groupings among the Italians were less marked and, out of the towns, the local populations were on the side of the partisans. Tilman's biographer J.R.L. Anderson described his first four months in Italy as "the most prolonged physical and mental strain of Tilman's life."[46]

The mission did not begin well as it was only on the third attempt to land his party, on 31st August 1944, that a successful landing was achieved. Tilman's entire mission landed wide of the target, with Tilman swinging violently on the way down and hitting a rock on landing, injuring the base of his spine. Ross had to be cut down out of a tree and Marini sprained his ankle. As the weather had closed in, their supplies were not dropped, and it was to be four more months before any further supplies were received. This made Tilman's position very difficult as the partisans were looking to him to improve the morale of their groups by providing much needed arms and ammunition. Tilman had to persuade them that the failure to drop supplies was not a deliberate attempt to weaken the communists as a fighting force. In this task of persuasion he was helped by the fact that he was obviously sharing in the difficulties and dangers of the group. He had to wear the same shirt for four months. Tilman put the repeated failure of the attempts to bad navigation, as not all the failures occurred in bad weather. It was a far cry from the efficient dropping of regular supplies that he had experienced in Albania.

Tilman and his men were at first posted to the Nanetti Division, but a 'rastrallamento' or comb out by the Germans resulted in them being unable to reach the headquarters of this division and Tilman decided to stay with the Gramsci Brigade in the mountains of

---

45   Ross interview, IWM Sound Archive ref 27077, 1445-551, cited in David Stafford, *Mission Accomplished, SOE and Italy 1943-1945* (London, 2011), p.190.

46   Anderson, *High Mountains and Cold Seas*, p.198.

the La Vette area. The local partisan commander retired to a mountaintop stronghold at La Vette in between bouts of guerrilla activity, believing his mountaintop position to be impregnable. Tilman realised, however that the paths leading up to the position made it in fact a trap, as they were the only exits. As the German 'comb outs' were getting nearer Tilman thought it advisable to withdraw from La Vette for a while. The local commander did not agree, as he wanted to stand and fight and was also awaiting a fresh supply drop. Tilman commented: "It was now a question of which would arrive first, the arms, the winter or the Germans; and the odds were heavily on the last."[47]

On 29th September the German forces set fire to a partisan store in the valley below, and by the evening were firing at La Vette. Tilman and his group withdrew to the plateau, taking with them ten escaped British prisoners of war who had been fighting with the partisans as the 'Churchill Company'. They were now, as Tilman had predicted, trapped on the plateau. A party of sixteen including the Churchill company, then went with Tilman to scale the north face of La Vette, either to find another way down, or to hide high in the rocks until the Germans had gone. After reaching 7,000 feet they found a path looking as if it would lead down, but found themselves on a ledge where the cliff fell away. They stayed on the mountain for three nights without food, until Tilman sent a scout who reported that the Germans had gone.

The Nanetti division was now re-establishing itself in the Cansiglio Forest and Tilman's mission set out to join them by a difficult and dangerous journey throughout October. Throughout the autumn difficulties in dropping supplies continued. Tilman recounted how the morale of the partisans was low and how they decided to reduce numbers for the winter, keeping only groups of the able and trustworthy men in the mountains. In November they received a radio message from General Alexander, urging that the resistance operation be scaled down and partisan groups bide their time until the worst of the winter was over. This decision, although well-meant, gave the partisans the idea that the Allies had no further use for them. David Stafford, in his book on the SOE in Italy, *Mission Accomplished,* considered that "it was a needless mistake"[48], as in addition to upsetting the partisans it made the SOE personnel feel abandoned.

At last a successful drop was made to Tilman's area on 26th December and with them arrived another British mission. At this point Tilman decided to move further north to the Belluno Division. He believed that when the Allied troops arrived in the Po Valley, that the Belluno Division could play a useful, if not vital, role in harassing the German retreat and blocking roads. His journey north was difficult as the Germans were very much in control of this area and there were many checkpoints and military posts to circumvent. At one stage he had to hide in a house for over a week before moving on. He arrived at the headquarters of the Belluno Division on 9th January and his first job was to arrange a drop for them. This was impracticable in the immediate area so Tilman, Ross Gozzer and the wireless operator spent January in a very cold cave as they prepared to find a suitable landing place. They travelled to the Forno area in the mountains to the north-west of Belluno and arranged a drop in the Val de Gares, a valley between steep walls of 7,000 feet. As the aeroplanes could not fly low because of the steep cliffs, there was a distinct possibility that the drop would land wide of the target, so Tilman asked for delayed action parachutes to be used. In the event the supplies came down with great accuracy and two more planes repeated the success

---

47   Ibid., p.204.
48   D. Stafford, *Mission Accomplished*, p.252.

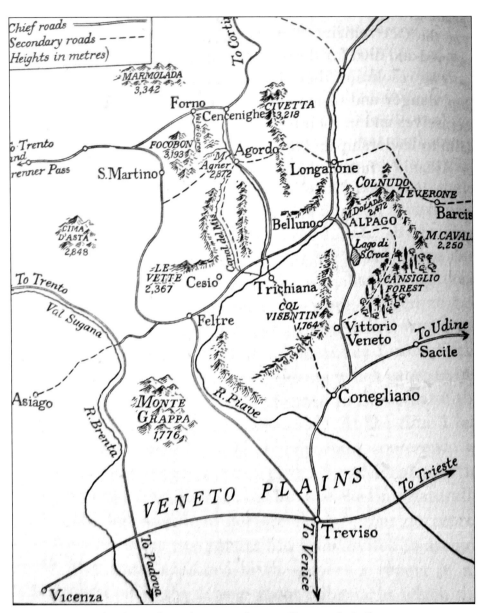

Sketch map drawn by H.W. Tilman to illustrate the Belluno
area of Italy. (*When Men and Mountains Meet*)

a few days later on 17th February. Ross remembered the drop, and how the plane "circled around our steep and hidden valley for, to us, a worryingly long time before accurately dropping its load. The containers whistled down for some time before the chutes opened."[49] He described how the supplies were taken down to Belluno for distribution hidden beneath loads of wood in lorries. The American crews who had completed the drops were later given medals for their accurate delivery.

In addition to the supplies that were dropped, Tilman and his party also travelled back to Belluno protected by coffin-like boxes under huge loads of logs. Tilman now decided to become a liaison officer to the partisan HQ, which was a farm in the Alpago area, about 3,000 feet into the mountains. Both Tilman and the partisan leaders thought that, in view of the expected breakthrough by the Allies, the HQ was the best place for Tilman to be. American troops captured Verona on 26th April and Tilman was kept busy organising the resistance forces to block the German retreat. The German garrison at Belluno was still holding out and fighting continued in the area. Tilman was involved in an operation to make sure that the Germans did not blow a bridge vital to the Allied advance, and narrowly avoided being shot by the partisans holding the bridge, who mistook him for a German trying to demolish the bridge.

On 2nd May the Germans in Belluno surrendered and Tilman, with two partisans, entered the city on a captured motorcycle. He now helped to establish a provisional Italian administration and was instrumental in recommending partisans from the committees of National Liberation for posts in the new civilian administration. Three weeks later, Tilman was made a freeman of Belluno, an honour shared only by Garibaldi and a few others.

---

49   John Ross papers, IWM ref O6/18/1 p.23, cited in Stafford, *Mission Accomplished*, p.283.

Conclusion

We have seen how a group of talented and adventurous men who had grown up in the shadow of the Great War not only contributed to the progress of exploration and scientific innovation in the inter-war period, but also took a full part in the defeat of Hitler and his regime in the Second World War. The group of men examined in this book are representative of a generation that was determined to make its mark on the world. It must be remembered that there were many more men who were of inestimable service to their country in the Second World War because of the way in which they made the most of their backgrounds and opportunities to meet new challenges and explore new territory in the years before the war.

Every individual was motivated by different circumstances, but there are some motivations in common to most of the men. In both Oxford and Cambridge Universities there was a strong inter- war interest in polar exploration guided by men who had been on Scott's and Shackleton's, expeditions, such as James Wordie and Frank Debenham. In the close-knit circle of Oxbridge university life it was perhaps inevitable that students who stood out as men of determination and character would be sought out for inclusion in university exploration expeditions. However, there was a definite sense of randomness and chance that introduced some of the characters to their future adventures. George Binney became committed to helping organise his first Spitsbergen expedition after bumping into Julian Huxley in a bookshop, Glen became interested in Polar exploration after a chance conversation in a queue for a bath. Spencer Chapman, although already experienced in Arctic matters, was recruited by Gino Watkins after meeting him on the ski slopes at Davos. Croft became involved in Glen's expedition to Spitsbergen while talking to the pretty female administrator, Nina Greville, at a party and nearly not accepting an invitation to join because of his mistaken belief that it was to be a mixed expedition. Different motivations existed in the ranks of those individuals that were or had been in the services. Martyn Sherwood and Robert Ryder needed a break from disciplined naval life, Tilman's adventures stemmed from a sense of restlessness after his teenage years had been spent fighting the Great War. Gino Watkins can be credited with bringing together the members of the BARRE expedition, who were handpicked by Watkins for their potential and the probability that they would fit in with his methods of Arctic exploration based on the use of initiative and cooperation rather than on stringent leadership.

A sense of fun and enjoyment is apparent in all the personal accounts of the men's experiences. Writing of the members of Watkins's second expedition of 1932 Courtauld said, "they would be the first to admit that he objects of the expedition ... were the means of living the life they like to live, rather than ends in themselves."[1] Peter Fleming described his adventures in Brazil as "great fun." [2] Martin Lindsay, on setting sail for Greenland to join Croft and take command of the Trans-Greenland Expedition enthused "I had enlisted for adventure and that was all I asked for. I had no responsibilities and was as carefree as a

---

1   Courtauld in Introduction to F. Spencer Chapman, *Watkins's Last Expedition*, p.13.
2   P. Fleming, *Brazilian Adventure* (London, 1933), p.409.

kitten."[3] Quintin Riley wrote in his diary at the end of the BARRE expedition: "well, it has been a wonderful year, full of interest and I have enjoyed every minute of it."[4] It should be remembered that most of the members of the various expeditions in the 1920s and 1930s were only in their twenties, the average age of the BARRE expedition, for example, being twenty-five years old, and they were inevitably filled with a sense of invulnerability and confidence.

However young and light-hearted these men were however, they were all to face dangers and experiences from which they would learn and which would mould their characters. At some stage in their exploring careers most of the individuals considered in this book faced life-threatening events, perhaps the most serious being Binney's aeroplane crash into the sea and Courtauld's incarceration at the ice cap station. Spencer Chapman and Riley had the traumatic experience of losing their leader, Gino Watkins, and then carrying on the work of the expedition. From the ice caps of Spitsbergen and Greenland to the Sahara desert they all had to face situations where only flexibility, resolve, endurance and courage could help them. They had varied experiences of leadership. All the men on Watkins's BARRE expedition were expected to make on-the-spot autonomous decisions, Binney, Ryder, Croft, Glen and, to some extent, Peter Fleming, were the leaders of their expeditions. Binney, Spencer Chapman, Lancelot Fleming, Riley, Ryder, Croft, Courtauld and Glen were all awarded the Polar Medal for their contribution to polar exploration. Riley also received a bar to his polar medal for his Antarctic BGLE expedition.

The contribution of these individuals in the Second World War involved working in many of the major theatres of war on land and sea, often with combined operations and special forces.

George Binney, although too old to join up at the beginning of the war, played the leading role in a remarkable series of operations to bring much needed war supplies from Sweden, overcoming many difficulties with flexibility and a stubborn determination. His knowledge of meteorology and experience in Arctic seamanship helped him to plan and assess the risks of these voyages. From the beginning of his blockade running he was supported by the Special Operations Executive, who worked with the Ministry of Supply to put Binney's plans into operation. Binney led from the front, accompanying each mission, and was awarded a DSO for his leadership skills.

Freddie Spencer Chapman was also awarded a DSO in recognition of his sabotage work and survival for three years behind Japanese lines in the Malayan jungle. He commented several times in his book *The jungle is neutral* on the way in which his Greenland experiences had given him the psychological courage and practical skills to withstand the rigours of his jungle existence.

Quintin Riley used his arctic skills and boat-handling abilities in working behind enemy lines in the invasion of Norway and in training Special Forces troops for Arctic warfare and commando landings on the enemy coast. His major contribution to the work of combined operations was the organising, training and action of No 30 Commando, later 30 Assault Unit. Here his logistical skills were to the fore, deploying the units in close cooperation with invasion forces to obtain maximum early intelligence of the enemy's technology.

Peter Fleming's war took him firstly to Norway, under the direction of MI (R),

3   M. Lindsay, *Three Got Through – Memoirs of an Arctic Explorer* (London, 1946), p.113.
4   J. Riley, *Pole to Pole* (Huntingdon, 1989), p.41.

where he had the distinction of being the first British soldier to land. He took part in the clandestine development of the auxiliary resistance forces before being involved in the withdrawal from Greece. He spent the rest of the war in military intelligence in the Far East where his knowledge of languages and the political geography of the area helped him plot numerous military deception operations to help confuse of the enemy forces. He was awarded the OBE as recognition of his efforts in this field. His wartime career showed the same characteristics as the swashbuckling 'Elizabethan adventurer' who had made a name for himself as a travel writer in the pre-war years.

Andrew Croft's Arctic experience resulted in his involvement with special operations at the beginning of the war when he was sent by MI (R) to supervise the shipment of supplies to help the Finns in their fight against Russia. Following this he was involved in Major Gubbins's independent companies as intelligence officer in the invasion of Norway, going behind the enemy lines to carry out reconnaissance and sabotage. His expertise in small boat-handling led him to his involvement with training commando troops for seaborne landings and eventually to the command of special services operations based at Corsica, landing agents and supplies on enemy coasts in the Mediterranean. In this operation and in his subsequent one, landing by parachute to disrupt German communications in southern France at the time of the Allied landings, he felt that his previous experiences had prepared him for 'running his own show'. He was awarded the DSO in 1945.

Alexander 'Sandy 'Glen's wartime career was to be directly linked to knowledge and expertise gained on expeditions to Spitsbergen in the 1930s. His knowledge of both the geography and climate of the archipelago was directly useful in the wartime operations, firstly to evacuate and then retake bases in Spitsbergen. His expertise in aerial meteorological reconnaissance also contributed to the safety of Atlantic convoys. In the Balkan theatre of war he worked for SOE in Yugoslavia in the early days of the war and in Yugoslavia at the end of the war when he was involved with some of the earliest encounters with the Russian army. He was awarded a DSC in 1942 and a bar to that medal in 1945.

Robert Ryder was a young Lieutenant in the Royal Navy when setting off in the company of three other young naval officers to sail the wrong way around the world in 1933. The talent for deception he showed in disguising certain clandestine aspects of their voyage was to be used again in preparations for the raid on St Nazaire. The courage and flexibility shown in a difficult few years as captain of the *Penola* on the BGLE expedition were to stand him in good stead in his wartime naval career, being torpedoed and sunk as the captain of a Q ship and later commanding "the greatest raid of them all" at St Nazaire. For his part in this raid he was awarded the VC.

Martyn Sherwood, Ryder's companion on the *Tai Mo Shan* and the chronicler of the voyage, had retired from the Navy, but returned during the war to take command of a group of anti-submarine trawlers. Following the sinking of his ship, the *Cape Passaro*, he was appointed to command a group of corvettes on convoy and anti-submarine duties in the Mediterranean. He was awarded the DSO in 1941 following action in Piraeus harbour during the Allied forces' withdrawal.

Augustine Courtauld was too much of an individualist to fit well in to the RNVR, which he joined at the outbreak of war. His arctic experience was put to good use initially as he worked in Military Intelligence, often giving advice on climatic and ice conditions over the Arctic Ocean. However this life did not suit him and he gained a transfer to serve in the difficult area of Coastal Command and later as navigating officer on convoy duties. He felt perhaps that his talents were not being used in his wartime role and that his defining experience was still that of his epic adventure on the ice cap.

Lancelot Fleming, who had contributed to the pastoral and spiritual well-being of the members of the BGLE expedition, joined up as a naval chaplain and saw service on the battleship the HMS *Queen Elizabeth*. His role in the expedition and his knowledge of men under stressful conditions was to stand him in good stead in gaining the trust of the men to whom he ministered in the Navy and he was instrumental in encouraging naval ordination candidates to follow their vocation.

H.W. 'Bill' Tilman is the only man of this group of adventurers to have fought in the Great War, earning a Military Cross and bar by the age of twenty-one. His extraordinary toughness and staying power made him a mountaineering legend in the 1930s. Following a period with his old regiment in the artillery, serving in Italy, Tilman was able to use his mountaineering and survival skills and his unflappable personality to good effect in SOE missions in Albania and Italy, where his taciturn nature was to reveal significant qualities of leadership, for which he was awarded the DSO.

The careers of the men considered in this book are similar in many ways, many of them coming from comparable backgrounds and educational institutions. The fact that several served together at various points in the war is not coincidence but indicative of the strong links created by their shared polar experiences. We are able to examine their careers as nearly all of them wrote books detailing their explorations and/or their war service, and the major events in which they took part are documented in archives. They are representative of a generation who, having thrown themselves into exploration and adventure, perhaps as a reaction to missing the Great War, found themselves taking a significant role in the Second World War. The individuals described here covered most of the major theatres of war on land and at sea from Norway and Dunkirk to the end of the war in the Far East and the surrender of the Japanese. A family member of one of them emphasised the message that such accounts as those contained in this book are not for the glorification of individuals, impressive though their conduct may have been. They represent the service of many of their countrymen who will not have their story told to a wide audience, yet who nevertheless served their country and are remembered in the hearts of their friends and families.

Appendix A

Members of the Oxford University Arctic Expedition 1924

Oxford University
G. Binney, Leader, No. 3 sledging party.
C.S. Elton, Chief Scientist, Biologist.
H.M. Clutterbuck, Assistant Organiser, No 2 sledging party.
F.A. Montague, Zoologist, No 1 sledging party.
K.S. Sandford, Geologist, Glaciologist, No 2 sledging party.
Dr H. Florey, Medical Officer.
A.T. Rankin, Bird Photographer.
R.Thorneycroft, in charge of motor-boat, mechanic.

Cambridge University
R.A. Frazer (National Physical Laboratory), Surveyor, leader of No 2 sledging party.
Lieut. H. Baker RN (Ret.), in charge M/S *Oiland*, Surveyor.
W.B. Carslake, Mountaineer, No 1 sledging party.
T. Stoneborough, Reserve Sledger.

Services and Government Departments
Lieut Col. Sir I. Colquhoun, DSO, No. 3 sledging party.
Col J.E. Tennant, DSO, Surveyor, Second-in-Command M/S *Polar Bjorn*.
Capt. F. Tymms (Air Ministry), Seaplane Observer and Navigator, Meteorologist.
Capt. J.C. Taylor (RAF Reserve), Ground Engineer.
A.G.B. Ellis, (ex-RAF) Seaplane Pilot.
Lieut. J.R.T. Aldous, MC (Royal Engineers), Surveyor, leader No 1 sledging party.
E. Relf (National Physical Laboratory), Physicist, Surveyor, Assistant Wireless Operator.
E. Law, Wireless Operator.
J.C.B. Mason, Cinematographer.

Norwegians
Capt H. Hansen (Amundsen South Pole Expedition), in charge of dogs, No 3 sledging party.
A. Eilertsen, interpreter, navigator, No 3 sledging party.
G. Lindquist, dog driver, No 1 sledging party.
H. Schmidt, dog driver, No 2 sledging party.

Appendix B

Oxford University Expedition to Spitsbergen 1924

The Use of Wireless for Sledging Parties[1]

G. Binney, from the data of E. Relf.

1924 Expedition

Following the successful use of a wireless receiving set by the sledging party in 1923, experiments were carried out in 1924 with a view to further development. The northern party was equipped with both receiving and transmitting gear. The receiving gear was of the same pattern as used in 1923. Power for transmission was made by hand generator. The whole equipment weighed approximately 40 1lbs. Owing to the illness of the wireless operator, it was not possible to give a thorough test to the experiment. While the gear was satisfactory under good conditions in England, it was not practical for summer use in the Arctic,

Two main faults were: (a) the difficulty of carrying an aerial with a fair radiation efficiency on a sledge;(b) the hand generators did not give a sufficiently steady high-tension voltage. Consequently they gave a very variable wavelength (which would not matter on spark transmission, but is hopeless on a continuous wave).

For reliable transmission of wireless messages by sledging parties the following suggestions are made:

1. The use of a much shorter wave-length (say 100 metres). Amateur experimenters are daily communicating thousands of miles on 75-90 metres. With 20-50 watts input it should therefore be possible to do 100-200 miles with 5 watts.
2. This would allow batteries to be used instead of generators, getting rid of the unsteadiness of the latter.
3. It is unlikely that a single valve transmitter on short wave will ever be steady. One would have to develop a concentrated transmitter of the "master oscillator" type, in which one valve controls the wavelength and the other does the radiating. The wavelength then does not depend on the varying capacity of an aerial swinging in the breeze and continuous wave working becomes easier in consequence. The receiving gear would need to be constructed for the shorter wave, and would probably be reduced to two valves instead of three. In fact the high frequency amplifier (first valve of our existing sets) would be probably impossible to handle on 100 metres. The weight of such a set would be very little (if at all) greater than the one used by the northern sledging party.

---

1   Appendix G, G. Binney, *With Seaplane and Sledge in the Arctic* (London, 1925), p.276.

It is hardly necessary to comment on the extreme value of a wireless transmitting set to a sledging party in any serious emergency.

Appendix C

The Oxford University Arctic Expedition 1924

The Flying Work of the Expedition

Per Ardua ad Astra – **Report on the Flying Work of the Expedition**

Following the ditching of the seaplane on its first operational flight on 14th July (see Chapter One), Taylor and Tymms made strenuous efforts to repair the damage. One of the piston heads had to be replaced and the entire engine had to be stripped down, and washed free of the duraluminium of the piston head. Binney considered the accident to have been a one in a hundred chance. The engine gave no further trouble during the expedition and Binney was only glad that it had happened at the beginning of it. He recalled "we were no longer harbouring blind delusions of mechanical perfection in flight".[1]

The seaplane was then loaded, fully-rigged, on the *Polar Bjorn* and taken to the base at Leifde Bay and then to Whalenberg Bay. On 2nd August a test flight was made to record climbing ability and fuel consumption. It was realised that the seaplane took 30 minutes to reach 4,000 feet, which was the minimum height for photographic surveying. It had been thought that the range of the seaplane was 400 miles at an average speed of 80 mph, but it was then discovered that the petrol tanks did not actually hold the amount of petrol they were supposed to. This effectively reduced the range to 275 miles at 70 mph. The slow rate of climb also took off time to be devoted to photography. It was therefore realised that, factoring in the safety margin for fuel consumption necessary for flying over uninhabited areas, that the planned aerial surveys could not take place from their present base.

Another problem was the weight of the emergency equipment carried on board the seaplane, with 28 days rations for two men and 3,232 1bs of emergency equipment including a sledge. With this weight on board the seaplane just would not take off. After the removal of some of these emergency supplies, cutting the ration to 14 days and removing the sledge and w/t systems altogether, the seaplane performed significantly better.

It was therefore decided by Tymms to move the base of the aerial survey to Treurenberg Bay, from where they would be able to survey the coast of North East Land and keep within their range. They planned to use the *Oiland* as a base. However the weather patterns at Treurenberg Bay were more unpredictable, with changing ice conditions. On two occasions the seaplane escaped serious damage. On 8th August she dragged her anchor and was almost swept away by a gale and was also later threatened by a 'growler' which missed colliding with her by inches. Binney commented as a result of the problems that the obvious answer would have been to have a bigger plane, but also added that they had not enough money to provide one so that they would have to make do with what they had.

The photographic survey was started on 9th August, when Tymms and Taylor took off and saw North East Land from above. Looking at the ground conditions, they congratulated

---

1   G. Binney, *With Seaplane and Sledge in the Arctic* (New York, 1926), p.96.

themselves on not being one of the sledging parties. On this flight the seaplane was in the air for 1 hour 15 minutes and returned safely. Each flight however, involved a day of repair work after landing. On 13th August, the weather having improved, a flight took off for Cape Sparre and Tymms started the aerial survey of the coastline. He managed to photograph a large strip of coastline.

The aerial survey did not consist of vertical photography, as vertical photographs of the featureless ice cap would not fit together. The object of the photographic survey was to photograph the coast with oblique photography of approximately 30°. The height of the seaplane was between 4 and 5 thousand feet, and it flew parallel with the coast, about a mile off it. Each photograph would overlap 50% with the previous one. Binney commented:

> It would be waste of both of time and money to attempt a very high degree of accuracy in the survey of uninhabitable and practically inaccessible regions. The most one can do is produce, in a short space of time and at comparatively small cost, a map which has a degree of accuracy sufficient for the needs of those who are likely to use it; and for this purpose aerial survey in the polar regions is admirable ... The aerial photographer can penetrate into regions where neither sledge or ship can follow [2]

At 6.30 on 26th August the seaplane took off to carry on the survey, and crashed soon after takeoff, losing height and hitting her undercarriage on a ridge of ice. Tymms and Ellis were unhurt, but it looked very much as if the seaplane was damaged beyond repair. Up to that date it had completed 7½ hours' flying time from Treurenberg Bay. However, after 120 hours skilled labour and 200 hours unskilled labour the seaplane was ready to take off again by 30th August. It completed a reconnaissance flight to gauge the extent of the pack ice and was about to take off again when it was realised that one of its floats was punctured. Repairs would take 24 hours, but time had run out and the seaplane's last flight had to be abandoned.

The seaplane was left on Spitsbergen, only its engine being brought back. It had flown on only two of the six days from 10th July to 1st September on which aerial photography was possible. It had surveyed, however, 70 miles of North East Land and had proved what Binney considered to be more important, that aircraft can play an important role, on their own and in conjunction with sledging, in exploration in polar districts.

---

2   Ibid., p.229.

Appendix D

Members of the British Arctic Air Route Expedition 1930-31

Leader, H.G. Watkins
Surgeon, Lieutenant E.W. Bingham, RN (Doctor)
Augustine Courtauld (Surveyor)
Flight Lieutenant H.I. Cozens, RAF (Photographer)
Flight Lieutenant N.H. D'Aeth, RAF (Pilot)
Captain P.H.M. Lemon, Royal Signals (Wireless Operator)
Lieutenant M. Lindsay, Royal Scots Fusiliers (Surveyor)
Q. Riley (Meteorologist)
J. Rymill (Surveyor)
J.M. Scott (Surveyor and in charge of dogs)
A. Stephenson (Chief Surveyor)
L.R. Wager (Geologist)

Appendix E

British Arctic Air Route Expedition – Sledging Rations

Summary of expedition report on sledging rations by H.G. Watkins[1]

Bovril Pemmican	8 ozs.
Maypole Margarine	8 ozs.
Plasmon Wholemeal Ship's Biscuits	5 ozs.
W. and D. Harvest's Prepared Flour	2 ozs.
Plasmon Powder	2 ozs.
Plasmon Oats	3 ozs.
Tate and Lyle Cube Sugar	4 ozs.
Cadbury's Cocoa and Milk powder	1 oz.
Cadbury's Milk Chocolate	3 ozs.
Horlicks Malted Milk	0.5 ozs.
Total	36.5 ozs.
Total Calories	6,000

Also small quantities of:
Cod Liver Oil
Dry Yeast Powder
Lemon Juice
Essential Salt

This ration contained correct proportions of carbohydrate fat and protein. The ratio differed from others in the small quantity of biscuit and a large quantity of margarine. This was the only way to increase the total calorific value of the rations without increasing their weight. These rations were more than enough for men travelling between 20 and 30 miles a day at low temperatures at a height of 8,000 feet. Sledging parties using these rations for up to two months were fit at the end of their journey.

On coast journeys where seal meat was available it was unnecessary to take rations as seal meat and blubber supply everything that is necessary to life.

Dog Sledging rations:
One pound of Bovril dog pemmican and a quarter of a pound of Maypole fat per dog per day.

---

1   Information from *Northern Lights, The Official Account of the British Arctic Air Route Expedition* (London, 1932), p.298.

Appendix F

The British Arctic Air Route Expedition 1930-31 – summary of climatological notes

The Climate of East Greenland

1. Coastal

The climate in the coastal area where the base camp was situated was neither too hot in summer nor too cold in winter. The highest and lowest recorded temperatures at our coastal station were 63° F. and – 3° F. respectively.

When the expedition arrived in the July of 1930 they reported warm weather. While unloading the ship, Spencer Chapman reported "working in the brilliant sunshine wearing only a shirt and trousers."[1] Riley mentioned that bathing was very pleasant apart from the mosquitoes. However, the fjord on which the base was positioned had ice pans and small icebergs which varied in size as the direction of the wind varied. From the middle of August showers of rain were experienced, leading up to the first gale on 31st August. Spencer Chapman called this the "first manifestation of evil weather."[2] This kind of autumn weather continued until the end of September, when the rain was replaced by snow. The upper end of the fjord near the inland ice became frozen over with new ice, and when the supporting party for Rymill's ice cap journey returned on 21st September they had to break a way through the ice with their oars. The coastal survey party, returning at the sea end of the fjord on 14th October, however, found that their entry was ice-free. By the end of October, most of the fjord north of the base was frozen. A gale on 8th October reached 120 mph and caused much damage around the base, including the loss of the anemometer and the toppling of the wireless mast. This blizzard blew away much of the newly formed ice in the fjord, which then reformed and was blown away by the next gale. This pattern continued until December 8th, when the fjord finally froze over and the boats were beached for the winter. From this date the aeroplane could take off with skis and winter hunting could begin

Snow alternated with fine weather during November, with a strong gale every few days. However, in December there were no gales. In January, February, March and the first half of April there a large number of fine days with a clear sky, intermingled with overcast days on which precipitation was generally experienced. Gales occurred two or three times a week. Quintin Riley described the onset of the gales. They "always came from the north, and always with the same procedure. First what appeared to be small puffs of smoke were seen coming from the tops of the mountains to the north of the base, some five miles away. This was snow blowing off, and resembled a semi-active volcano. It would gradually increase and a roaring sound would be heard."[3] They were always above 100 mph and it was impossible to stand up against them. Riley described how one had to crawl along holding

---

1   F. Spencer Chapman, *Northern Lights*, p.21.
2   Ibid., p.84.
3   Q. Riley, Appendix 'Climatological Notes' in F. Spencer Chapman, *Northern Lights*, p.282.

onto rocks. The gales were also extremely localised. On one occasion an aeroplane flight was being successfully made while a strong gale raged 15 miles away. They do not seem to have been of such intensity on the ice cap, only near the coast.

Plans for journeys down the coast by sledge were abandoned as the sea pack ice never froze firmly onto the new ice in the fjords. In the darkest days of winter the temperature varied between 5° F. to 38° F. After 15th April the maximum temperature was always above freezing, the snow began to melt, and no more gales were experienced. This fine spring weather continued till the end of May. By the beginning of June the whole fjord at base camp was ice-free. Stephenson, Wager and Bingham set out to climb Mount Forel on 6th May and found conditions on the way to Big Flag Depot so warm that in the day they were wearing only grey flannels and thin vests. Quintin Riley considered that summer began on 1st June. By 9th June the climbing party were at Big Flag depot on their return to base. Spencer Chapman remembered "summer had come since they were last at base. The Saxifrages and Alpine Azaleas were in flower among the rocks and the Arctic Terns were screaming over the Fjord."[4]

2. The Ice Cap and the Ice Cap Station

The ice cap station was set up on 8th September 1930 and meteorological observations were taken until 26th March. The station was 140 miles from the coast and at an altitude of 8,200 feet. It had a very much less variable climate than the base. The whole time when meteorological reading was taken, the precipitation was snow. Through most of September the temperature was below zero, with an average of 9° F. Throughout September and October the weather was stable, varying day by day from blue sky to co overcast with snowfall. The first change over in personnel took place without incident on 3rd October and observations continued until August Courtauld took over on his own on 3rd December. Courtauld experienced frequent gales in the period January to March, some as high as 9 on the Beaufort scale. These gales and regular snow precipitation contributed to the drifting of snow that was to eventually trap Courtauld inside the ice cap station.

As far as the use of aircraft on the ice cap, Riley commented on the poor visibility at ground level owing to the drift snow. He went on to add however that in many cases the drift snow was a shallow layer and that the zenith was clear. This would not interfere with aircraft passing over the ice cap which did not wish to land. If the pilot did wish to land Riley commented, rather casually, "it would only mean a drop of 10-15 feet, which although it might damage an aeroplane, would probably not wreck it."[5]

A full report on conditions on the ice cap was not obtained as the ice cap station was abandoned on 5th May 1931.

---

4   F. Spencer Chapman, *Northern Lights*.
5   Q. Riley, Appendix 'Climatological Notes' in F. Spencer Chapman, *Northern Lights*, p.282.

Appendix G

The British Arctic Air Route Expedition 1930-31 – report on flying operations

Personnel: Flt. Lt. N.H. D'Aeth, W.E. Hampton.
(G. Watkins, J. Rymill and H.I. Cozens also qualified pilots).
Aircraft: Two De Havilland 60 Moths G-AAUR and G-AAZR.
G-AAUR equipped with two undercarriages, one ski, one float, also a locker for emergency equipment.
G-AAZR of standard specification.

General Aims of Flying Programme

Aeroplanes were to be used for air photography, to assist mapping and to test flying conditions throughout the year in East Greenland. A demonstration flight along the whole route between England and Winnipeg.[1]

Projected Programme for Summer 1930

1. Photographing of coast from Angmagssalik to north of Kangerdlugssuaq fjord.
2. Reconnaissance flights over the ice cap to help planning a route to establish an ice cap station.

Some Difficulties

The limitations of a single engine aircraft were realised, as even though the engine was very reliable, there was always the possibility of a forced landing or crash many miles away from base. D'Aeth commented, "flying from the ice-filled waters of East Greenland in a single engine aircraft was, of necessity, a severe strain."[2]

There was always the danger that chosen take-off site would have frozen over or be closed in by moving ice by the time the aeroplane came in to land.

However, the discovery of a fresh water lake above Lake Fjord, further up the coast, at 66° 20' North, helped, as this proved very suitable for a seaplane base.

Achievements of summer programme

23 flights had been carried out in the 44 flying days available, with a total of 32 hours and 15 minutes flying time. Nine of the flights were for the purposes of photography and 450 plates were exposed. This photographic survey covered the coast from Björne Bugt (lat. 66° 05' N.) up to and including Kangerdlugssuaq (lat. 68° 10' N.) On 29th August D'Aeth and Watkins flew north of Kangerdlugssuaq fjord and noticed a range of mountains much higher than the surrounding peaks, at an estimated height of up to 14,000 feet. The following day they returned to photograph them. This range was to be named by the Danish

---

1   Gino Watkins, introduction to F. Spencer Chapman, *Northern Lights* (London, 1932), p.2.
2   N.H. D'Aeth, 'Report on flying work', Appendix II in F. Spencer Chapman, *Northern Lights* p.266.

Government the Watkins Mountains, and one of their peaks was eventually to be climbed by a party led by Courtauld in 1935. D'Aeth reported "the season can be considered as most successful."[3] The Moths were then overhauled and made ready for winter flying, skis being fitted to G-AAUR.

Projected Programme for Winter 1930-31
1. Flight of the moths from Angmagssalik to Winnipeg and back.
2. Flights over the ice cap station to drop supplies.
3. Photographic survey of coastal mountain belt.
   This was an ambitious programme, very little of which was carried out.

Some Difficulties
1. The large number of Föhn gales. These broke up newly-formed ice, making taking off and landing from the fjords and lake difficult. They also raised large wind-drifts on the ice cap surface of the ice cap, making landing on it impossible throughout the winter.
2. The gales were unpredictable, making it difficult to carry out longer flights from base. The fjord did not become safe to use until 19th December.
3. G-AAUUR was badly damaged in a gale while being secured out on the ice at Angmagssalik, when weather conditions prevented a return to base. Repair was possible but took two months, by which time the plan for the long flight to Winnipeg had to be abandoned.
4. All attempts to find the ice cap station by aeroplane and drop supplies failed. Flying on the ice cap had to be undertaken on sunny days, resulting in large black shadows from the plane obscuring clear vision of the ground. D'Aeth was annoyed at their failure to locate the ice station, but at that time he did not realise that the station was buried and out of sight.

Summary of Winter Flying
49 flights were carried out with 46 hours 50 minutes airtime. These flights were mainly ferrying trips, but some photographic reconnaissance was carried out, competing aerial survey objectives for the whole year and useful information obtained. D'Aeth pointed out that more flights had been carried out in the winter season than in the summer one. He commented on the relative comfort and warmth of the aeroplanes in winter due to the coupé heads and heated cockpits. He was full of praise for Hampton, assisted by Rymill, who kept the aeroplanes going in poor condition. There were only 20 days in which both aeroplanes were out of action.

Projected Flying Programme for Summer 1931
1. Completion of the photographic survey of Sermilik Fjord as far as the ground survey had been completed.
2. Photographic survey of the coat from Sermilik to Umivik.
3. Flight to Winnipeg in a multi-engine aeroplane.
4. D'Aeth and Watkins planned to fly home to England in one of the Moth aeroplanes.

---

3   Ibid., p.268.

Some Difficulties

1. The proposed flight to Winnipeg was cancelled as a larger aeroplane did not become available.
2. The London Committee of the expedition vetoed the flight back to England by Moth. The photographic survey plans for the summer, were however, completed.

Summary of Flying for the Whole Expedition

74 flights were made in the whole expedition with a total of 86 hours flying. 49 of the flights, with 46 hours and 50 minutes flying time were carried out from the ice.

The coastal photographic survey was complete from Umivik to Kangerdlugssuaq Fjord.

During summer flights, some new islands and a range of mountains were sighted.

The aeroplanes were used effectively for ferrying personnel and stores when needed.

The suitability of East Greenland for flying

At the end of the expedition D'Aeth came to some conclusions about the prospects of regular or commercial flying in Greenland. Because of the large amount of ice regularly to be found in the east coast waters, and the rapidly changing nature of this ice due to wind and tides, he considered that the fjords were not suitable to be used as bases for aircraft. However he recommended the two lakes in coastal areas, at Angmagssalik and Lake Fjord, as suitable bases. In summer both these lakes are ice-free, and calm enough for a seaplane. There were beaches for grounding an aeroplane for repair and the lake beds were suitable for anchoring. Although the weather conditions in summer were good, he recommended that multi-engine aircraft were used as "there is still the risk of a forced descent away from base. This can be overcome by a multi-engine aircraft that is capable of flying with one unit completely out of action.[4]"

Despite the Föhn-like gales that prevailed in winter, and the shortness of the days, D'Aeth recommended that the lakes would be suitable for bases as they would freeze over with a smooth surface, and also, being fresh water, they would freeze over more quickly than the sea. He mentioned that it would be impossible to arrange long distance flights to or from any one base on the coast, because of the unpredictability of the gales, but pointed out that as the gales were very localised it would usually be possible to land at one of the two lakes. He expressed the opinion that an aeroplane flying above Greenland and not wanting to land would not be affected by these localised gales.

---

4   Ibid., p.273.

Appendix H

Members of the Oxford University expedition to Spitsbergen 1933

Alexander Glen	Leader
John Benson	Geologist
R. Binney	Surveyor
J. Brough	Geologist
Jakes Edmonds	Geologist
J.M. McC. Fisher	Ornithologist
Lancelot Fleming	Chief Scientist
Oliver Gatty	Seismography
Alexander Geddes	Geologist
A.K. Gregson	Biologist
H.R. de B. Greenwood	Surveyor
J.H. Hartley	Ornithologist
A.S. Irvine	Surveyor
John de Lazlo	Wireless operator
E.E. Mann	Surveyor
Robert Robertson	Geologist
H.C. Smith	Surveyor
Fred Storr	Biologist

Appendix I

The Oxford University expedition to Spitsbergen 1933 – geological report by the Reverend W. Fleming

East Glaciology: The New Friesland Ice-Sheet[1]
by W.L.S. Fleming

The central part of New Friesland is covered by a continuous sheet of ice extending some 42 miles from north to south. In the north it is approximately 23 miles broad and narrows to a width of 7 miles at its southern margin, which is some 4 or 5 miles south of the southern end of Lomme Bay. The approximate area of the sheet is 650 square miles.

The ice-sheet does not form a true ice cap, since its surface is not completely independent of the underlying topography. The summit of the ice, instead of forming a level surface, comprises a number of broadly gently arched domes up to 7 or 8 miles in diameter. The domes are separated from each other by wide shallow sags, or valley-like depressions. Some of these extend right across the ice sheet and for convenience will be referred to as through-valleys. Their location is probably determined by preglacial valleys in the underlying terrain.

Near the margins of the ice –sheet there are several high independent domes, of which Valhal dome is one of the most prominent. This dome is separated from the main ice-sheet farther west by the north-to-south through-valley leading down to Duner Glacier. The dome, which was named Birfrost by the Swedish Arc of Meridian Expedition, and which appears in De Geer's[2] map as connected by unbroken ice with the central ice–sheet, is in point of fact separated from the latter by a glaciated valley bounded by rock walls.

The elevation of the snow line is not easy to estimate. On 11th July at Hecla Hook and Mossel Peninsula, the snow line extended down to about 1100 feet, whilst, three weeks later it was 300 feet higher. On both occasions snow was lying some 600-700 feet lower on glacial ice and in sheltered valleys. No marked difference was observed between the altitude of the snow-line on the east and the west of the ice-sheet, and the main divide is not eccentric. No crevasses, thaw pools, melt water streams or nunatakkr break the monotony of the central portion of the ice sheet. Various kinds of sastrugi are the only things that which from time to time diversify its surface.

The glaciers which are fed by the ice-sheet are of two main types. In the first place there are normal glaciers such as the Duner Glacier which head in through-valleys whilst the second class comprises glaciers which head in steep sided ice–corries forming embayments at the margins of the sheet. Some glaciers, however, such as Gullfaxe and Skinfaxe Glaciers might be grouped in either class, since each of them heads in an ice-corrie lying at the lower end of a through-valley, which is continued westward right across the ice-sheet to Wijde Bay.

---

1   Lancelot Fleming, Appendix Ia – New Friesland, in A. Glen, *Young Men in the Arctic* (London, 1934).

2   G. De Geer, *Missions scientifiques pour la mesure d'un arc de meridien au Spitzberg: Mission Suedoise* (Stockholm, 1923).

Crevasses occur near the top of some of three ice-corrie embayments and parallel to their flanks. The glaciers plunge steeply at 500-700 feet to the foot of the ice-corries, and then flow at more gentle gradients between precipitous frost- shattered rock walls, which dissect a glacially scoured peneplane. The ice-free surface of the bevelled hilltops is characterised by frost-weathered material which in many places has been sorted to form polygonal markings, stone stripes, etc.

The lower distal portions of the glaciers are free from snow throughout the summer to expose an ice-free surface marked by lines of long and narrow hummocks oriented parallel to the direction of the ice movement. In some places the hummocks may be attributed to pressure, but as a rule they appear to be due to thaw. Near the margins of many of the glaciers, however, there are lanes of smooth ice overlaying lateral morainic material. The gentle gradients of the glacier snouts may indicate that the glaciers are at present retreating. A great part of the dissipation of the glacial ice during the summer take place by melting, the melt water being carried away by superglacial and marginal streams, and less commonly in subglacial channels. Part of the glacial debris is deposited by streams as proglacial outwash, while part is transported either englacially or as lateral and medial moraines on the surface of the ice to be deposited at the snout of each glacier as end moraines.

The Oxford University expedition to Spitsbergen 1933 – Rations and equipment by A.R. Glen

(i) Sledging Parties and Coastal Survey Party.

The ration per man per day was: 8 oz. Bovril Pemmican, 4 oz. Van den Bergh's Margarine, 4 oz. Cadbury Chocolate, 4 oz. Tate and Lyle Granulated Sugar, 5 oz. mixture, Quaker Oats and Plasmon Powder. Total 25 oz.

Also, small quantities of concentrated lemon juice prepared by Messrs. Lyons; dried yeast by Messrs. Distillers Co.; cod-liver oil by Messrs. Fairbanks Kirby; and a salt mixture.

These were used by the two sledge parties, the base depot-laying party, the Coastal Survey party, and the Dickson Land party. The total weight of each man's daily ration was 26 oz. (including the extras), which is considerably less than the weight of most previously used rations. The ration contained the correct proportions of carbohydrate, fat, and protein. Vitamins A and D were supplied by the cod-liver oil, vitamin B by the dried yeast, vitamin C by the lemon juice. The best testimonial to the success of this ration is that the health of each member of the parties, who were living on this ration, remained consistently good.

In the choice of rations, it is all-important that full consideration be given to whether the party is equipped with dogs or is a manhauling party. It is also important that full allowance be made for the variation of Arctic summer or winter climates. In the case of a dog-sledging party, the above ration would be more than adequate, but it would have to be increased slightly for a winter manhauling party.

Several conclusions were reached concerning the use of these rations under summer Arctic conditions. Biscuit was badly missed and 4 oz. of wholemeal biscuits is suggested, while 2 oz. of margarine is ample. The possibility of obtaining vitamins in their pure form has simplified this part of the question. Variety can be introduced by taking brown, demerara, white, and barley sugar: also by using different kinds of oats. Light flavouring essences would have been much appreciated, and some toffee or other sweets are desirable. Luxury items (limited necessarily to a few Ibs.) are most successful when they are simple: cocoa, golden syrup, baked beans, or something similar.

(ii) Base Party

The food used by the base party was ordinary English diet. Plain corned beef was more popular than tinned pies, etc., and a good supply of this ought to be taken. Bacon is excellent for boat journeys, but a larger proportion of carbohydrates is required if non-active work, such as the laboratory work at Bruce City, is being done. Fresh bread was much appreciated.

Although seals and bird life were plentiful at the face of the Nordenskiold Glacier, this is exceptional in Spitsbergen, where any attempt to live off the country is impracticable as well as being a waste of time. Hunting can produce pleasant variations in the daily menu but cannot do more. A full-time cook ought to be taken on an expedition with a large personnel.

(iii) Sledging Equipment

Nansen sledges were used and were excellent in every way. They ought to be well soaked in a mixture of linseed oil and paraffin some time before leaving, and it was found that it was well worthwhile waxing their hickory runners. Decking and the fitting of handle-bars increase their efficiency. Ordinary climbing rope is as good as anything for lashings and harness ropes. It is important that manhauling harnesses fit easily round the hips. Finnesko are essential for winter sledging, but either ordinary nailed climbing boots or the hairless Lapp shoe are most suited for summer work. Ski binding for the last, as designed by Messrs. Lillywhite, is very satisfactory. Sohm or reinforced plush skins, as also supplied by Lillywhites, have the longest life. Pyramid tents supplied by Messrs. Camp & Sports were very successful; but a coastal party requires a rainproof tent. For summer sledging some kind of light collapsible beds, similar to that used by Dr. Ahlmann in North-East Land during 1932, are advisable, and waterproof covers for sleeping bags are necessary. Dogs ought to have been taken on all sledging parties, as they would have enabled considerably more work to have been attempted.

(iv) General Equipment

Sailing conditions in Ice Fjord were so good that properly rigged sailing boats would have been useful. The 'Seagull' outboard engine, lent by the kindness of Messrs. Imperial Chemical Industries, was very successful; but the whaleboat ought to have been semi-decked. Full boat stores are essential, as also mooring and landing apparatus.

In conclusion, I would like to thank the many people who helped me in the choice of rations and equipment, and many firms who assisted us by their generosity in supplying goods free or at reduced rates; and finally, in particular, Mr. J.M. Scott, who gave me details of the rationing used by the BAARE 1931-32; and Dr. S.S. Zilva, of the Lister Institute of Preventative Medicine, who very kindly calculated the ration ultimately adopted.

Members of the Oxford University Expedition to North East Land 1935-36

A.R. Glen	Leader and Glaciologist
N.A.C. Croft	Second-in-Command, Photographer, and in charge of dogs
A. Dunlop-Mackenzie	Organiser and Surveyor
K.S. Bengtssen	Trapper
A.S.T. Godfrey, R.E.	Surveyor
R.A. Hamilton	Physicist
D.B. Keith	Biologist
R. Moss	Physicist
A.B. Whatman, RC of Signals	Wireless Operator and in charge of the research on the Ionosphere
J.W. Wright	Surveyor
Hon Agent in England	George Binney, Esq.
Hon Agent in Norway	Carl Saether, OBE

Appendix L

The Oxford University Expedition to North East Land – some scientific aims and achievements

The Scientific Programme

1. Research on the Ionosphere

Previous research by Appleton (c 1927) had discovered that a layer high in the atmosphere reflected radio waves sent upwards. The existence of this highly ionized 'F' layer was thought to explain the fact that wireless signals could be heard at longer distances than would be expected taking into account the curvature of the earth, as in the upper atmosphere free electrons reflect wireless rays and because of this radio signals can travel around the world. Electrons in these higher layers of the atmosphere are ionized by solar radiation. The degree of ionization and the heights of the ionized layers fluctuate on a daily and a seasonal basis and show latitudinal variations. In 1936 research had not been carried out on the ionosphere at latitudes north the auroral belt and Glen was anxious to find out whether there was a difference in reflection for this layer in latitudes which did not see the sun at all for several months of the year. He considered that this part of the scientific programme would "bring results not only theoretical, but of immediate practical value."[1]

By 30th August 1935 the equipment needed to carry out this research was installed at base camp and the first readings from the transmitter and receiver were taken. The transmitter sent up small particles of electromagnetic energy in all directions. Those particles that went up to the atmosphere were reflected downwards by the conducting layer of the ionosphere. The receiver measured the difference in time taken by the direct and reflected pulse and the height of the layer was calculated. Glen called each transmission and reception a 'run' and these runs took place regularly at noon. Every two weeks runs were performed every two hours for a twenty-four hour period. At times, continuous runs were made for 24 hours. This meant that the echo pattern was being photographed continuously, indicating how the height of the ionosphere varied at different times of day.[2] When he spoke to the Royal Geographical Society in January 1937 Glen had not received the full results of the experiments, but he announced that "preliminary inspection has shown that they are both important and unexpected" and plans are being made for another expedition to continue this same research."[3]

---

1   A. Glen, 'The Oxford University Arctic Expedition, North East Land, 1935-36', *The Geographical Journal*, Vol. XC, No.3, 1937, p.198.

2   It is now known that the F layer consists of one layer at night, but during the day, a deformation often forms in the profile that is labelled F1. The F2 layer remains by day and night responsible for most skywave propagation of radio waves facilitating high frequency (HF, or shortwave) communications over long distances.

3   A. Glen, 'The Oxford University Arctic Expedition, North East Land', p.211.

Observations carried out on the aurora were important, as the presence of aurorae has an effect on the ionosphere results. General observations on the aurorae were made hourly, but Glen's experiments were also aimed at establishing the direction of the auroral arcs, by taking photographs which were then examined at the Auroral Observatory at Tromsö and the position and direction of the arcs computed. The direction of 16 arcs was established.

2. Meteorological Recording

Meteorological records were taken three times a day over the whole expedition period at base camp and at the two ice stations. The information was sent back to the Norwegian weather station at Bear Island 30 minutes after each reading. Observations of maximum and minimum temperature, snowfall, hoar frost, wind force and direction, and ablation were made at 07.00, 12.00 and 17.00 GMT, at base, the ice cap stations and on the sledging journeys. Self-recording instruments measured temperature, pressure and humidity at base and at the ice cap stations. The information sent to Bear Island was used in weather forecasting during the period of the expedition. A summary of the results showed that at the base camp, February was the only month in which average temperature at sea level was below 0° F. The wind average was high, and the consequent drifting snow made weather conditions worse. There were strong warm föhn winds which blew the ice out of the bay at base camp in January. The temperature only rose above 32° F. for eight days in June. At the central ice cap station the lowest recorded temperature was –39, once in February and once in March. The maximum temperature was 36° F. on 14th May. Wind averages varied from 15 mph in February to 20 mph in October. Drifting snow was continuous.

Glaciology at the Ice Cap Stations on the West Ice

The research Glen had planned for the ice cap stations was centred on the fact that there was little knowledge of weather conditions in the centre of the permanent ice cap. There was a need for meteorological observations to be made for as long a period as possible. The fact that the North East Land Ice cap was much smaller than the Greenland ice cap where most previous research had been carried out made it more suitable and manageable for research purposes.

The aims of the research were to continue the glaciological work on the area began by Ahlmann in 1931, and to investigate the nature of the violent winds which are present on the North East Land Ice cap. The research looked at the gain and loss of the ice cap over the winter, spring and summer. Precipitation, ablation and thaw needed to be accurately measured, and the action of the strong winds taken into consideration. The small-scale structure of the ice crystals and the development of snow into firn over a period of time was to be examined.

It was discovered that at a depth of twenty-five metres the temperature remained constant at 32° F. during the year. The time required for the change of snow into firn was measured, and the relative roles played by accumulation and ablation in the results examined. The thermal conductivity of snow, firn and ice was estimated. The large crevasse discovered in proximity to the ice cap station tunnels gave an opportunity to examine the layers of ice and firn and also to establish, by the use of meters inserted in the walls of the shaft, the speed at which the crevasse was opening. By examining the bands of ice in the crevasse and tunnel, it was decided that firn finally turned to ice at a depth of 30 feet below the surface. A continuous record of the temperature of the ice on different levels had been noted.

The West Ice as a Sub-Arctic Glacier

During a lecture give to the Royal Geographical Society in 1941, Glen gave further insights into the aims and achievements of the 1935-1936 expedition. In it he categorised the region of the West Ice North East Land as a "Sub Arctic Glacier". He estimated that the average thickness of the glacier faces to be between 20 and 30 metres, and worked out from the regularity of nunatakkr that the region consisted of a rock plateau covered with ice of about 30 to 40 metres thick. The marginal zones of the glacier cap did not have a depth of more than 50 metres, and only in the valleys was there a thickness of ice which was more than 300 metres.

Glen considered the West Ice to be 'generally static' and considered that the 'stagnancy of the ice cap'[4] was proven by the fact that there were no icebergs in the sea or in the bays that had glaciers at their head. He had observed that many of the glaciers facing the sea were stranded and melting where they were. Moreover, the movement of the glaciers seemed to be two feet per day, which was considered by Glen to be "dynamically inactive".[5] The ice foot of each glacier thought to be an' instrument of abrasion', an abrasion which had over time formed the coastal plain area of Svalbard.

The relative lack of movement in the ice cap might be due, according to the research carried out in 1936, to be due to the undramatic gradients, therefore, the glacier was not exerting much downward pressure. This was compared with the east coast of Greenland, where the glaciers have to force themselves downwards through steep gaps in the coastal mountain ranges. The expedition monitored the precipitation and the ablation over the period of time it was researching on the West Ice and reached the conclusion that snowfall over the ice cap was insufficient to make up for the loss by ablation.

Glen and his colleagues' overall conclusion was stated to the Royal Geographical Society in 1941:

> The present accumulation/ablation balance seems to be negative, and the West Ice can be seen to be in a gradually recessive condition, little movement occurring and the marginal areas slowly melting away in situ.[6]

---

4   A. Glen, 'A Sub-Arctic Glacier Cap: The West Ice of North East Land', *The Geographical Journal* Vol XCVIII, August 1941, p.70.
5   Ibid.
6   Ibid., p.145.

Appendix M

Members of the British Graham Land Expedition 1934-37

John Rymill	Leader
W.E. Hampton	Second-in-Command
Surgeon Lt. Commander E.W. Bingham	Doctor
The Reverend W. Fleming	Chaplain and Geologist
J.L. Moore	Engineer and Surveyor
Q. Riley	Quartermaster and in charge of small boats
B. Roberts	Ornithologist

Crew of the *Penola*

Lt. R.E.D. Ryder	Captain
J.H. Martin	First Mate
Captain L.C.D. Ryder	Second Mate
G.C.L. Bertram	Biologist and Sailor
N. Gurney	Sailor

Appendix N

The British Graham Land Expedition 1934-37 – sledging rations[1]

Our sledging rations were base on those used by the British Arctic Air Route Expedition, but owing to the experience gained in Greenland we were able to make a considerable reduction in weight. Our daily ration for one man was:

Biscuits	2.7 ozs.
Cocoa	0.8 ozs.
Oats	2.0 ozs.
Chocolate	2.4 ozs.
Pemmican	5.6 ozs.
Sugar	3.2 ozs.
Yeast	0.4 ozs.
Milk Powder	1.6 ozs.
Margarine	5.6 ozs.
Pea Flour	1.6 ozs.
Total	25.9 ozs.

Also 1 tablespoon of Califorange (concentrated orange juice prepared by the California Fruit Growers Exchange Ltd.), and 1 Adeloxin capsule (halibut oil).

These rations were packed in three-ply boxes, each containing the right amount to last 2 men for 10 days.

---

1   Information from Appendix on p.285 in J. Rymill, *Southern Lights* (London, 1939).

Appendix O

The British Graham Land Expedition 1934-37 – sledging equipment[1]

The equipment on a sledge journey varies with the time of the year and type of country through which the journey is made, but some idea of the things carried may be of interest. The following lists show practically everything other than food and fuel which Bingham and I carried on the eastern journey.

1 pyramid tent
1 pup tent
1 groundsheet
1 pressure stove and spare parts including prickers
2 pots with lids
2 cups
2 plates
2 spoons
2 dish cloths
1 packet matches (containing 12 boxes)
24 candles
1 2-pint tin of methylated spirits
1 medical outfit
2 thermos flasks
2 climbing ropes
1 shovel
1 .22 rifle

Repair outfit including:
12 spare harnesses
12 spare traces
Tent patching material
6 leather thongs
1 small roll of lamp wick for repairing harnesses
1 cigarette tin containing assorted screws and nails
1 ball of cod-line
1 ball of twine
1 pair of pliers
1 screwdriver
1 bradawl
1 small spanner

---

1   Information from Appendix on p.278, Rymill, *Southern Lights* (London, 1939).

1 marlins spike

Surveying equipment
1 wireless set
1 sledge wheel
2 spare cyclometers
1 p 4 compass
1 Watts $3\frac{1}{4}$ inch theodolite
2 prismatic compasses (1 dry and 1 liquid)
1 torch with spare battery and bulbs
2 thermometers
3 aneroids
1 nautical almanac
1 'hints to travellers' volume 1
1 angle book, R.G.S. pattern
2 traverse books
2 notebooks
1 meteorological notebook
1 canvas roll with compartments for parallel ruler, metal diagonal scale, dividers, protractor and pencils
Navigating sheets carried between two 3-ply boards which fit into a canvass case
1 Leica camera and films

Appendix P

The British Graham Land Expedition 1934-37 – emergency equipment[1]

Emergency equipment for two men carried in the aeroplane on all flights

Summer

Inflatable rubber boat to carry 275 kilos.	
Inflating apparatus and two light paddles	36 lbs
Light double tent complete	7lbs
24 days rations at 16 oz. per day, small primus and cooking pot	25 lbs
2 double down sleeping bags	5 lbs
1 gallon kerosene and tin	10 lbs
Air Ministry pattern anchor	25 lbs
20 fathoms 1¼-inch rope	17 lbs
Boat hook	3 lbs
Very pistol and 8 cartridges	5 lbs
Box spares and float repair outfit	5 lbs
2 signal flags	½ lb
Total	138½ lbs

Winter

Light double tent, complete	7 lbs
24 days rations at 15 oz. per day	25 lbs
Spare footwear and socks	3 lbs
2 reindeer-fur sleeping bags	18 lbs
1 gallon kerosene and tin	10 lbs
4 mooring bags and rope	22 lbs
Small shovel	3½ lbs
Ice chisel	1½ lbs
Engine muff and blow lamp	25 lbs
Can for draining oil from tank	4 lbs
Box spares (plugs, rubber pipe joints, repair outfit for fabric, etc)	5 lbs
Very pistol and 8 cartridges	5 lbs
2 pairs snowshoes	8 lbs
Total	137 lbs

---

1   Information from Appendix on p.285 of J. Rymill, *Southern Lights* (London, 1939).

Appendix Q

The voyage of the *Tai mo Shan* – medical aspects and equipment[1]

By Lt. Surgeon B. Ommanney-Davis

In any ocean trip one does not expect to have illness, but minor complaints are bound to arise, while accidents may happen at any time. During the earlier part of the trip of *Tai mo Shan*, sunburn and prickly heat were our only troubles. At sea, cuts and abrasions did not become septic, nor did any of us suffer from common colds. Presumably, fresh air and sunlight killed off any pathogenic bacteria that may have accompanied the yacht as extra passengers from the last port of call. At different times cuts required sutures, and off the coast of Alaska one member of the crew suffered such violent toothache that, although he was not at all sure of the operative abilities in dental surgery of the doctor, he submitted himself as a victim. Under local anaesthesia the tooth was removed quite painlessly and successfully, so much so that at Victoria, when X-rays showed that four more molars must go, he was quite content for the yacht to be the surgery.

During the two weeks which we were forced to spend on the beach at Crooked Island, we were all working very hard and living under most uncomfortable conditions. We received numerous cuts and abrasions on our hands and feet, to which we had no time to give attention. Added to this was the intolerable irritation caused by sand fly and mosquito bites, which resulted in septic sores. When we arrived at Nassau only one of the crew was clear of these troubles; of the other four, one had a considerable number of boils, two had chronic ulcers on their hands and feet, and the last was unfortunate enough to get some virulent infection through an abrasion which resulted in a cellulitis, necessitating his leg being opened in hospital. The enforced four weeks' stay at Bermuda due to his sickness was enough to put us all in good health again. However, we can hardly blame yachting for these things, and the deep-sea yacht is not liable to meet with them.

The minor things that are likely to occur are constipation, toothache, sunburn, prickly-heat and small abrasions, of which more will be said later.

A complete list of medical stores is given, and may be considered excessive, but as one of the crew was a medical man, chloroform, ether and surgical instruments were taken, so that a major operation or an amputation could be performed if necessary. The following is a list of medical stores which are recommended for a yacht undertaking a similar ocean cruise, and is followed by a few first-aid hints on their use and the methods of treatment.

Bandages—2-inch	24
Boric Lint	1 lb
Cotton-Wool	1 lb
Mackintosh Tissue	2 yards

---

1 Appendix X in *The voyage of the Tai Mo Shan* (London 1935), p.263.

Adhesive Tape	4 yards
Gauze	½ lb
Tincture of Iodine	1 lb
Horsehair (for sutures) tubes	12
Morphia Ampoules	12
Syringe with needles	1
Nikalgin Jelly (for sunburn	1 lb
Epsom Salts	1 lb
Bicarbonate of Soda	1 lb
Aspirin Gr. V tablets	50
Quinine Sulphate Gr. V tablets	50
Dovers Powder Gr. V tablets	50
Calomel Gr. I tablets	50
Boracic Ointment	4 ozs.
Carbolic Acid (pure	2 ozs.
Surgical Spirit	1 lb
Knife	1
Artery Forceps (pair)	1
Dressing Forceps (pair)	6
Scissors (pair	1
Gutta Percha	

Morphia comes under the Dangerous Drugs Act and will necessitate the Captain's signature.

Carbolic Acid is strong and should be carefully stowed and used with caution.

Septic Spots or Abrasions. Treat by hot fomentations. Soak a piece of Boric Lint in boiling water, wring out and apply while hot to the affected part. Cover the lint with a piece of mackintosh tissue to prevent soaking up the bandage; cover this with cotton-wool and bandage up. Repeat this two or three times a day, until there is no further purulent discharge. Afterwards dress with dry lint until healed.

Burns. Apply a thick layer of Nikalgin Jelly on a piece of gauze and place this on the affected part. Bandage lightly.

Cuts. When a cut extends completely through the skin and the wound gapes, it should be sutured.

First scrub the hands and nails well; clean the wound inside and out with Tincture of Iodine; next break a tube of horsehair and thread it on to a needle which has been previously boiled for ten minutes. Then, starting at about a quarter of an inch from the edge of the cut, pass the horsehair downwards through the skin on one side and up through the skin on the other side; cut the horsehair at a convenient length, draw the edges of the wound together and tie with a reef-knot. A long cut may require several sutures like this, and, if such is the case, place them about half an inch apart. Afterwards swab again with Tincture of Iodine and apply a dry gauze dressing secured in position by a bandage or adhesive tape.

Toothache. If the pain is due to a cavity, relief may be obtained temporarily by placing in it a piece of cotton-wool soaked in carbolic acid. This must be done carefully, as a drop of the acid on the gums will cause a painful burn. Next, soften a small piece of gutta percha in a flame and press into the cavity, afterwards smoothing off the edges with the warmed handle of the dressing-forceps.

Broken Bone. Provided the skin is intact, the limb should be splinted to prevent further injury and the patient kept in his bunk until medical assistance can be obtained. If the skin has been broken it is important that antiseptic dressings should be kept on the wound, in addition to the splints. Only when pain is extremely severe should morphia be given.

Method of Administering Morphia. The syringe is assembled with a needle, spirit is drawn up and pumped out several times to sterilise it. Remove plunger and allow a few minutes for it to dry. Next, cut through the neck of one of the ampoules with the file provided, and draw up the contents. Clean an area of the outer part of the arm with spirit or Tincture of Iodine, then push needle through the skin at an angle of fifteen degrees with the surface—inject slowly.

Constipation. Epsom Salts or two grains of Calomel. We also found that the Alophen pills of Parke, Davis and Co were excellent.

Food Poisoning. To get rid of the poison give large doses of salt-water or mustard in water. This will promote vomiting. Afterwards give Epsom Salts.

Sickness or Flatulence. Gastric discomfort can often be cured by giving a teaspoonful of Bicarbonate of Soda in water every three hours.

Sunburn. Smear Nikalgin Jelly on the affected part; it will give relief rapidly.

Prickly Heat. This is a common complaint in the Tropics; it is caused by excessive perspiration and is characterised by a rash, appearing usually at the bends of joints. There is a good deal of soreness and tenderness associated with it. Weak carbolic acid usually clears the condition in a few days. The strength of solution is a teaspoonful of the pure acid dissolved in half a pint of water. It should be dabbed on the skin with a piece of cotton-wool, three or four times a day.

Sore Throat. Gargle with the carbolic-acid solution as above.

Crushed Finger. Swab with Iodine and cover with gauze dressing. Dress the wound twice a day. If the finger is very badly lacerated it may be necessary to amputate the injured part. If so, clean the finger with spirit and cut through one of the joints with the surgical knife, trying if possible to leave a flap of skin to cover the end of the bone.

Vitamins

As the average person has a very vague idea of vitamins, it may be as well to give a rough explanation of them.

Natural foods contain certain constituents, the lack of which gives rise to various diseases. They have nothing to do with the digested food; they have no bodybuilding value, neither do they supply any energy. Hence they are called 'Accessory Food Factors'. They are not present in synthetic foods, no matter how carefully they may have been prepared.

VITAMIN A is comparatively resistant to heat and is present in milk, eggs, cabbages, peas, beans and many other vegetables, also in fat fish and fat meat. An adult can do without this vitamin for a long time, but ultimately the lack of it gives rise to septic complications.

VITAMIN B is resistant to boiling for two hours; it is present in eggs, yeast, potatoes, beans, peas, and many other vegetables. Lack of it gives rise to the disease known as Beri Beri.

VITAMIN C is sensitive to heat and drying. It is present in cabbages, onions, potatoes (raw or cooked), fruit-juices and milk. Dried beans and peas allowed to soak in water and germinate for a few days develop Vitamin C. Lack of this vitamin gives rise to scurvy.

Lime-juice was formerly used to avoid this, and in fact did so, until 1850, when the cordial was made from Mediterranean lemons. Since then, however, West Indian limes have been used, the juice of which is useless in preventing scurvy.

As potatoes, onions, carrots and eggs will last up to six weeks, the yachtsman need have no worry on the score of vitamins. If the proposed voyage is going to last a longer period, it is advisable to purchase a preparation such as Allen and Hanbury's 'Halib-orange', which is a concentrated combination of liver oil and orange-juice.

Appendix R

Operation Performance 1942[1]

Ships

B.P. *Newton*

Tanker of 10,324 tons. Speed 14 knots. Norwegian Captain[2] E.R. Blindenheim, British Captain, J.W. Calvert.

Arrived in Britain carrying 5,000 tons of ball bearings. 27% of total cargo for operation

Rigmor

Tanker of 6,300 tons. Speed 11 knots. Norwegian Captain P.K. Monson, British Captain W. Gilling.

Attacked by German planes with bombs and torpedoes, abandoned and eventually sunk by British destroyer who took crew on board.

Cargo of 600 tons of ball bearings lost.

Buccaneer

Tanker of 6,222 tons. Speed 12 knots. Norwegian Captain, B. Reksten, British Captain, G.D. Smail.

Attacked by German patrol vessel, abandoned ship but managed to scuttle her.

Cargo of 4,000 tons lost.

Captain Smail fatally injured during evacuation.

Storsten

Tanker of 5,343 tons. Speed 10 knots. Norewgian Captain R. Bull Neilsen, British Captain J. Reeve.

Survived attack by German plane and two German patrol boats but hit mine. Then sank by German patrol boat.

One lifeboat of crew landed on the Norwegian coast. Some were captured but 9 escaped and were helped to Sweden by resistance workers. The second lifeboat was lost at sea.

Lind

Tanker of 5,461 tons. Speed 8 knots. Norwegian Captain H.A. Trovick, British Captain, J.R Nicol.

Arrived in Britain carrying 1% of total cargo.

---

1   Based on material found in R. Barker, *The Blockade Busters* (New York, 1976).

2   Because of legal complications, each ship had two captains. The ships would leave harbour under the control of British captains, but the Norwegian captains were supposed to take over when Swedish waters had been cleared.

Lionel

Tanker of 5,653 tons. Speed 10 knots. Norwegian Captain H. Schnitler, British Capatain F.W. Kershaw.

Returned to Gothenburg.

Dicto

Tanker of 5,263 tons. Speed 14 knots. British Captain, D.J. Nicholas. No Norwegian Captain.

Returned to Gothenburg.

Dicto and *Lionel* were carrying 45% of total cargo.

Skytteren

Factory whaler of 12,355 tons. Speed 10 knots.

Steering failed (possible sabotage at Gothenburg). Attacked by German patrol boat and scuttled by captain. Two lifeboats taken in tow by the German trawler. Two lifeboats escaped, but were illegally captured in Swedish waters and taken on board the trawler.

Gudvang

Cargo steamship of 1,470 tons. Speed 9 knots. Norwegian captain H.C.Seeberg, British Captain J.W. Macdonald.

Attacked by German patrol boat and scuttled.

Charante

Cargo steamship of 1,282 tons. Speed 11 knots. Norwegian Captain K.M. Nordby, British Captain J.W. Donald.

Challenged by German patrol boats, and scuttled.

Operation Performance 31st March 1942 – Order of the Day

To Masters, Officers, Crews and other volunteers on board:
M/T *Buccaneer* M/T *Lind* M/T *Rigmor* M/T *Charante* M/T *Lionel* M/T *Skytteren* M/T *Dicto* M/T B.P. *Newton* M/T *Storsen* M/T *Gudvang*
From Sir George Binney

Today at long last we are going to England determined, come what may, to render a staunch account of our voyage, as befits Norwegian and British seamen. Indeed we run a risk, but what of it? If we succeed, these splendid ships will serve the Allied cause and with their cargoes we shall aid the task of supplies.

To sink our ships and cargoes rather than see them captured by the enemy is of course our duty, and on your behalf I have taken such measures as you would wish.

Should we encounter misfortune at sea, remember that in our home and among our countrymen it will be said with simple truth that we have done our best for the honour and freedom of Norway and Britain; but I, for one, have never held with this blockade and look once more to our success, believing that before two days have passed your laughter will resound in a British port

So let us merchant seamen – 400 strong – shape a westerly course in good heart counting it an excellent privilege that we have been chosen by Providence to man these ships in the immortal cause of freedom. God speed our ships upon this venture,

Long live King George, long live King Hakon.
M.S. *Dicto*. Gothenburg

Appendix S

Arctic Warfare: A Lecture Given by Lieutenant Commander Q.T.P.M. Riley on 13th October 1942 at Chatham House[1]

The Arctic must not be interpreted in a strict geographical sense. For our purposes we are considering all countries and districts where snow prevails for at least half the year. The main problem confronting the training of men for winter warfare is the fact that we have no mountain people used to existing in severe weather. The French draw their Chasseurs Alpins from the Alpine district of France; the Germans from Tyrol; the Italians from the Alps. All these people have the right outlook: it is comparatively easy to train a man to be a soldier but very difficult to live in a new environment. You cannot, for example, take a miner who thinks it is quite normal to live and work underground, give him a month's course and expect him to be a mountaineer – he has not got the right attitude. As an illustration I quote a remark made by quite an efficient soldier in Iceland in a letter to his wife: "I have had enough of mountains and snow darling, and when this is over darling, I promise you darling that I will never leave Leeds again". However hard that man tries he will never be much good for winter warfare.

Now General Winter may be a valuable ally if you know how to use him, and to do this you must get people out of their pre-conceived ideas – the hardest part of training. The first thing to combat is the conception of the Arctic as an area of ice and snow, intense cold, absence of life, light, where people only live because they are criminals or beaten races. What is the snow white truth? There are fewer deserts in the Arctic than in many other parts of the world. In summer, any amount of plants flourish in constant sunshine, the seas abound with life, and on land, millions of caribou, wolves, musk oxen, bears, birds and insects have their being. The Eskimos are the happiest people on earth – Englishmen who visit them always want to go back. Can the same be said of darkest Africa? In the Yukon, Norway and Russia there are large flourishing towns. The coldest temperature on earth was recorded in the Siberian town of Verchoyansk, -92° F, not in Antarctica or the North Pole. A healthy man can adapt to this 124 degrees of frost, a sick or starved man feels cold even in a warm room. I have experienced –62° F and only noticed it from the thermometer, but have felt cold and miserable in Suffolk.

What about the other imaginary disadvantages? Isn't the food monotonous? Cold weather diets contain a large proportion of fat with a high calorific value, most unpleasant in ordinary life but ideal and not monotonous in the cold. I remember dining with Lincoln Ellsworth after his transatlantic flight. We were eating oysters. "Don't you wish this was

1   From the Quintin Riley Papers, Liddell Hart Centre for Military Archives.

pemmican?" he asked. "If you do," I replied, "you had better give me your oysters". But I'd rather eat naked margarine in the Arctic than oysters. People often imagine that frostbite is inevitable; I have spent seven years in the polar regions and have never been frostbitten. Frost bite is nearly always due to punishable carelessness, as is snow blindness. Scurvy, the one-time scourge of polar expeditions, is now completely avoidable by eating fresh meat, or Vitamin C tablets, which are supplied in the army's Arctic ration.

Now the advantages. Health – there are no germs in the polar region, colds appear with mail from home, or after one's return. Comfort – let me describe the day of an Arctic traveller. Breakfast in bed – no need to shave and he is wearing most of his clothes – no dressing. He then packs up and starts when ready- no rush to catch the train. He will start the day's march wearing lots of clothes, and gradually take some off. This is important to avoid frostbite. He travels on at an unhurried pace until lunch: chocolate, biscuit with margarine, sugar. He will not stop long enough to get cold. At the end of the day he pitches camp. The primus will be soon be giving out its cheering heat and he will take off some clothes, scrape the ice out of his socks with a spoon, and settle down in his sleeping bag and await the brewing of his supper of pemmican thickened by flour or pea flour.

Some of you may wonder what pemmican is: it is an extract of beef with fat added- very rich in protein. It looks like a large oxo cube and can be eaten raw (rather thirst-making) or cooked in water. It tastes like oxo but nicer. I have found soldiers won't eat it if it is called pemmican, but are quite content if it is called 'special Bovril'. So much for advertising! After his supper, a few puffs on his pipe and a few verses from his poetry book and the explorer falls into a restful sleep. Plenty of insulation underneath is unnecessary: brushwood is good if in a wooded country.

Now let me tell you what a winter warfare soldier must leave behind. His present ideas about taste. Sledging rations are designed for special conditions, not those of home. Casualness – everything must be checked. Dependence on others – he must learn to look after himself and know where he is, all these regardless of rank. Untidy habits – he must know where everything is, tempers become short in tiny tents. Intolerance of others. Luxuries, they have to be carried. Alcohol – rum to keep out the cold is a myth, have good spirits yourself! Your supposed physical limitations – they probably don't exist.

Now this is what you must take: only such clothes as you could conceivably wear all at once apart from socks and gloves. An easily readable book. Attention to detail in the smallest degree. Lots of optimism. Experimental mindedness, especially over food. Above all a sense of humour, and the Englishman's amused intolerance of discomfort.

You know about the 5th Scots Guards. After their disbandment, work on Arctic Warfare was not allowed to lapse and today there are sledges, snow shoes, clothing, tents, and other things being turned out on a scale to make an explorer's mouth water. When this equipment is required is not something on which I can comment, but I am proud to say that all this gear has been produced as a result of the researches of those who spent time in the service of polar exploration before the war. You owe the safety of your sons and husbands, and the successful prosecution of a winter war, to those of all three services who laboured for the prosecution of science in the polar regions.

But polar war is not polar exploration. There are many problems which have to be solved in war which do not confront an expedition. For example, bamboo is used for tent poles and in sledges. The stock of bamboo in this country is governed by the pre-war demand- a mere nothing. Now ask for a large quantity and the Ministry of Supply says they haven't got any, and it does not grow here. The Ministry of Shipping is not going to fill up ships with bamboo, so we have to think of a substitute. Another thing which distinguishes the Arctic soldier from the explorer is that the soldier's job is to fight, and so he requires weapons, ammunition, wireless – all bulky and heavy, and which allow for little modification. If you make a mortar bomb lighter then you have less explosive to annoy the enemy. Experiments have been carried out hauling guns etc, when the snow becomes impossible for wheels. A transport system based on sledges instead of trucks gives food for thought. My own view is that dogs will be essential.

To the untrained men, travel over snow is tiring torment, while to the skilled man properly equipped it gives joy and exhilaration; snow shoes and skis are therefore essential. The mobility of a good skier makes ski troops' tactics similar to those of cavalry. In 1891 a ski detachment of the 20th Russian Infantry division performed a 10-day march of 1,115 miles. At the end of their first month's training, cadets of the Chasseurs Alpins are expected to cover 37½ miles in full marching order in a day. Ski warfare is not new. The first known military use of skis was the Battle of Isen, near Oslo, in 1200, when ski patrols under King Sverre were instrumental in his victory. In 1781 ski training was introduced into the curriculum of the Swedish and Norwegian armies and 15 years later into the Prussian army.

The first British military attempt at ski was in 1914, when McGill University mustered a ski detachment. Ski platoons were formed in units stationed in Iceland last year and good progress was made, although owing to the warmth of the Icelandic winter it is not really good skiing ground. Each unit had Norwegian ski instructors attached and they were quite favourably impressed with the standard reached by ordinary British soldiers. The trouble is that skiing is not like shooting; one bad man will hold up a whole platoon so care must be taken to weed out the weak. Some people will never learn, although this is no fault of their own, just inadaptability to that accomplishment. From my own experience, I am quite sure that a reasonably large number of our men can be ski-trained, but they must be selected. I would also suggest that the core of ski units be formed from skiers serving in Norwegian army units in this country. Military skiing is not like downhill skiing using spectacular turns. The soldier must learn to carry weight, to run under control, and to go uphill easily. Speed is less essential than remaining on one's feet. The Norwegians do not use skis for going uphill – in Iceland they were quite impressed at the ease with which quite inexpert British soldiers could go uphill under load using them – ski troops may be looked upon as cavalry and will be used to patrol. And guard flanks while slower units move along tracks with snowshoes. Much may also be done in the construction of snow roads, and the passage of a few men on skis soon hardens the surface so that those following on walk unaided. Ponies and horses can be taught to wear snowshoes, the Canadian type is probably the best standard. The soldier must also learn to live comfortably in the snow: to pitch his tent, to cook with the primus stove, to build a snow house and improvise shelter. At all times he must think of the enemy and conceal himself and his movements, keep to one track, not throw away rubbish. He must learn what protection various thicknesses of ice and snow will give against small arms, what thickness of ice will bear him, a horse, a lorry, a tank, and how to get out if he falls in. A soldier must learn to navigate, to improvise a sledge from skis to carry wounded, how to look after his weapons lest they become useless. He will probably need to know how to go down screes, scale mountains and lower loads over precipices. It is obvious that men for Arctic warfare must be fit and strong, and kept so. Unlike other armies which employ Arctic troops, the particular difficulty of the British Army is that it seldom knows where it is going to fight and thus the training problem is very great: [it is not]for Arctic warfare alone we have to devise equipment and train men ... we have to endeavour to give so much all-round training that wherever a unit is sent they will give a good account of themselves. And experience had taught us that if we are to undertake any operations against the Germans then we must put very large forces into the field, whether it be in the jungle, the desert, the mountains or the Arctic.

Appendix T

Summary of topics to be covered on the Arctic warfare course 1941[1]

Lt. Q. Riley's notes on the topics to be covered during the Arctic Warfare course at Skogar Camp Iceland 1941

1. Friendly Arctic.
2. Military aspects of travel and bivouacs in snow.
3. Improvisation of shelters.
4. Snow transport.
5. Sledges.
6. Local map reading.
7. Keeping direction
8. Mountain craft.
9. Snow and ice climbing.
10. Snow.
11. Concealment and camouflage in snow.
12. Care of equipment and arms.
13. Clothing and its care.
14. Personal care.
15. Food values, diet and vitamins.
16. Disposal of casualties.
17. Lifting and lowering loads.
18. Internal combustion engines in the cold.
19. Interception and ambush.
20. Weights of various items of equipment.
21. Selected exercises.
22. Tent cooking.
23. Hill walking and river crossing.
24. Skis and skiing equipment.
25. Notes on care of horses and mules in extreme cold.

---

1   From the Quintin Riley Papers, Liddell Hart Centre for Military Archives.

No 30 Commando – Summary by Lieutenant Commander Q.T.P.M. Riley on activities in the Naples area up to September 24th 1943[1]

1. Salerno

a. Captured field German wireless set, together with codists' working papers and code books.

b. Took sundry papers, etc., possibly of some value, from abandoned vehicles.

2. Capri

a. Captured Salverini, suspected of being the principal fascist in the area.

b. Captured secret radio station reported as being engaged in communicating with the Germans on the mainland, together with special codes.

c. Took other secret papers from radio and coast guard stations.

d. Temporarily immobilised radio stations by removal of valves, this with a view to preventing unauthorised transmissions pending the arrival of regular troops of occupation.

e. Searched wreckage of former German R T. Station, and removed items of wreckage likely to be of interest to our technicians.

3. Ischia

a. Landed at Sant Anglo at dawn on 14.IX.43 and raided Hotel Roma and its environs with a view to discovering an alleged German secret R.T. station, without success, however.

b. Examined Italian Semaphore station and R/T station but decided to leave them intact in view of the fact that the cipher and codes operated by such stations can no longer be regarded as secret documents, and the possibility of their being employed in due course by the Allied nations.

c. Enquired generally into the possibility of the continuation of German activities in the area and decided that no direct evidence in support thereof was forthcoming.

4.Procida

a. Landed and enquired into the possibility of shore batteries being employed against the enemy on the mainland.

b. In collaboration with the local Italian naval authorities, made a survey of all shipping on the island and submitted a detailed report thereon to N.O.I.C. Ischia.

c. Made contact with Italian artillery officers and ascertained spot where obturators and

---

1   From the Quintin Riley Papers, Liddell Hart Centre for Military Archives.

firing piers were buried; arranged for transport of responsible officers from Ischia order to bring the Procida batteries into battle order, handed over this business to Lieut. Taylor, R.N.

5. Mainland
a. Landed at San Martino, reconnoitred torpedo testing ranges, removed Admiral Minisini, Italy's foremost torpedo expert and inventor of the safety launch and other devices, to Capri, at the same time took charge of blueprints and other secret papers, these were handed to Lt. Cdr. Austin on his arrival on Capri to see Admiral Minisini.

b. Landed again at San Martino, climbed cliffs and reconnoitred area of Monts Procida, but failed to establish contact with any German forces.

c. With L.C.I. No. 249 attacked German positions around Monte Cuma from the sea and established positions of machine gun posts, silenced enemy positions and started satisfactory fires, including a petrol and ammunition dump. There were two slight casualties to personnel.

Appendix V

A summary of the report of Captain Sverdrup, Royal Norwegian Forces, and Lt. Glen of reconnaissance flight 4th-5th April 1942, prior to Operation Fritham[1]

1. Weather conditions encountered on the flight have been discussed with D.N.M.S and the Forecast Division at the Admiralty. They show clearly the necessity for meteorological stations in Spitsbergen and, if possible in Bear Island. The information available on 4th-5th April gave a misleading forecast of conditions in the North Barents Sea. The area of high pressure reported over Jan Meyen Island and Greenland must have had a trough to the north-east, on the far side of which, over Spitsbergen and Fridtjof Nansen Land, was an area of intense high pressure. Accordingly between 65° and 70° N., N.W. winds of up to 50 mph were encountered, while beyond 72° N. the wind was in the N.E., its force steadily increasing until, in the vicinity of Horsund, it had attained a strength of between 80 and 120 mph.

2. The Barents Sea was open up to 74° 30' N, at longitude 10° 00' N. At this loose drift ice was encountered, its edge orientated E-W and extended indefinitely in each direction. This zone of loose drift ice persisted until 76° North at longitude 11° N. and consisted of individual floes up to 500 metres in width and 50 cms. in thickness, the density of the ice to water being of the order of 3:10. Navigation in this zone is possible for ships of every type, provided expert ice pilots are carried.

3. Northwards of 76° heavier drift ice extended from the west coast of Spitsbergen indefinitely westwards. This ice is impenetrable except by ice breaker.

4. Hornsund, Bellsund and Isfjord were covered with smooth bay ice of up to 60 cms in thickness. No leads or other area of open water existed inside any of these fjords or inside their inner bays. Outside each of these bays however, was a zone of open water, extending some 15 kilometres westwards and a similar distance from north to south. Across the surface of these, lanes of small ice floes were being streamed by the strong N.E. wind, the strength of which, in the region of Hornsund, was estimated at between 80 and 100 mph.

5. Storfjord was filled with heavy drift and bay ice, and no leads of water were observed.

6. The sea ice conditions can be summarised as relatively unfavourable and comparable to those existing in the 1918-1919 period of medium to bad ice years. It should be emphasised however that the sea ice conditions in this area are at their most severe in March and April. Strong N.E. winds and a warm spring could bring about a rapid change by May.

---

1   Based on TNA Air 15/211.

7. The reconnaissance showed that there was no one in occupation at Kap Linn, Grumantsby, Barentsberg, Longyearbyen or Hjorthavn.

8. It was impossible to ascertain whether the coal seams at Barentsberg were on fire, but it was evident that the town was destroyed. The coal seam at Grumantsby were burning with such intensity that the flames were easily visible from a height of 3,000. At Longyearbyen it appeared that some of the coal stocks were still in existence, and no fire or smoke could be seen. This coal may therefore be available for bunkering or shipping.

9. The results of the reconnaissance can therefore be applied to the forthcoming Fritham operation in the following respects.

    a. That prevailing sea ice conditions indicate that it will be possible, by the beginning of May, for the M/S *Salis* and the *Polaric* to penetrate the drift ice and reach Qaude Hoek (sic.) and Isfjord.

    b. That no enemy forces are now in Spitsbergen.

    c. That air reconnaissance of sea ice conditions can give accurate information, and further flights could be of great value in connection with the north Russian convoy route.

10. It should be emphasised that this flight is one of the most difficult attempted in Arctic history. No long distance flight has been made so early in the year and the conditions encountered were as severe as might have been anticipated. Between 70° N and 77° N heavy cloud caused the aircraft to ice badly, and in Spitsbergen itself wind velocities of between 80 and 120 mph made the low flying which was necessary to complete the reconnaissance extremely hazardous. It is earnestly hoped that the officers of the aircraft, captain Flt. Lt. Hawkins and navigator F.O. Wright may receive suitable recognition for this notable flight.

Appendix W

Training in preparation for the raid on St Nazaire[1]

12th, Thurs.
MLs from Portsmouth Command carry out sleeve-firing off Weymouth and then proceed to Falmouth. Remainder of MLs arrive Falmouth p.m.

13th, Fri.
P.M. MLs exercise station keeping and manoeuvring under orders of S.O. MLs. H.M.S. *Princess Josephine Charlotte* arrives Falmouth with troops.

14th, Sat.
MLs sail at dusk and exercise manoeuvring after dark, returning about 2300 and practise going alongside in the dock area under orders of Commander Ryder. MTB 74 arrives Plymouth and is towed to Falmouth to test towing gear.

15th, Sun.
MLs operating in harbour with exercise landing troops in the dock area, under the orders of S/ O MLs (1000 to 2300).

16th, Mon.
0900 – Sail for extended cruise with troops on board MLs. Exercising day and night formations.

17th, Tues.
2200 – Return to Falmouth. MGB 314 arrives Plymouth and is towed to Falmouth the next day.

18th, Wed.
MGB 314 arrives Falmouth. Sleeve-target practise on passage, *Sturgeon* arrives Plymouth.

19th, Thurs.
CO *Campbeltown* to practise handling his ship, sleeve-target firing, and going alongside after dark. Sleeve–target practise for 2nd Flotilla MLs by day. 3 miles west of Eddystone. 1400. ST4.

20th, Fri.
Spare day.

---

1   Based on material found in R. Ryder, *The Attack on St Nazaire, 28th March 1942* (London, 1947).

21st, Sat.
Approx. 1500 all available forces sail from Falmouth so as to arrive off Plymouth breakwater half an hour after sunset.

22nd, Sun.
Exercise Defences of Devonport Dockyard. The force is to withdraw and return to Falmouth by 0400/22. *Sturgeon* being used as navigational beacon off end of swept channel.

23rd, Mon.
Local night training, going alongside after dark and landing troops. *Atherstone* and *Tyndale* arrive Falmouth.

24th, Tues.
Sleeve target firing/or storing, 1st flotilla MLs. *Campbeltown* arrives Falmouth.

25th, Wed.
(Spare day) sleeve-target firing/or storing.

26th, Thurs.
Spare day (sailed one day earlier than planned).

Appendix X

The main clandestine boating operations from Corsica 1943-44[1]

28th November – *Operation Valentine*. Three SOE agents were to be put ashore near Spezia. Major Croft and Sgt. Arnold were the boat party to land the agents.

ML 576 was used under the command of Lt. Commander Whinney, but rough weather led to postponement

2nd December – Second attempt at *Operation Valentine*. MAS 541 was used under the command of Lt Kusolich. Croft and Arnold were the boat party. The agents were safely landed.

28th December – two OSS agents were to be put ashore in a 'blind landing' near St Tropez. Croft and Seaman Miles were the boat party. The mission successfully landed the agents.

2nd January 1944. The first attempt at *Operation Fragrant*. Four SOE agents were to be landed at Moneglia. The PTs boat alerted the coastal defences and the operation was abandoned.

3rd January – Second attempt at *Operation Fragrant*. Croft and Sgt. Coltman were the boat party, but the attempt had to be abandoned due to the absence of a suitable landing ground.

15th January – *Operation Big Game*. Stores were taken by MAS 541 to the island of Gorgona to a forward SOE observation post.

17th January – *Operation Richmond* using PT 215 and PT 203 attempted to land four agents and supplies to Porto Ercole, 70 miles north of Rome. PT 125 broke down but PT 203 succeeded in the landing.

19th January – Third attempt at *Operation Fragrant*. Failed due to unreliability of MAS boat's compass.

20th January – *Operation Richmond 2*. Using MAS 541 landed six agents at Porto Ercole. Embarked seven other agents and an escaped prisoner of war.

21st January – Fourth attempt at *Operation Fragrant*. Croft and Cpt. Cooper accompanied agents but broken fuel pipe on MAS 543 resulted in abandonment of operation.

---

1 From information in A. Cecil Hampshire, *Undercover Sailors, Secret Operations of World War Two* (London, 1981).

Operation Possum. MAS 507 landed stores for the Allied forward position on Capraia. This operation was to be repeated over ten times.

22nd January – *Operation Barley*. MAS 543 landed two agents south of Leghorn.

28t^h January – *Operation Tail Lamp* attempted to land two SOE Agents at Voltri Pier near the docks at Genoa. Croft and Seaman Miles were the landing party. The mission was abandoned when the MAS retreated after being challenged.

Operation Furtive. MAS 543 successfully landed two SIS agents at Cape Camaret, near St Tropez.

29th January – *Operation Ladbroke* attempted to land French SOE agents on Capraia. Croft, Petty Officer Smalley and Cpl. Bourne-Newton were the boat party. The operation was abandoned because of PT217s unwillingness to provide a diversion, and Croft's unwillingness to go along with the suggestion that the agents be sent in to shore alone. No compromise was reached, so the operation failed.

31st January – *Operation Tail Lamp* was repeated, with Croft, Coltman, Miles and Ashton as the shore party. Three agents were successfully landed at Voltri.

18th February – *Operation Jolly* using MAS 509 failed to land an SIS agent near Capo delle Melle due to bad weather conditions.

Two operations, *Benello* and *Youngstown*, successfully landed agents at different pinpoints near Portofino.

Operation Doughboy, using MAS 576, landed three French agents and their wireless equipment on Elba.

21st February – *Operation Maryland*. Croft led this operation on an Italian MS boat (63 tons and capable of 34 knots) to the Moneglia area near Spezia and successfully landed eight Italian Commandos.

Operation Possum XI using MAS 546 and P403 took a reconnaissance party to Capraia. MAS 546 hit an acoustic mine at the beginning of her return journey and sank with only five survivors.

17th March – *Operations Anstey, Zeal and Flack* were carried out in one trip using MS 24. Croft oversaw the landing of ten agents near Genoa in this multiple mission.

Operation Amloch landed five SOE agents at Castiglioncello.

Operations Sand and Mario, after having landed three agents near Spezia, ran into an attack by three E-boats and narrowly escaped due to the speed of MAS 543.

19th 21st 24th and 26th March – *Operation Cromer* made four unsuccessful attempts to land a woman SOE agent near Marseilles.

21st March – *Operation Cadex*. Using MAS 541 set out to land two French Commandos with explosives near Cape Arenzano. MAS 541 did not return from this operation and was lost at sea. It was thought she had probably hit a mine.

22nd March – *Operation Ginny* landed a party of 15 OSS men near Sestri Levante to blow up a railway tunnel. The PT boats returned to pick up the party but were prevented from doing so by an enemy patrol craft.

Operation Ginny A returned on the 25th but was unable to locate them. They had been captured by the Germans and killed by firing squad two days later.

18th and 24th April – *Operation Gooseberry* attempted to pick up prisoners of war from Montalo. Both attempt failed as no prisoners turned up, but enemy aircraft did.

23rd April – *Operations Arctic and Nostrum*, using PT boats 207 and 215, landed three French agents on the south west coast of Elba. Four days later they were picked up having obtained valuable information for the invasion of Elba.

26th April – *Operation Abraham* attempted for the second time to land SIS agents at Cape Camaret. This was abandoned due to a hostile enemy reception committee.

15th May – *Operation Ashwater*, using MTB375 with Croft in charge of the boat party, attempted to land three SOE agents at Capo delle Melle. The landing boats were driven back by enemy fire. A repeat of *Ashwater* was tried on the 17th but again had to be abandoned due to enemy presence at landing points.

19th June – *Operations Scram* and *Ferret*, both using ARB403. French agents were landed at Bonassola but the arranged rendezvous with prisoners of war to be taken off failed. In the confusion ARF 403 lost touch with the dinghy, manned by Jones and Bourne-Newton, who had to row to Capraia, having rowed 120 miles in 90 hours.

24th June – *Operation Gorge 2,* using PT556 with Croft and Smally as landing party, attempted to land SOE agents in the St Tropez region, but compass faults on PT resulted in abandonment of the operation.

15th July – *Operation Skid* set out to pick up 30 prisoners of war from Vernazza, near Spezia in MTB 357, escorted by two other PT boats and an MTB. The prisoners were picked up, but the supporting vessel became engaged in a short battle with an enemy force of a corvette, two E boats and two destroyers. The PT boats and the MTB covered the retreat of MTB 357, which escaped back to base.

24th July – *Operation Kingston*, using MAS 543, attempted to land two French agents at Mesco Porto. The dinghy party and the MAS were attacked by three E boats, and while the MAS managed to withdraw, the dinghy and its occupants were captured.

The 'Balaclava' mission was disbanded in September 1944. From December 1943 until July 1944 fifty-two sorties had been attempted, off which twenty four had been successful. Nearly 100 agents had been infiltrated into occupied territory and around 50 had been taken out. Wireless sets, stores and ammunition had also been taken in.

Appendix Y

Supplies infiltrated into Albania by air and sea during the period May 1943 to January 1945[1]

1. **Arms**
   Anti-Tank Rifles 244
   Rifles 6, 839
   LMGs 1,790
   MMGs 57
   SMGs 4,933
   Pistols 119
   PIATs 59
   Mortars (81mm and 3") 192
   Mortars (45mm and 2") 45
2. **Ammunition**
   SAA 16,532,811
   Mortar Bombs (81mm and 3") 12,957
   Mortar Bombs (45mm and 2") 10,604
   Grenades No. 36 23,062
   Bombs (PIAT) 1,870
   20mm AA/AT 3,040
   75mm Mountain Gun 400
3. **Explosives**
   808 52,062 lbs
   Ammonal 23,940 lbs
   PHE 40,940 lbs
   Gun Cotton 2,368lbs
   Gelignite 210 lbs
   Clams 125 lbs
   Beehives 842 lbs
   Mines 2,699 lbs
   Camouflet sets 7 lbs
   Tyrebusters 8,200 lbs
4. **Signal Stores**
   W/T Sets Bmk 1 and 2 43
   W/T Sets No. 22 22
   Petrol Generators 91

---

1 Based on TNA HS5/128, Albania S LO Report F.

	Hand and Pedal Generators	31
	Turbo Generators	4
	Decca Receivers	11
	Batteries	244
	S Phones	9
	Telephones	97
	Switchboards	9
	Aldis Lamps	11
	Cable	161 miles
5.	**Food**	
	Dehydrated Food	299,041 lbs
	Coffee	818 lbs
	Flour	362,380 lbs
	Rice	214,998 lbs
	Oatmeal	119,334 lbs
	Sugar	70 lbs
	P meat	132,907 lbs
	Biscuits	16,333 lbs
	Milk	21,591 lbs
	Fats	15,515 lbs
	Wheat	305,734 lbs
	Tea	204 lbs
	Salt	2,426 lbs
	Mule Fodder	100,810 lbs
	Bran	4,770 lbs
6.	**Medical**	
	Medical Packs	743
7.	**Clothing etc.**	
	Battle Dress	28,157
	Boots (pairs)	56,834
	Socks (pairs)	111,814
	Shirts	49,360
	Underwear (sets)	12,820
	Great Coats	24,819
	Pullovers	25,440
	Blankets	14,220
	Groundsheets and Capes A/G	2,404
	Caps F.S.	350
	Anklets, web	5,550
	Towels	2,000
	Haversacks, web	5,000
8.	**Miscellaneous**	
	Torches	390
	Binoculars	53
	Compasses	7
	Bivouacs	29

Welbikes	20
Jeeps	6
Trailers	5
Motorcycles	1
Petrol	3,116 gallons
Derv	3,216 gallons
Oil	196 gallons
Kerosene	570 gallons
Cordage 1½"	450 fathoms
Cordage 3"	310 fathoms
Pulley Blocks 1 ½ snatch	2
Shovels G.S	24
Crowbars	6
Saws, Cross Cut	1
Assault Boats, Mk II	12
Mine Detectors	4

Bibliography

Archival Sources
The National Archives
ADM 1/24 248 Report on Operation Bridford
ADM 199/478 Report on action at Namsos Fjord, May 1940
ADM 199/730 Operation Gauntlet 1941
ADM 16849 Reports on the Dolphin Mission
War Cabinet Minutes relating to Events in Norway April/May 1940:
    CAB 65/6/39
    CAB 65/7/3
    CAB 65/12/25
    CAB 65/12/25
    CAB 65/12/31
    CAB 65/112/26
FO 371/2942 Report on the Gothenburg shipment plan by George Binney 12th February 1941
FO 371/2924 Report on Operation Rubble by J.M. Addis, Foreign Office, dated 29th January 1941
FO 371/2924 Account of Operation Rubble written by George Binney
H/59 Glen in Albania
HS 5/128 Report by Major H.W. Tilman on mission to Gjinokastre 30th May, 1944
HS 5/912 A report by Alexander Glen on his relations with the Yugoslavs, November 1941
HS 3/30 Report by Major A. Croft on Operation Snow White
WO 106/1996 Operations on Spitsbergen

The Imperial War Museum
Doc 60/30/1 The papers of R.E.D. Ryder V.C.

Liddell Hart Centre for Military Archives, King's College London
GB0099 Quintin Riley Papers

The Scott Polar Research Institute, University of Cambridge
GB 15 The George Binney Papers

The Andrew Croft Archive – unpublished papers of A. Croft DSO (private collection)
Personal scrapbook created by A. Croft relating to his experiences in the Second World War.
Letters and papers of A. Croft.

Unpublished Papers of R.E.D. Ryder VC (private collection)
Intelligence report from Officers of the *Tai Mo Shan* to the Admiralty 7th January 1934
Undated Lecture given by R.E.D. Ryder entitled "A Voyage to the Antarctic"
R.E.D. Ryder's diary "British Graham Land Expedition- Yacht *Penola*" August 1934-
April 1937

Newspapers and Journals/Journal Articles
After The Battle magazine no. 126, 2004
Classic Boat
The Times
Croft, Andrew, 'Across the Greenland Ice-Cap', *Geographical*, Vol. 1 (1935).
Glen, A. & F. Selinger, 'Arctic Meteorological operations and counter operations during
World War', *Polar Record,* no. 21, 1983.
Glen, A. 'The Oxford University Arctic Expedition, North East Land , 1935-1936', *The
Geographical Journal,* vol. XC, no. 3 , 1937.
Glen, A., 'A Sub-Arctic Glacier Cap: The West Ice of North East Land.' *The Geographical
Journal*, vol. XCVIII,no.2, 1941.
Onslow, Susan, 'Britain and the Belgrade Coup of 27th March 1941 revisited', *Electronic
Journal of International History,* Institute of Historical Research, University of
London, 2005.

Published Primary Sources
Astley, Joan Bright, *The Inner Circle* (London, Hutchinson, 1971).
Binney, G., *With Seaplane and Sledge in the Arctic* (New York, George Doran, 1926).
Calvert, Michael, *Prisoners of Hope* (London, Jonathan Cape, 1952)
Carton de Wiart, Adrian, *Happy Odyssey* (London, Jonathan Cape, 1950).
Courtauld, A., *Man the Ropes,* (London, Hodder and Stoughton, 1957).
Croft, A., *A Talent for Adventure* (Worcester, SPA, 1991).
Fell, W.R., *The Sea Our Shield* (London, Cassell, 1966).
Fleming, P., *Brazilian Adventure* (New York, Charles Scribner's and Sons, 1934).
Fleming, P., *News From Tartary : A Journey from Peking to Kashmir* (London, Jonathan
Cape, 1936).
Fuchs, Vivian, *A Time to Speak: An Autobiography* (Oswestry, Anthony Nelson, 1990).
Glen, Alexander, *Young Men in the Arctic* (London, Faber and Faber, 1934).
Glen, Alexander, *Under the Pole Star. The Oxford University Arctic Expedition, 1935-6*
(London, Methuen, 1937).
Glen, Alexander, *Footholds against the Whirlwind* (London, Hutchinson, 1975).
Glen, Alexander & Leighton Bowen, *Target Danube: A River not Quite Too Far* (Lewes,
The Book Guild, 2002).
Lindsay, Martin, *Those Greenland Days* (London, William Blackwood & Sons, 1932).
Lindsay, Martin, *Sledge: The British Trans-Greenland Expedition 1934* (London, Cassell,
1935).
Lindsay, Martin, *Three Got Through, Memoirs of an Arctic Explorer* (London, The Falcon
Press, 1946).
Maillart, Ella, *Forbidden Journey* (London, William Heinemann, 1937).
Ryder, R., *The Attack on St Nazaire, 28th March 1942* (London, John Murray, 1947).

Scott, J., *Portrait of an Icecap with Human Figures* (London, Chatto and Windus, 1953).

Sherwood, Martyn, *The voyage of the Tai –Mo- Shan* (London, Geoffrey Bless, 1935).

Sherwood, Martyn, *Coston Gun* (London, Geoffrey Bless, 1946).

Spencer Chapman, F., *Northern Lights, The Official Account of the British Arctic Air route expedition* (London, Chatto and Windus, 1934).

Spencer Chapman, F. *Watkins' Last Expedition* (London, Penguin, 1938).

Spencer Chapman, F., *Living Dangerously* (London, Chatto and Windus, 1953).

Tilman, H.W., *Snow on the Equator* (London, G. Bell & Sons Ltd, 1937).

Tilman, H.W., *When Men and Mountains Meet* (Cambridge, CUP, 1947).

Tilman, H.W., *Mount Everest 1938* (Cambridge, CUP, 1948).

Warwick, C., *Really Not Required* (Edinburgh, The Pentland Press, 1997).

Published Secondary Sources

Anderson, J.R.L., *High Mountains and Cold Seas: A biography of H.W. Tilman* (London, Gollancz, 1980).

Bailey, Roderick, *The Wildest Province, SOE In the Land of the Eagle* (London, Vintage, 2008).

Barnett, Correlli, *Engage the Enemy More Closely, the Royal Navy in the Second World War* (London, Hodder and Stoughton, 1991).

Barker, Ralph, *One Man's Jungle: A Biography of F. Spencer Chapman, D.S.O* (London, Chatto and Windus, 1975).

Barker, Ralph, *The Blockade Busters* (Chatto and Windus, New York, 1976).

Binney, Marcus, *Secret War Heroes: The Men of Special Operations Executive* (London, Hodder and Stoughton, 2005).

Cecil Hampshire, A., *On Hazardous Service* (London, Kimber, 1974).

Cecil Hampshire, A., *Undercover Sailors, Secret Operations of World War Two* (London, William Kimber, 1981).

Gilbert, Martin, *The Second World War: A Complete History,* (New York, Henry Holt, 1989).

Hart-Davis, Duff, *Peter Fleming: A Biography* (Oxford, OUP, 1987).

Hayes, G., *The Conquest of the North Pole* (London, Macmillan, 1934).

Hopton, Richard, A *Reluctant Hero: The Life of Captain Robert Ryder VC* (Barnsley, Pen and Sword, 2011).

Hunt, Giles, *Lancelot Fleming, a Portrait* (Canterbury, Norwich Press, 2003).

Lindsay, Donald, *Friends for Life, a Portrait of Lancelot Fleming* (Seaford, Lindel Publishing Company, 1981).

Moynahan, Brian, *Jungle Soldier* (London, Quercus, 2009).

Lucas Phillips, C.E., *The Greatest Raid of all* (London, Heinemann, 1958).

Rankin, Nicholas, *Ian Fleming's Commandos: The Story of the Legendary 30 Assault Unit in WWII* (London, Faber and Faber, 2011).

Riley, J.P., *Pole to Pole* (Huntingdon, Bluntisham Books, 1989).

Roskill, S.W., *The War at Sea* Volume I (London, HMSO, 1954).

Rymill, J., *Southern Lights. The Official Account of the British Graham Land Expedition 1934–1937* (London, The Travel Book Club, 1939).

Schofield, E. & R. Conyers Nesbit, *Arctic Airmen, The RAF in Spitsbergen and North Russia 1942* (London, William and Kimber, 1987).

Scott, Jeremy, *Dancing on Ice: A Stirring Tale of Adventure, Risk and Reckless Folly* (London, Old St Publishing, 2008).

Smith, Sir M., *James Wordie, Polar Explorer* (Edinburgh, Birlinn, 2004).

Stafford, David, *Mission Accomplished, SOE and Italy 1943-1945* (London, Random House, 2011).

Wollaston, N., *The Man on the Ice Cap . The life of August Courtauld* (London, Constable, 1980).

Web Sites

Dix Noonan Web, Medal Auction Site. http://www.dnw.co.uk/medals/auctionarchive/viewspecialcollections/itemdetail.lasso?itemid=60285

Royal Naval Patrol Service Association Newsletter 2010 http://www.rnps.lowestoft.org.uk/newsletter/newsletter_index.htm

Naval History Net

http://www.naval-history.net

Us Navy Blimps and dirigibles

http://bluejacket.com/usn_avi_lta.html

U-boat Net

uboat.net

Index

Military units/formations/establishments

For individual ships *see* 'Miscellaneous/Other Index below'. Listed In numeric order, then alphabetical order.

Related titles published by Helion & Company

Battlefield Rations. The food given
to the British soldier for marching
and fighting 1900-2011
Anthony Clayton
ISBN 978-1-909384-18-7

Striking Back. Britain's Airborne
and Commando Raids 1940-42
Niall Cherry
ISBN 978-1-906033-41-5

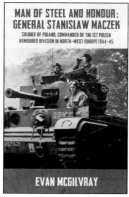

Man of Steel and Honour. General
Stanislaw Maczek. Soldier of Poland,
Commander of the 1st Polish Armoured
Division in North-West Europe 1944-45
Evan McGilvray
ISBN 978-1-908916-53-2

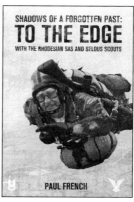

Shadows of a Forgotten Past. To the edge
with the Rhodesian SAS and Selous Scouts
Paul French
ISBN 978-1-908916-60-0

HELION & COMPANY

26 Willow Road, Solihull, West Midlands B91 1UE, England
Telephone 0121 705 3393   Fax 0121 711 4075
Website: http://www.helion.co.uk